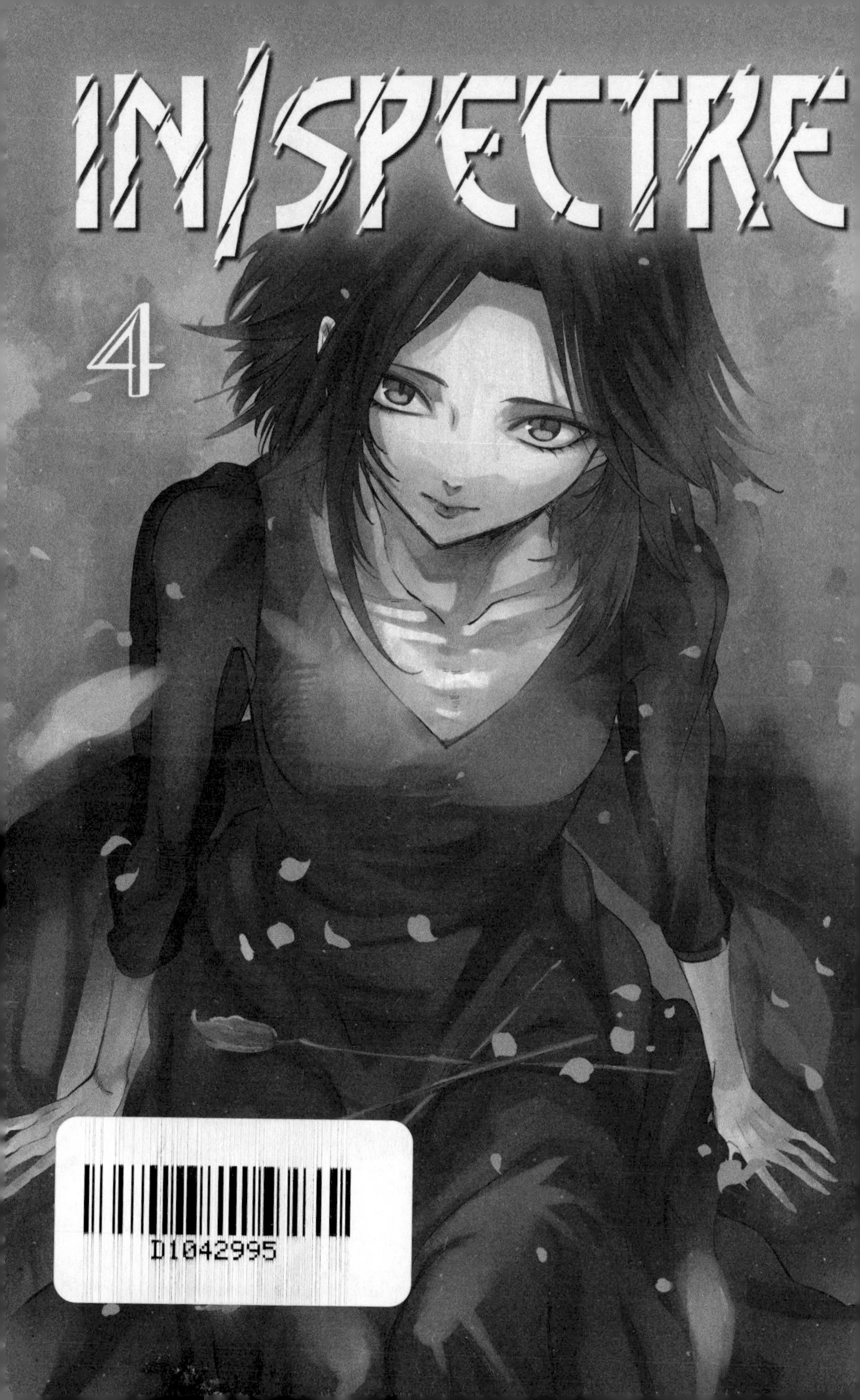
IN/SPECTRE
4

# CONTENTS

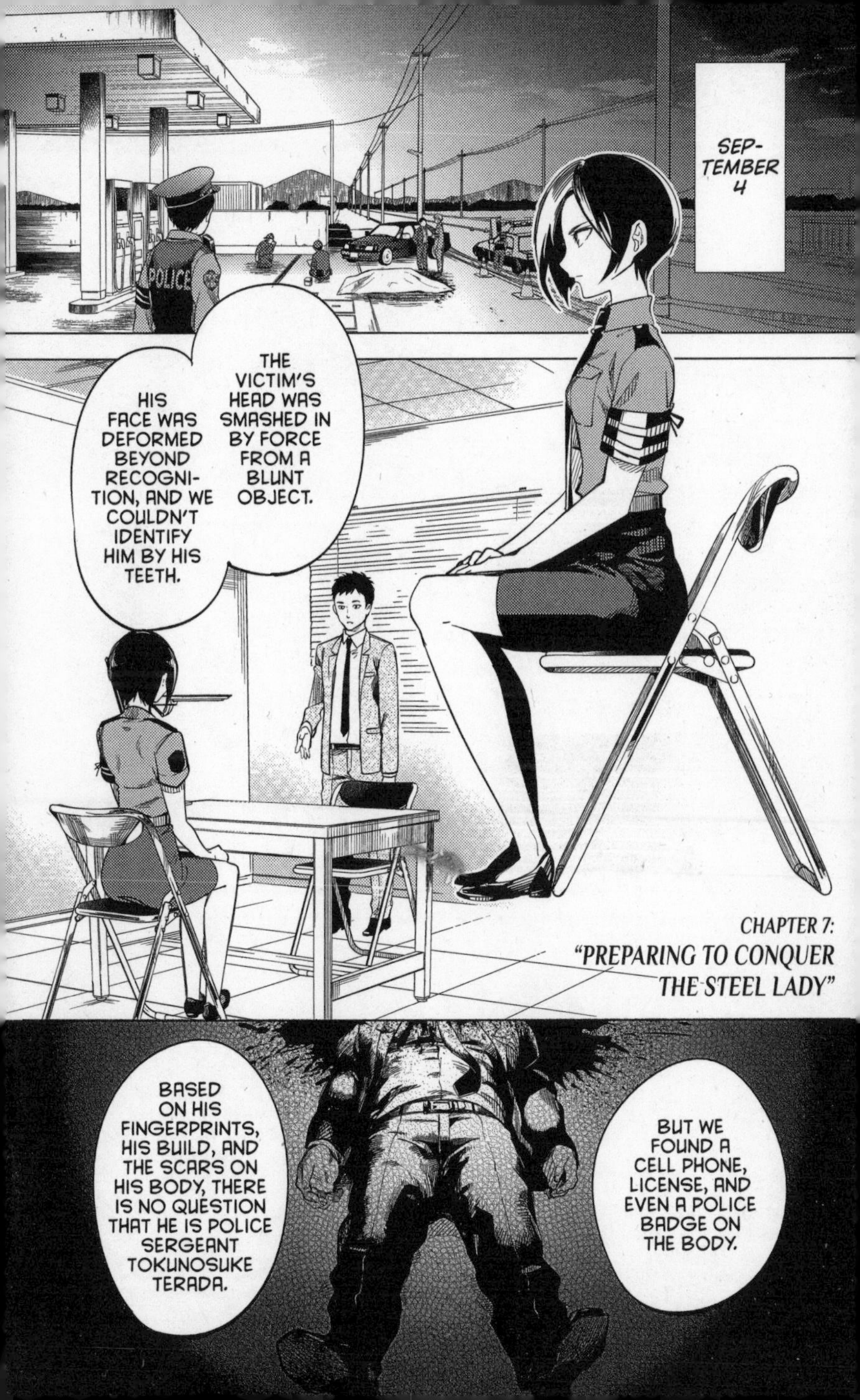
SEP-TEMBER 4
THE VICTIM'S HEAD WAS SMASHED IN BY FORCE FROM A BLUNT OBJECT.
HIS FACE WAS DEFORMED BEYOND RECOGNI-TION, AND WE COULDN'T IDENTIFY HIM BY HIS TEETH.
CHAPTER 7: "PREPARING TO CONQUER THE STEEL LADY"
BUT WE FOUND A CELL PHONE, LICENSE, AND EVEN A POLICE BADGE ON THE BODY.
BASED ON HIS FINGERPRINTS, HIS BUILD, AND THE SCARS ON HIS BODY, THERE IS NO QUESTION THAT HE IS POLICE SERGEANT TOKUNOSUKE TERADA.

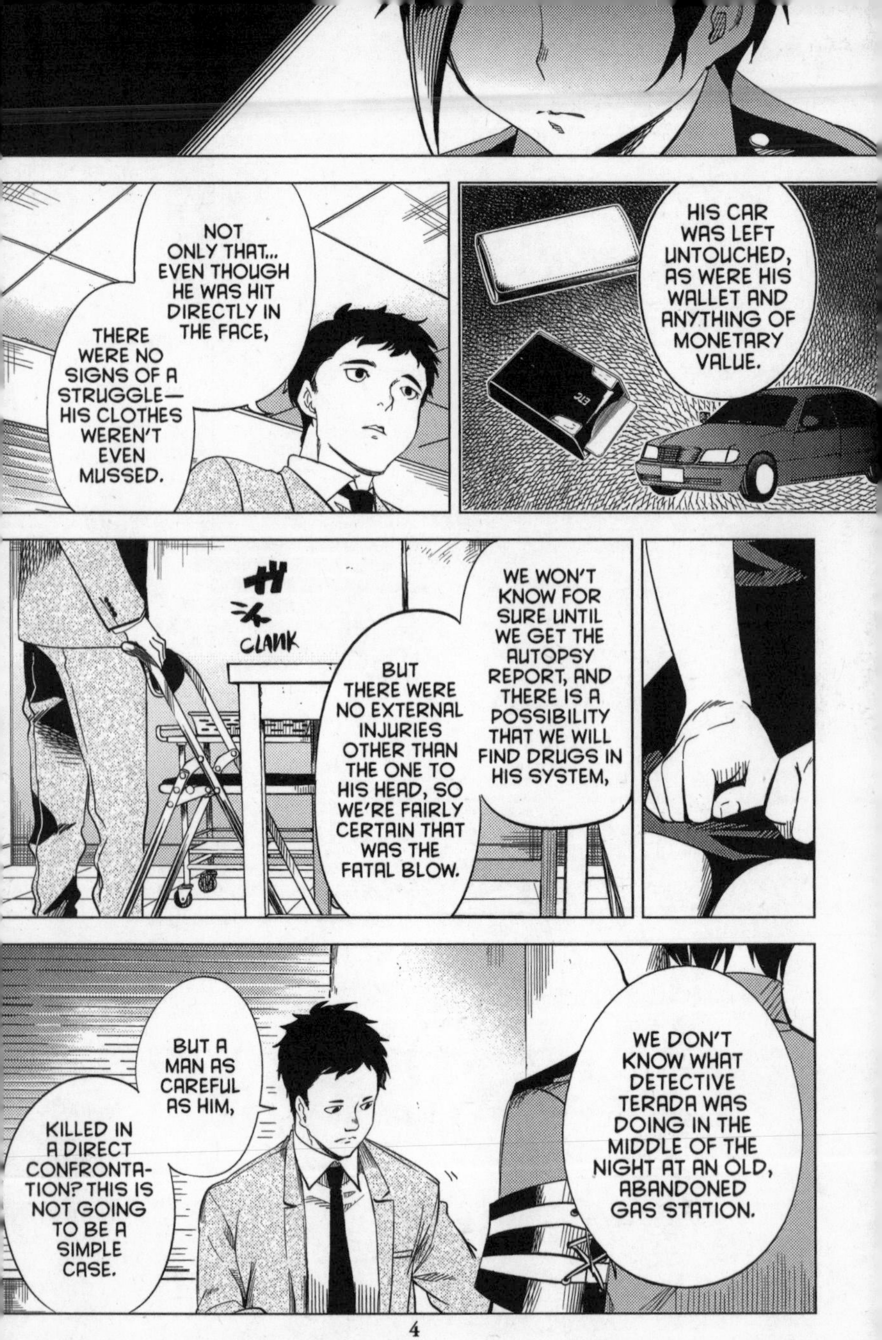
HIS CAR WAS LEFT UNTOUCHED, AS WERE HIS WALLET AND ANYTHING OF MONETARY VALUE.
NOT ONLY THAT... EVEN THOUGH HE WAS HIT DIRECTLY IN THE FACE,
THERE WERE NO SIGNS OF A STRUGGLE—HIS CLOTHES WEREN'T EVEN MUSSED.
WE WON'T KNOW FOR SURE UNTIL WE GET THE AUTOPSY REPORT, AND THERE IS A POSSIBILITY THAT WE WILL FIND DRUGS IN HIS SYSTEM,
BUT THERE WERE NO EXTERNAL INJURIES OTHER THAN THE ONE TO HIS HEAD, SO WE'RE FAIRLY CERTAIN THAT WAS THE FATAL BLOW.
CLANK
WE DON'T KNOW WHAT DETECTIVE TERADA WAS DOING IN THE MIDDLE OF THE NIGHT AT AN OLD, ABANDONED GAS STATION.
BUT A MAN AS CAREFUL AS HIM,
KILLED IN A DIRECT CONFRONTATION? THIS IS NOT GOING TO BE A SIMPLE CASE.

EITHER THE MURDERER WAS SOMEONE VERY CLOSE TO HIM,

OR THE TIMING OF THE ATTACK WAS SO UNEXPECTED THAT HE WAS LITERALLY STUNNED.

ON HIS PHONE, WE FOUND WHAT WE BELIEVE TO BE A PRIVATE EMAIL EXCHANGE WITH YOU.

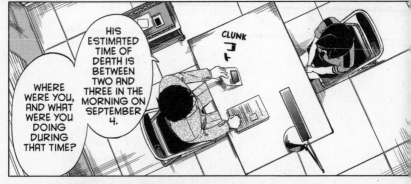

HIS ESTIMATED TIME OF DEATH IS BETWEEN TWO AND THREE IN THE MORNING ON SEPTEMBER 4.

WHERE WERE YOU, AND WHAT WERE YOU DOING DURING THAT TIME?

CLUNK

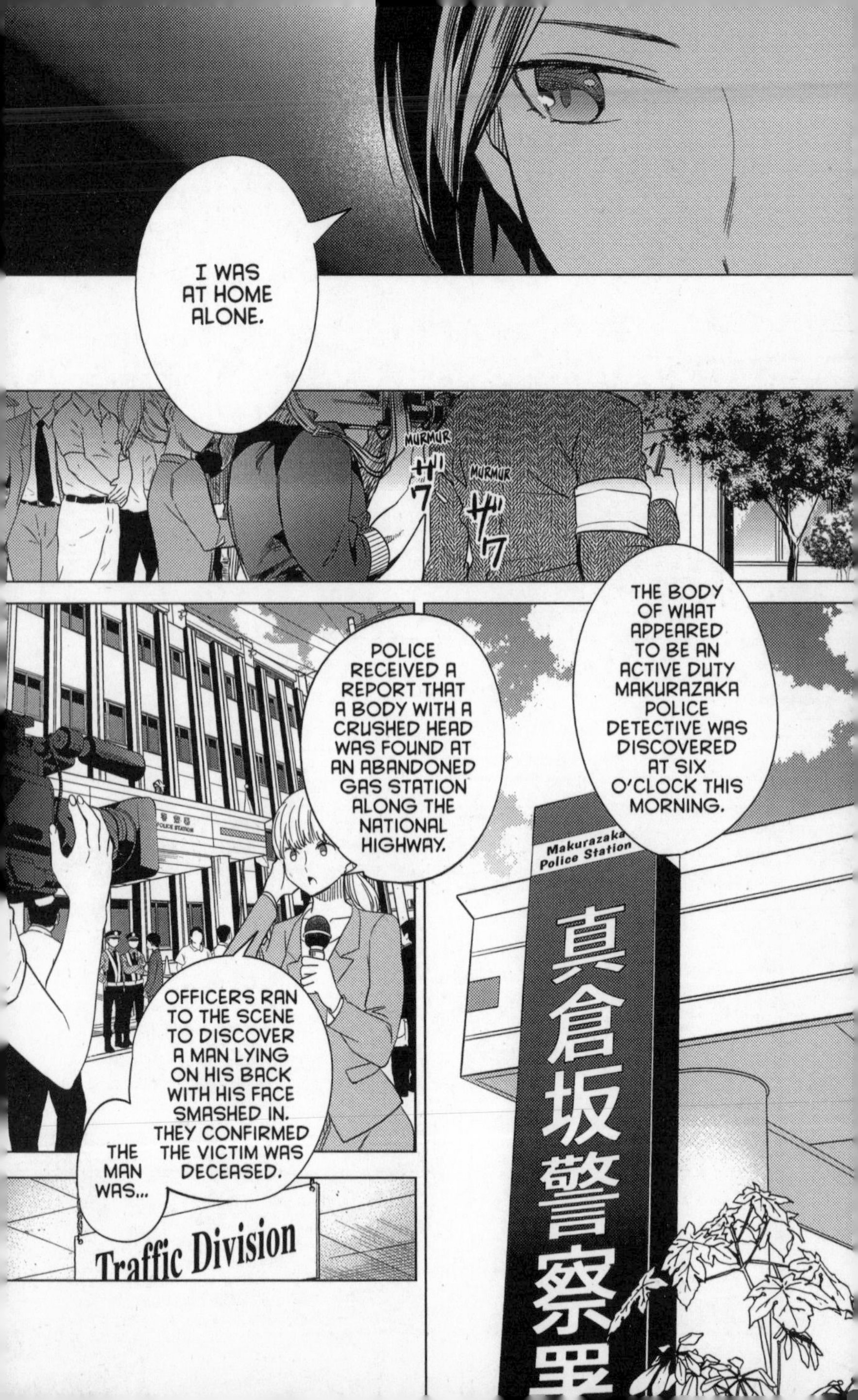
I WAS AT HOME ALONE.
MURMUR
ザワ
MURMUR
ザワ
THE BODY OF WHAT APPEARED TO BE AN ACTIVE DUTY MAKURAZAKA POLICE DETECTIVE WAS DISCOVERED AT SIX O'CLOCK THIS MORNING.
Makurazaka Police Station
真倉坂警察
POLICE RECEIVED A REPORT THAT A BODY WITH A CRUSHED HEAD WAS FOUND AT AN ABANDONED GAS STATION ALONG THE NATIONAL HIGHWAY.
OFFICERS RAN TO THE SCENE TO DISCOVER A MAN LYING ON HIS BACK WITH HIS FACE SMASHED IN. THEY CONFIRMED THE VICTIM WAS DECEASED.
THE MAN WAS...
Traffic Division

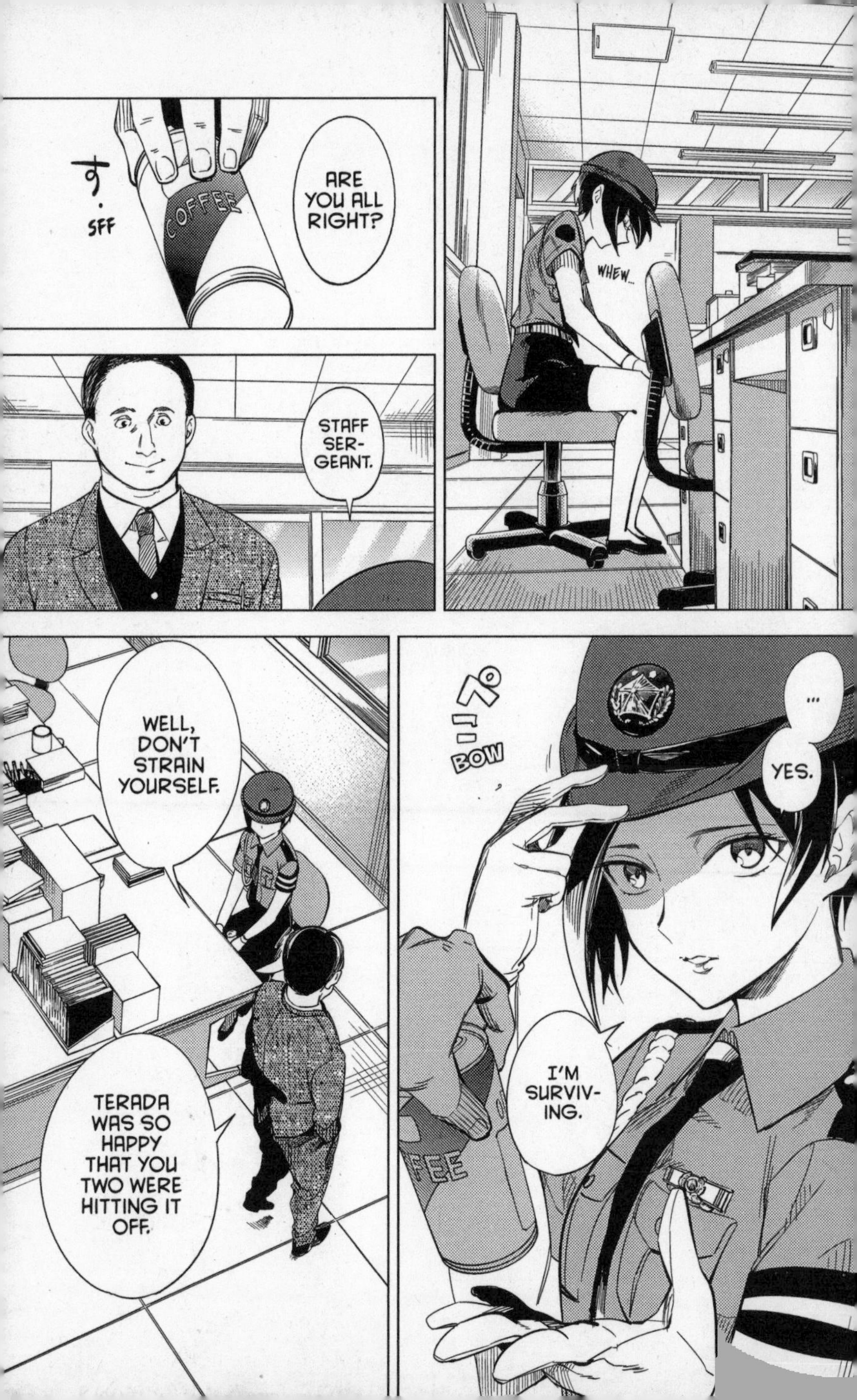

WHEW...
ARE YOU ALL RIGHT?
す
SFF
STAFF SER-GEANT.
...
YES.
ペコ
BOW
I'M SURVIV-ING.
WELL, DON'T STRAIN YOURSELF.
TERADA WAS SO HAPPY THAT YOU TWO WERE HITTING IT OFF.

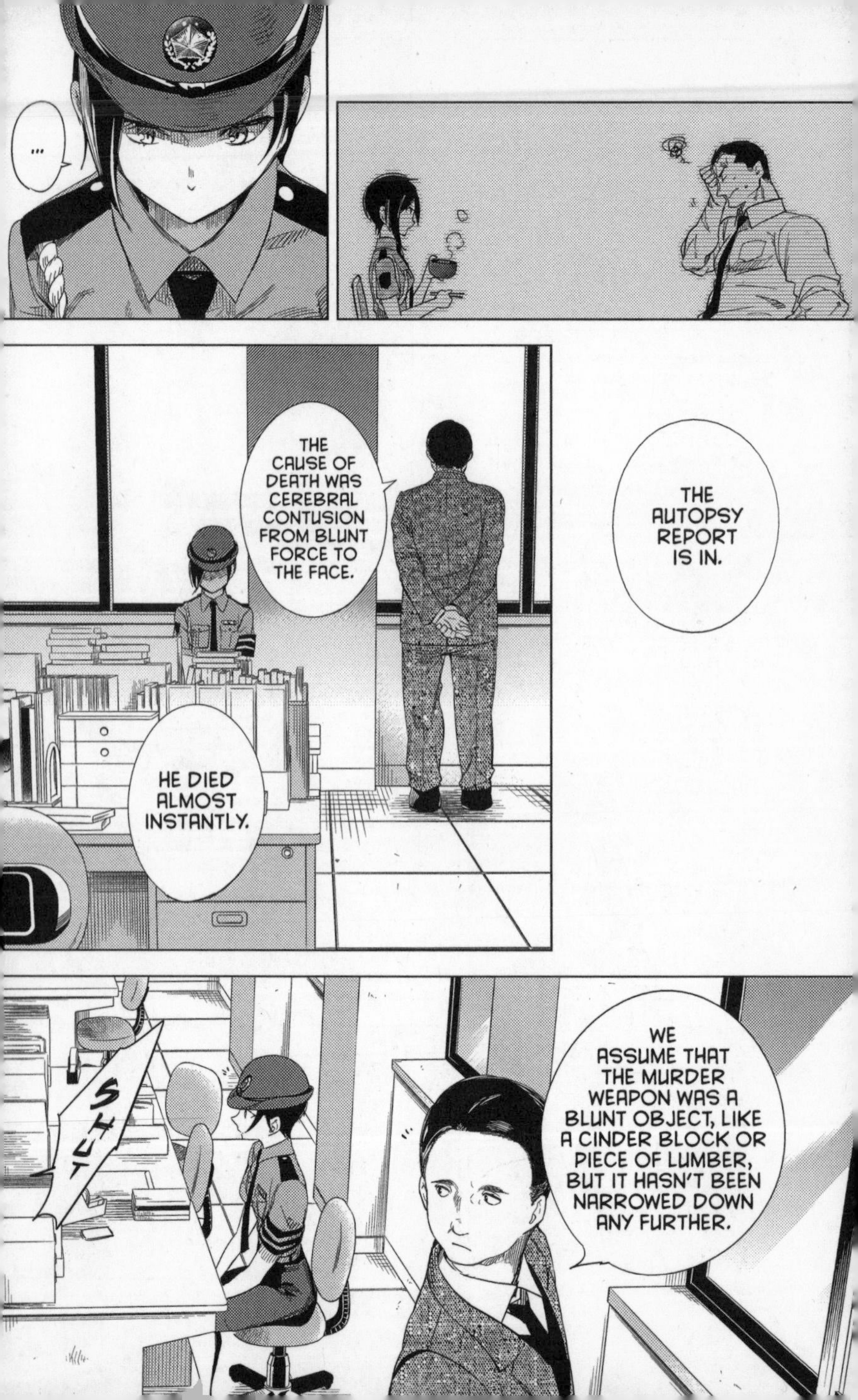
...
THE AUTOPSY REPORT IS IN.
THE CAUSE OF DEATH WAS CEREBRAL CONTUSION FROM BLUNT FORCE TO THE FACE.
HE DIED ALMOST INSTANTLY.
WE ASSUME THAT THE MURDER WEAPON WAS A BLUNT OBJECT, LIKE A CINDER BLOCK OR PIECE OF LUMBER, BUT IT HASN'T BEEN NARROWED DOWN ANY FURTHER.
SHUT

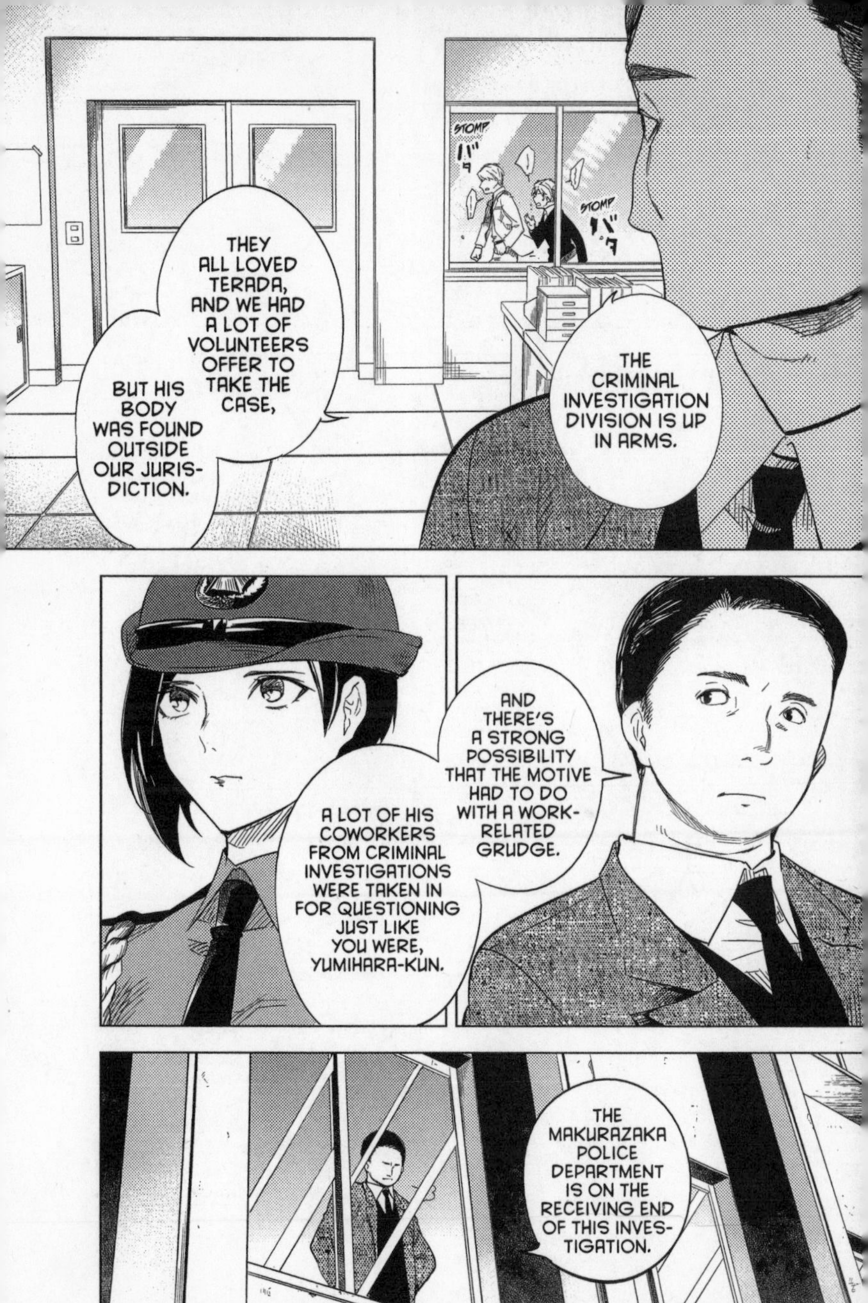
STOMP
STOMP
THE CRIMINAL INVESTIGATION DIVISION IS UP IN ARMS.
THEY ALL LOVED TERADA, AND WE HAD A LOT OF VOLUNTEERS OFFER TO TAKE THE CASE,
BUT HIS BODY WAS FOUND OUTSIDE OUR JURIS-DICTION.
AND THERE'S A STRONG POSSIBILITY THAT THE MOTIVE HAD TO DO WITH A WORK-RELATED GRUDGE.
A LOT OF HIS COWORKERS FROM CRIMINAL INVESTIGATIONS WERE TAKEN IN FOR QUESTIONING JUST LIKE YOU WERE, YUMIHARA-KUN.
THE MAKURAZAKA POLICE DEPARTMENT IS ON THE RECEIVING END OF THIS INVES-TIGATION.

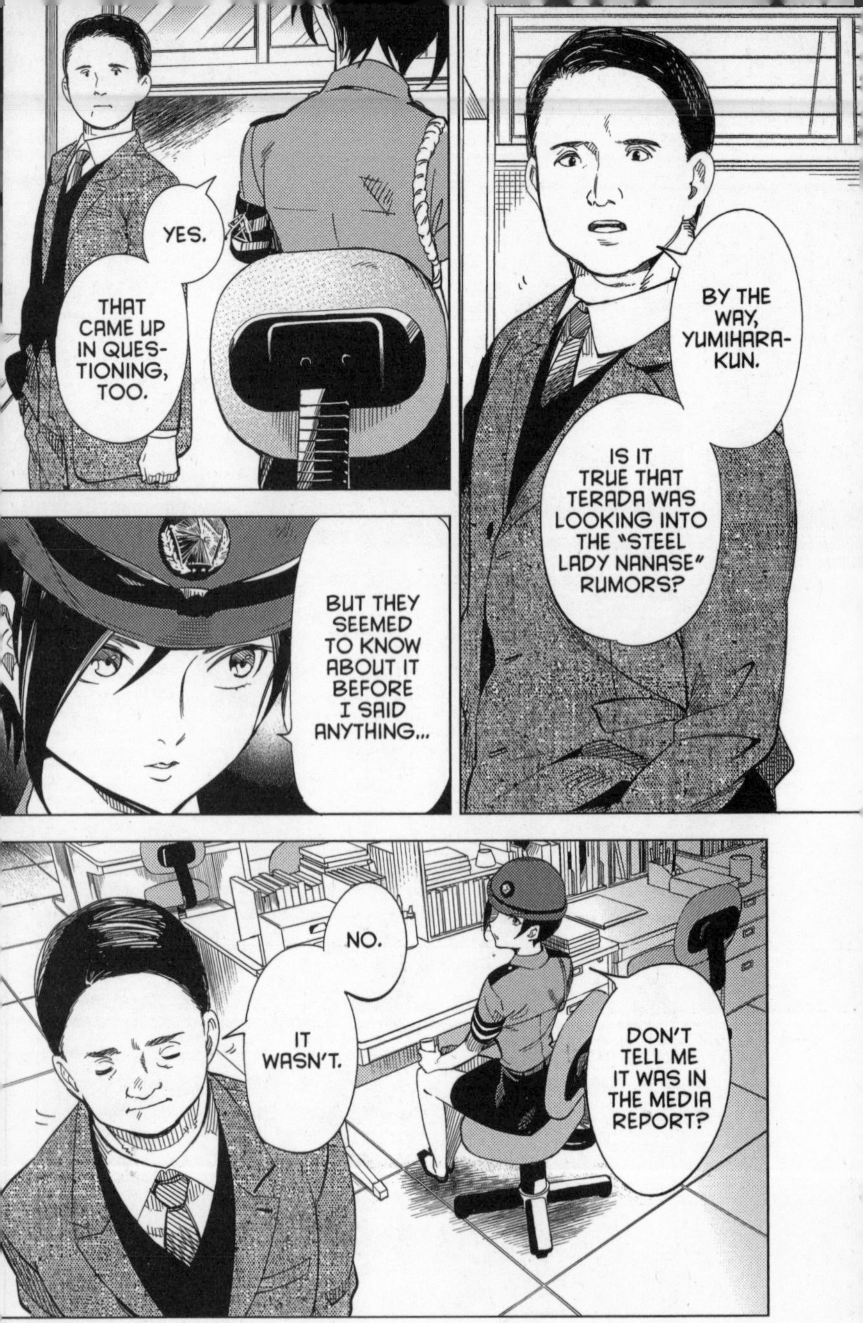

BY THE WAY, YUMIHARA-KUN.
IS IT TRUE THAT TERADA WAS LOOKING INTO THE "STEEL LADY NANASE" RUMORS?
YES.
THAT CAME UP IN QUES-TIONING, TOO.
BUT THEY SEEMED TO KNOW ABOUT IT BEFORE I SAID ANYTHING...
DON'T TELL ME IT WAS IN THE MEDIA REPORT?
NO.
IT WASN'T.

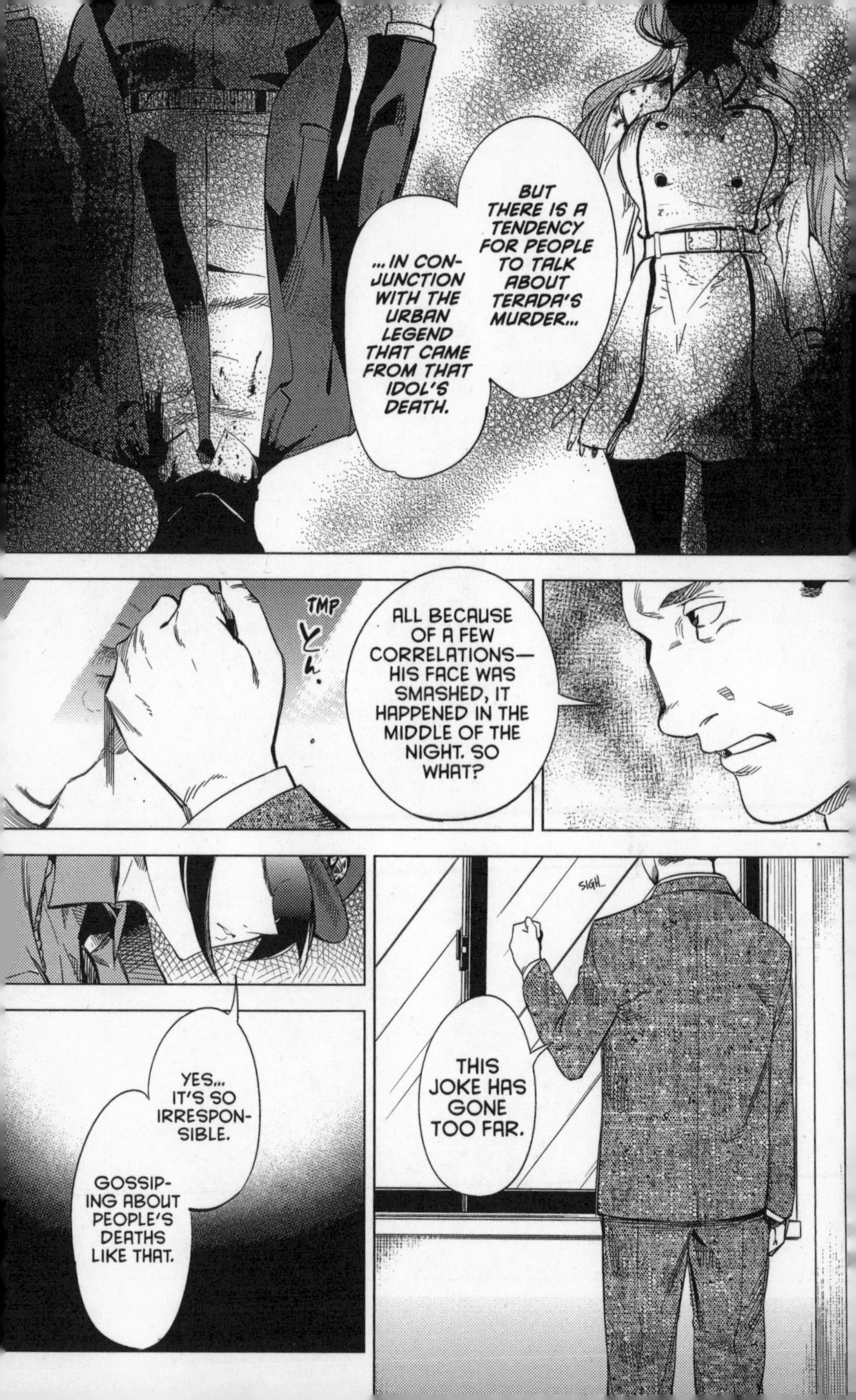
BUT THERE IS A TENDENCY FOR PEOPLE TO TALK ABOUT TERADA'S MURDER...
...IN CONJUNCTION WITH THE URBAN LEGEND THAT CAME FROM THAT IDOL'S DEATH.
ALL BECAUSE OF A FEW CORRELATIONS— HIS FACE WAS SMASHED, IT HAPPENED IN THE MIDDLE OF THE NIGHT. SO WHAT?
TMP
SIGH...
THIS JOKE HAS GONE TOO FAR.
YES... IT'S SO IRRESPONSIBLE.
GOSSIPING ABOUT PEOPLE'S DEATHS LIKE THAT.

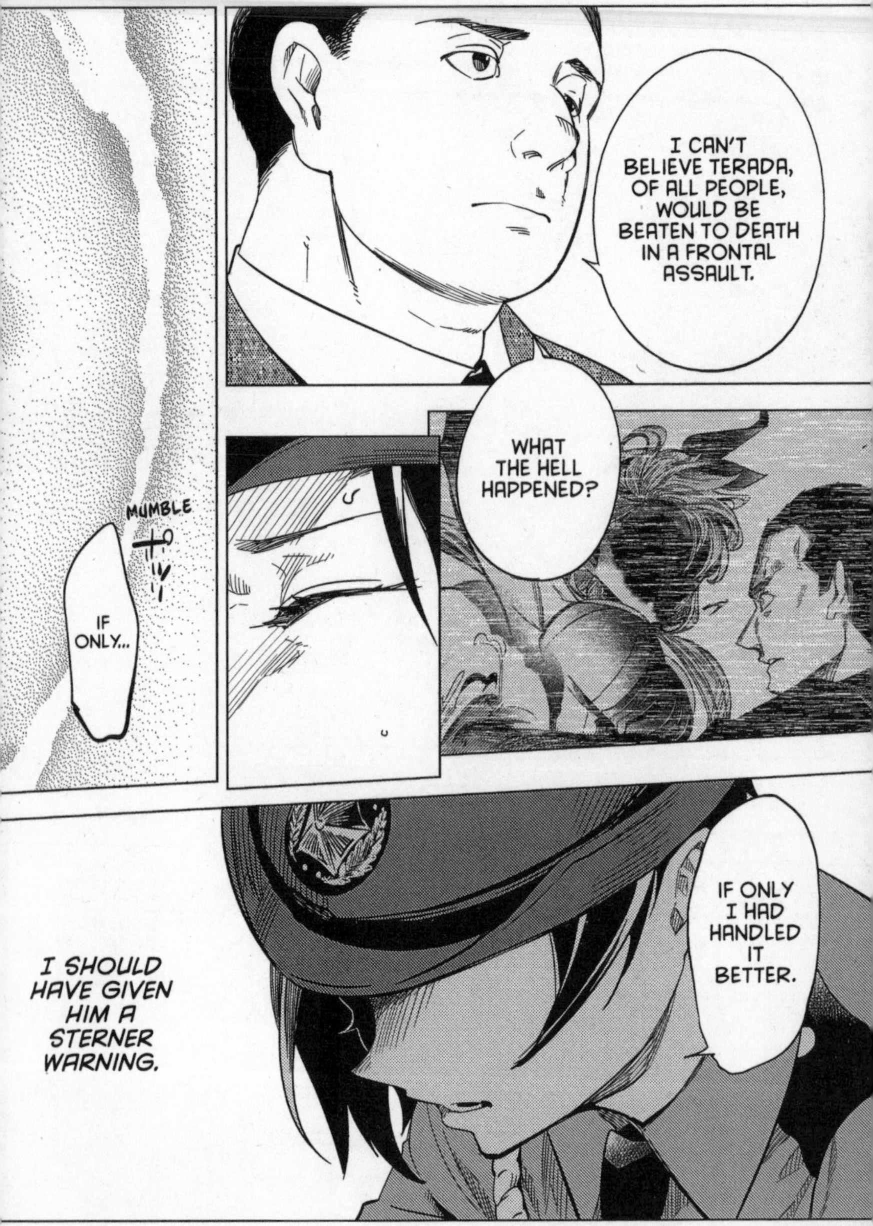
I CAN'T BELIEVE TERADA, OF ALL PEOPLE, WOULD BE BEATEN TO DEATH IN A FRONTAL ASSAULT.
WHAT THE HELL HAPPENED?
MUMBLE
IF ONLY...
IF ONLY I HAD HANDLED IT BETTER.
I SHOULD HAVE GIVEN HIM A STERNER WARNING.

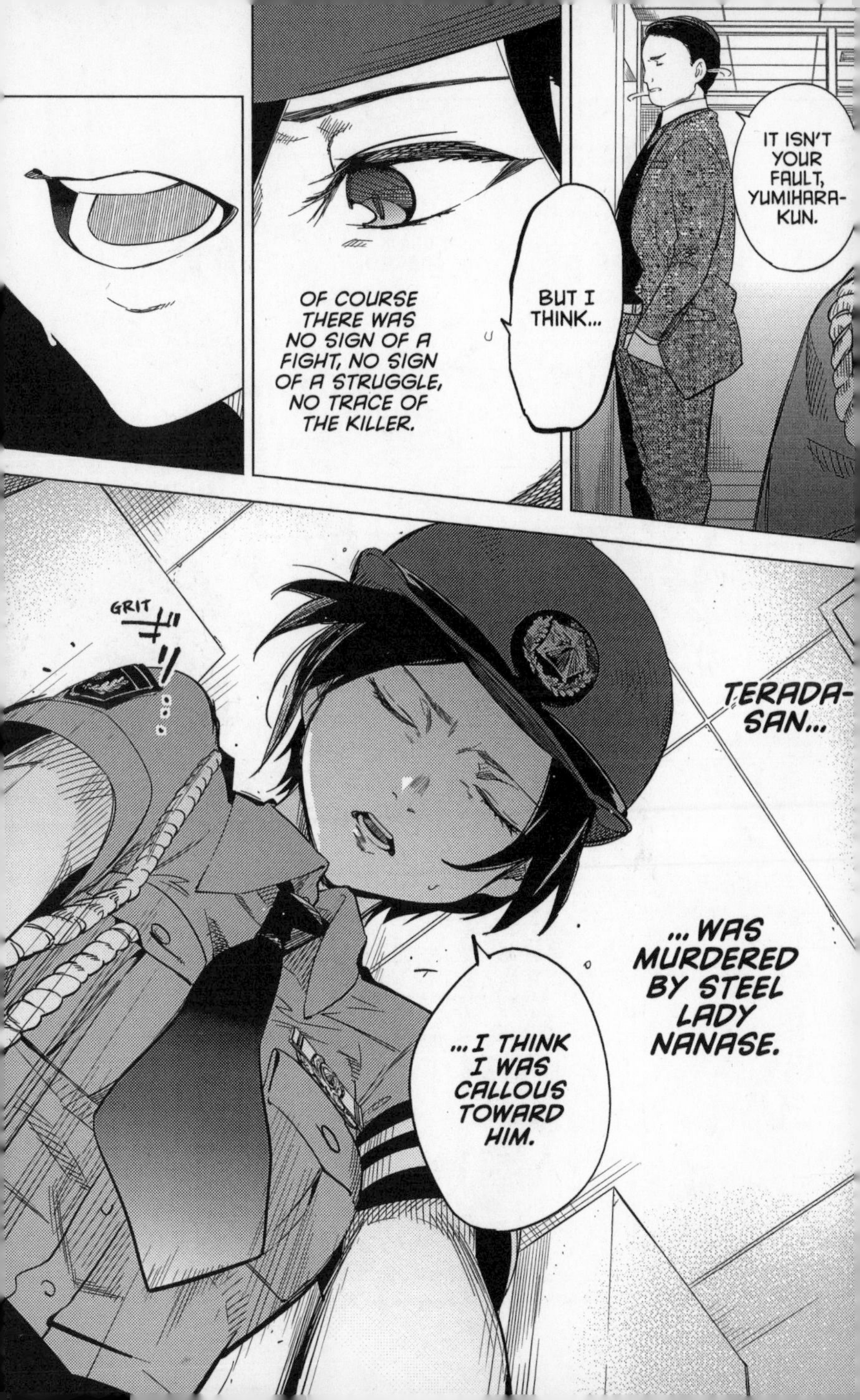
IT ISN'T YOUR FAULT, YUMIHARA-KUN.
BUT I THINK...
OF COURSE THERE WAS NO SIGN OF A FIGHT, NO SIGN OF A STRUGGLE, NO TRACE OF THE KILLER.
TERADA-SAN...
...WAS MURDERED BY STEEL LADY NANASE.
GRIT
...I THINK I WAS CALLOUS TOWARD HIM.

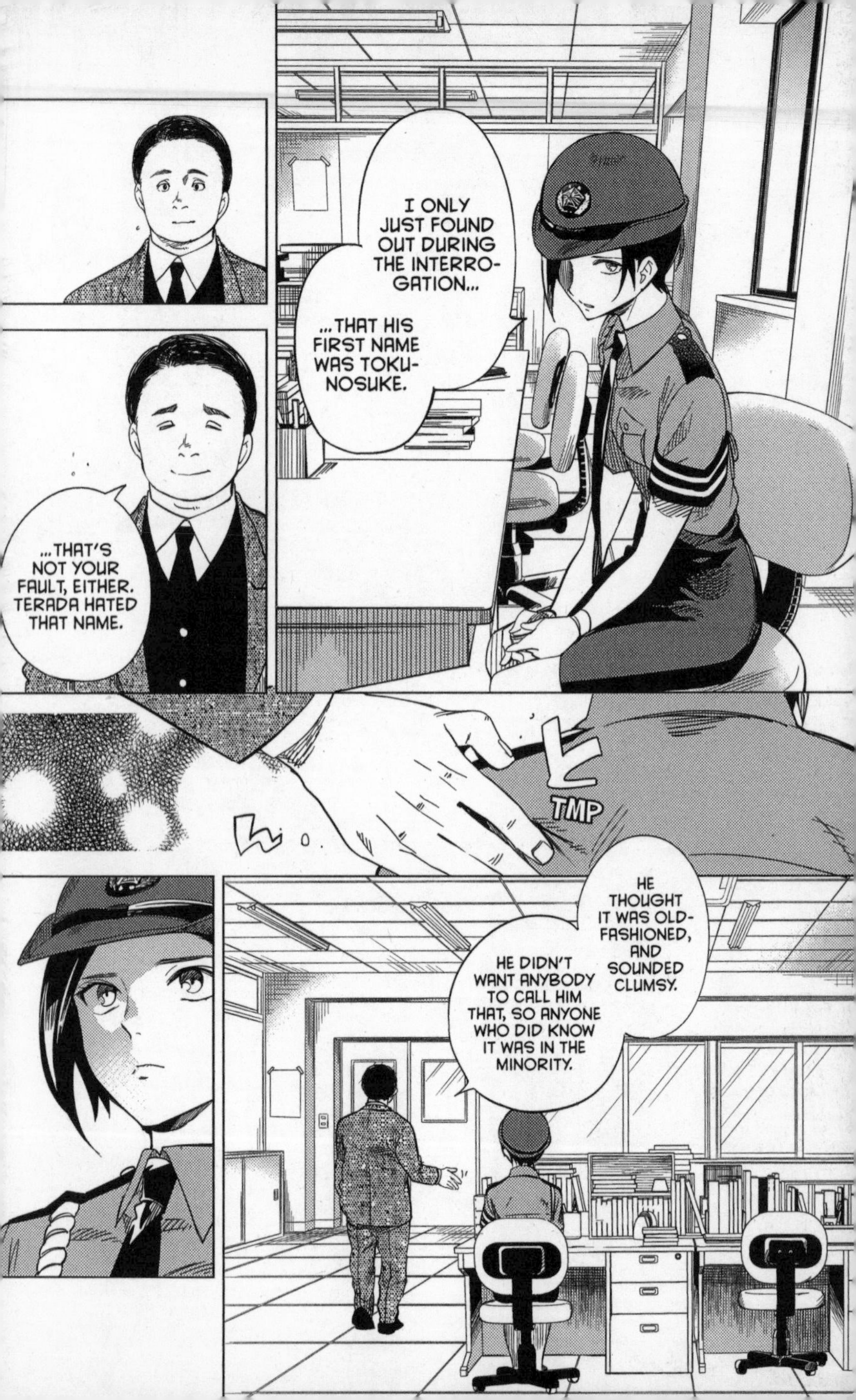
I ONLY JUST FOUND OUT DURING THE INTERROGATION...
...THAT HIS FIRST NAME WAS TOKUNOSUKE.
...THAT'S NOT YOUR FAULT, EITHER. TERADA HATED THAT NAME.
TMP
HE THOUGHT IT WAS OLD-FASHIONED, AND SOUNDED CLUMSY.
HE DIDN'T WANT ANYBODY TO CALL HIM THAT, SO ANYONE WHO DID KNOW IT WAS IN THE MINORITY.

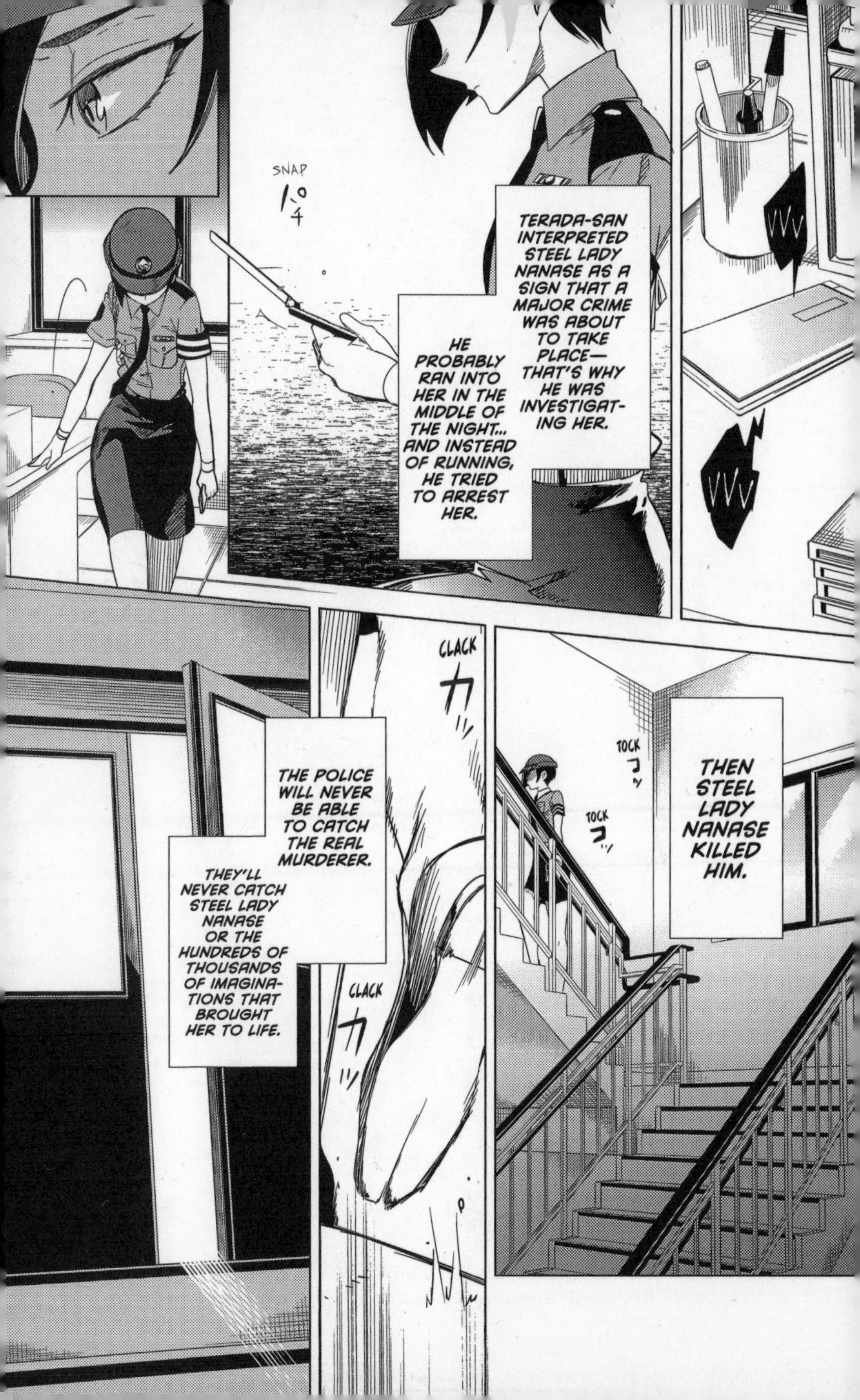
TERADA-SAN INTERPRETED STEEL LADY NANASE AS A SIGN THAT A MAJOR CRIME WAS ABOUT TO TAKE PLACE—THAT'S WHY HE WAS INVESTIGAT-ING HER.
SNAP
HE PROBABLY RAN INTO HER IN THE MIDDLE OF THE NIGHT... AND INSTEAD OF RUNNING, HE TRIED TO ARREST HER.
THEN STEEL LADY NANASE KILLED HIM.
TOCK
TOCK
CLACK
CLACK
THE POLICE WILL NEVER BE ABLE TO CATCH THE REAL MURDERER.
THEY'LL NEVER CATCH STEEL LADY NANASE OR THE HUNDREDS OF THOUSANDS OF IMAGINA-TIONS THAT BROUGHT HER TO LIFE.

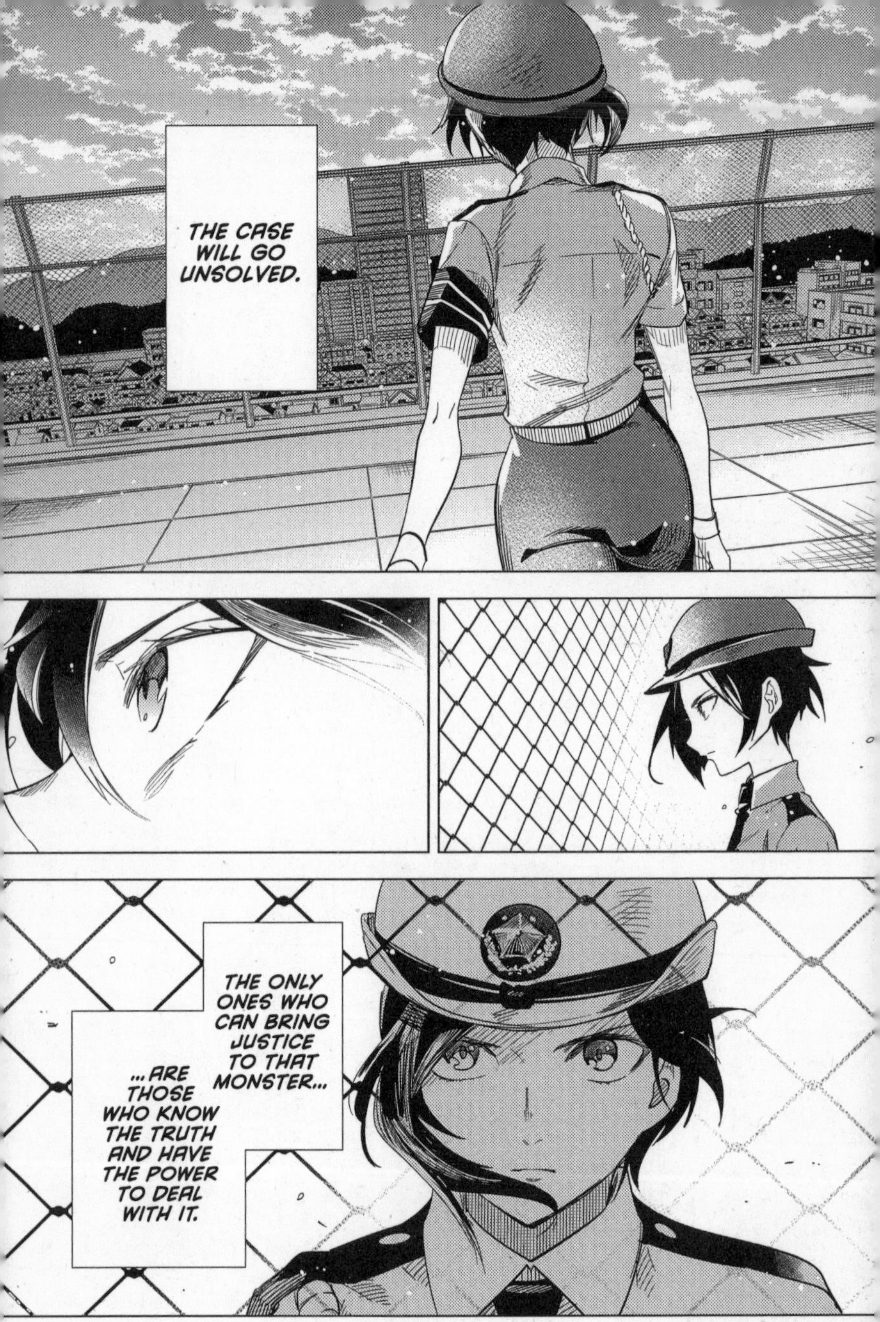
THE CASE WILL GO UNSOLVED.
THE ONLY ONES WHO CAN BRING JUSTICE TO THAT MONSTER...
...ARE THOSE WHO KNOW THE TRUTH AND HAVE THE POWER TO DEAL WITH IT.

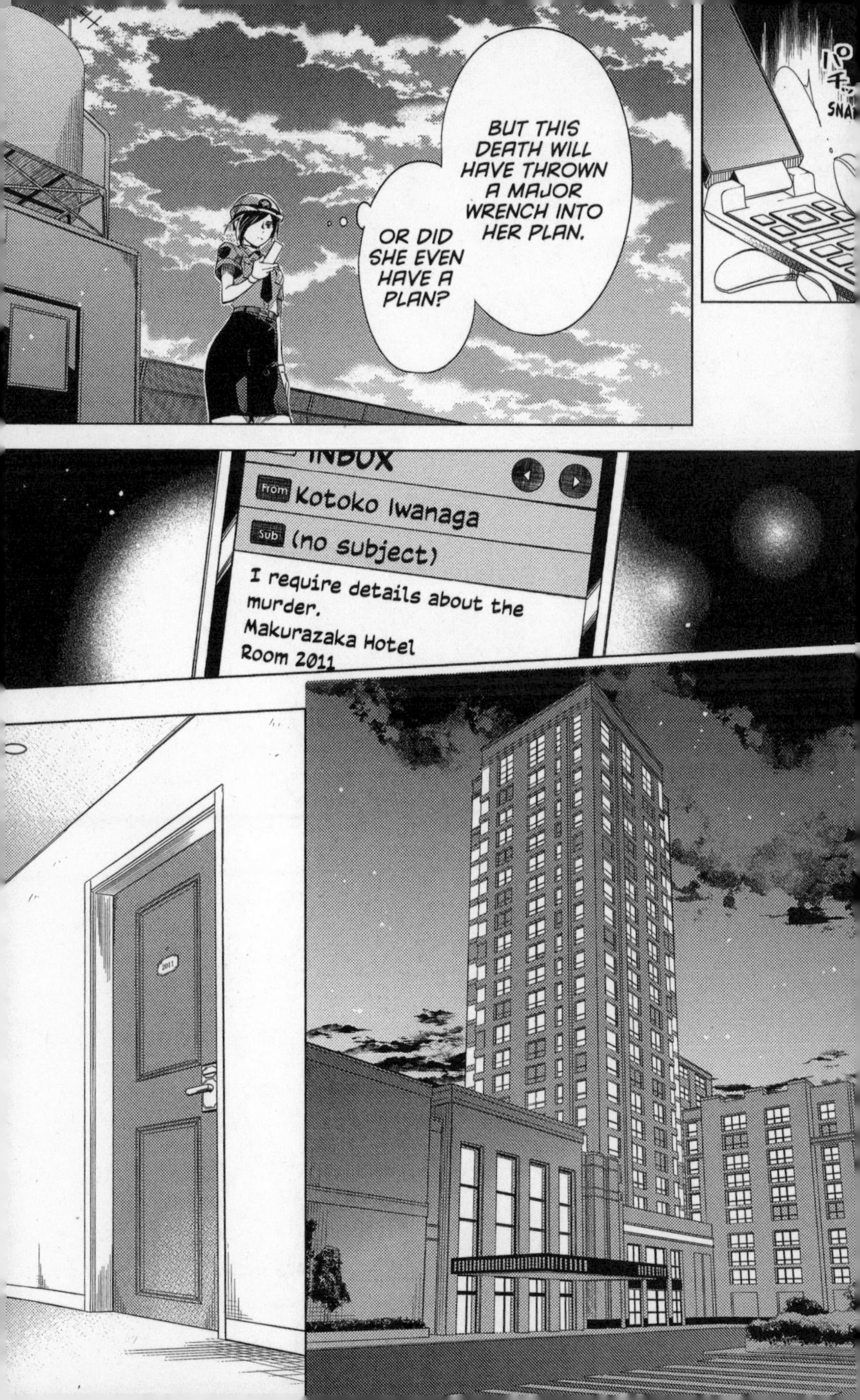
パチッ
SNA
BUT THIS DEATH WILL HAVE THROWN A MAJOR WRENCH INTO HER PLAN.
OR DID SHE EVEN HAVE A PLAN?
INBOX
From Kotoko Iwanaga
Sub (no subject)
I require details about the murder.
Makurazaka Hotel
Room 2011
2011

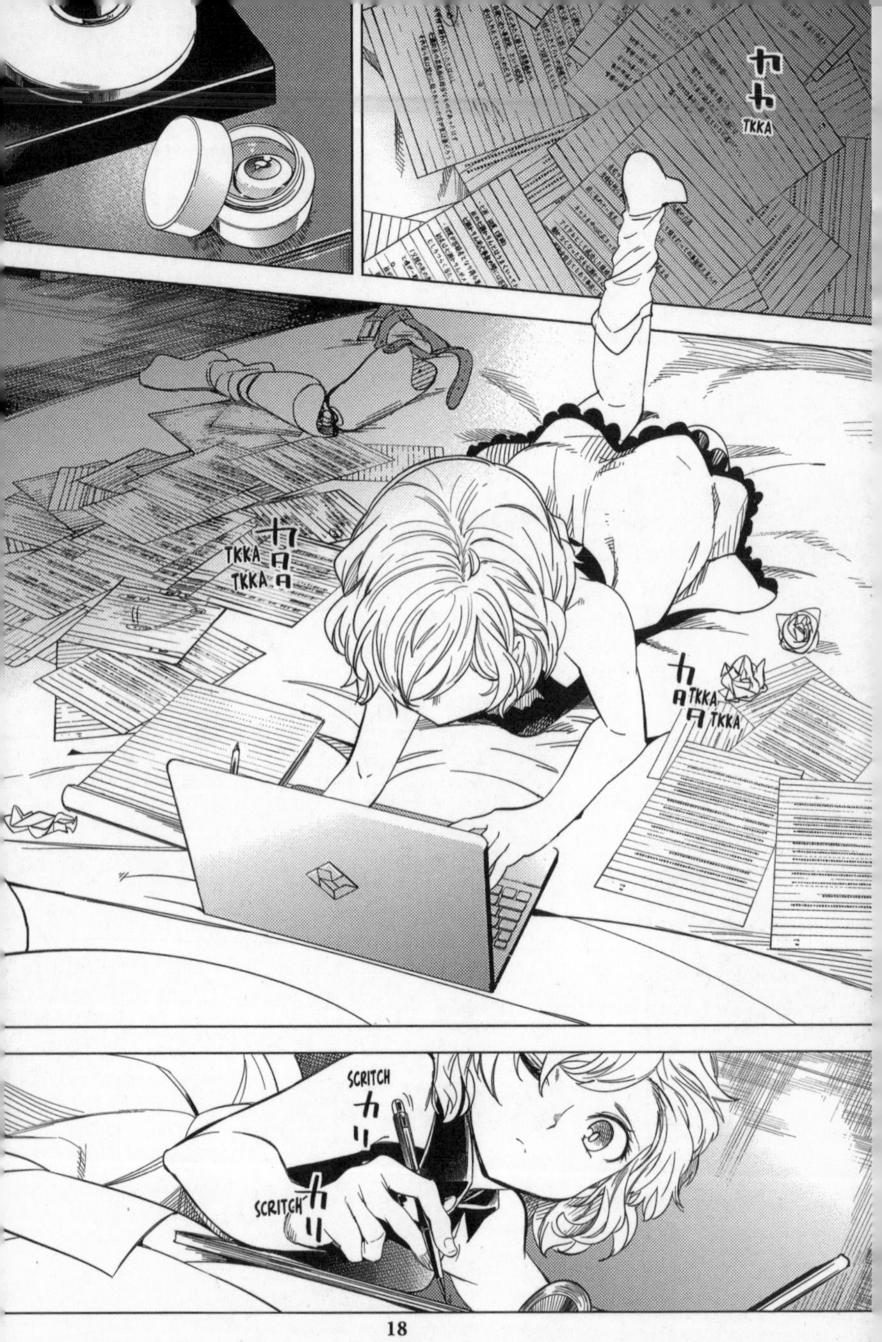
TKKA
TKKA
TKKA
TKKA
TKKA
SCRITCH
SCRITCH

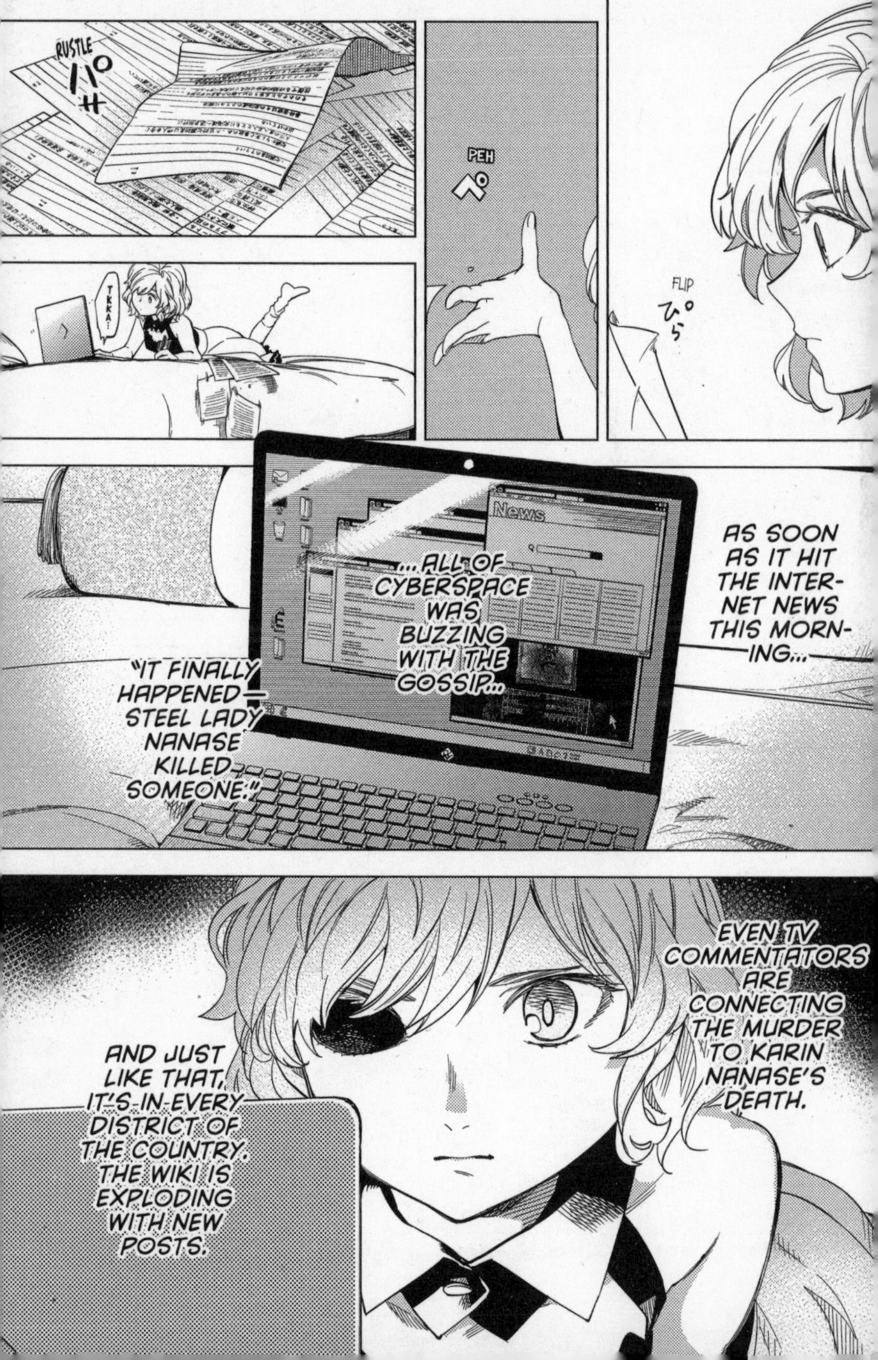
FLIP
ぴら
PEH
ぺ
RUSTLE
パサ
TKKA...
AS SOON AS IT HIT THE INTERNET NEWS THIS MORNING...
...ALL OF CYBERSPACE WAS BUZZING WITH THE GOSSIP...
"IT FINALLY HAPPENED—STEEL LADY NANASE KILLED SOMEONE."
EVEN TV COMMENTATORS ARE CONNECTING THE MURDER TO KARIN NANASE'S DEATH.
AND JUST LIKE THAT, IT'S IN EVERY DISTRICT OF THE COUNTRY. THE WIKI IS EXPLODING WITH NEW POSTS.

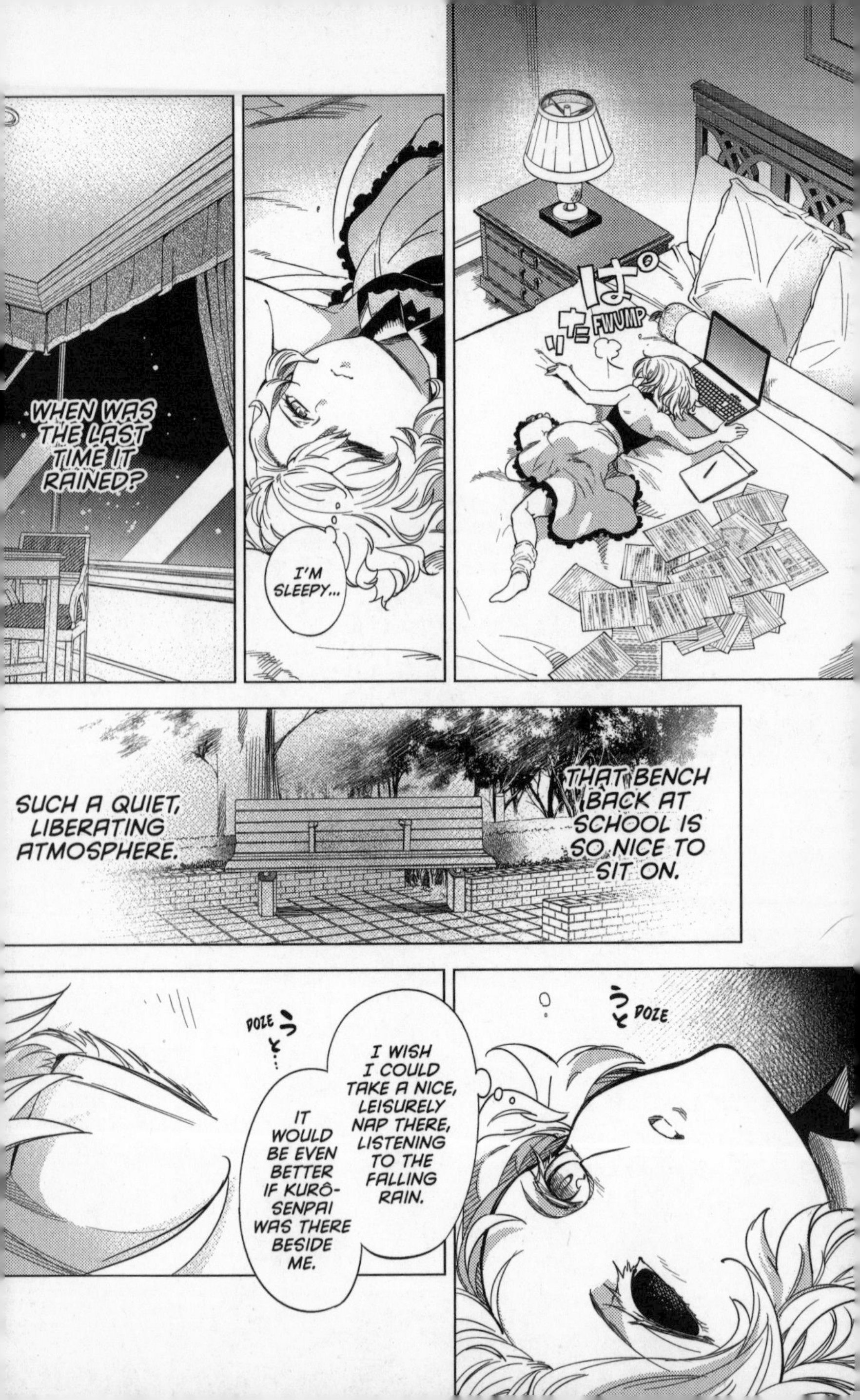

FWUMP
I'M SLEEPY...
WHEN WAS THE LAST TIME IT RAINED?
THAT BENCH BACK AT SCHOOL IS SO NICE TO SIT ON.
SUCH A QUIET, LIBERATING ATMOSPHERE.
DOZE
DOZE
I WISH I COULD TAKE A NICE, LEISURELY NAP THERE, LISTENING TO THE FALLING RAIN.
IT WOULD BE EVEN BETTER IF KURÔ-SENPAI WAS THERE BESIDE ME.

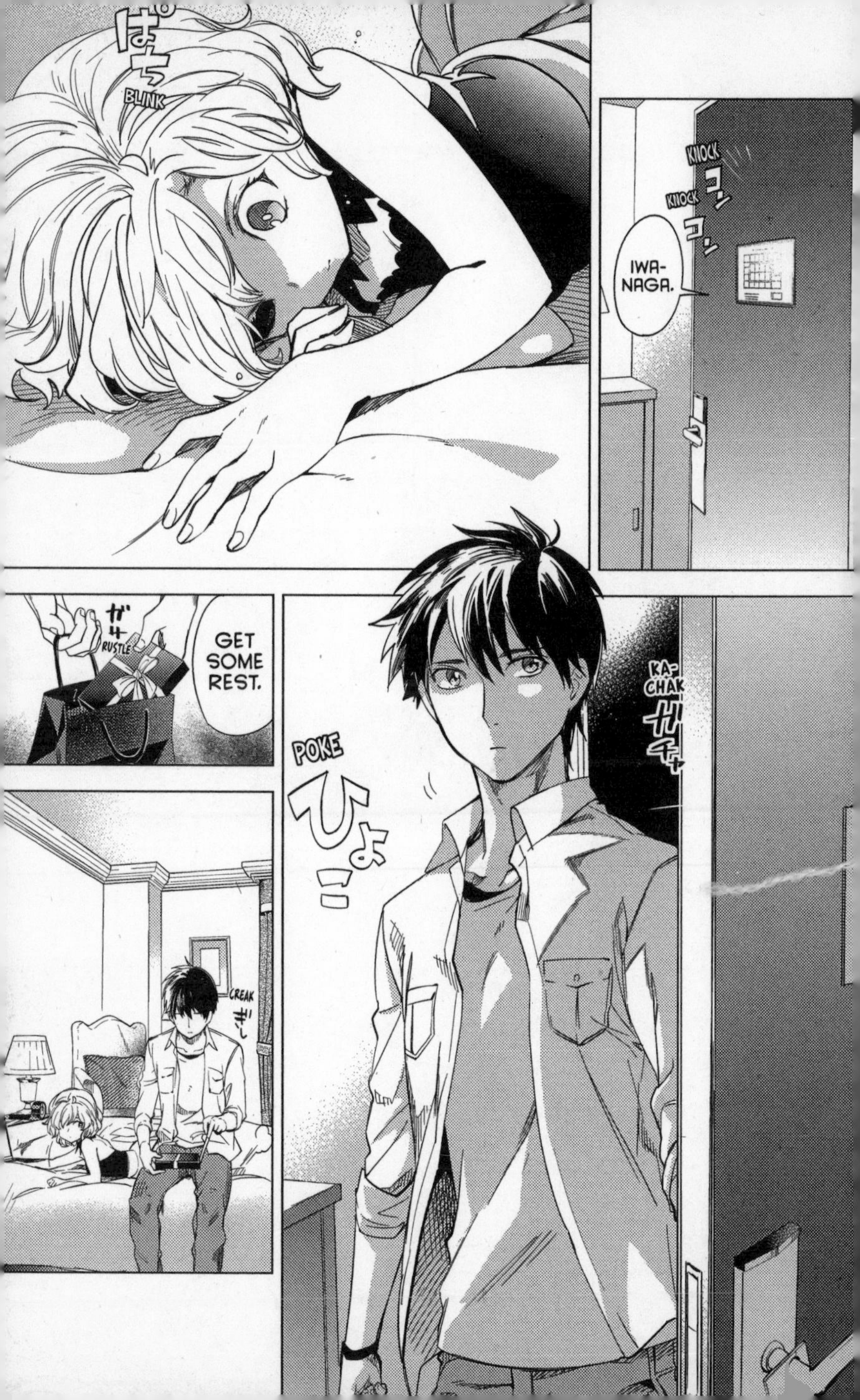
KNOCK
コン
KNOCK
コン
IWA-NAGA.
ぱち
BLINK
KA-CHAK
ガチャ
POKE
ひょこ
ガサ
RUSTLE
GET SOME REST.
CREAK
ぎし

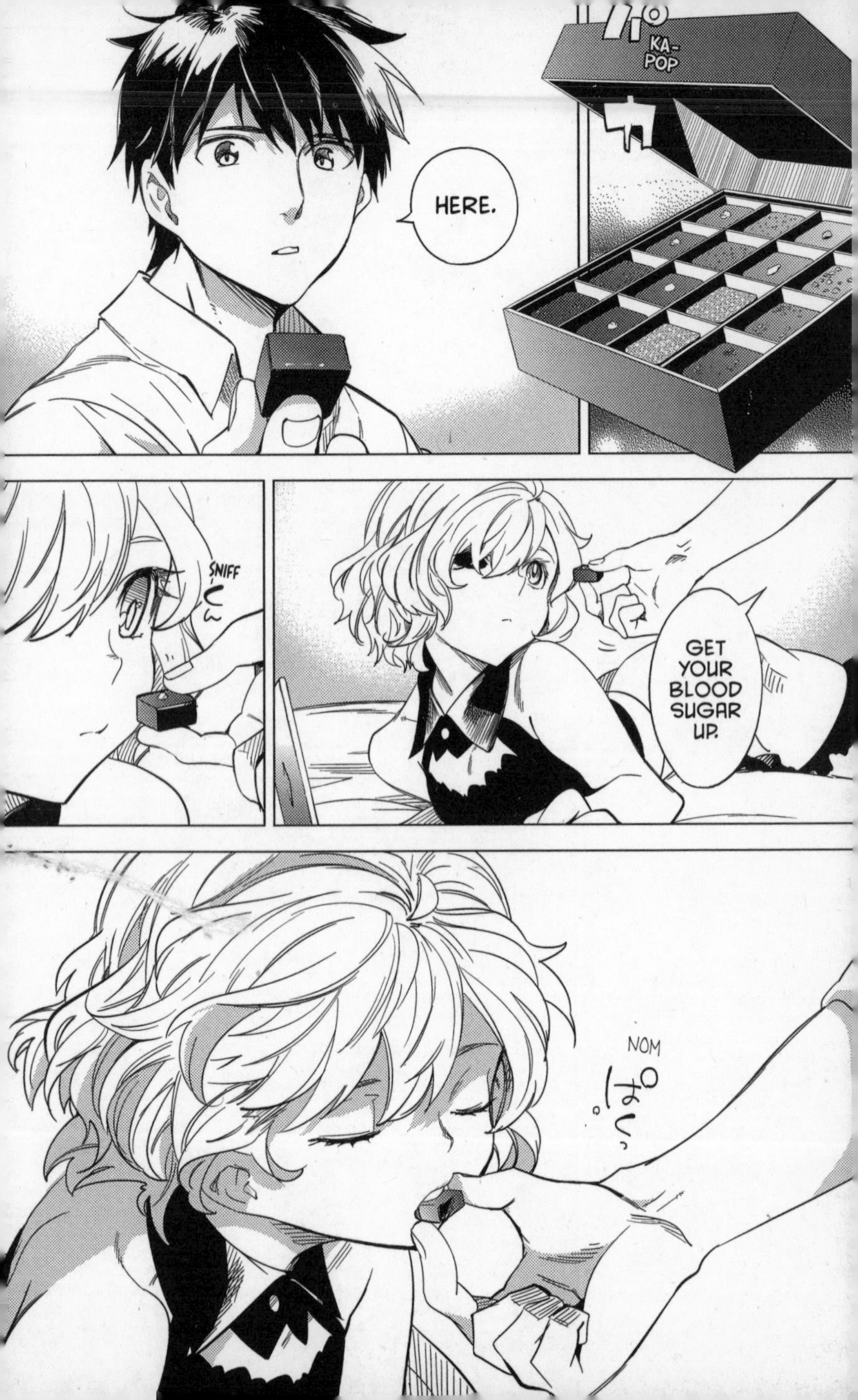
KA-POP
HERE.
GET YOUR BLOOD SUGAR UP.
SNIFF
NOM

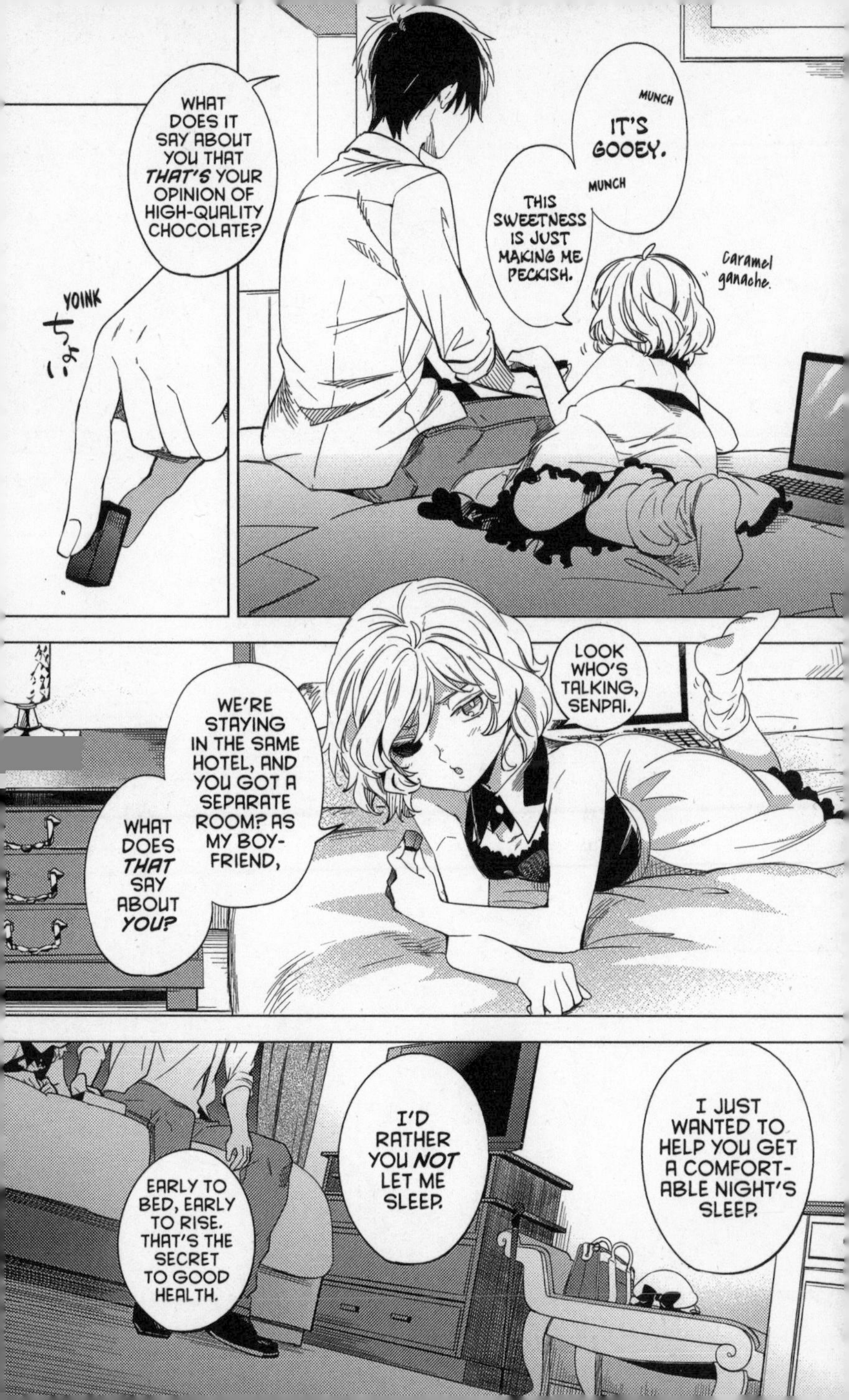
MUNCH
IT'S GOOEY.
MUNCH
THIS SWEETNESS IS JUST MAKING ME PECKISH.
Caramel ganache.
WHAT DOES IT SAY ABOUT YOU THAT *THAT'S* YOUR OPINION OF HIGH-QUALITY CHOCOLATE?
YOINK
ちょい
LOOK WHO'S TALKING, SENPAI.
WE'RE STAYING IN THE SAME HOTEL, AND YOU GOT A SEPARATE ROOM? AS MY BOY-FRIEND,
WHAT DOES *THAT* SAY ABOUT *YOU?*
I JUST WANTED TO HELP YOU GET A COMFORT-ABLE NIGHT'S SLEEP.
I'D RATHER YOU *NOT* LET ME SLEEP.
EARLY TO BED, EARLY TO RISE. THAT'S THE SECRET TO GOOD HEALTH.

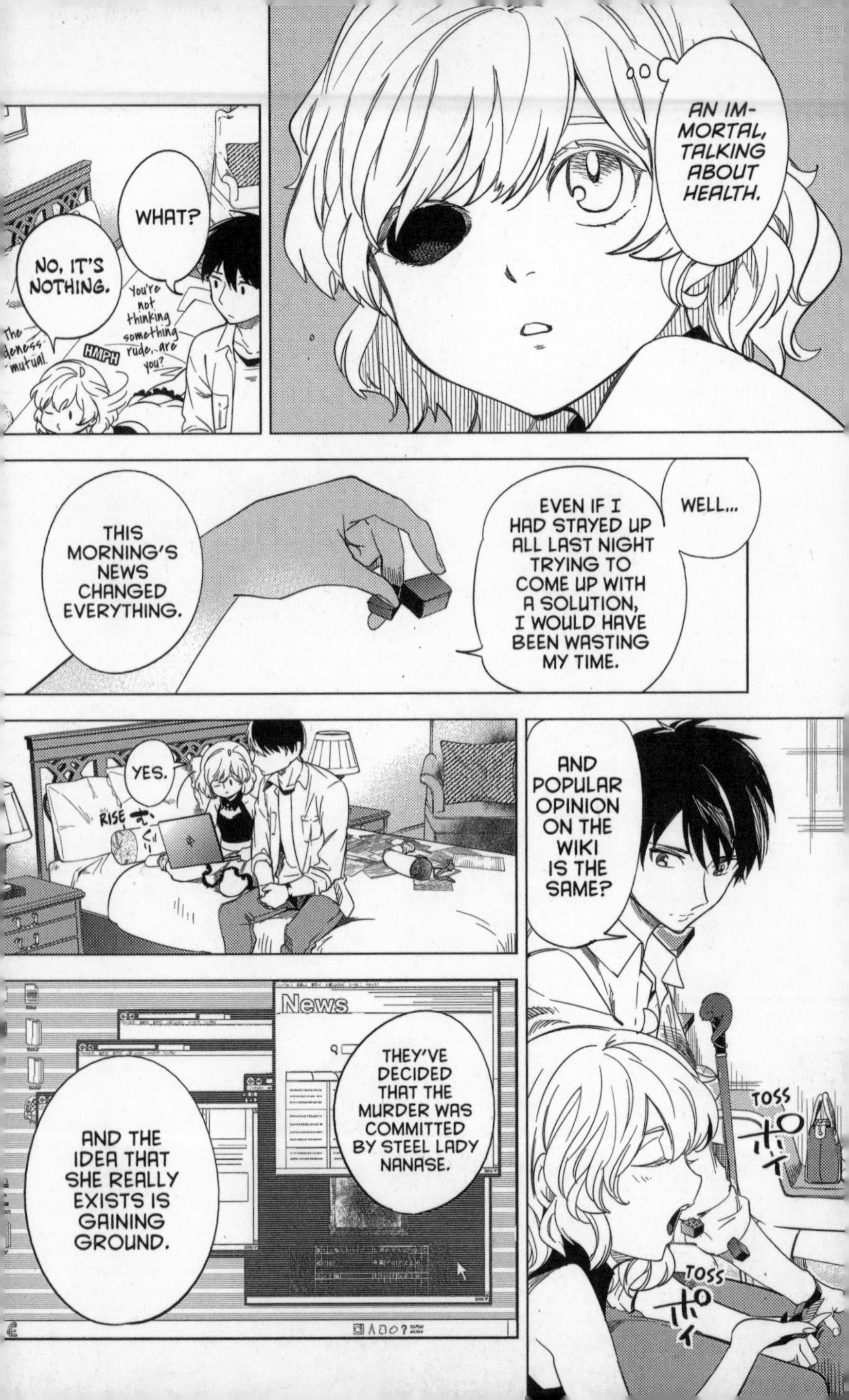

AN IM-MORTAL, TALKING ABOUT HEALTH.
WHAT?
NO, IT'S NOTHING.
You're not thinking something rude, are you?
HMPH
The deness mutual.
WELL...
EVEN IF I HAD STAYED UP ALL LAST NIGHT TRYING TO COME UP WITH A SOLUTION, I WOULD HAVE BEEN WASTING MY TIME.
THIS MORNING'S NEWS CHANGED EVERYTHING.
AND POPULAR OPINION ON THE WIKI IS THE SAME?
TOSS
TOSS
YES.
RISE
News
THEY'VE DECIDED THAT THE MURDER WAS COMMITTED BY STEEL LADY NANASE.
AND THE IDEA THAT SHE REALLY EXISTS IS GAINING GROUND.

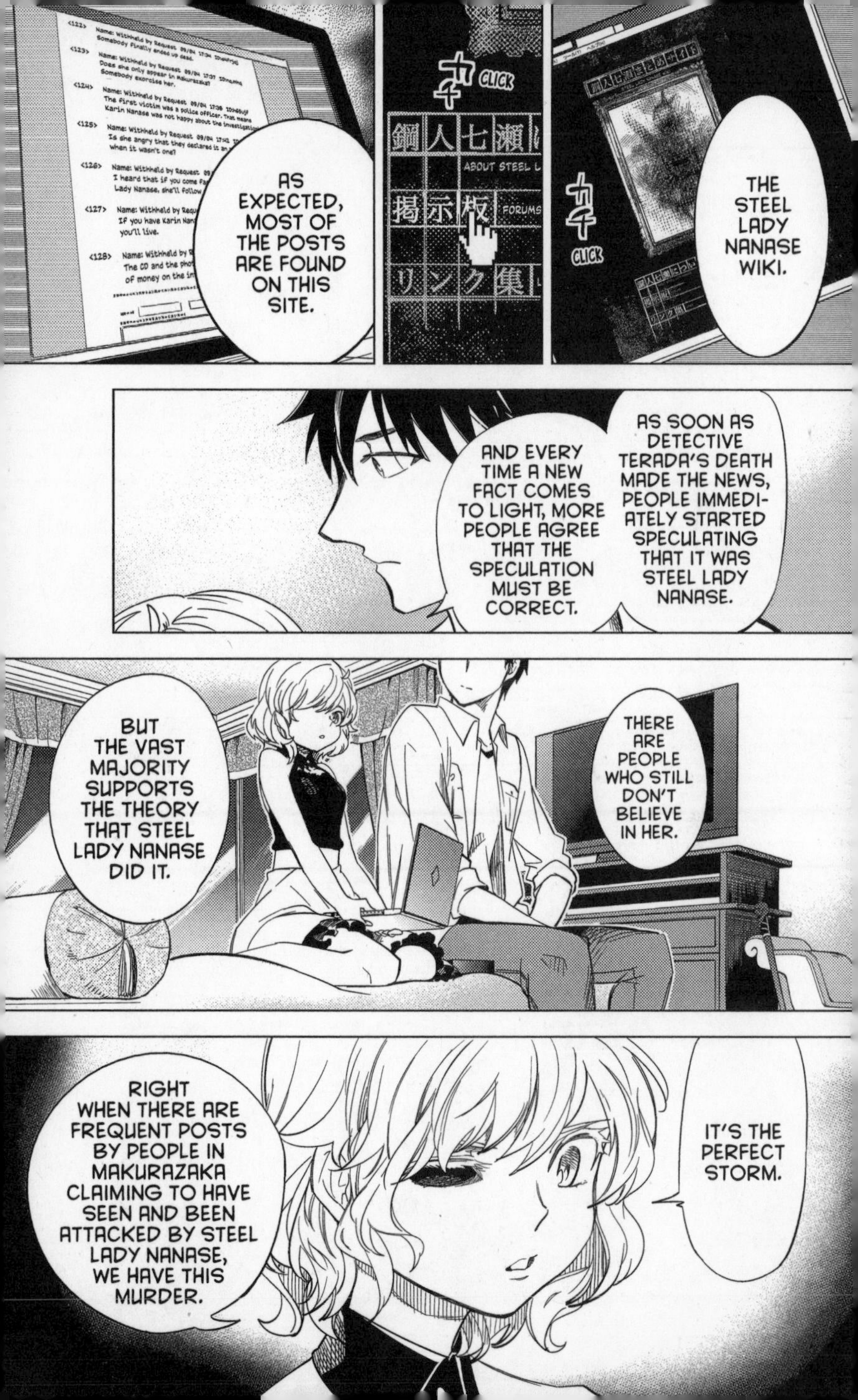
カチ
CLICK
THE STEEL LADY NANASE WIKI.
カチ
CLICK
鋼人七瀬
掲示板
FORUMS
リンク集
<122> Name: Withheld by Request 09/04 17:34
Somebody finally ended up dead.
<123> Name: Withheld by Request 09/04 17:37
Does she only appear in Makurazaka?
Somebody exorcise her.
<124> Name: Withheld by Request 09/04 17:38
The first victim was a police officer. That means
Karin Nanase was not happy about the investigation
<125> Name: Withheld by Request 09/04 17:42
Is she angry that they declared it an
when it wasn't one?
<126> Name: Withheld by Request
I heard that if you come
Lady Nanase, she'll follow
<127> Name: Withheld by
If you have Karin
you'll live.
<128> Name: Withheld by
The CD and the
of money on the
AS EXPECTED, MOST OF THE POSTS ARE FOUND ON THIS SITE.
AS SOON AS DETECTIVE TERADA'S DEATH MADE THE NEWS, PEOPLE IMMEDIATELY STARTED SPECULATING THAT IT WAS STEEL LADY NANASE.
AND EVERY TIME A NEW FACT COMES TO LIGHT, MORE PEOPLE AGREE THAT THE SPECULATION MUST BE CORRECT.
THERE ARE PEOPLE WHO STILL DON'T BELIEVE IN HER.
BUT THE VAST MAJORITY SUPPORTS THE THEORY THAT STEEL LADY NANASE DID IT.
IT'S THE PERFECT STORM.
RIGHT WHEN THERE ARE FREQUENT POSTS BY PEOPLE IN MAKURAZAKA CLAIMING TO HAVE SEEN AND BEEN ATTACKED BY STEEL LADY NANASE, WE HAVE THIS MURDER.

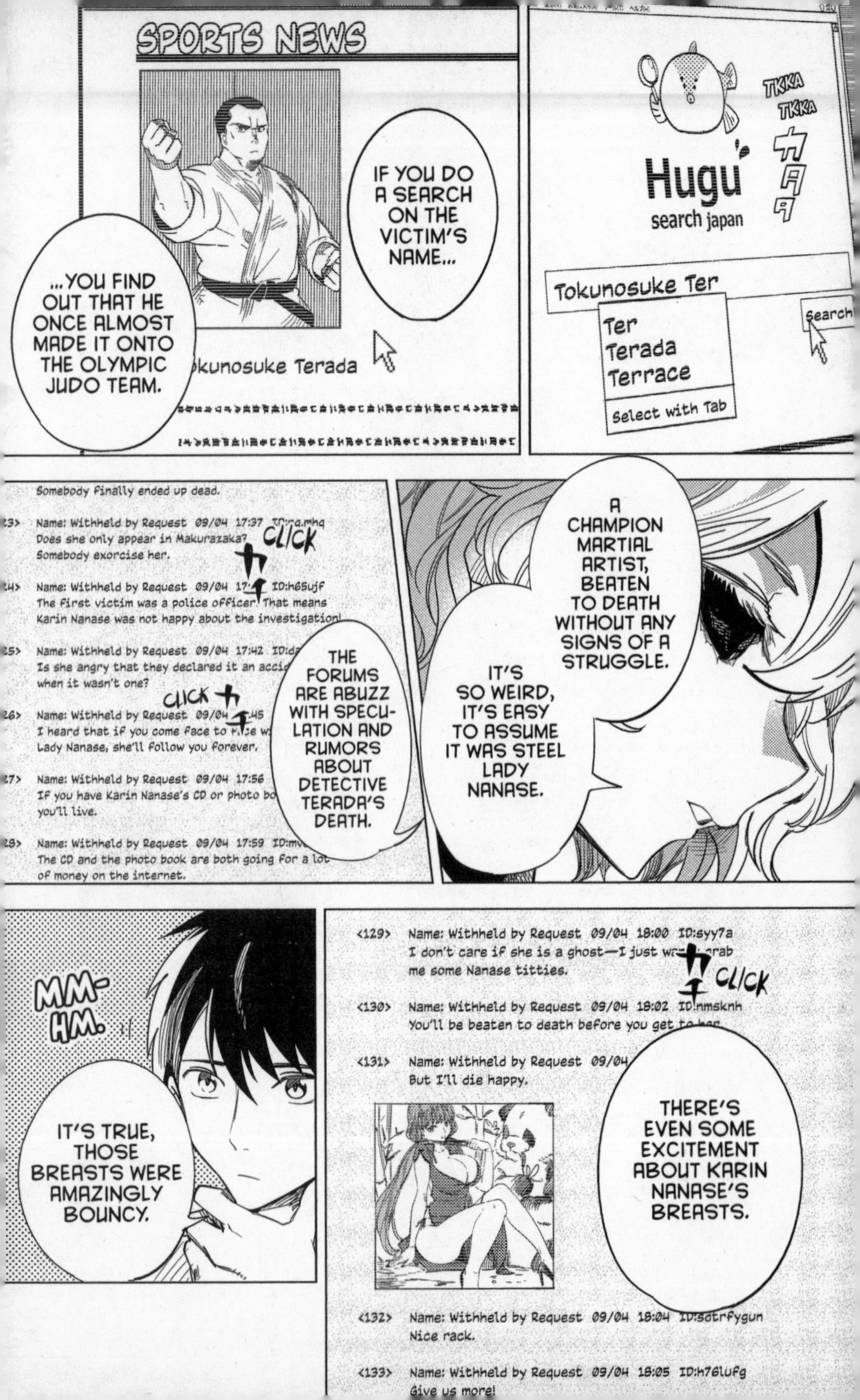
TKKA TKKA
カタタ
Hugu
search japan
Tokunosuke Ter
Ter
Terada
Terrace
Select with Tab
Search
SPORTS NEWS
IF YOU DO A SEARCH ON THE VICTIM'S NAME...
okunosuke Terada
...YOU FIND OUT THAT HE ONCE ALMOST MADE IT ONTO THE OLYMPIC JUDO TEAM.
A CHAMPION MARTIAL ARTIST, BEATEN TO DEATH WITHOUT ANY SIGNS OF A STRUGGLE.
IT'S SO WEIRD, IT'S EASY TO ASSUME IT WAS STEEL LADY NANASE.
THE FORUMS ARE ABUZZ WITH SPECULATION AND RUMORS ABOUT DETECTIVE TERADA'S DEATH.
Somebody finally ended up dead.
23> Name: Withheld by Request 09/04 17:37
Does she only appear in Makurazaka?
Somebody exorcise her.
CLICK カチ
24> Name: Withheld by Request 09/04 ID:h65ujf
The first victim was a police officer. That means
Karin Nanase was not happy about the investigation!
25> Name: Withheld by Request 09/04 17:42
Is she angry that they declared it an acci
when it wasn't one?
CLICK カチ
26> Name: Withheld by Request 09/04
I heard that if you come face to
Lady Nanase, she'll follow you forever.
27> Name: Withheld by Request 09/04 17:56
If you have Karin Nanase's CD or photo bo
you'll live.
28> Name: Withheld by Request 09/04 17:59
The CD and the photo book are both going for a lot
of money on the internet.
<129> Name: Withheld by Request 09/04 18:00 ID:syy7a
I don't care if she is a ghost—I just w
me some Nanase titties.
カチ CLICK
<130> Name: Withheld by Request 09/04 18:02 ID:nmsknh
You'll be beaten to death before you get
<131> Name: Withheld by Request 09/04
But I'll die happy.
THERE'S EVEN SOME EXCITEMENT ABOUT KARIN NANASE'S BREASTS.
<132> Name: Withheld by Request 09/04 18:04 ID:sdtrfygun
Nice rack.
<133> Name: Withheld by Request 09/04 18:05 ID:h76lufg
Give us more!
MM-HM.
IT'S TRUE, THOSE BREASTS WERE AMAZINGLY BOUNCY.

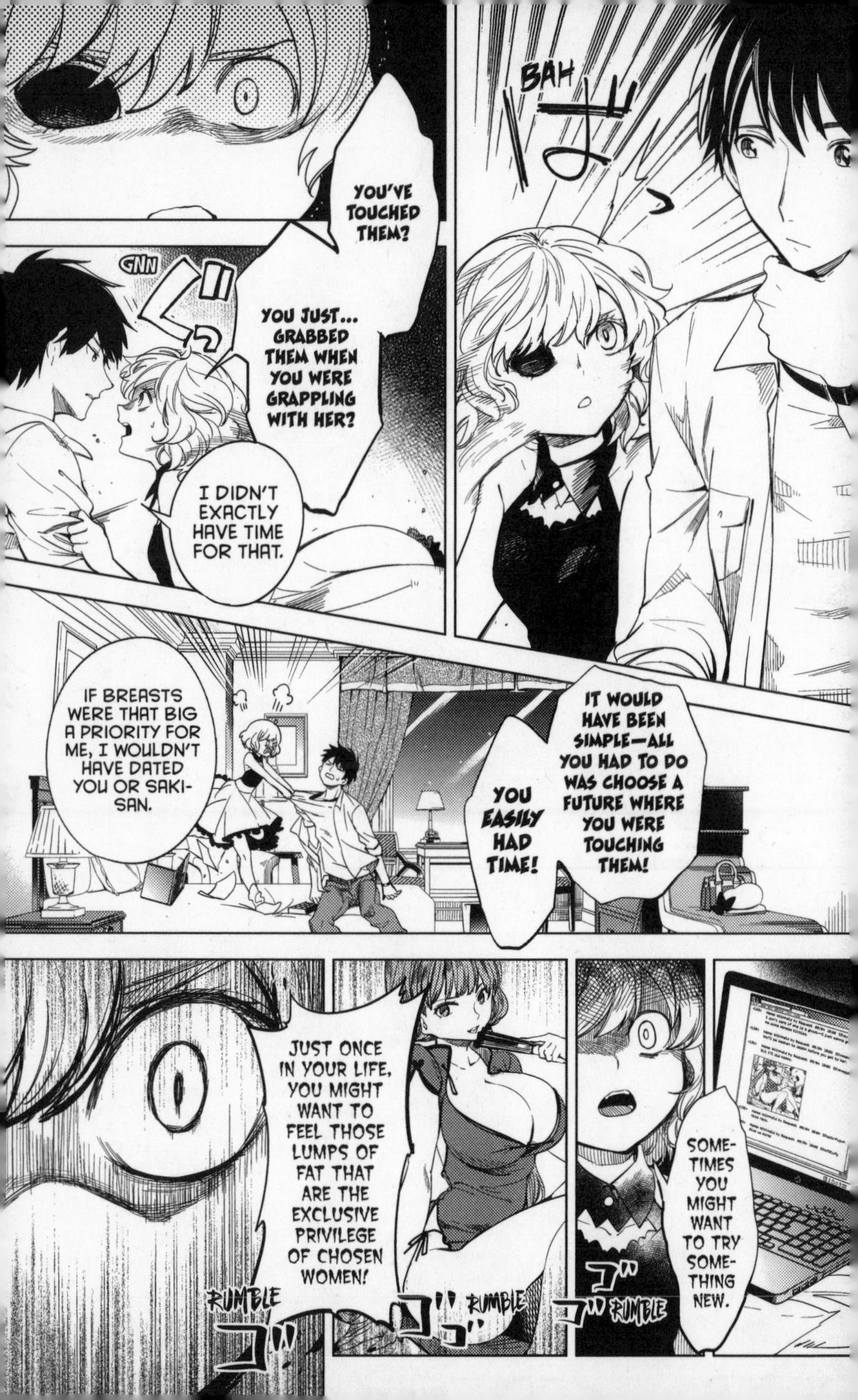
BAH
YOU'VE TOUCHED THEM?
GNN
YOU JUST... GRABBED THEM WHEN YOU WERE GRAPPLING WITH HER?
I DIDN'T EXACTLY HAVE TIME FOR THAT.
IT WOULD HAVE BEEN SIMPLE—ALL YOU HAD TO DO WAS CHOOSE A FUTURE WHERE YOU WERE TOUCHING THEM!
YOU EASILY HAD TIME!
IF BREASTS WERE THAT BIG A PRIORITY FOR ME, I WOULDN'T HAVE DATED YOU OR SAKI-SAN.
SOME-TIMES YOU MIGHT WANT TO TRY SOME-THING NEW.
RUMBLE
JUST ONCE IN YOUR LIFE, YOU MIGHT WANT TO FEEL THOSE LUMPS OF FAT THAT ARE THE EXCLUSIVE PRIVILEGE OF CHOSEN WOMEN!
RUMBLE
RUMBLE

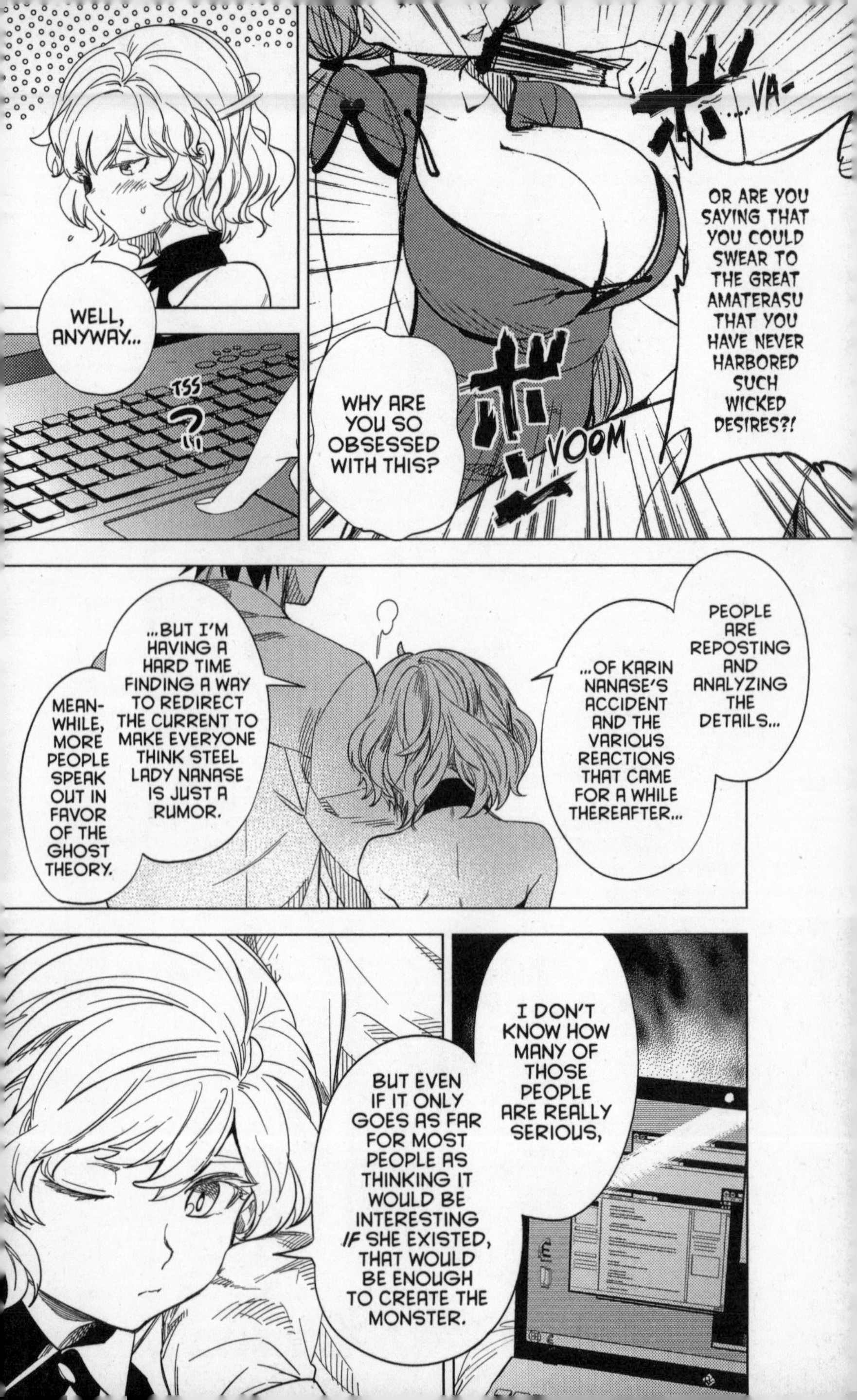
...VA-
OR ARE YOU SAYING THAT YOU COULD SWEAR TO THE GREAT AMATERASU THAT YOU HAVE NEVER HARBORED SUCH WICKED DESIRES?!
WHY ARE YOU SO OBSESSED WITH THIS?
VOOM
WELL, ANYWAY...
TSS
PEOPLE ARE REPOSTING AND ANALYZING THE DETAILS...
...OF KARIN NANASE'S ACCIDENT AND THE VARIOUS REACTIONS THAT CAME FOR A WHILE THEREAFTER...
...BUT I'M HAVING A HARD TIME FINDING A WAY TO REDIRECT THE CURRENT TO MAKE EVERYONE THINK STEEL LADY NANASE IS JUST A RUMOR.
MEAN-WHILE, MORE PEOPLE SPEAK OUT IN FAVOR OF THE GHOST THEORY.
I DON'T KNOW HOW MANY OF THOSE PEOPLE ARE REALLY SERIOUS,
BUT EVEN IF IT ONLY GOES AS FAR FOR MOST PEOPLE AS THINKING IT WOULD BE INTERESTING *IF* SHE EXISTED, THAT WOULD BE ENOUGH TO CREATE THE MONSTER.

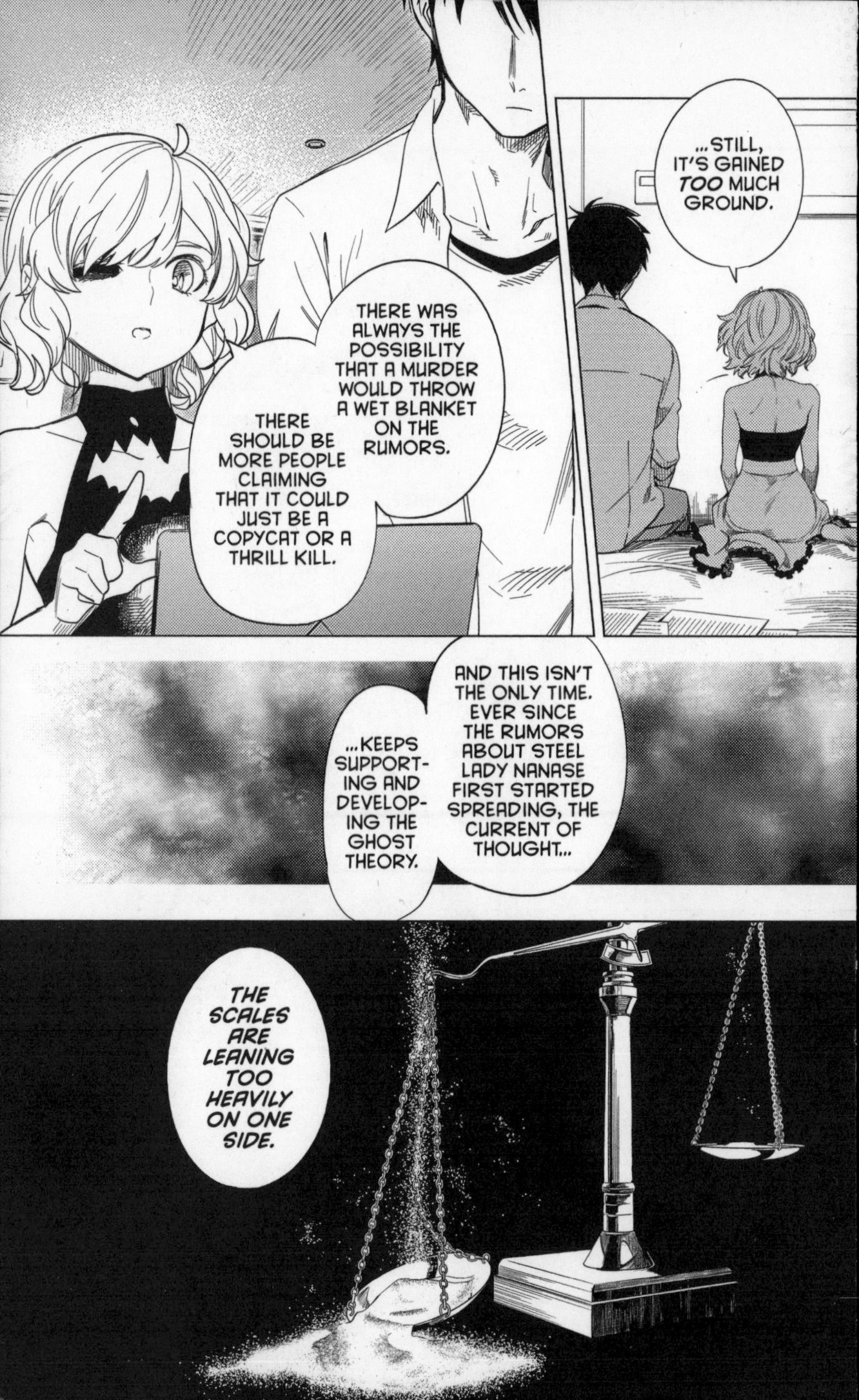
...STILL, IT'S GAINED *TOO* MUCH GROUND.
THERE WAS ALWAYS THE POSSIBILITY THAT A MURDER WOULD THROW A WET BLANKET ON THE RUMORS.
THERE SHOULD BE MORE PEOPLE CLAIMING THAT IT COULD JUST BE A COPYCAT OR A THRILL KILL.
AND THIS ISN'T THE ONLY TIME. EVER SINCE THE RUMORS ABOUT STEEL LADY NANASE FIRST STARTED SPREADING, THE CURRENT OF THOUGHT...
...KEEPS SUPPORTING AND DEVELOPING THE GHOST THEORY.
*THE SCALES ARE LEANING TOO HEAVILY ON ONE SIDE.*

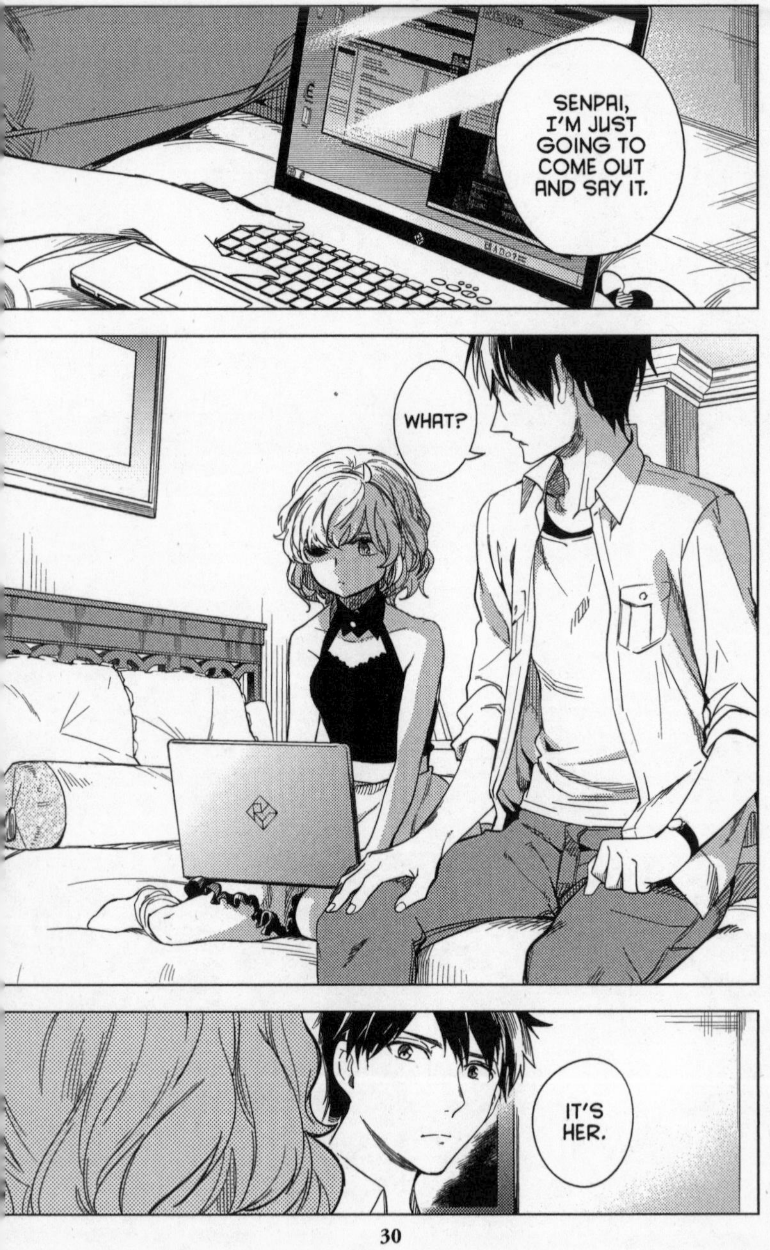
SENPAI, I'M JUST GOING TO COME OUT AND SAY IT.
WHAT?
IT'S HER.

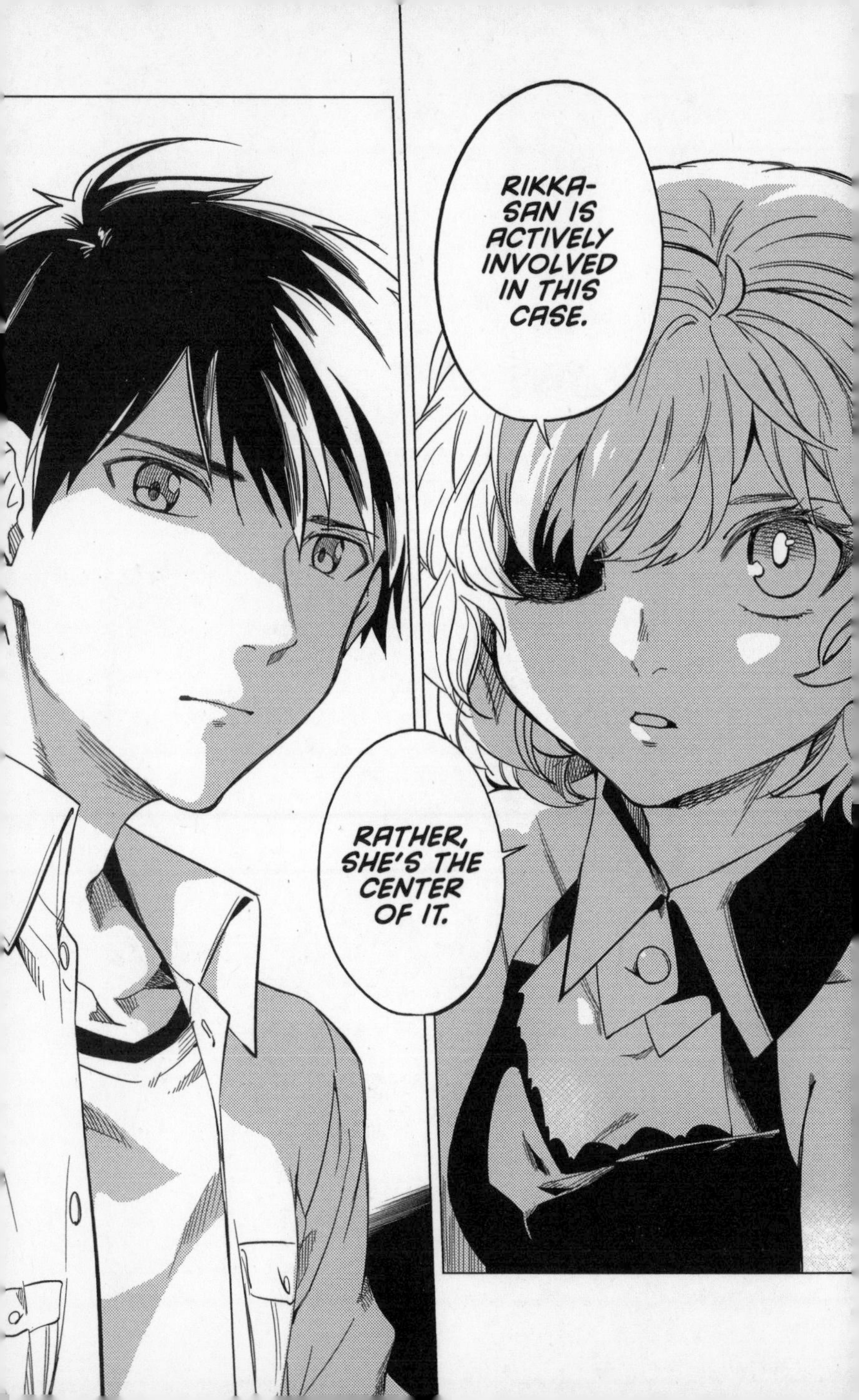
RIKKA-SAN IS ACTIVELY INVOLVED IN THIS CASE.
RATHER, SHE'S THE CENTER OF IT.

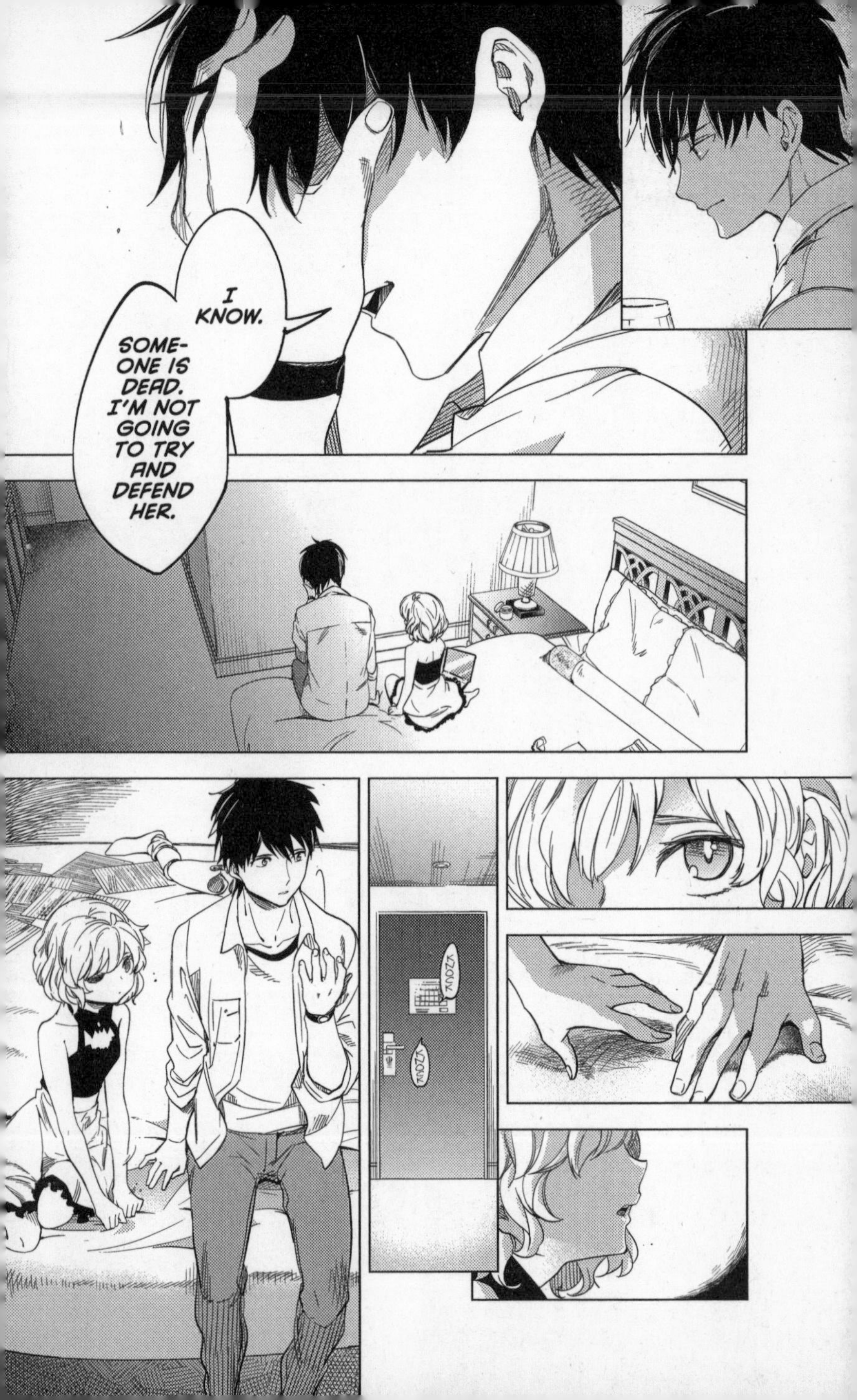
I KNOW.
SOME-ONE IS DEAD. I'M NOT GOING TO TRY AND DEFEND HER.
KNOCK
KNOCK

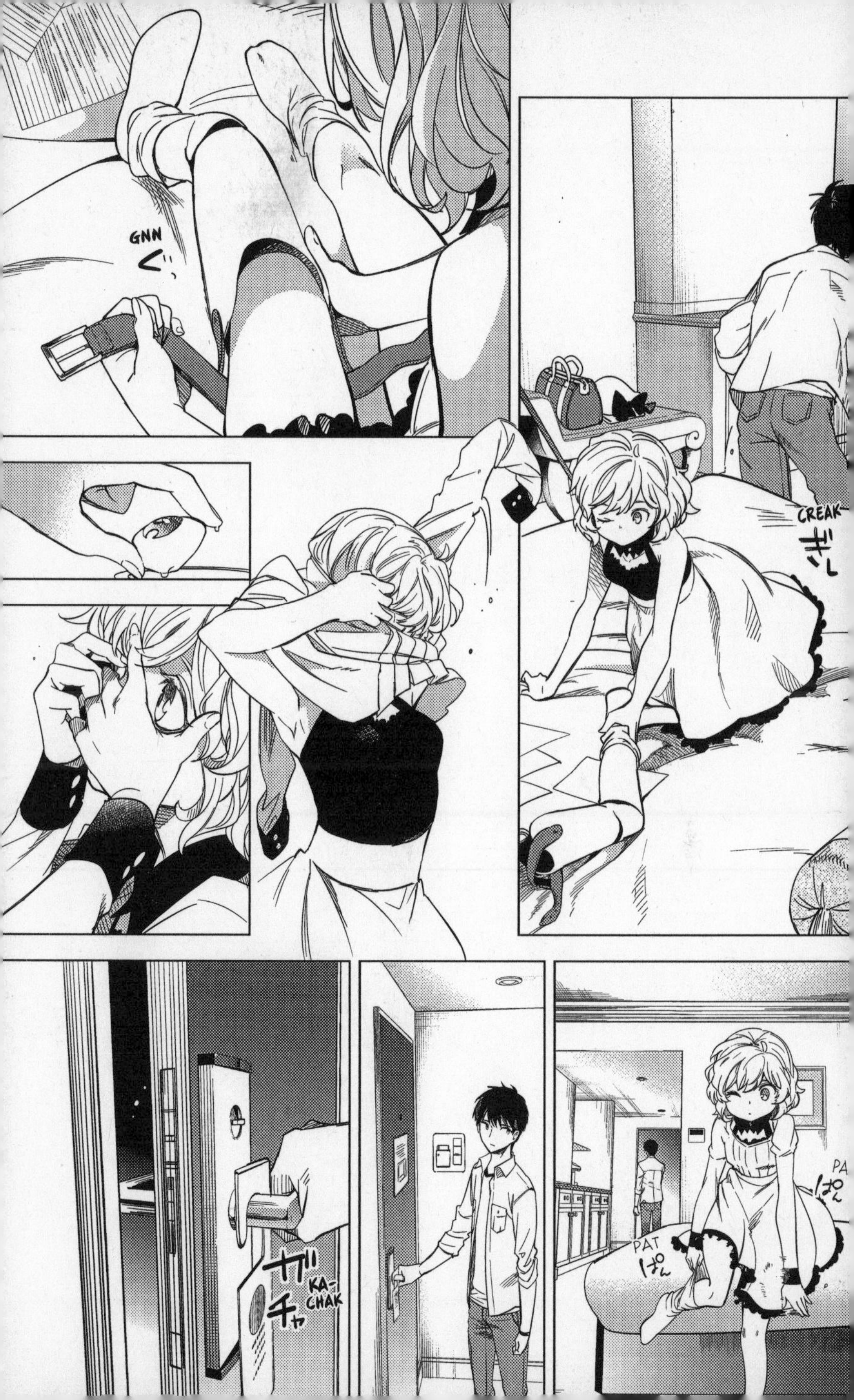
CREAK
ぎし
GNN
ぐ
PA
ぱん
PAT
ぱん
KA-CHAK
ガチャ

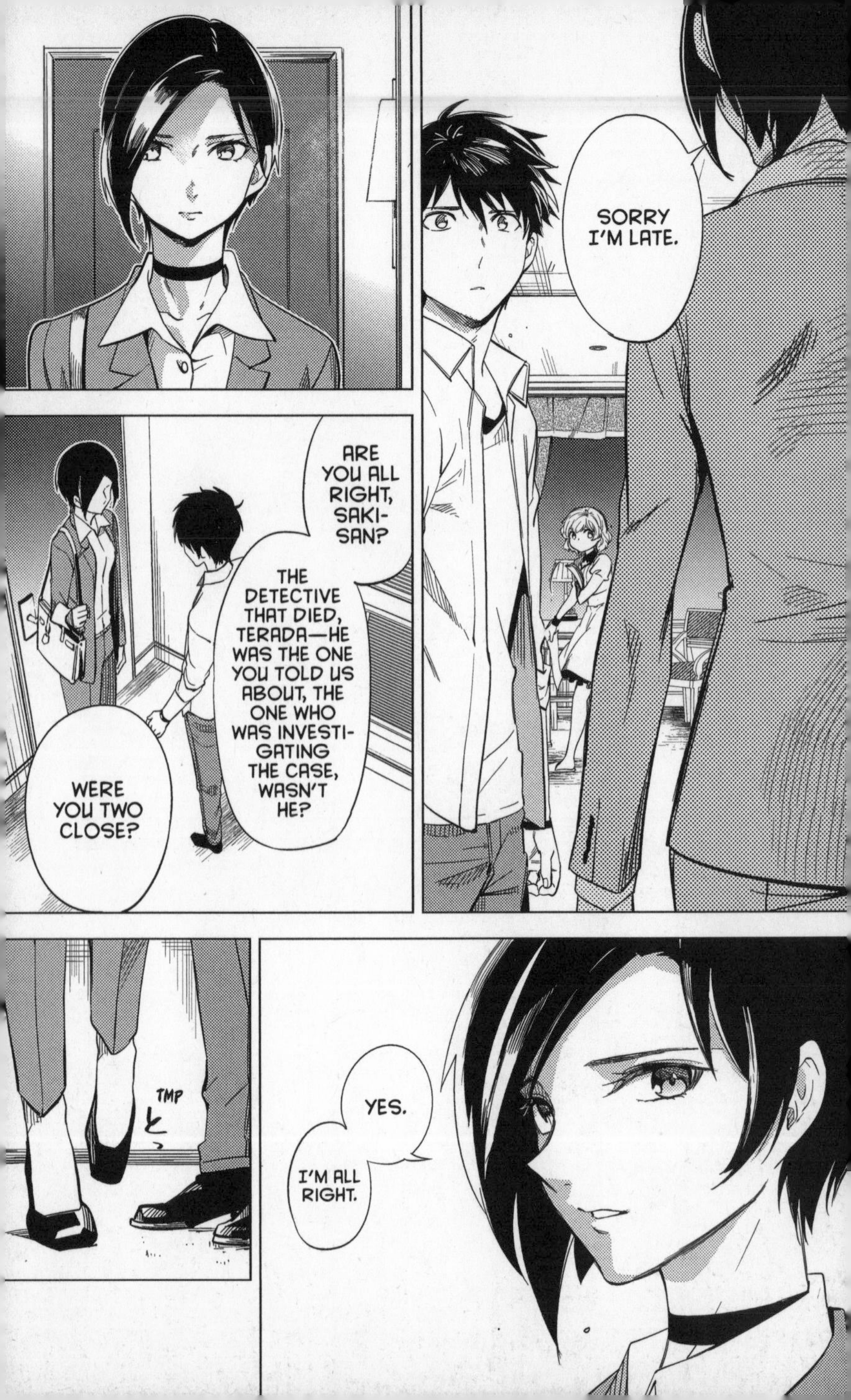
SORRY I'M LATE.
ARE YOU ALL RIGHT, SAKI-SAN?
THE DETECTIVE THAT DIED, TERADA—HE WAS THE ONE YOU TOLD US ABOUT, THE ONE WHO WAS INVESTIGATING THE CASE, WASN'T HE?
WERE YOU TWO CLOSE?
YES.
I'M ALL RIGHT.
TMP

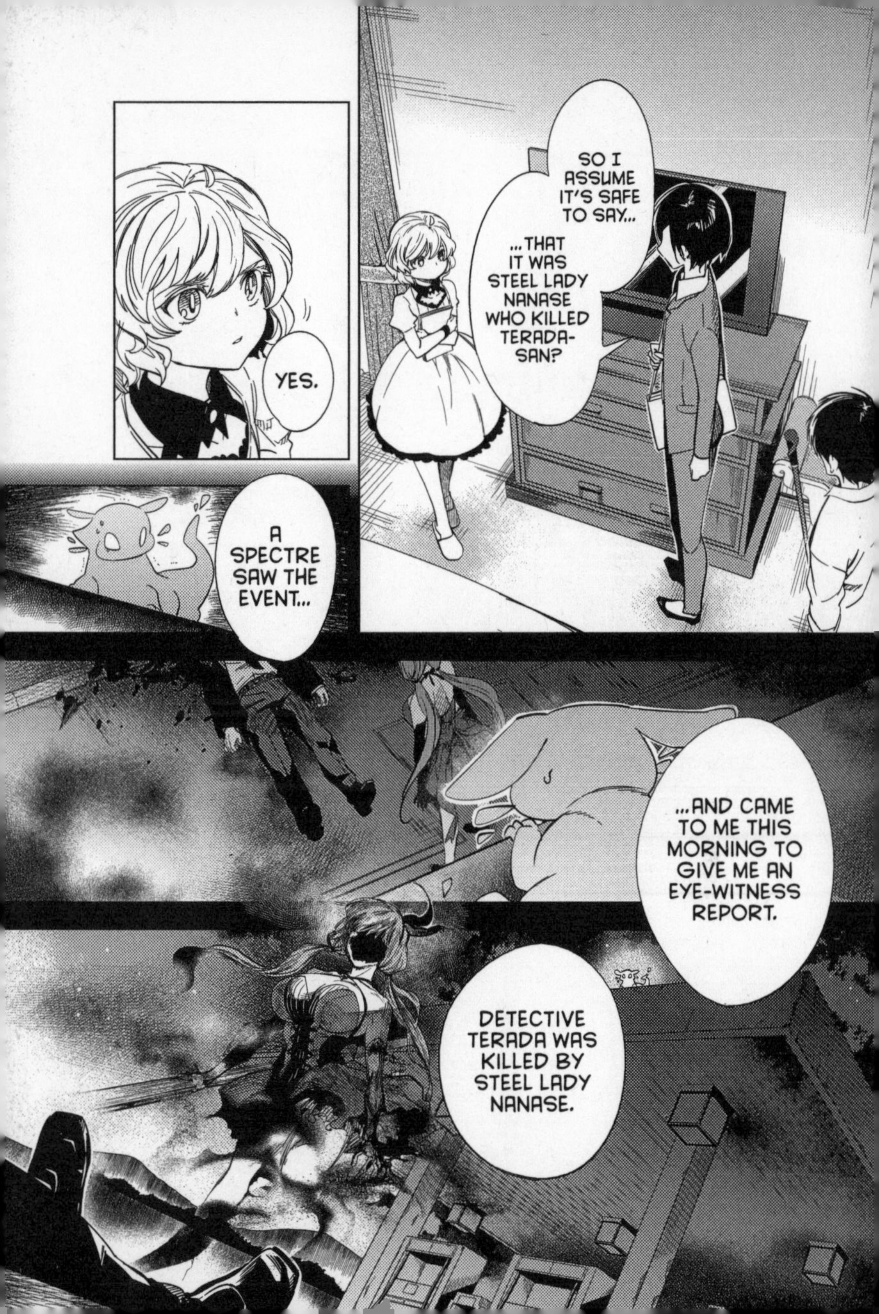
SO I ASSUME IT'S SAFE TO SAY...
...THAT IT WAS STEEL LADY NANASE WHO KILLED TERADA-SAN?
YES.
A SPECTRE SAW THE EVENT...
...AND CAME TO ME THIS MORNING TO GIVE ME AN EYE-WITNESS REPORT.
DETECTIVE TERADA WAS KILLED BY STEEL LADY NANASE.

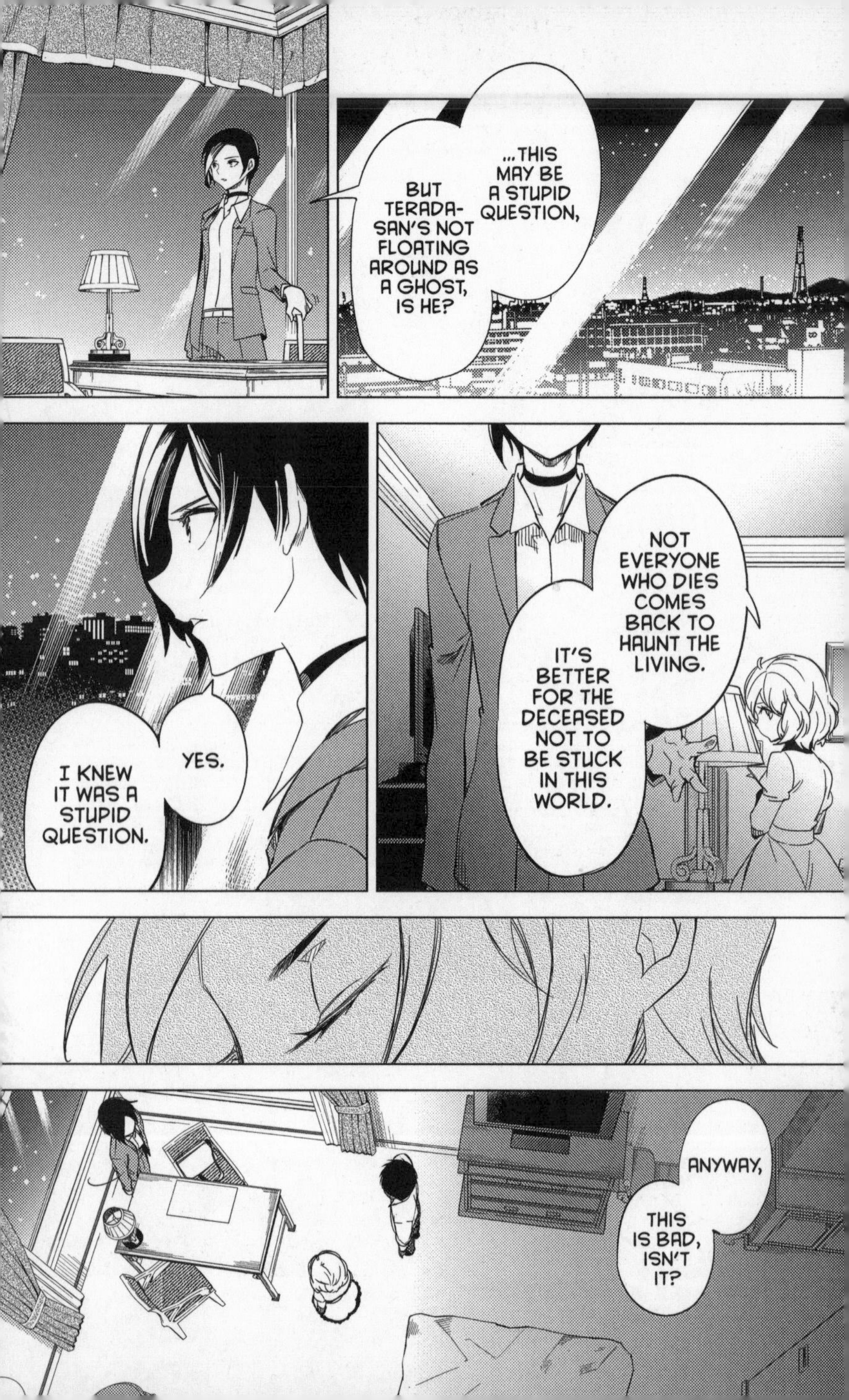
...THIS MAY BE A STUPID QUESTION,
BUT TERADA-SAN'S NOT FLOATING AROUND AS A GHOST, IS HE?
NOT EVERYONE WHO DIES COMES BACK TO HAUNT THE LIVING.
IT'S BETTER FOR THE DECEASED NOT TO BE STUCK IN THIS WORLD.
YES.
I KNEW IT WAS A STUPID QUESTION.
ANYWAY,
THIS IS BAD, ISN'T IT?

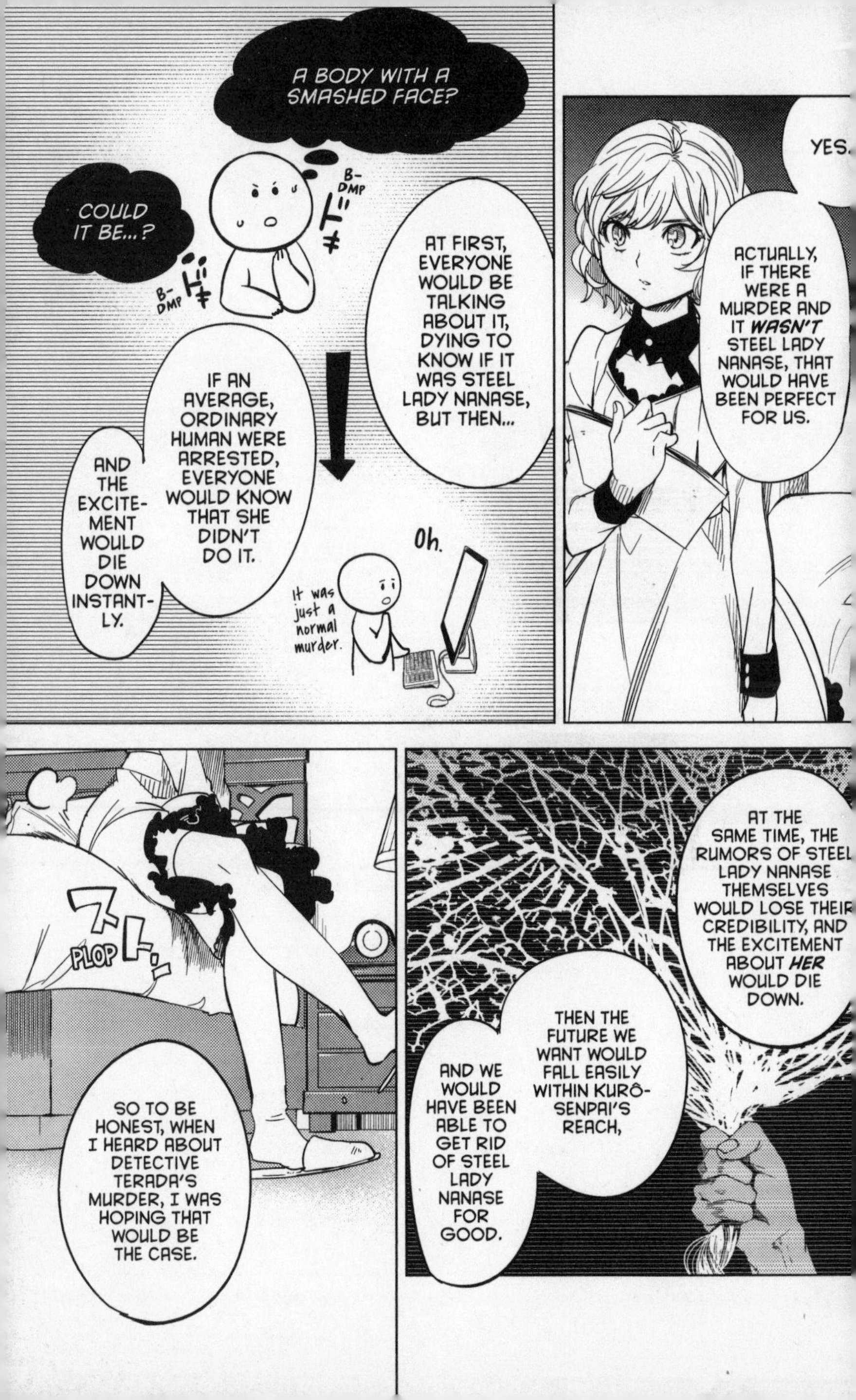

YES.
ACTUALLY, IF THERE WERE A MURDER AND IT *WASN'T* STEEL LADY NANASE, THAT WOULD HAVE BEEN PERFECT FOR US.
A BODY WITH A SMASHED FACE?
B-DMP
COULD IT BE...?
B-DMP
AT FIRST, EVERYONE WOULD BE TALKING ABOUT IT, DYING TO KNOW IF IT WAS STEEL LADY NANASE, BUT THEN...
IF AN AVERAGE, ORDINARY HUMAN WERE ARRESTED, EVERYONE WOULD KNOW THAT SHE DIDN'T DO IT.
AND THE EXCITE-MENT WOULD DIE DOWN INSTANT-LY.
Oh.
It was just a normal murder.
AT THE SAME TIME, THE RUMORS OF STEEL LADY NANASE THEMSELVES WOULD LOSE THEIR CREDIBILITY, AND THE EXCITEMENT ABOUT *HER* WOULD DIE DOWN.
THEN THE FUTURE WE WANT WOULD FALL EASILY WITHIN KURÔ-SENPAI'S REACH,
AND WE WOULD HAVE BEEN ABLE TO GET RID OF STEEL LADY NANASE FOR GOOD.
PLOP
SO TO BE HONEST, WHEN I HEARD ABOUT DETECTIVE TERADA'S MURDER, I WAS HOPING THAT WOULD BE THE CASE.

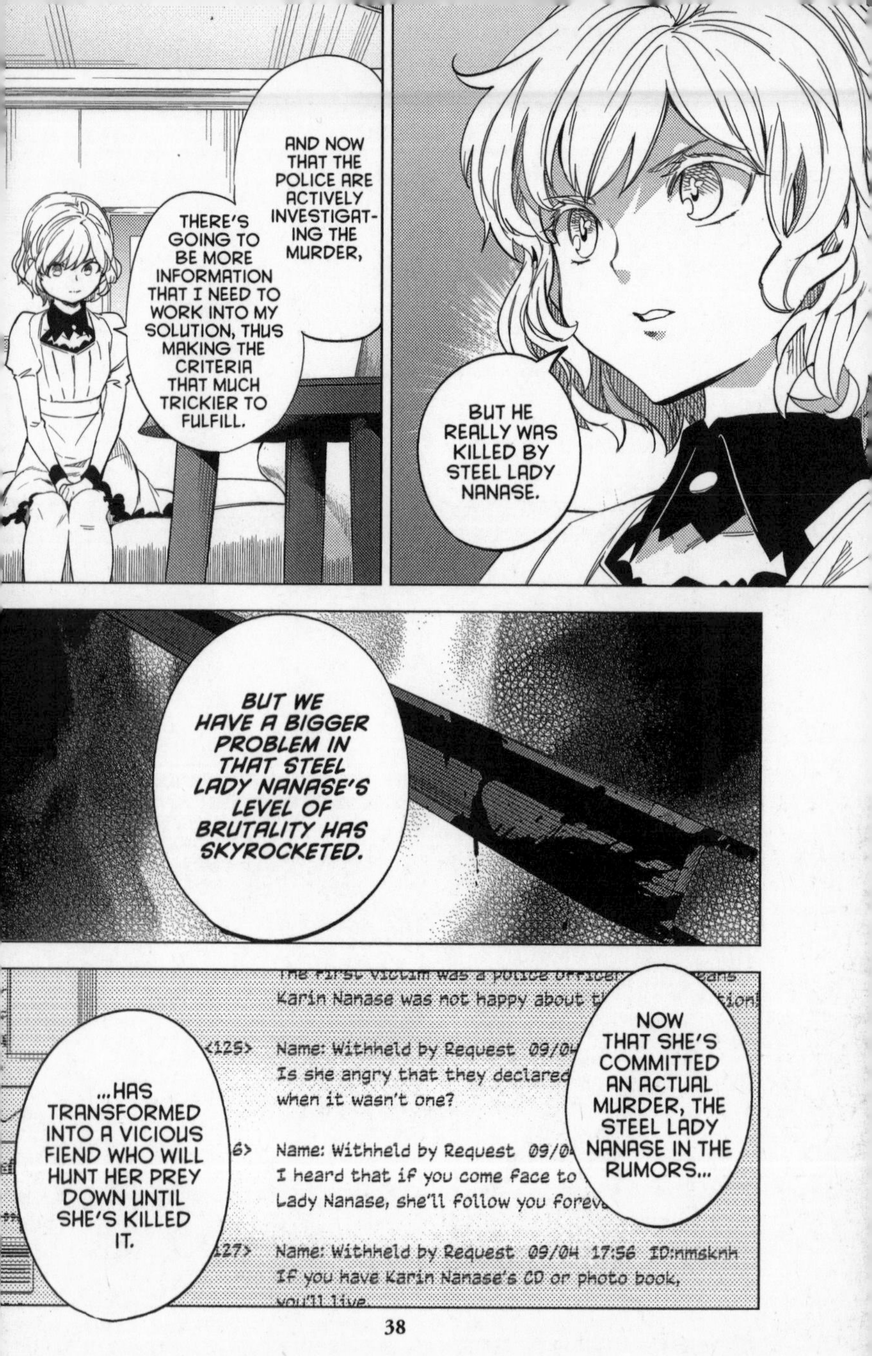
BUT HE REALLY WAS KILLED BY STEEL LADY NANASE.
AND NOW THAT THE POLICE ARE ACTIVELY INVESTIGATING THE MURDER,
THERE'S GOING TO BE MORE INFORMATION THAT I NEED TO WORK INTO MY SOLUTION, THUS MAKING THE CRITERIA THAT MUCH TRICKIER TO FULFILL.
BUT WE HAVE A BIGGER PROBLEM IN THAT STEEL LADY NANASE'S LEVEL OF BRUTALITY HAS SKYROCKETED.
NOW THAT SHE'S COMMITTED AN ACTUAL MURDER, THE STEEL LADY NANASE IN THE RUMORS...
<125> Name: Withheld by Request
Is she angry that they declared
when it wasn't one?
Name: Withheld by Request
I heard that if you come face to
<127> Name: Withheld by Request 09/04 17:56 ID:nmsknh
If you have Karin Nanase's CD or photo book,
...HAS TRANSFORMED INTO A VICIOUS FIEND WHO WILL HUNT HER PREY DOWN UNTIL SHE'S KILLED IT.

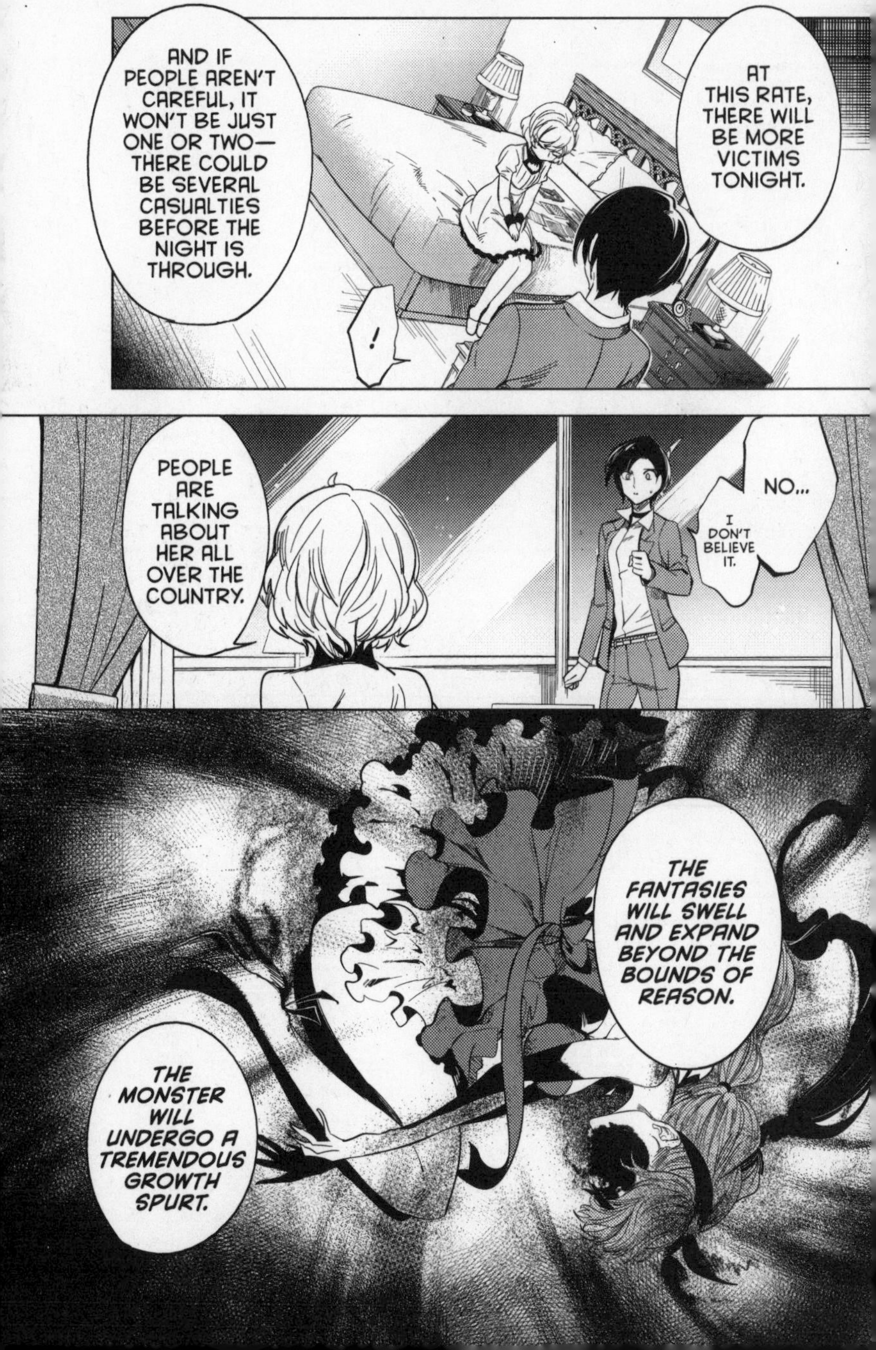
AT THIS RATE, THERE WILL BE MORE VICTIMS TONIGHT.
AND IF PEOPLE AREN'T CAREFUL, IT WON'T BE JUST ONE OR TWO—THERE COULD BE SEVERAL CASUALTIES BEFORE THE NIGHT IS THROUGH.
!
NO...
I DON'T BELIEVE IT.
PEOPLE ARE TALKING ABOUT HER ALL OVER THE COUNTRY.
THE FANTASIES WILL SWELL AND EXPAND BEYOND THE BOUNDS OF REASON.
THE MONSTER WILL UNDERGO A TREMENDOUS GROWTH SPURT.

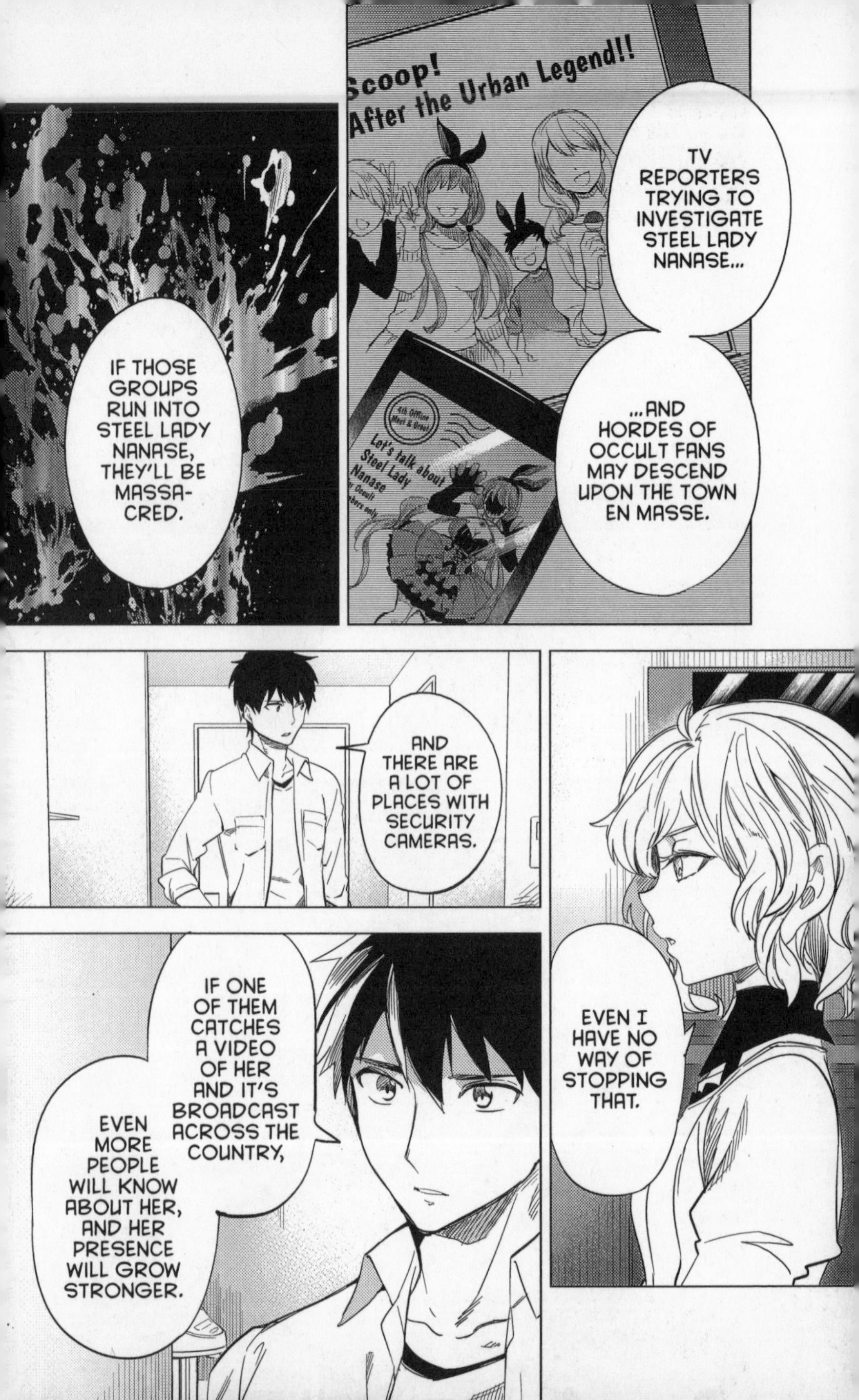

Scoop! After the Urban Legend!!
TV REPORTERS TRYING TO INVESTIGATE STEEL LADY NANASE...
Let's talk about Steel Lady Nanase
...AND HORDES OF OCCULT FANS MAY DESCEND UPON THE TOWN EN MASSE.
IF THOSE GROUPS RUN INTO STEEL LADY NANASE, THEY'LL BE MASSA-CRED.
EVEN I HAVE NO WAY OF STOPPING THAT.
AND THERE ARE A LOT OF PLACES WITH SECURITY CAMERAS.
IF ONE OF THEM CATCHES A VIDEO OF HER AND IT'S BROADCAST ACROSS THE COUNTRY,
EVEN MORE PEOPLE WILL KNOW ABOUT HER, AND HER PRESENCE WILL GROW STRONGER.

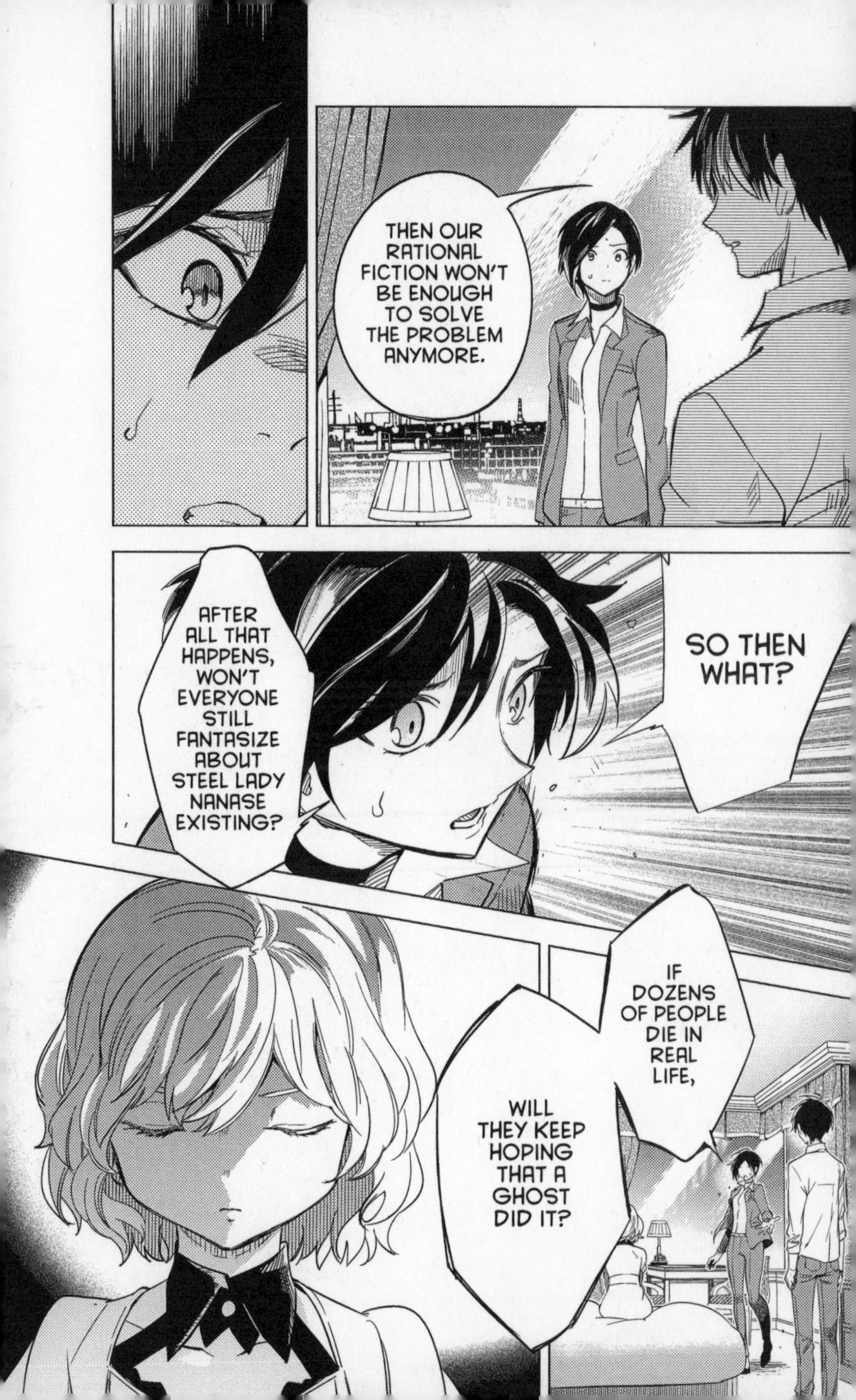
THEN OUR RATIONAL FICTION WON'T BE ENOUGH TO SOLVE THE PROBLEM ANYMORE.
SO THEN WHAT?
AFTER ALL THAT HAPPENS, WON'T EVERYONE STILL FANTASIZE ABOUT STEEL LADY NANASE EXISTING?
IF DOZENS OF PEOPLE DIE IN REAL LIFE,
WILL THEY KEEP HOPING THAT A GHOST DID IT?

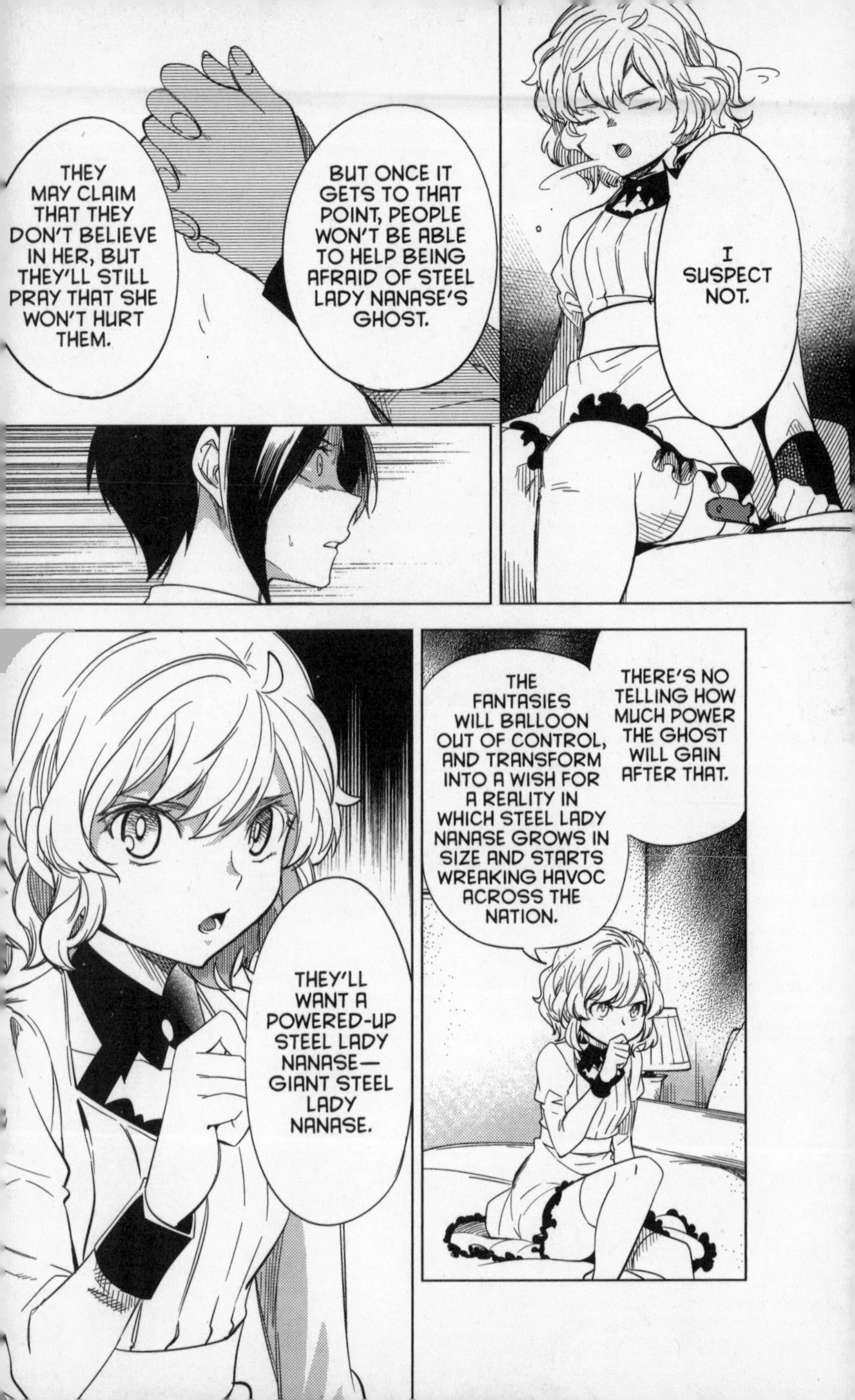
I SUSPECT NOT.
BUT ONCE IT GETS TO THAT POINT, PEOPLE WON'T BE ABLE TO HELP BEING AFRAID OF STEEL LADY NANASE'S GHOST.
THEY MAY CLAIM THAT THEY DON'T BELIEVE IN HER, BUT THEY'LL STILL PRAY THAT SHE WON'T HURT THEM.
THERE'S NO TELLING HOW MUCH POWER THE GHOST WILL GAIN AFTER THAT.
THE FANTASIES WILL BALLOON OUT OF CONTROL, AND TRANSFORM INTO A WISH FOR A REALITY IN WHICH STEEL LADY NANASE GROWS IN SIZE AND STARTS WREAKING HAVOC ACROSS THE NATION.
THEY'LL WANT A POWERED-UP STEEL LADY NANASE—GIANT STEEL LADY NANASE.

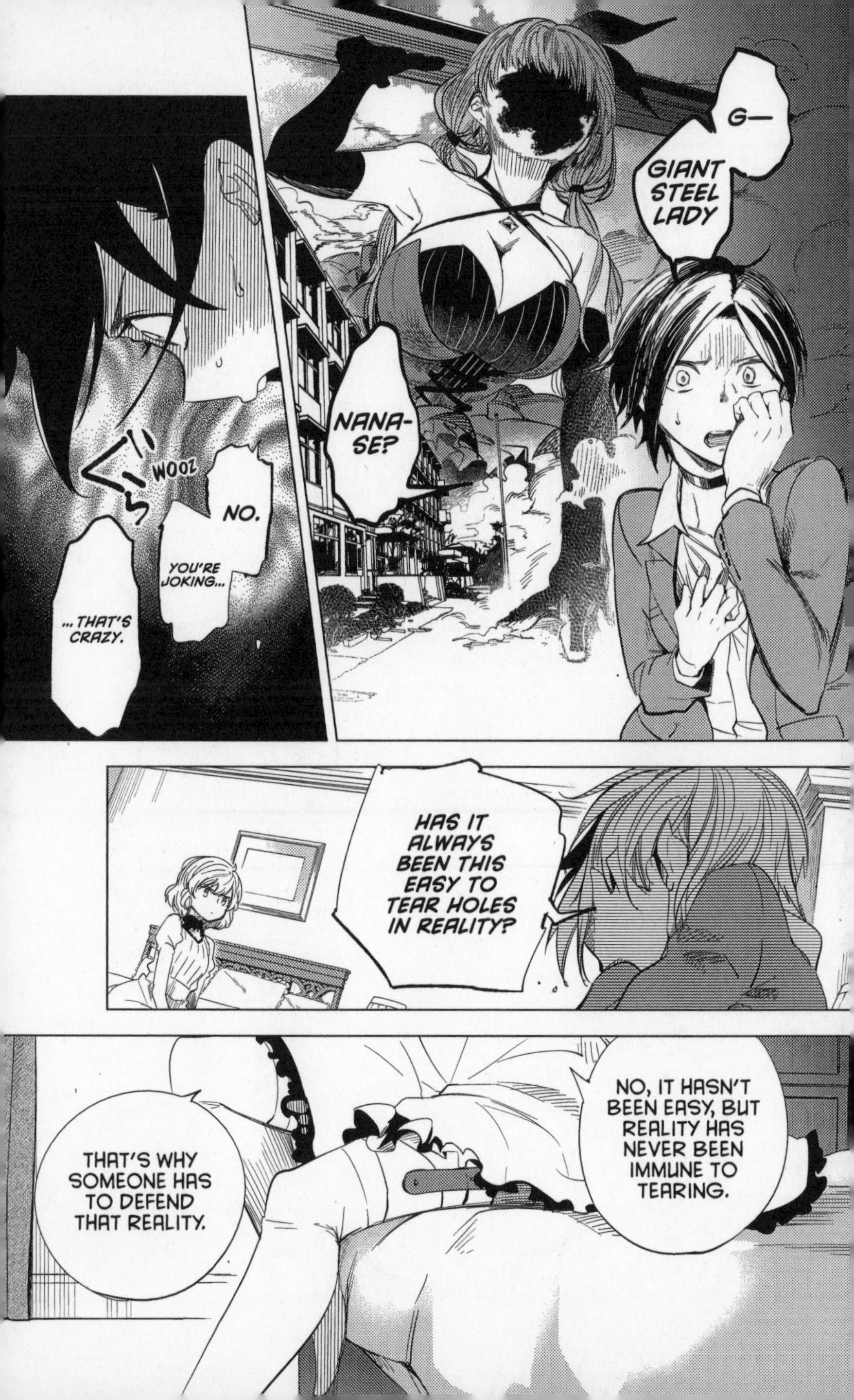
G— GIANT STEEL LADY
NANA-SE?
WOOZ
NO.
YOU'RE JOKING...
...THAT'S CRAZY.
HAS IT ALWAYS BEEN THIS EASY TO TEAR HOLES IN REALITY?
NO, IT HASN'T BEEN EASY, BUT REALITY HAS NEVER BEEN IMMUNE TO TEARING.
THAT'S WHY SOMEONE HAS TO DEFEND THAT REALITY.

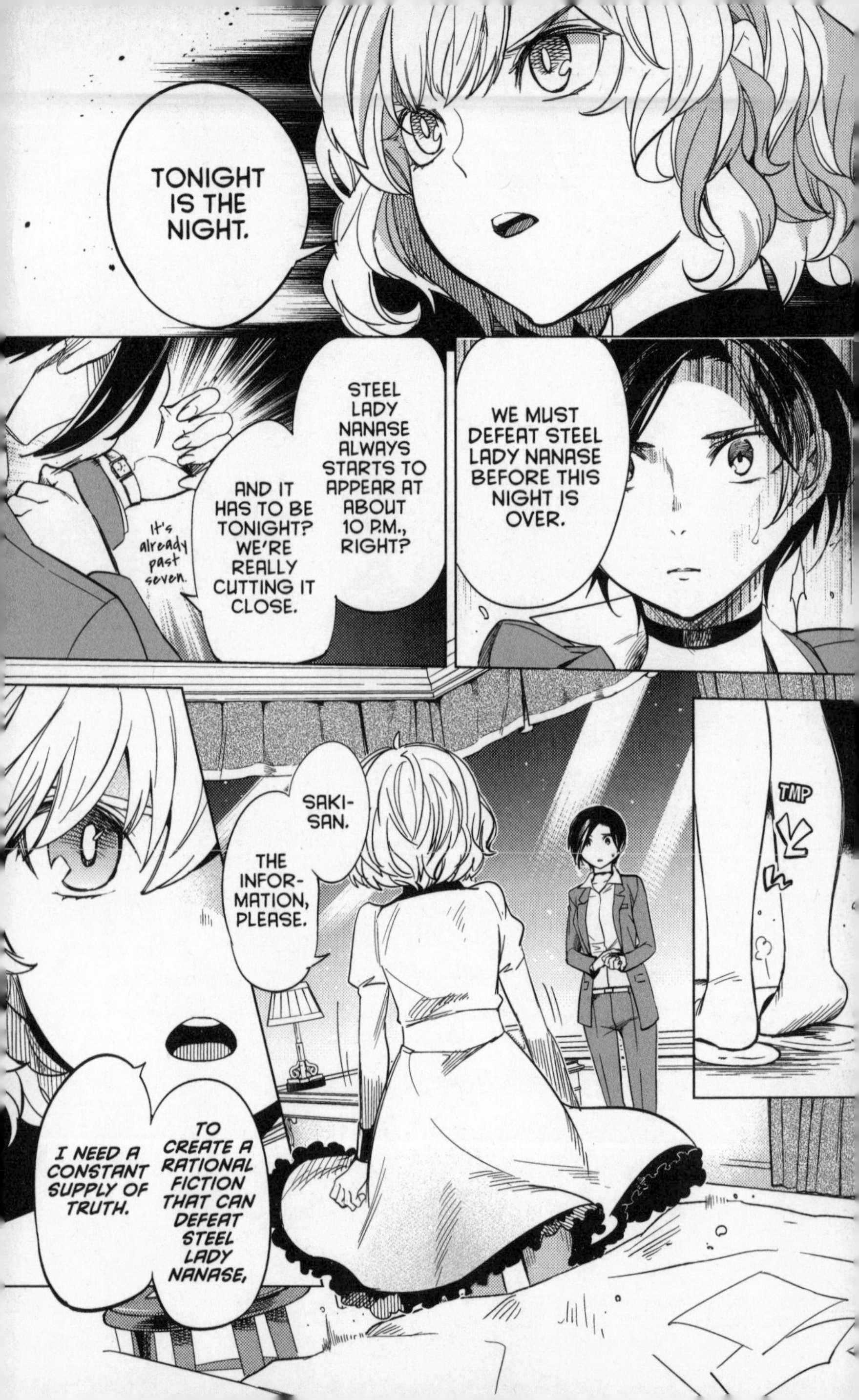
TONIGHT IS THE NIGHT.
WE MUST DEFEAT STEEL LADY NANASE BEFORE THIS NIGHT IS OVER.
STEEL LADY NANASE ALWAYS STARTS TO APPEAR AT ABOUT 10 P.M., RIGHT?
AND IT HAS TO BE TONIGHT? WE'RE REALLY CUTTING IT CLOSE.
It's already past seven.
TMP
SAKI-SAN.
THE INFORMATION, PLEASE.
TO CREATE A RATIONAL FICTION THAT CAN DEFEAT STEEL LADY NANASE,
I NEED A CONSTANT SUPPLY OF TRUTH.

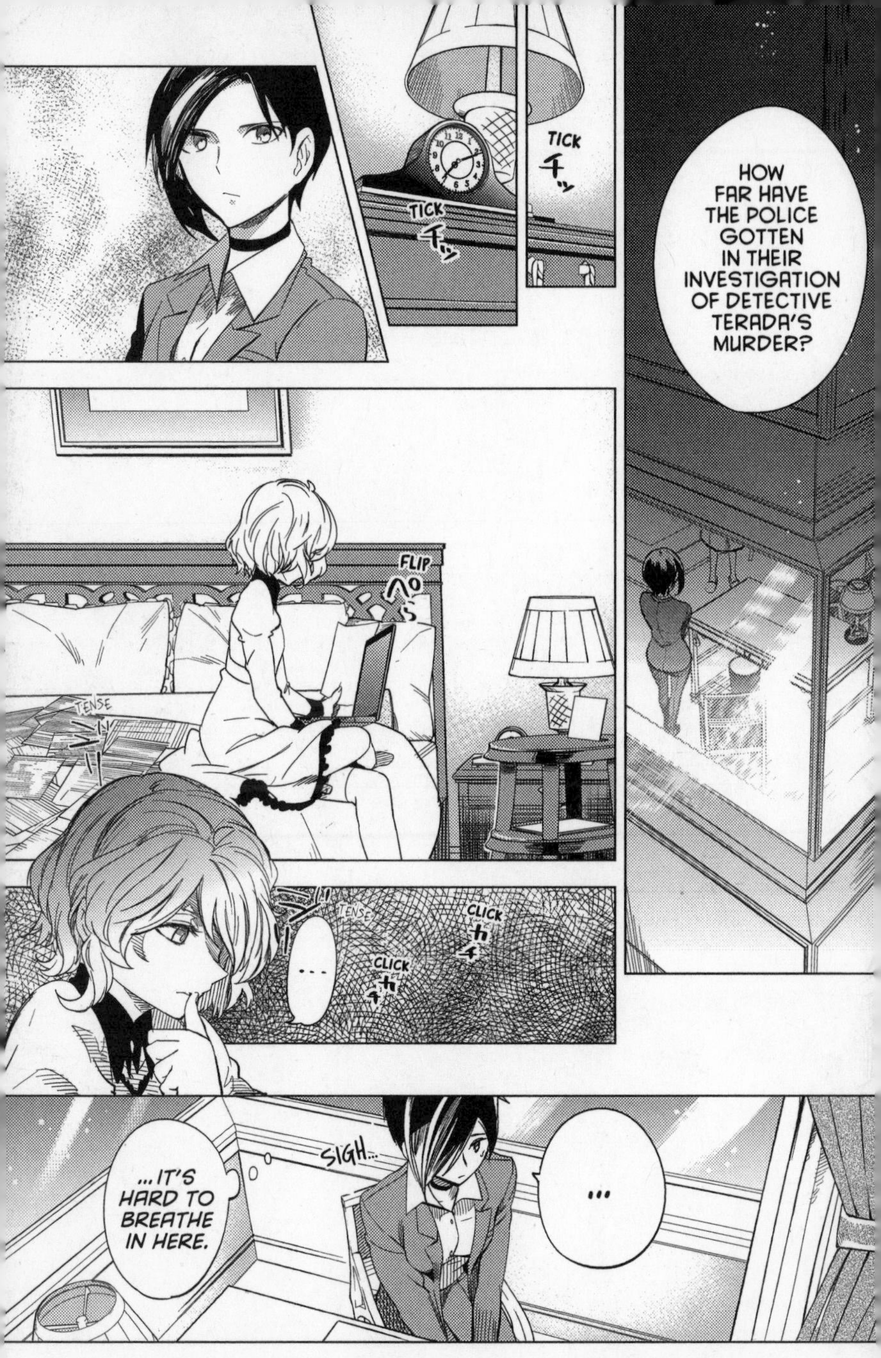
HOW FAR HAVE THE POLICE GOTTEN IN THEIR INVESTIGATION OF DETECTIVE TERADA'S MURDER?
TICK
TICK
FLIP
TENSE
TENSE
CLICK
CLICK
...
...
SIGH...
...IT'S HARD TO BREATHE IN HERE.

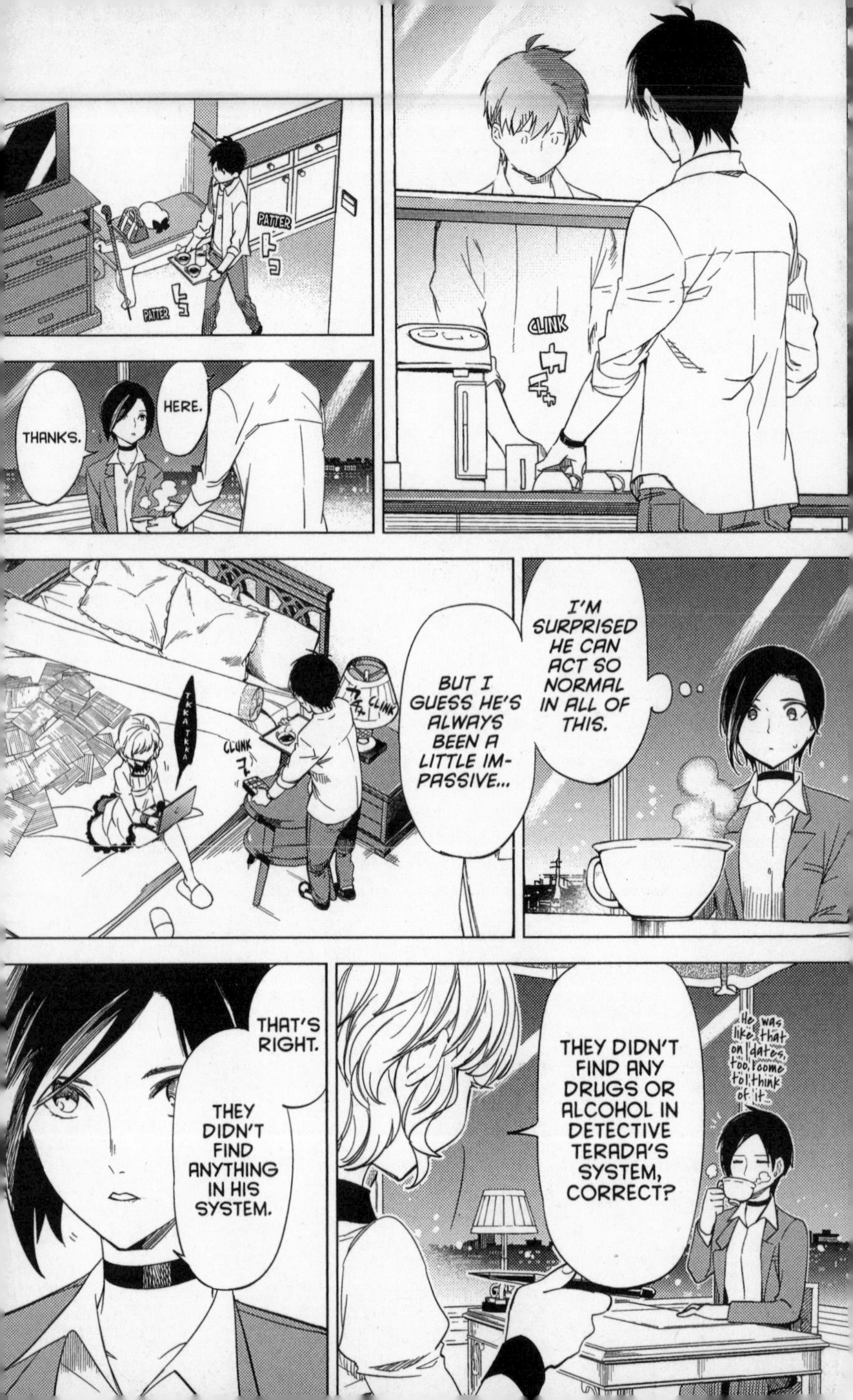
CLINK
PATTER
PATTER
HERE.
THANKS.
I'M SURPRISED HE CAN ACT SO NORMAL IN ALL OF THIS.
BUT I GUESS HE'S ALWAYS BEEN A LITTLE IM-PASSIVE...
CLINK
TKKA TKKA
CLUNK
He was like that on dates, too, come to think of it...
THEY DIDN'T FIND ANY DRUGS OR ALCOHOL IN DETECTIVE TERADA'S SYSTEM, CORRECT?
THAT'S RIGHT.
THEY DIDN'T FIND ANYTHING IN HIS SYSTEM.

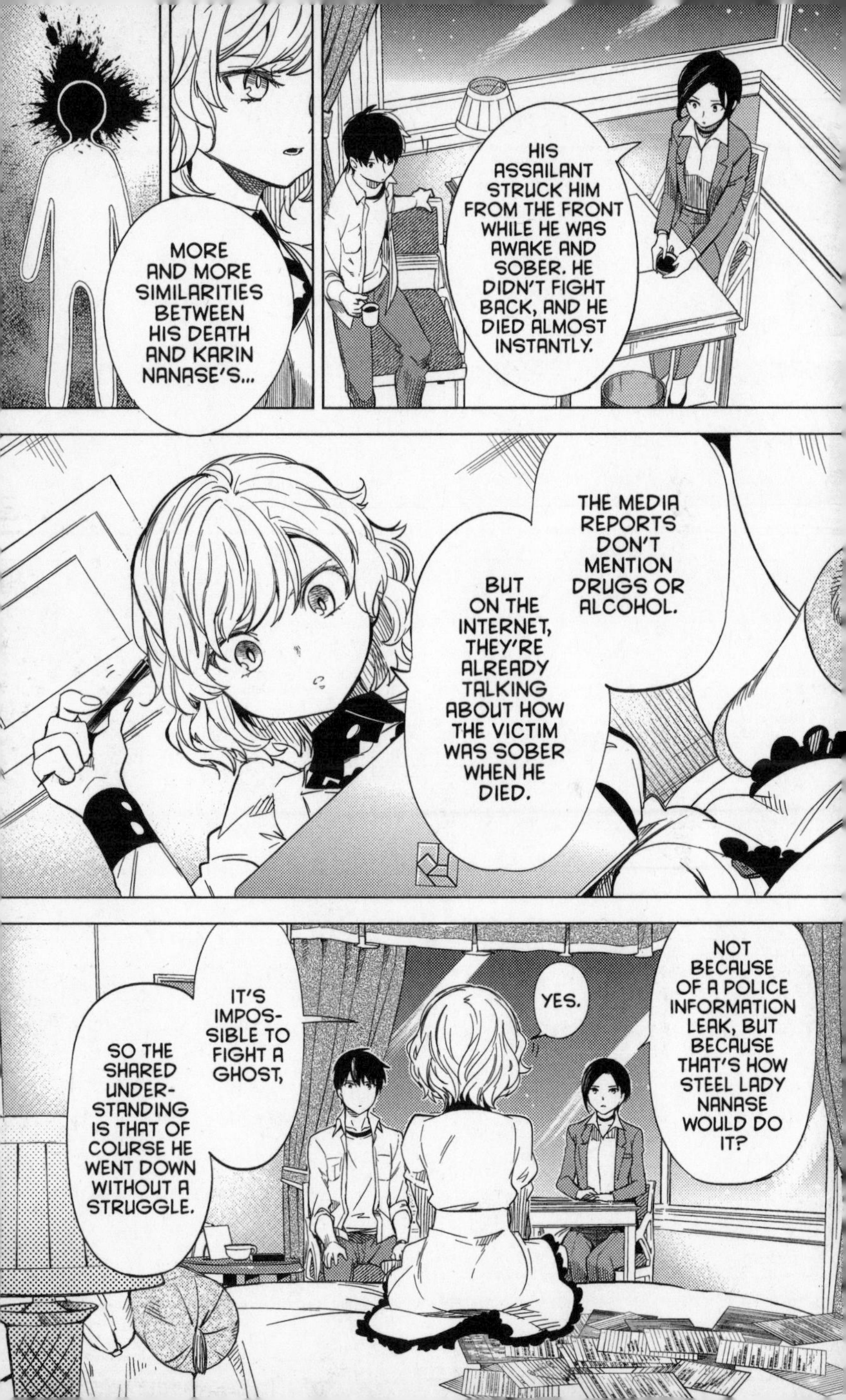
HIS ASSAILANT STRUCK HIM FROM THE FRONT WHILE HE WAS AWAKE AND SOBER. HE DIDN'T FIGHT BACK, AND HE DIED ALMOST INSTANTLY.
MORE AND MORE SIMILARITIES BETWEEN HIS DEATH AND KARIN NANASE'S...
THE MEDIA REPORTS DON'T MENTION DRUGS OR ALCOHOL.
BUT ON THE INTERNET, THEY'RE ALREADY TALKING ABOUT HOW THE VICTIM WAS SOBER WHEN HE DIED.
NOT BECAUSE OF A POLICE INFORMATION LEAK, BUT BECAUSE THAT'S HOW STEEL LADY NANASE WOULD DO IT?
YES.
IT'S IMPOS-SIBLE TO FIGHT A GHOST,
SO THE SHARED UNDER-STANDING IS THAT OF COURSE HE WENT DOWN WITHOUT A STRUGGLE.

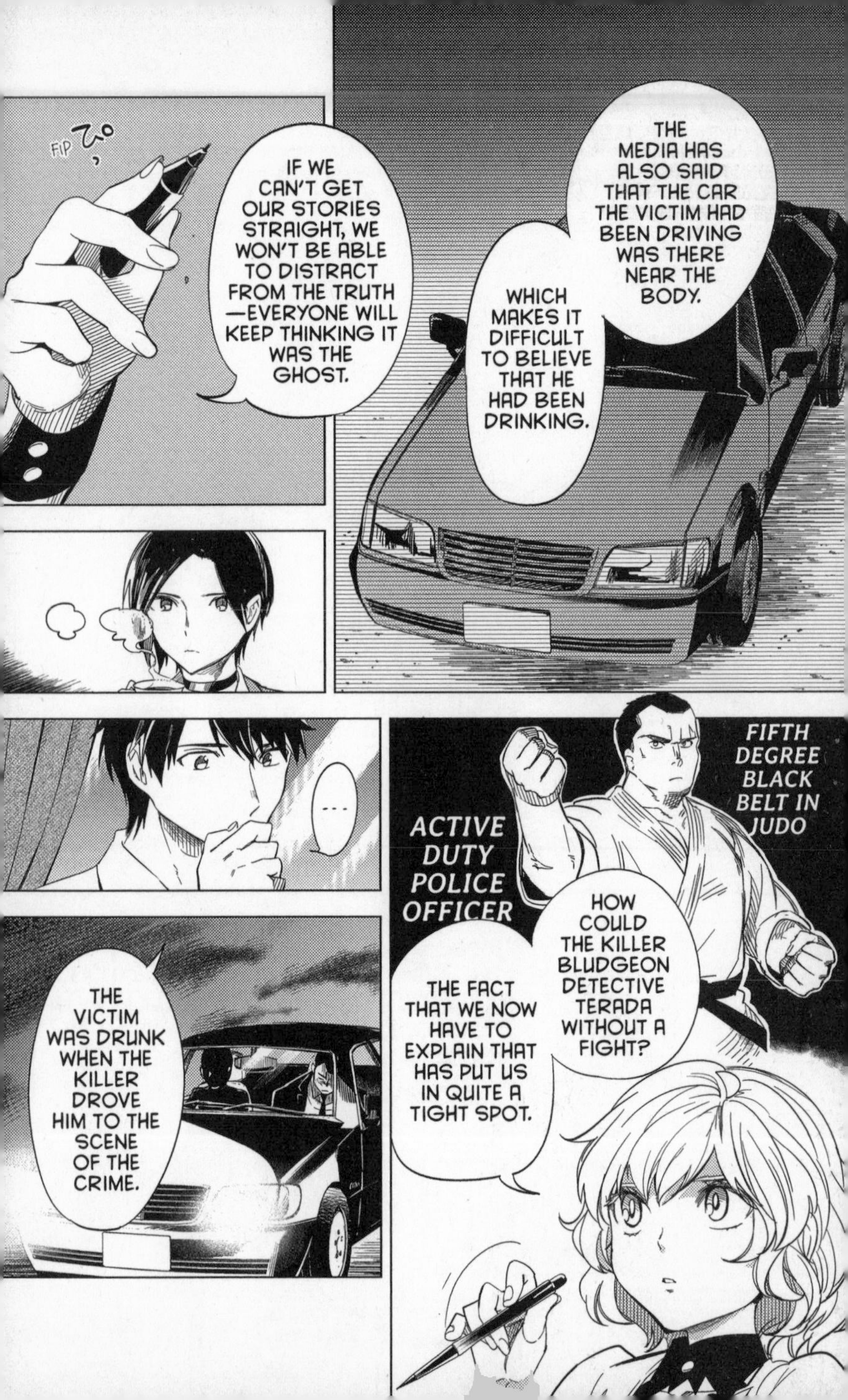
THE MEDIA HAS ALSO SAID THAT THE CAR THE VICTIM HAD BEEN DRIVING WAS THERE NEAR THE BODY.
WHICH MAKES IT DIFFICULT TO BELIEVE THAT HE HAD BEEN DRINKING.
FLIP ぴっ
IF WE CAN'T GET OUR STORIES STRAIGHT, WE WON'T BE ABLE TO DISTRACT FROM THE TRUTH —EVERYONE WILL KEEP THINKING IT WAS THE GHOST.
FIFTH DEGREE BLACK BELT IN JUDO
ACTIVE DUTY POLICE OFFICER
HOW COULD THE KILLER BLUDGEON DETECTIVE TERADA WITHOUT A FIGHT?
THE FACT THAT WE NOW HAVE TO EXPLAIN THAT HAS PUT US IN QUITE A TIGHT SPOT.
...
THE VICTIM WAS DRUNK WHEN THE KILLER DROVE HIM TO THE SCENE OF THE CRIME.

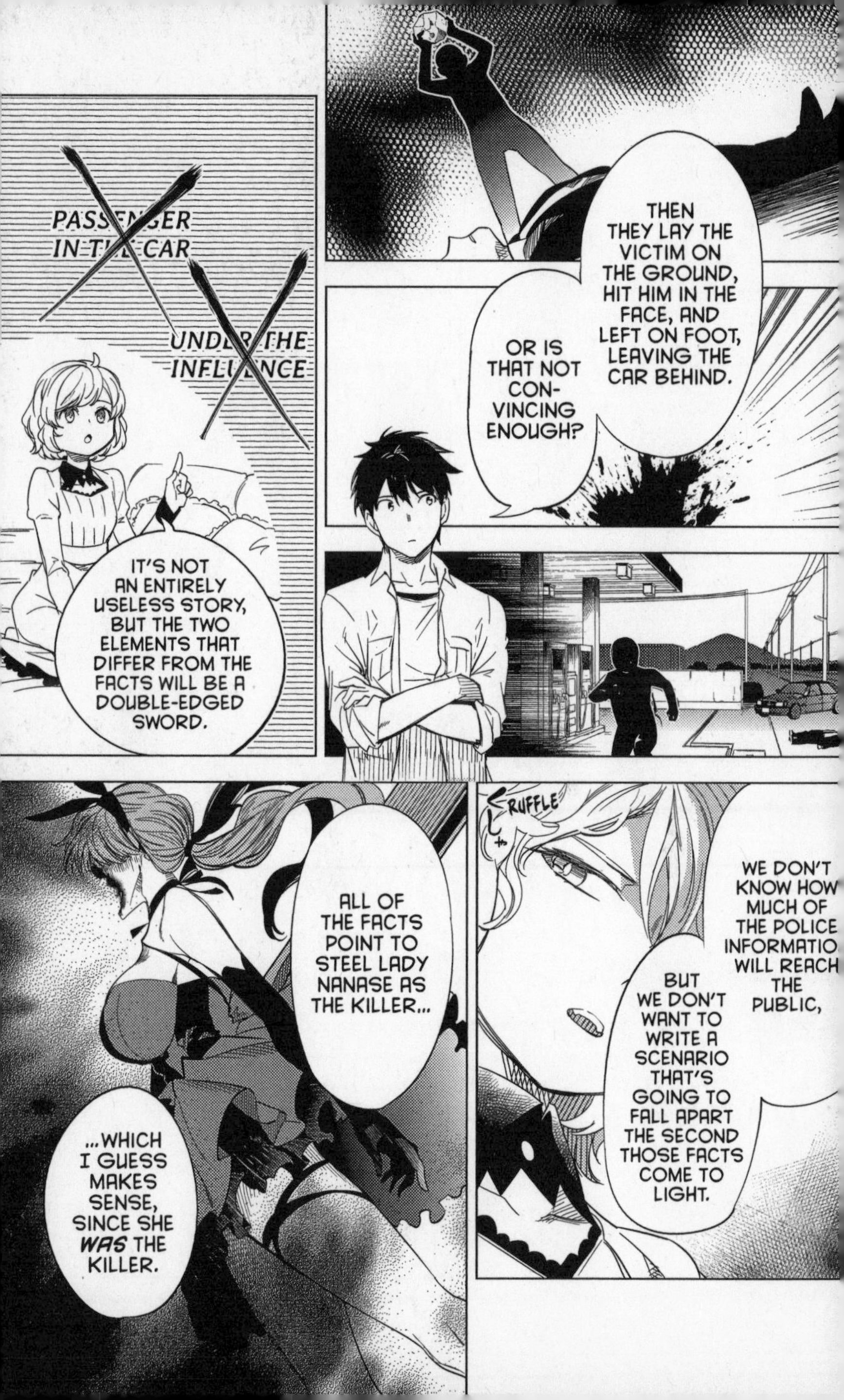
THEN THEY LAY THE VICTIM ON THE GROUND, HIT HIM IN THE FACE, AND LEFT ON FOOT, LEAVING THE CAR BEHIND.
OR IS THAT NOT CON-VINCING ENOUGH?
PASSENGER IN THE CAR
UNDER THE INFLUENCE
IT'S NOT AN ENTIRELY USELESS STORY, BUT THE TWO ELEMENTS THAT DIFFER FROM THE FACTS WILL BE A DOUBLE-EDGED SWORD.
RUFFLE
WE DON'T KNOW HOW MUCH OF THE POLICE INFORMATIO WILL REACH THE PUBLIC,
BUT WE DON'T WANT TO WRITE A SCENARIO THAT'S GOING TO FALL APART THE SECOND THOSE FACTS COME TO LIGHT.
ALL OF THE FACTS POINT TO STEEL LADY NANASE AS THE KILLER...
...WHICH I GUESS MAKES SENSE, SINCE SHE *WAS* THE KILLER.

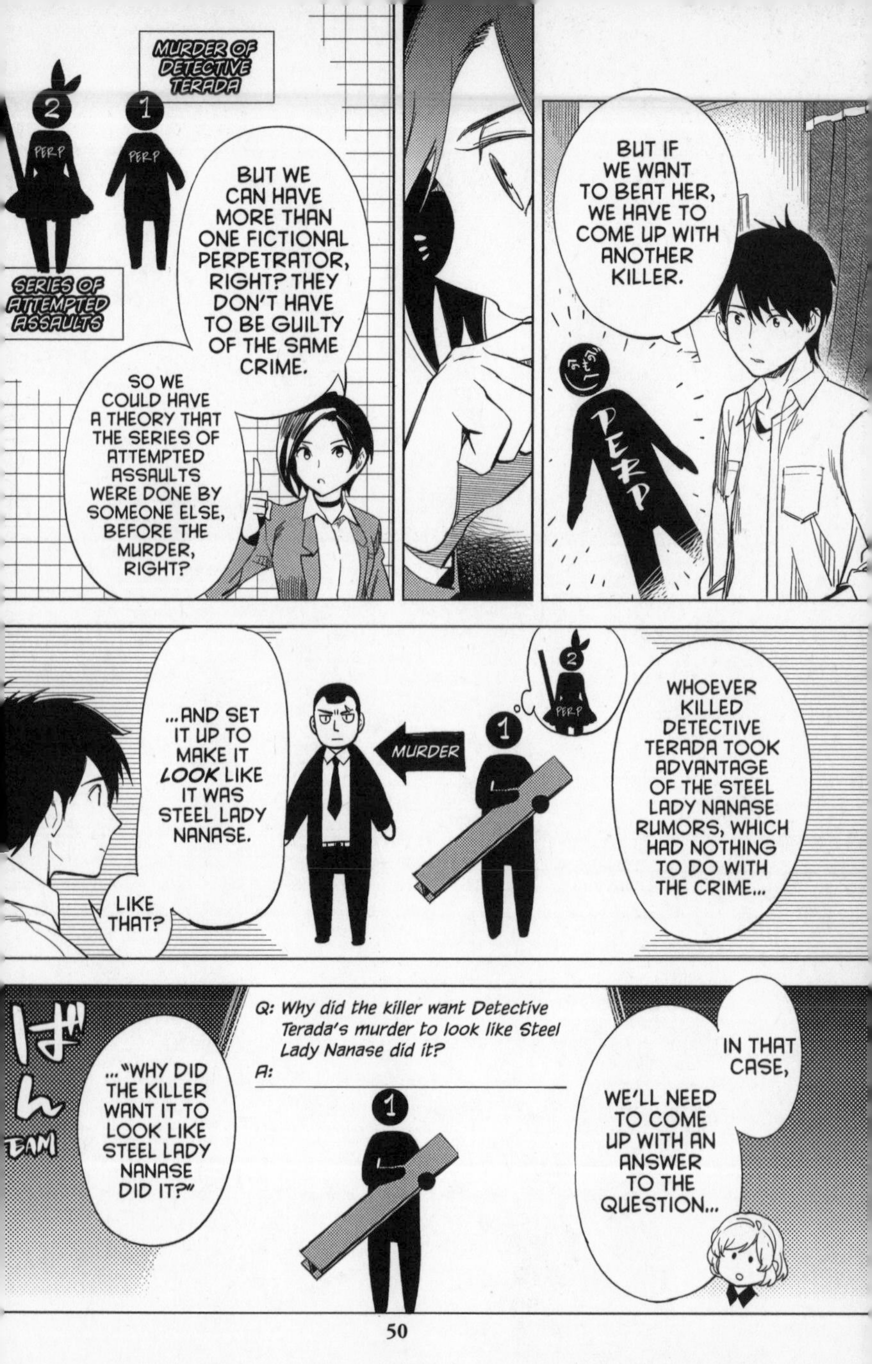
BUT IF WE WANT TO BEAT HER, WE HAVE TO COME UP WITH ANOTHER KILLER.
PERP
MURDER OF DETECTIVE TERADA
BUT WE CAN HAVE MORE THAN ONE FICTIONAL PERPETRATOR, RIGHT? THEY DON'T HAVE TO BE GUILTY OF THE SAME CRIME.
1
PERP
2
PERP
SERIES OF ATTEMPTED ASSAULTS
SO WE COULD HAVE A THEORY THAT THE SERIES OF ATTEMPTED ASSAULTS WERE DONE BY SOMEONE ELSE, BEFORE THE MURDER, RIGHT?
WHOEVER KILLED DETECTIVE TERADA TOOK ADVANTAGE OF THE STEEL LADY NANASE RUMORS, WHICH HAD NOTHING TO DO WITH THE CRIME...
2
PERP
1
MURDER
...AND SET IT UP TO MAKE IT *LOOK* LIKE IT WAS STEEL LADY NANASE.
LIKE THAT?
IN THAT CASE,
WE'LL NEED TO COME UP WITH AN ANSWER TO THE QUESTION...
Q: Why did the killer want Detective Terada's murder to look like Steel Lady Nanase did it?
A:
1
..."WHY DID THE KILLER WANT IT TO LOOK LIKE STEEL LADY NANASE DID IT?"
ばん
BAM

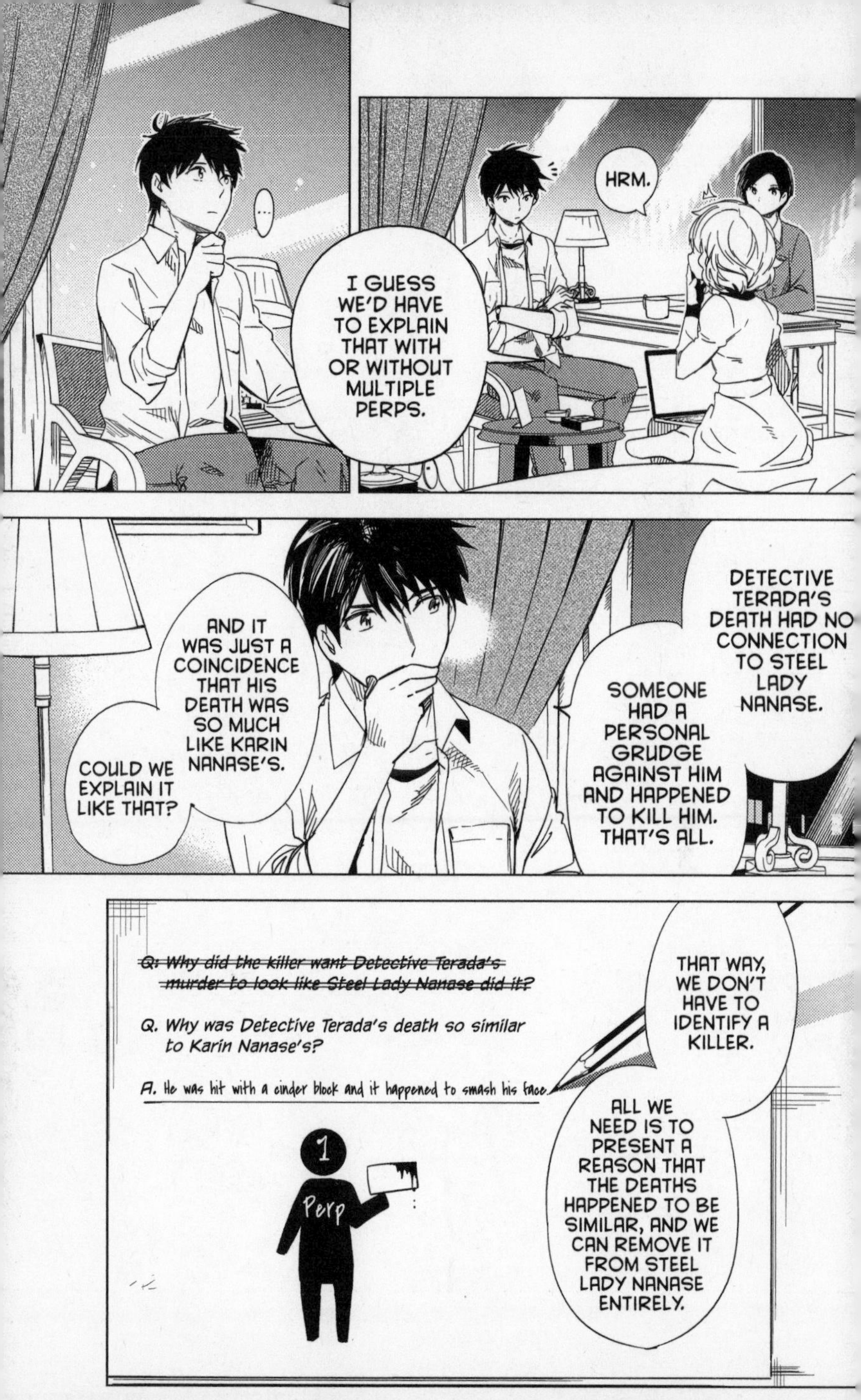
HRM.
I GUESS WE'D HAVE TO EXPLAIN THAT WITH OR WITHOUT MULTIPLE PERPS.
...
DETECTIVE TERADA'S DEATH HAD NO CONNECTION TO STEEL LADY NANASE.
SOMEONE HAD A PERSONAL GRUDGE AGAINST HIM AND HAPPENED TO KILL HIM. THAT'S ALL.
AND IT WAS JUST A COINCIDENCE THAT HIS DEATH WAS SO MUCH LIKE KARIN NANASE'S.
COULD WE EXPLAIN IT LIKE THAT?
THAT WAY, WE DON'T HAVE TO IDENTIFY A KILLER.
ALL WE NEED IS TO PRESENT A REASON THAT THE DEATHS HAPPENED TO BE SIMILAR, AND WE CAN REMOVE IT FROM STEEL LADY NANASE ENTIRELY.
~~Q: Why did the killer want Detective Terada's murder to look like Steel Lady Nanase did it?~~
Q. Why was Detective Terada's death so similar to Karin Nanase's?
A. He was hit with a cinder block and it happened to smash his face.
1
Perp

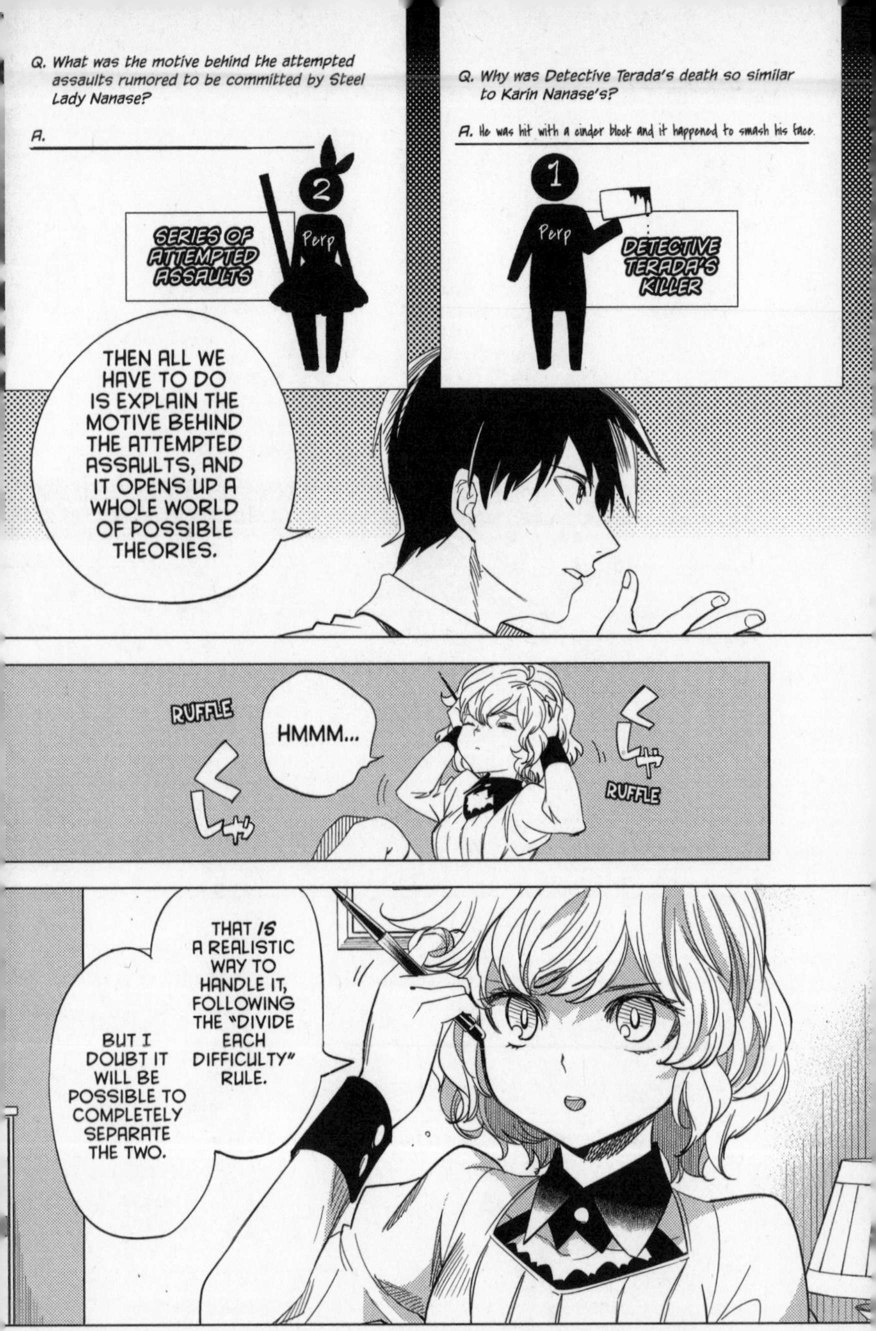
Q. Why was Detective Terada's death so similar to Karin Nanase's?
A. He was hit with a cinder block and it happened to smash his face.
1
Perp
DETECTIVE TERADA'S KILLER
Q. What was the motive behind the attempted assaults rumored to be committed by Steel Lady Nanase?
A.
2
Perp
SERIES OF ATTEMPTED ASSAULTS
THEN ALL WE HAVE TO DO IS EXPLAIN THE MOTIVE BEHIND THE ATTEMPTED ASSAULTS, AND IT OPENS UP A WHOLE WORLD OF POSSIBLE THEORIES.
くしゃ
RUFFLE
HMMM...
RUFFLE
くしゃ
THAT *IS* A REALISTIC WAY TO HANDLE IT, FOLLOWING THE "DIVIDE EACH DIFFICULTY" RULE.
BUT I DOUBT IT WILL BE POSSIBLE TO COMPLETELY SEPARATE THE TWO.

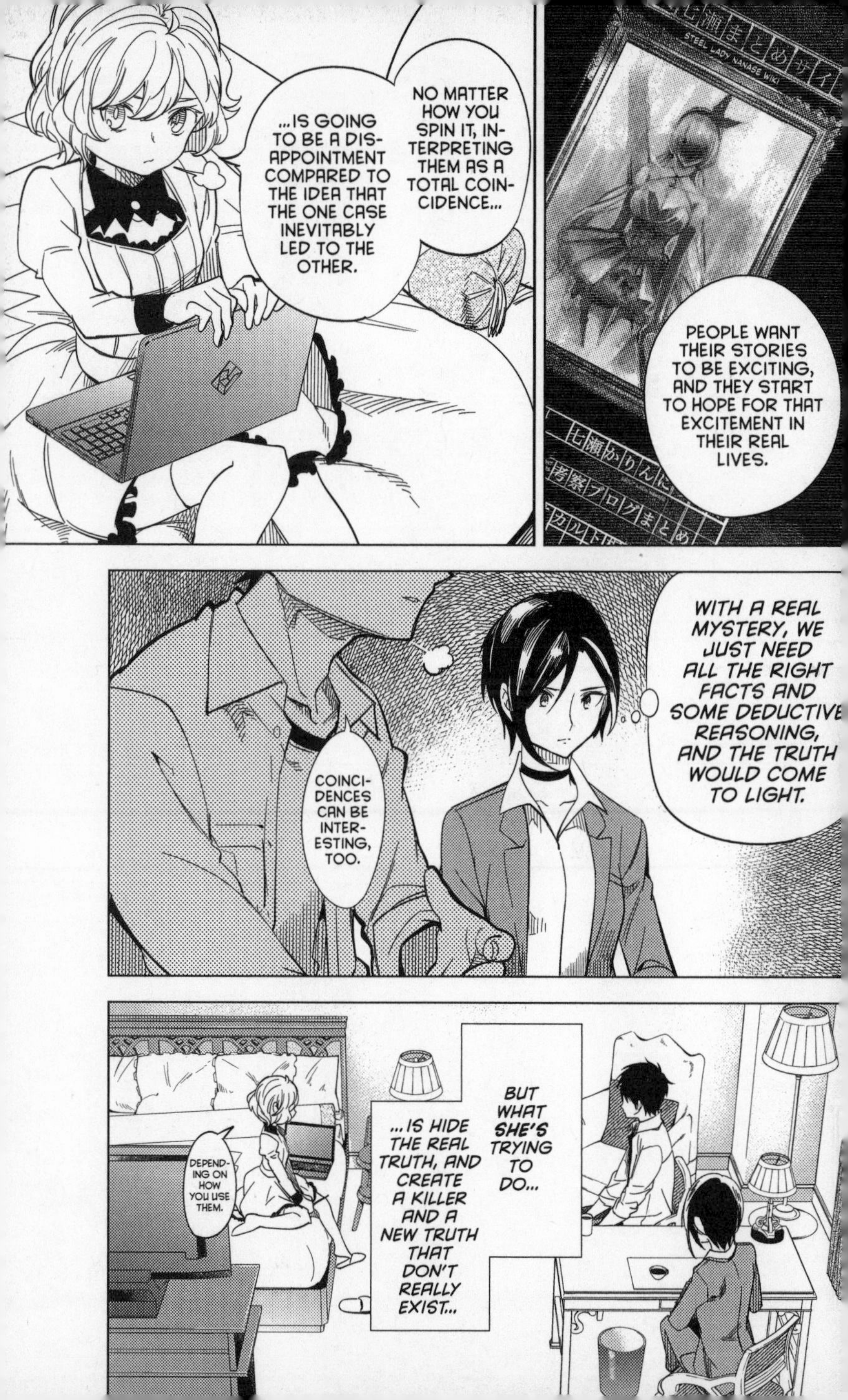
STEEL LADY NANASE WIKI
七瀬かりんに
考察ブログまとめ
PEOPLE WANT THEIR STORIES TO BE EXCITING, AND THEY START TO HOPE FOR THAT EXCITEMENT IN THEIR REAL LIVES.
NO MATTER HOW YOU SPIN IT, INTERPRETING THEM AS A TOTAL COINCIDENCE...
...IS GOING TO BE A DISAPPOINTMENT COMPARED TO THE IDEA THAT THE ONE CASE INEVITABLY LED TO THE OTHER.
WITH A REAL MYSTERY, WE JUST NEED ALL THE RIGHT FACTS AND SOME DEDUCTIVE REASONING, AND THE TRUTH WOULD COME TO LIGHT.
COINCIDENCES CAN BE INTERESTING, TOO.
BUT WHAT SHE'S TRYING TO DO...
...IS HIDE THE REAL TRUTH, AND CREATE A KILLER AND A NEW TRUTH THAT DON'T REALLY EXIST...
DEPENDING ON HOW YOU USE THEM.

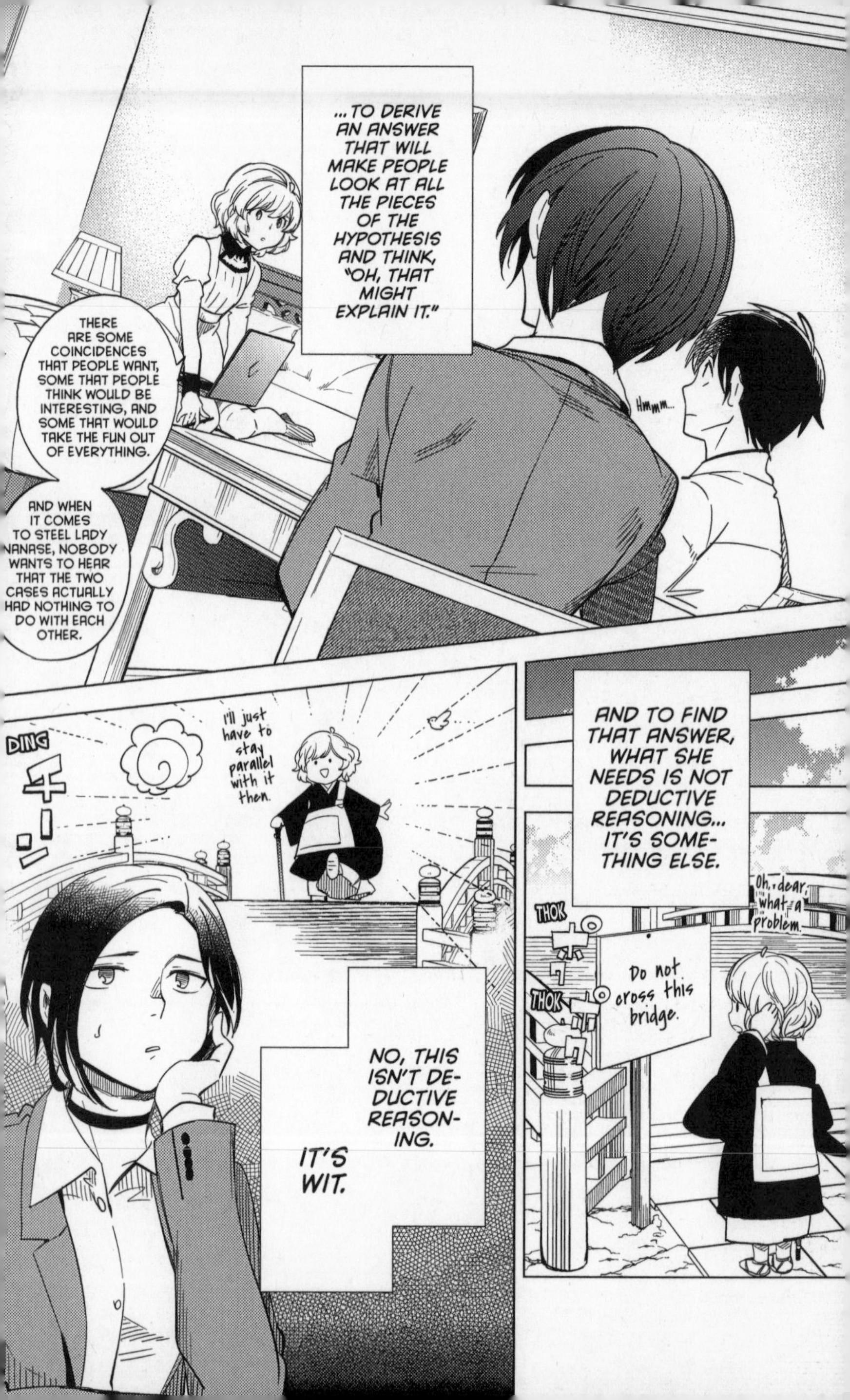
...TO DERIVE AN ANSWER THAT WILL MAKE PEOPLE LOOK AT ALL THE PIECES OF THE HYPOTHESIS AND THINK, "OH, THAT MIGHT EXPLAIN IT."
Hmmm...
THERE ARE SOME COINCIDENCES THAT PEOPLE WANT, SOME THAT PEOPLE THINK WOULD BE INTERESTING, AND SOME THAT WOULD TAKE THE FUN OUT OF EVERYTHING.
AND WHEN IT COMES TO STEEL LADY NANASE, NOBODY WANTS TO HEAR THAT THE TWO CASES ACTUALLY HAD NOTHING TO DO WITH EACH OTHER.
AND TO FIND THAT ANSWER, WHAT SHE NEEDS IS NOT DEDUCTIVE REASONING... IT'S SOMETHING ELSE.
Oh, dear, what a problem.
THOK
THOK
Do not cross this bridge.
DING
I'll just have to stay parallel with it then.
NO, THIS ISN'T DEDUCTIVE REASONING.
IT'S WIT.

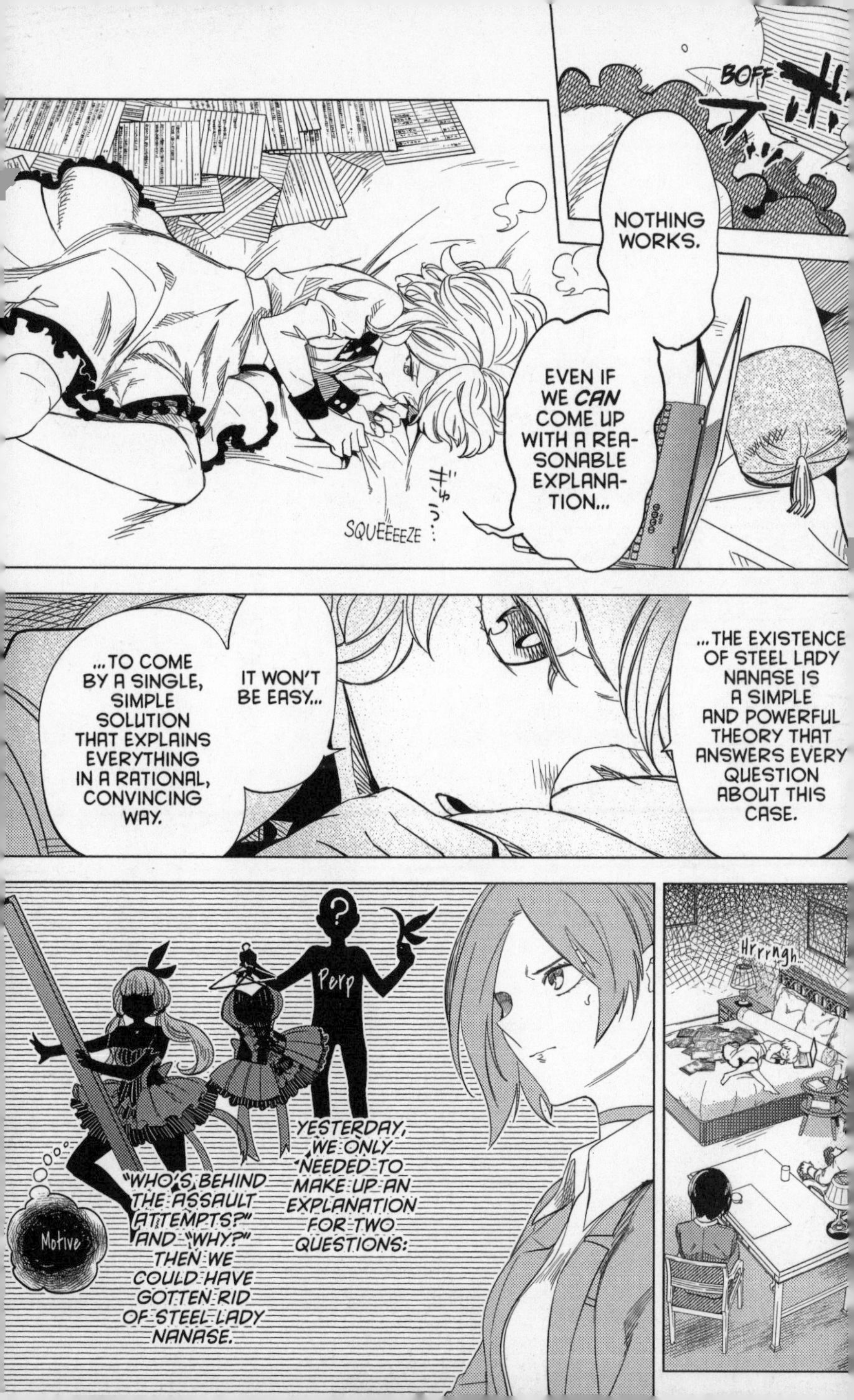
BOFF
NOTHING WORKS.
EVEN IF WE *CAN* COME UP WITH A REA-SONABLE EXPLANA-TION...
SQUEEEEZE
ぎゅっ…
...THE EXISTENCE OF STEEL LADY NANASE IS A SIMPLE AND POWERFUL THEORY THAT ANSWERS EVERY QUESTION ABOUT THIS CASE.
IT WON'T BE EASY...
...TO COME BY A SINGLE, SIMPLE SOLUTION THAT EXPLAINS EVERYTHING IN A RATIONAL, CONVINCING WAY.
Hrrrngh
YESTERDAY, WE ONLY NEEDED TO MAKE UP AN EXPLANATION FOR TWO QUESTIONS:
?
Perp
"WHO'S BEHIND THE ASSAULT ATTEMPTS?" AND "WHY?" THEN WE COULD HAVE GOTTEN RID OF STEEL LADY NANASE.
Motive

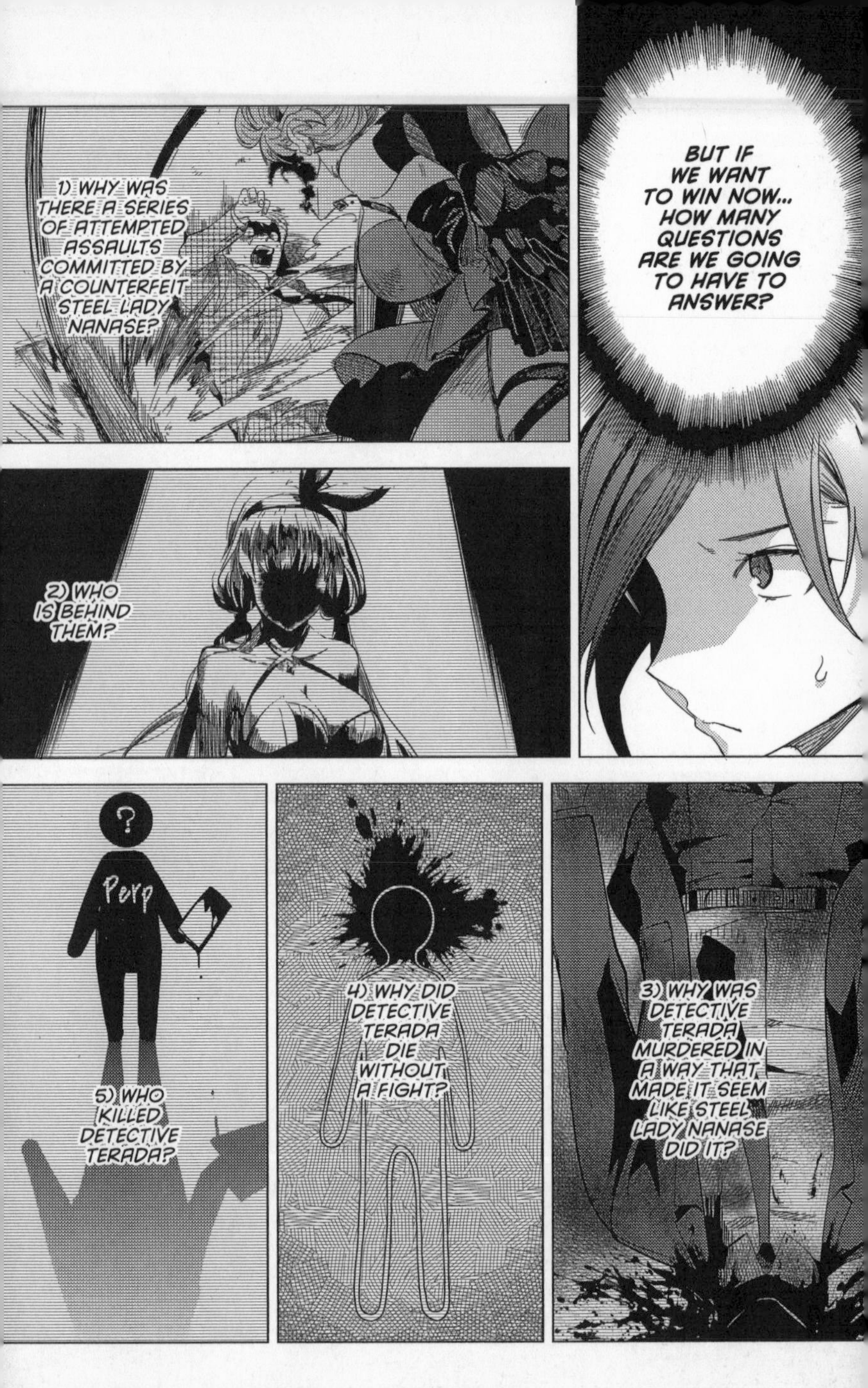
BUT IF WE WANT TO WIN NOW... HOW MANY QUESTIONS ARE WE GOING TO HAVE TO ANSWER?
1) WHY WAS THERE A SERIES OF ATTEMPTED ASSAULTS COMMITTED BY A COUNTERFEIT STEEL LADY NANASE?
2) WHO IS BEHIND THEM?
3) WHY WAS DETECTIVE TERADA MURDERED IN A WAY THAT MADE IT SEEM LIKE STEEL LADY NANASE DID IT?
4) WHY DID DETECTIVE TERADA DIE WITHOUT A FIGHT?
Perp
5) WHO KILLED DETECTIVE TERADA?

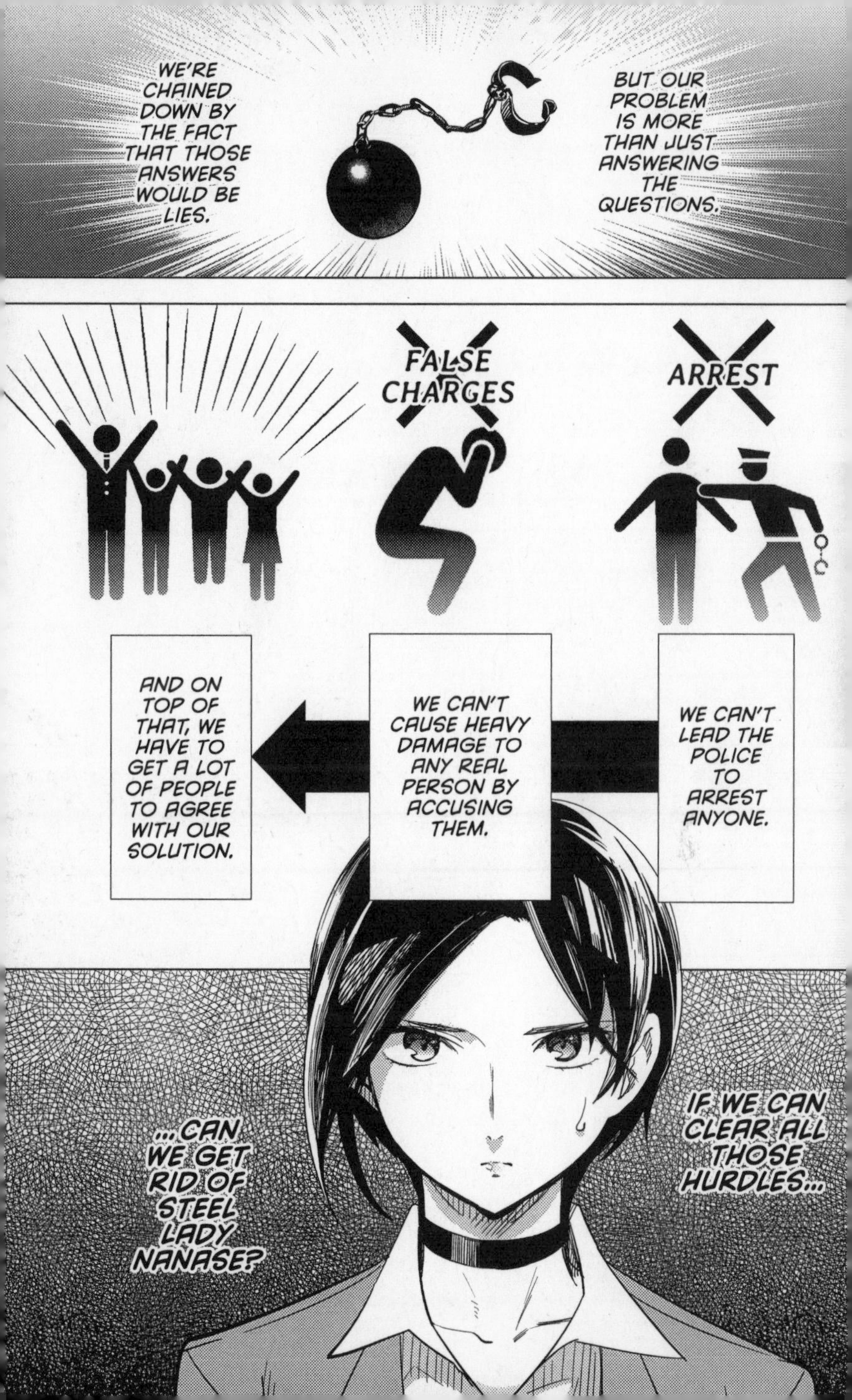
BUT OUR PROBLEM IS MORE THAN JUST ANSWERING THE QUESTIONS.
WE'RE CHAINED DOWN BY THE FACT THAT THOSE ANSWERS WOULD BE LIES.
ARREST
FALSE CHARGES
WE CAN'T LEAD THE POLICE TO ARREST ANYONE.
WE CAN'T CAUSE HEAVY DAMAGE TO ANY REAL PERSON BY ACCUSING THEM.
AND ON TOP OF THAT, WE HAVE TO GET A LOT OF PEOPLE TO AGREE WITH OUR SOLUTION.
IF WE CAN CLEAR ALL THOSE HURDLES...
...CAN WE GET RID OF STEEL LADY NANASE?

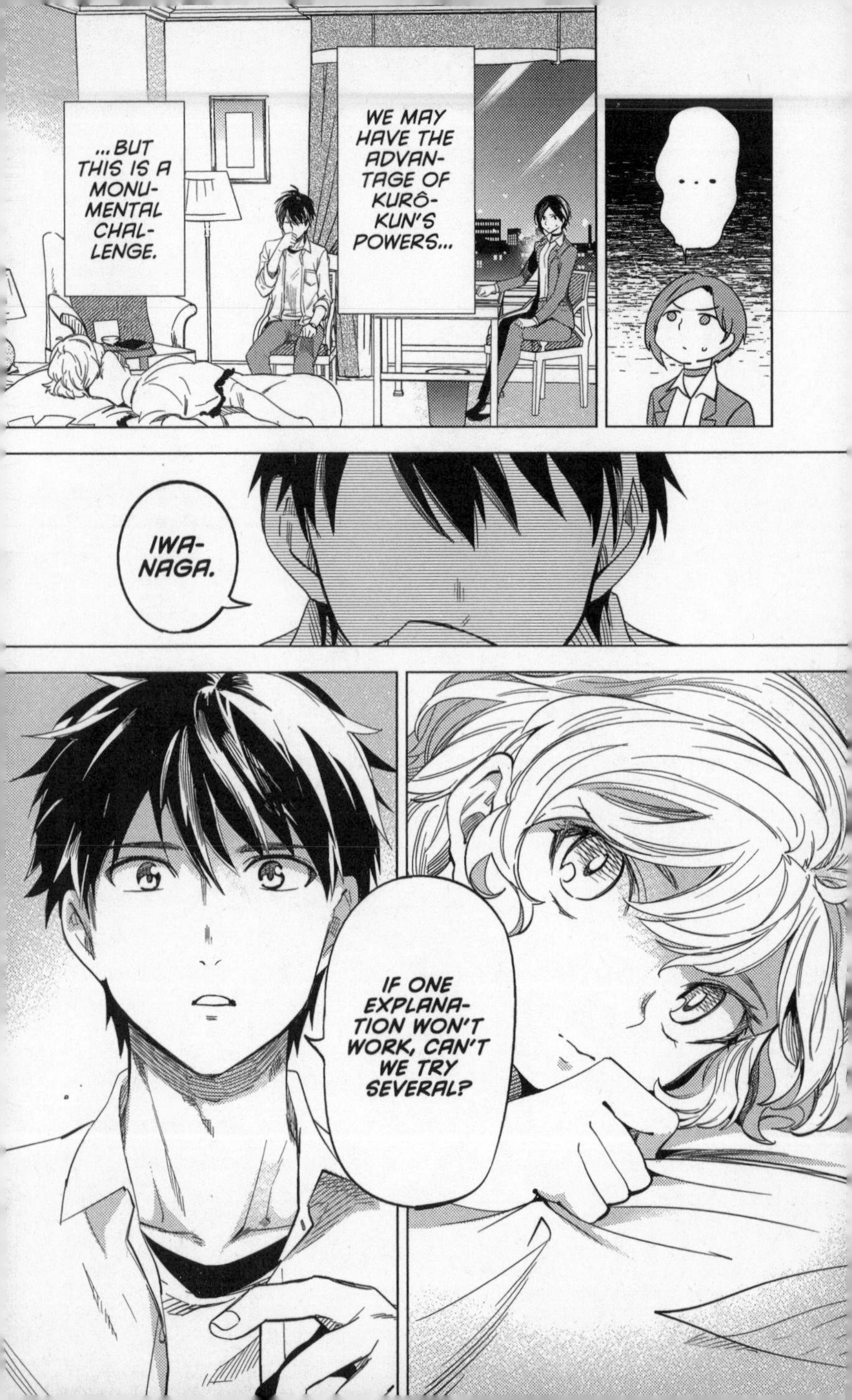
...
WE MAY HAVE THE ADVANTAGE OF KURÔ-KUN'S POWERS...
...BUT THIS IS A MONUMENTAL CHALLENGE.
IWANAGA.
IF ONE EXPLANATION WON'T WORK, CAN'T WE TRY SEVERAL?

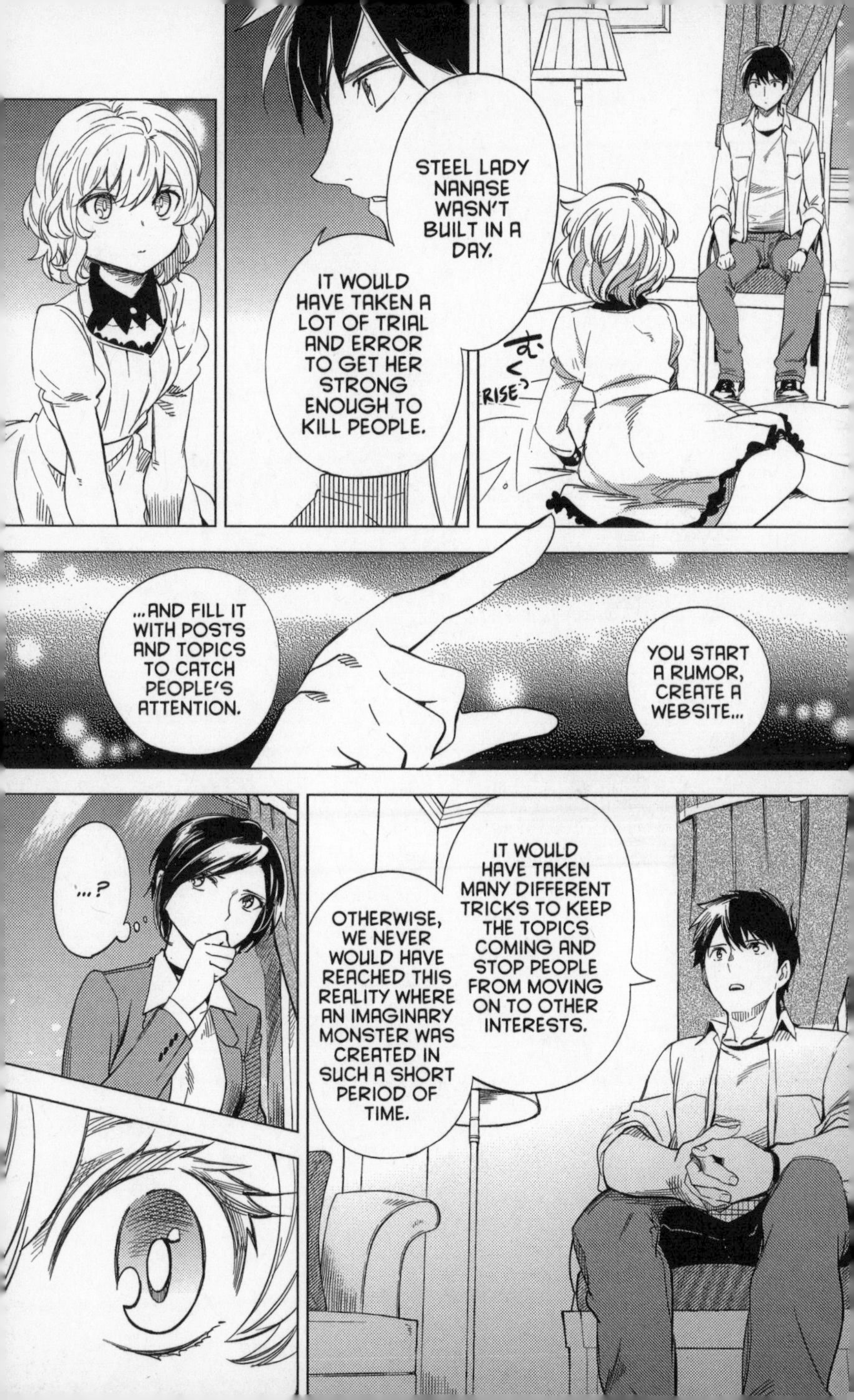
むく
RISE
STEEL LADY NANASE WASN'T BUILT IN A DAY.
IT WOULD HAVE TAKEN A LOT OF TRIAL AND ERROR TO GET HER STRONG ENOUGH TO KILL PEOPLE.
YOU START A RUMOR, CREATE A WEBSITE...
...AND FILL IT WITH POSTS AND TOPICS TO CATCH PEOPLE'S ATTENTION.
IT WOULD HAVE TAKEN MANY DIFFERENT TRICKS TO KEEP THE TOPICS COMING AND STOP PEOPLE FROM MOVING ON TO OTHER INTERESTS.
OTHERWISE, WE NEVER WOULD HAVE REACHED THIS REALITY WHERE AN IMAGINARY MONSTER WAS CREATED IN SUCH A SHORT PERIOD OF TIME.
...?

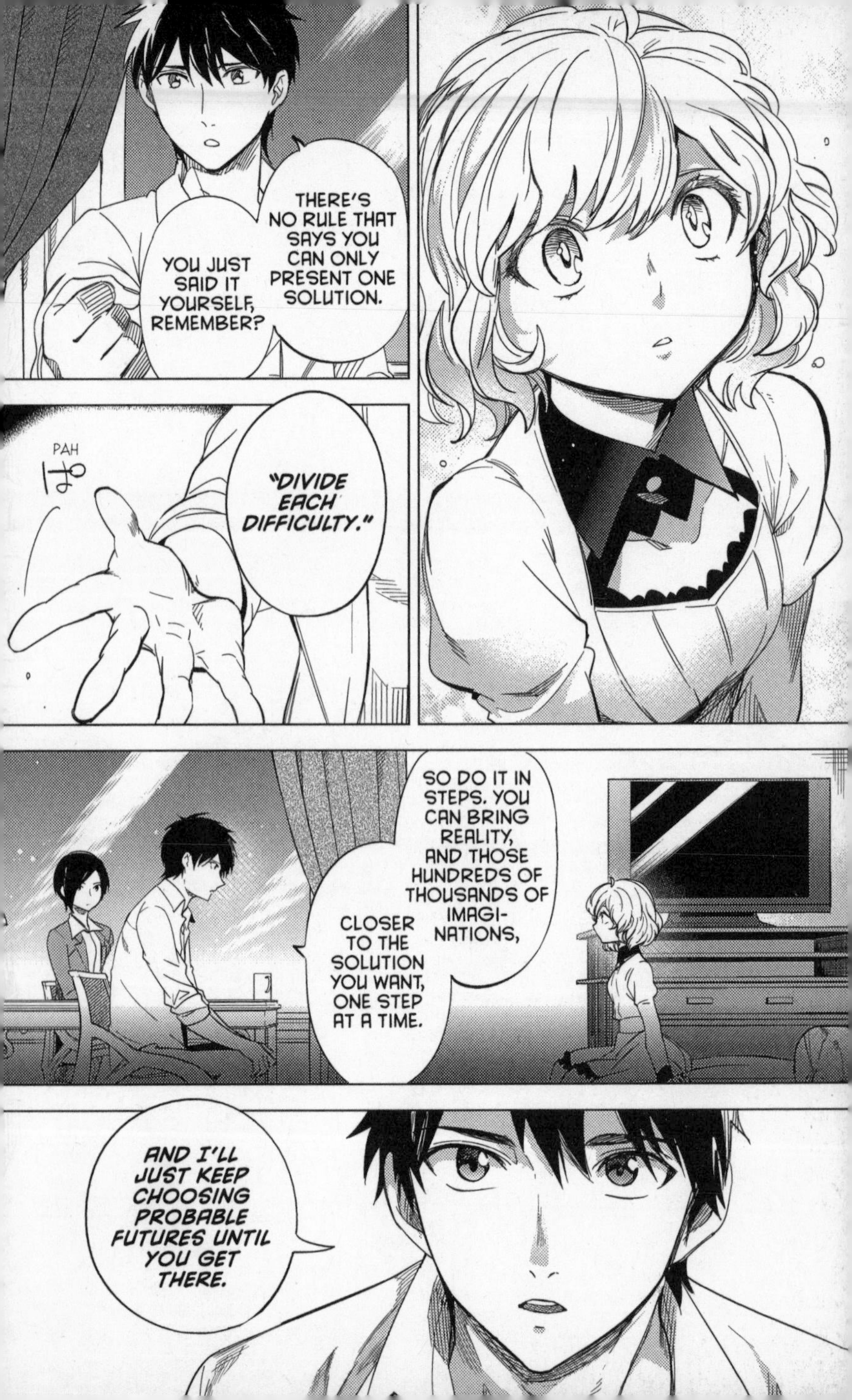
THERE'S NO RULE THAT SAYS YOU CAN ONLY PRESENT ONE SOLUTION.
YOU JUST SAID IT YOURSELF, REMEMBER?
"DIVIDE EACH DIFFICULTY."
PAH
ぱ
SO DO IT IN STEPS. YOU CAN BRING REALITY, AND THOSE HUNDREDS OF THOUSANDS OF IMAGI- NATIONS,
CLOSER TO THE SOLUTION YOU WANT, ONE STEP AT A TIME.
AND I'LL JUST KEEP CHOOSING PROBABLE FUTURES UNTIL YOU GET THERE.

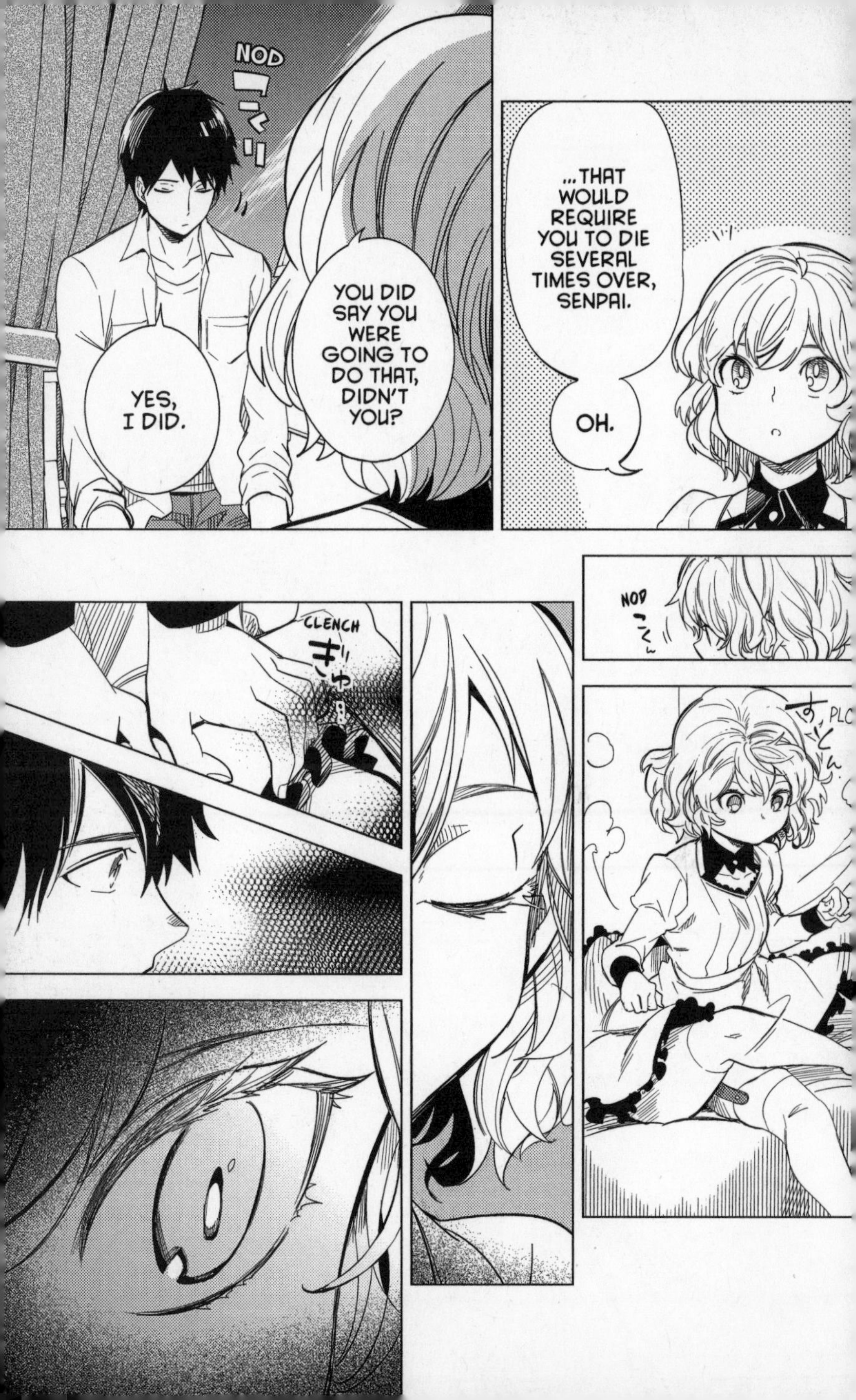
...THAT WOULD REQUIRE YOU TO DIE SEVERAL TIMES OVER, SENPAI.
OH.
NOD
YOU DID SAY YOU WERE GOING TO DO THAT, DIDN'T YOU?
YES, I DID.
NOD
CLENCH

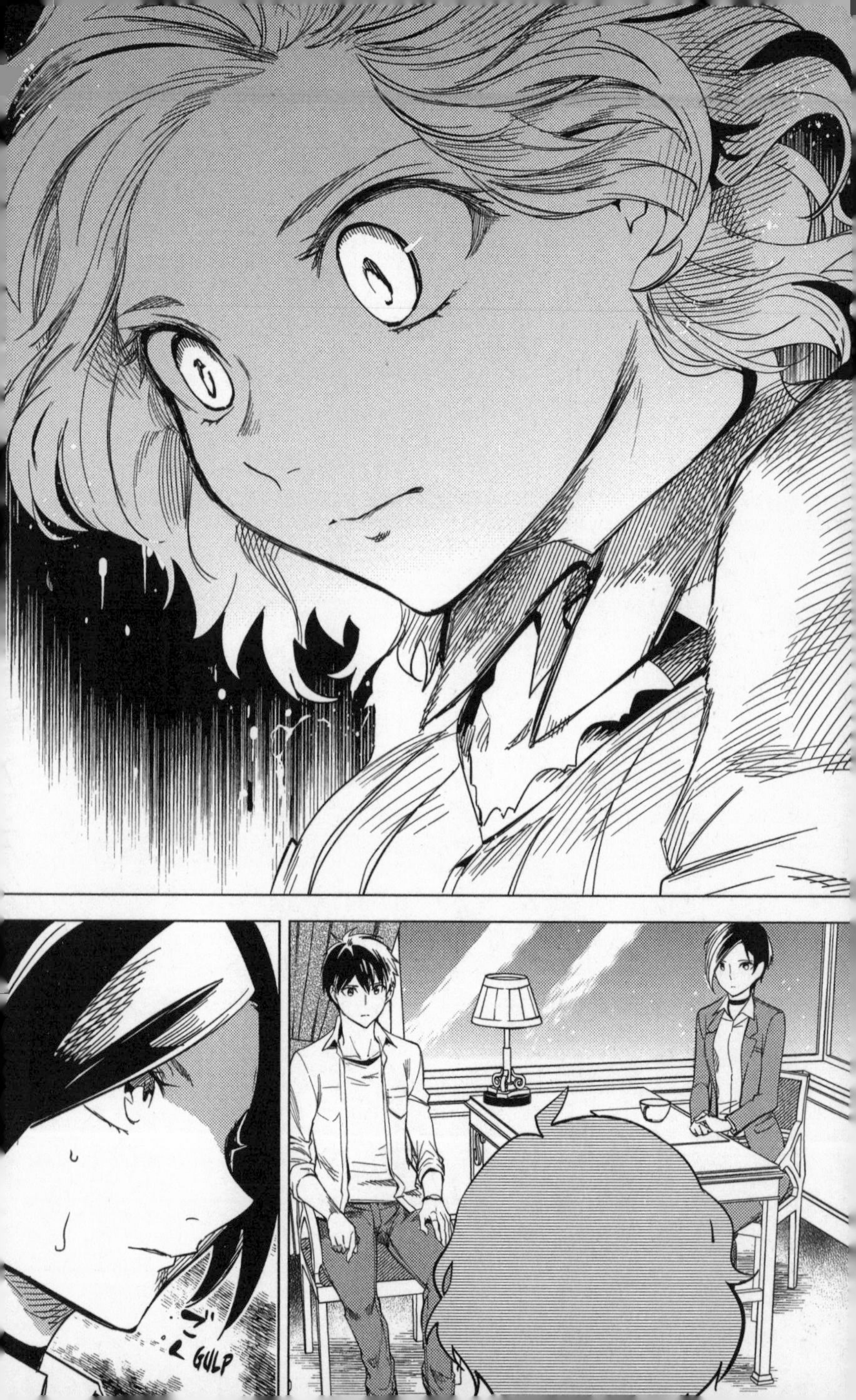
ゴクッ
GULP

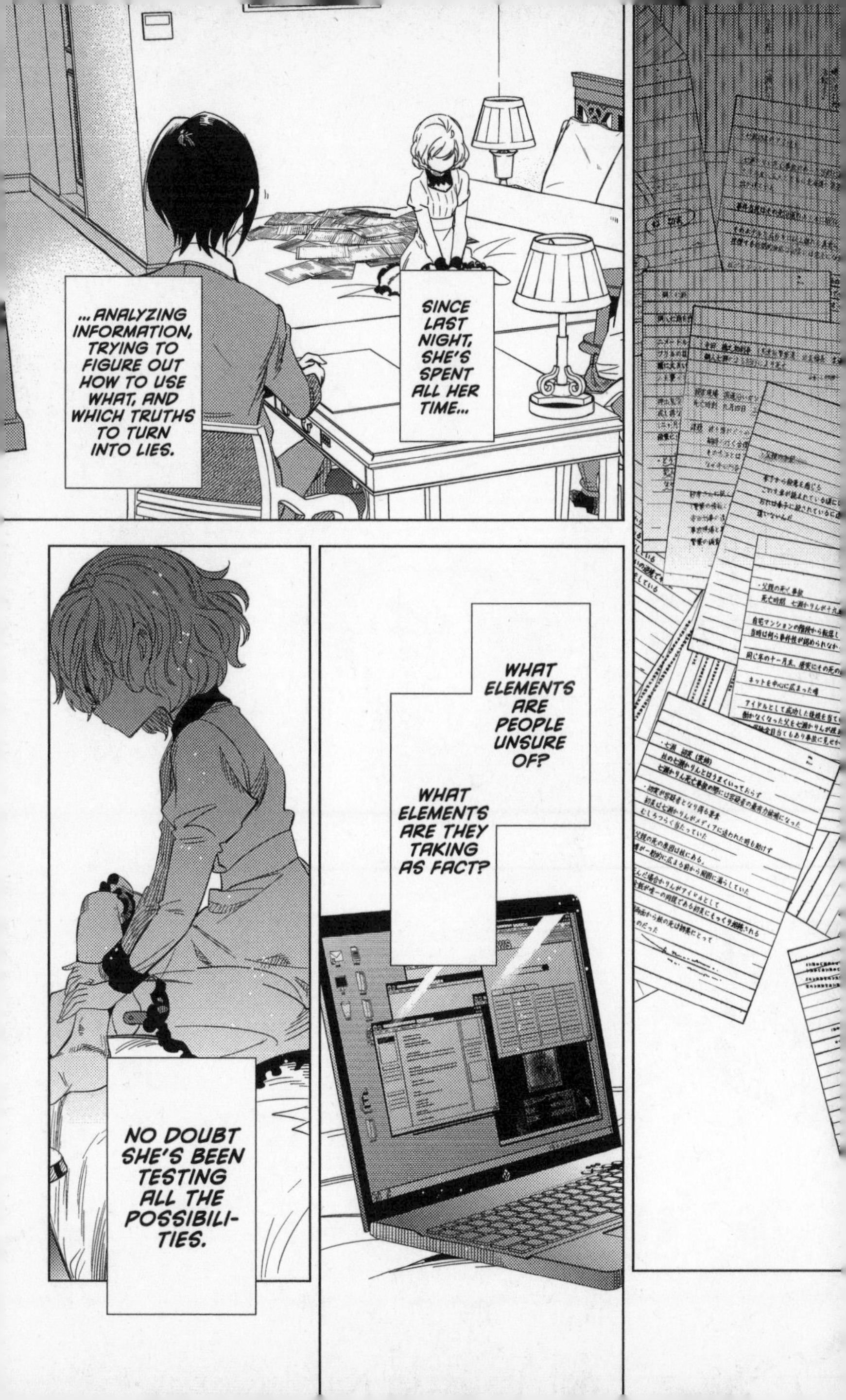
SINCE LAST NIGHT, SHE'S SPENT ALL HER TIME...
...ANALYZING INFORMATION, TRYING TO FIGURE OUT HOW TO USE WHAT, AND WHICH TRUTHS TO TURN INTO LIES.
WHAT ELEMENTS ARE PEOPLE UNSURE OF?
WHAT ELEMENTS ARE THEY TAKING AS FACT?
NO DOUBT SHE'S BEEN TESTING ALL THE POSSIBILI-TIES.

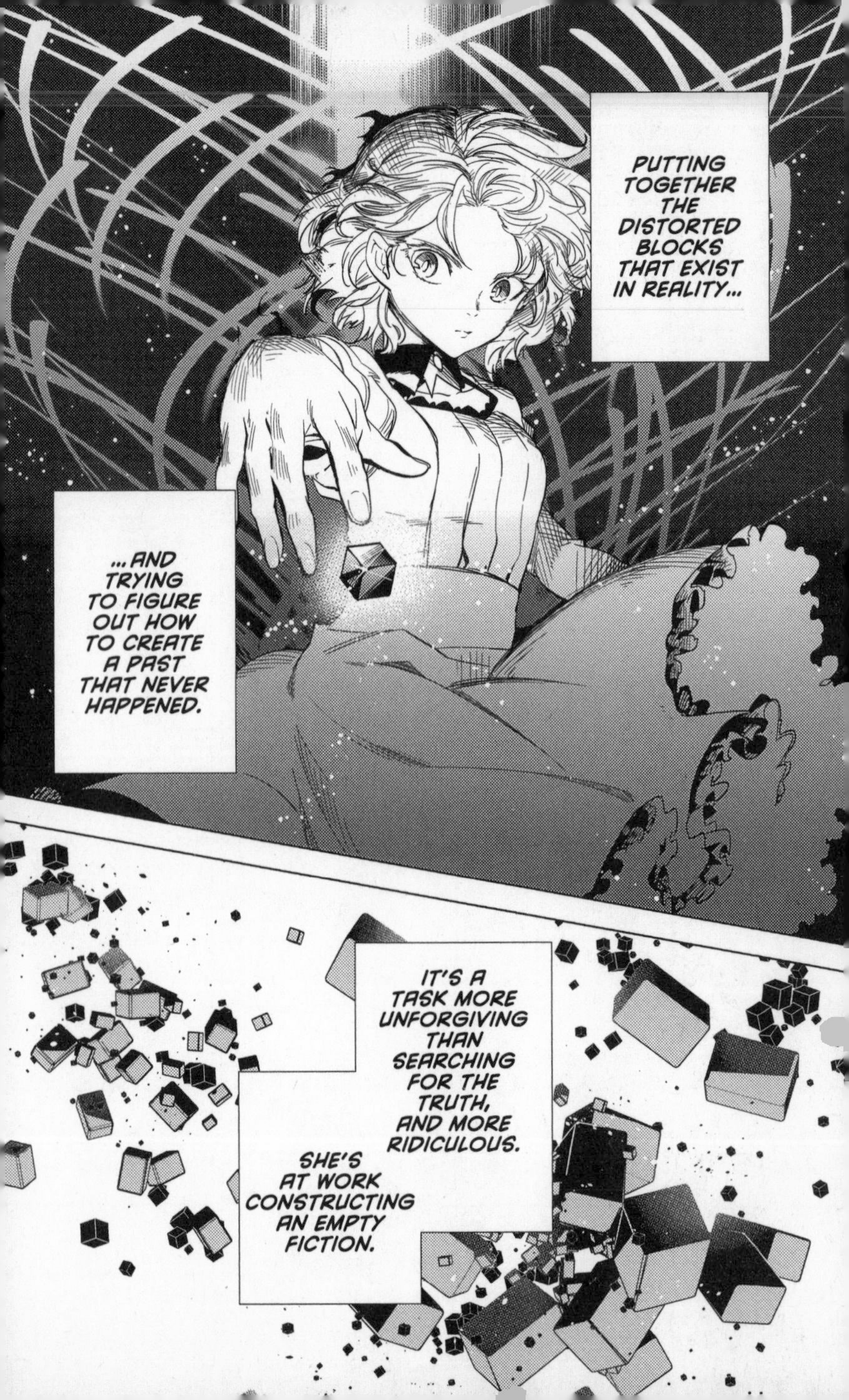
PUTTING TOGETHER THE DISTORTED BLOCKS THAT EXIST IN REALITY...
...AND TRYING TO FIGURE OUT HOW TO CREATE A PAST THAT NEVER HAPPENED.
IT'S A TASK MORE UNFORGIVING THAN SEARCHING FOR THE TRUTH, AND MORE RIDICULOUS.
SHE'S AT WORK CONSTRUCTING AN EMPTY FICTION.

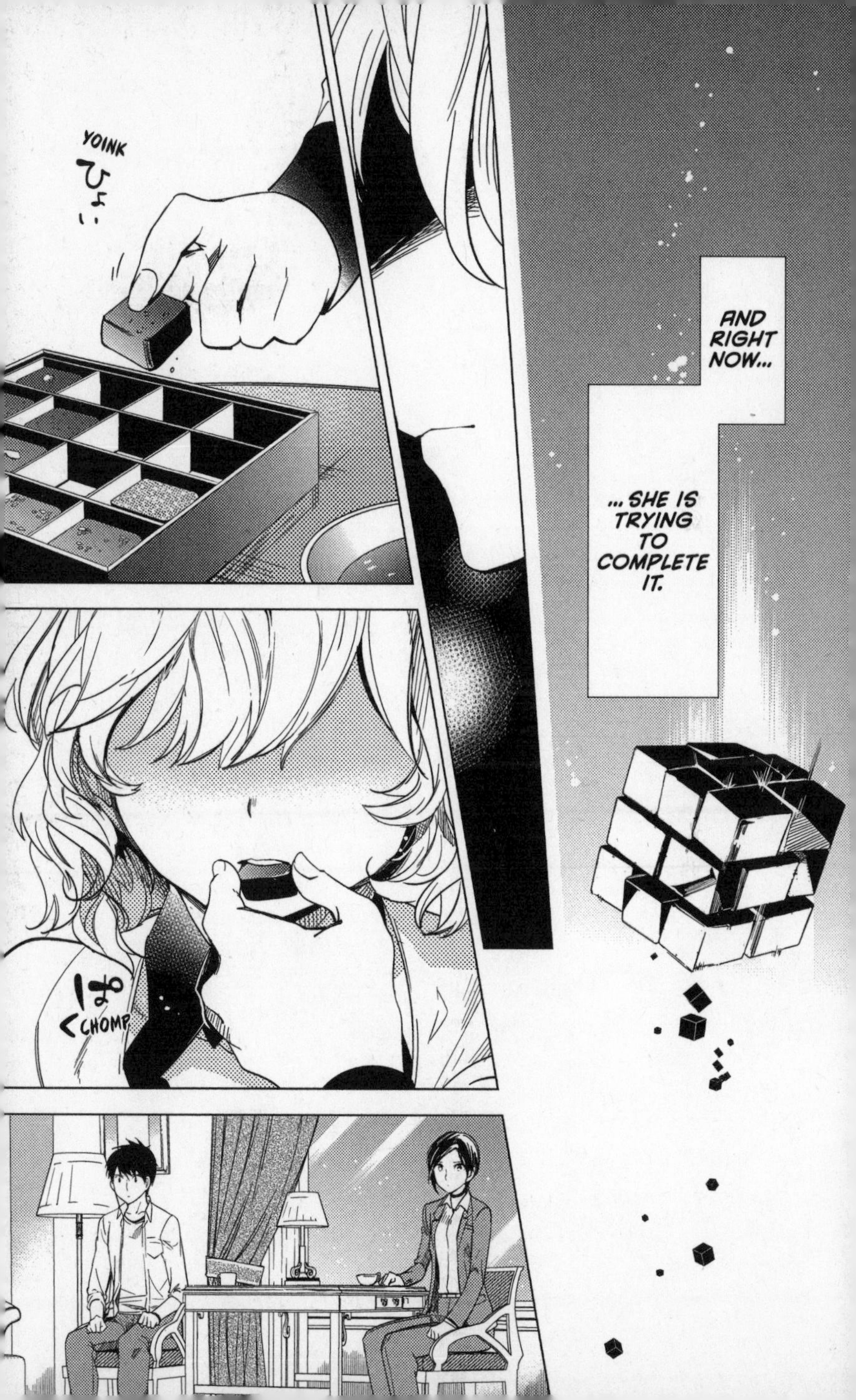
AND RIGHT NOW...
...SHE IS TRYING TO COMPLETE IT.
YOINK
ひょい
ぱく
CHOMP

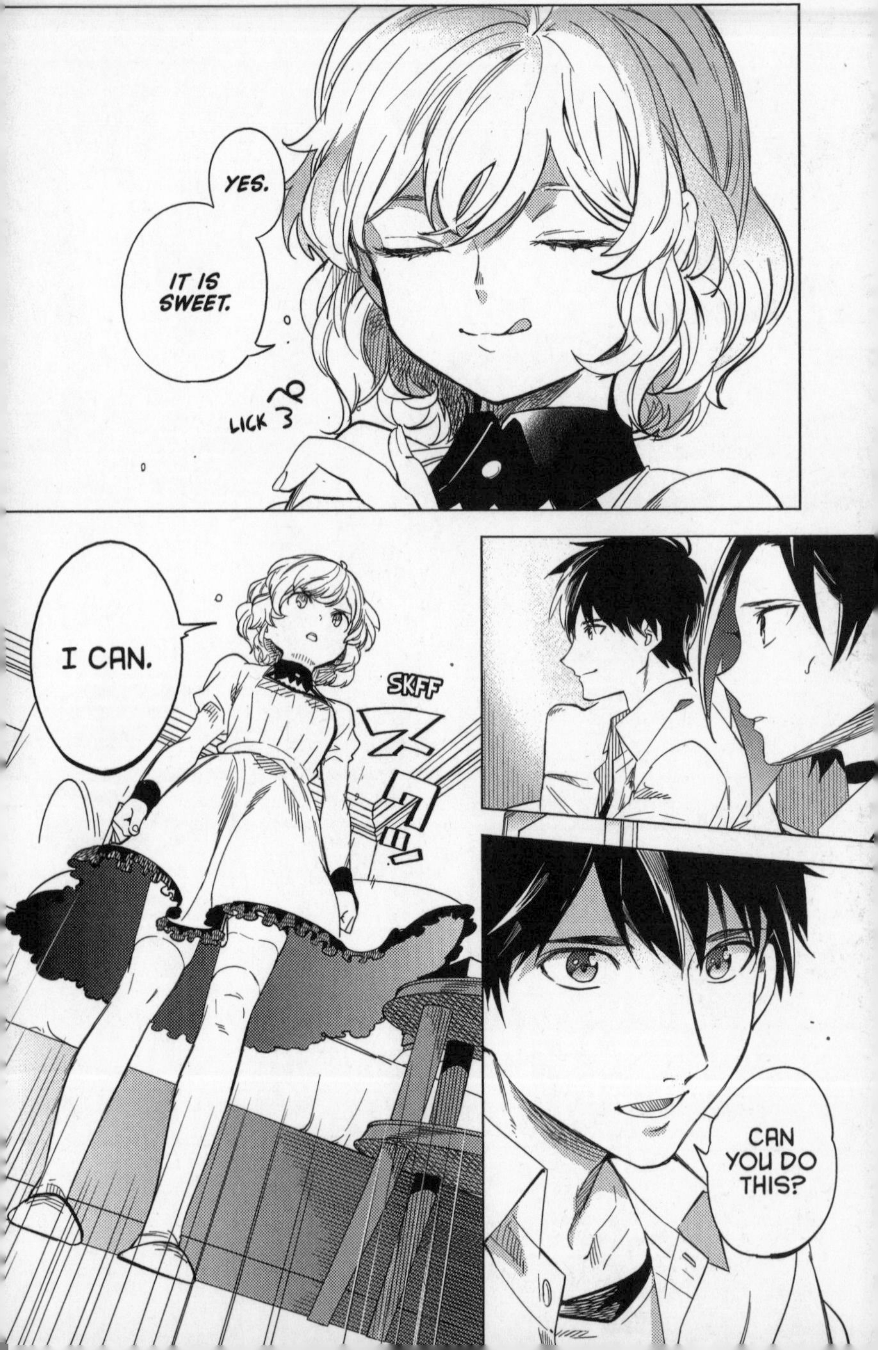
YES.
IT IS SWEET.
LICK
CAN YOU DO THIS?
I CAN.
SKFF

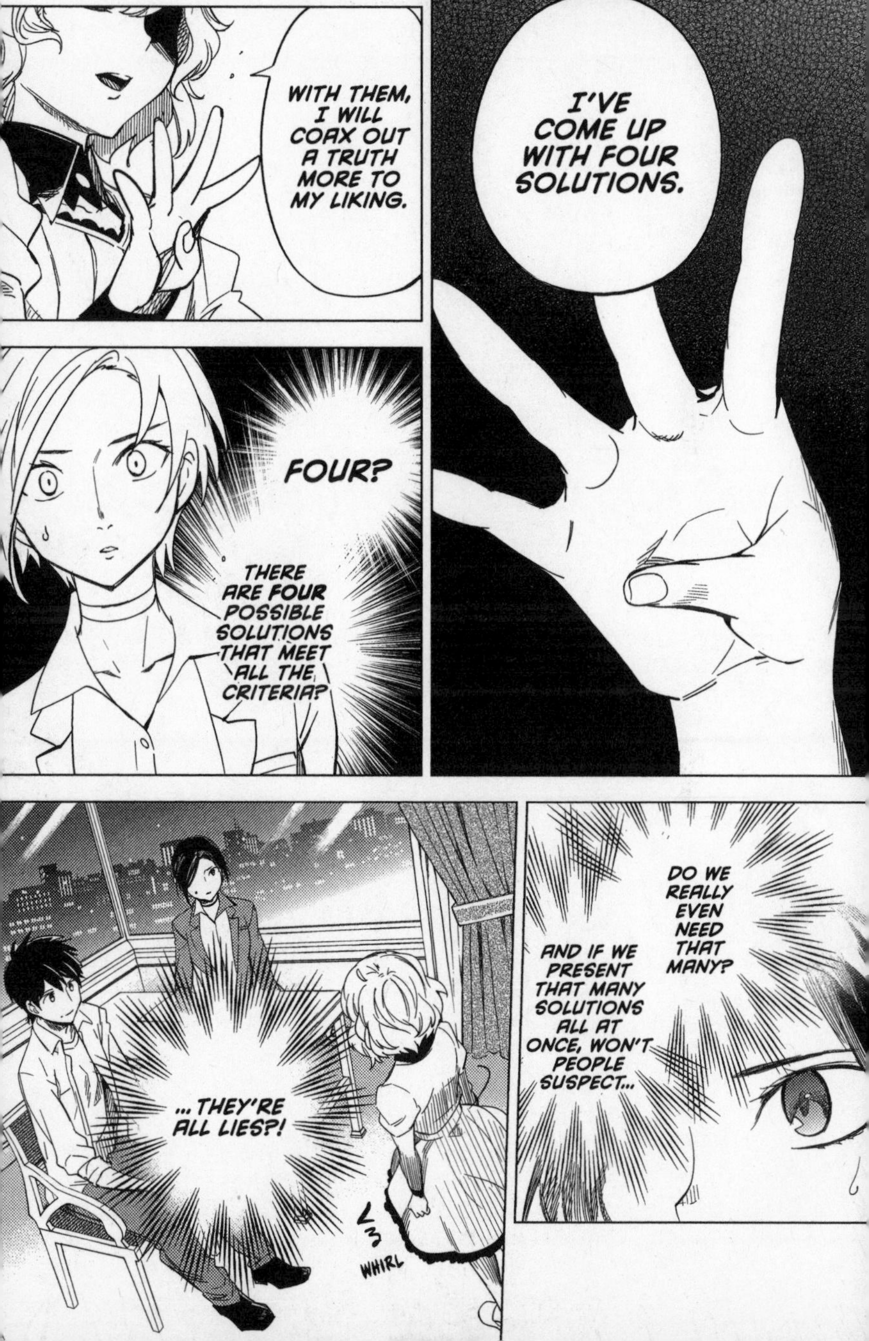
I'VE COME UP WITH FOUR SOLUTIONS.
WITH THEM, I WILL COAX OUT A TRUTH MORE TO MY LIKING.
FOUR?
THERE ARE FOUR POSSIBLE SOLUTIONS THAT MEET ALL THE CRITERIA?
DO WE REALLY EVEN NEED THAT MANY?
AND IF WE PRESENT THAT MANY SOLUTIONS ALL AT ONCE, WON'T PEOPLE SUSPECT...
...THEY'RE ALL LIES?!
WHIRL

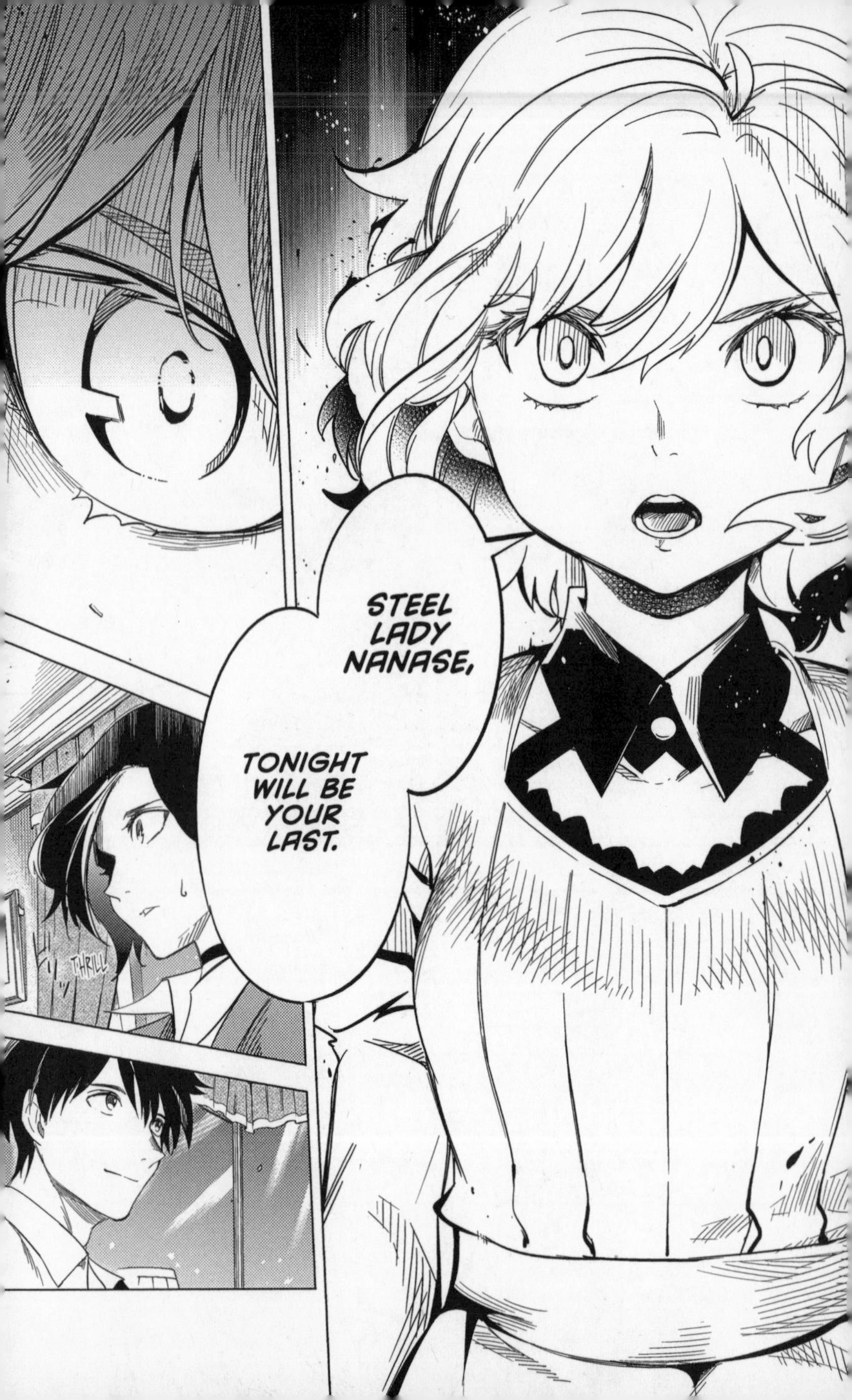
STEEL LADY NANASE,
TONIGHT WILL BE YOUR LAST.
THRILL

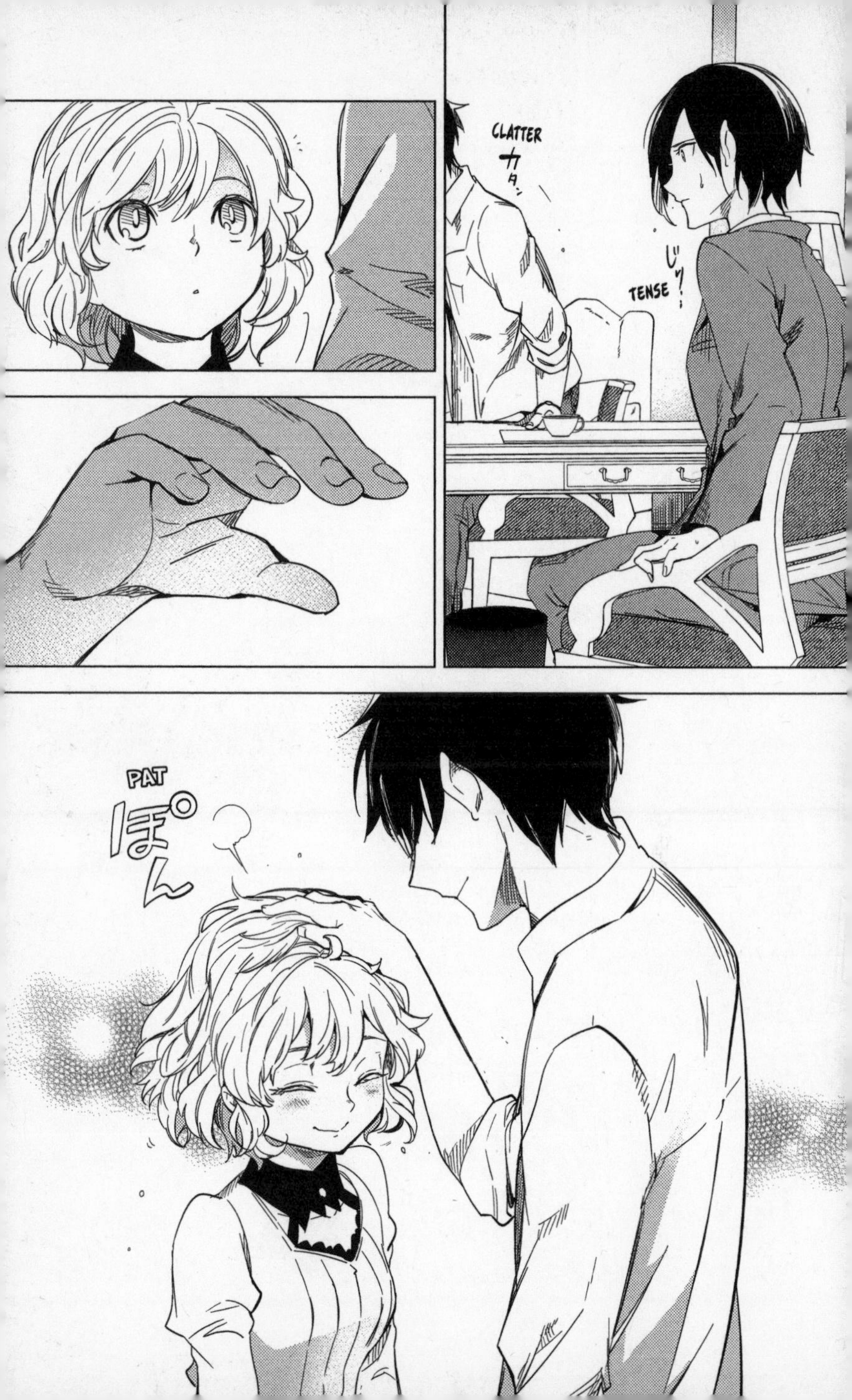
CLATTER
カタッ
TENSE
じッ!
PAT
ぽん

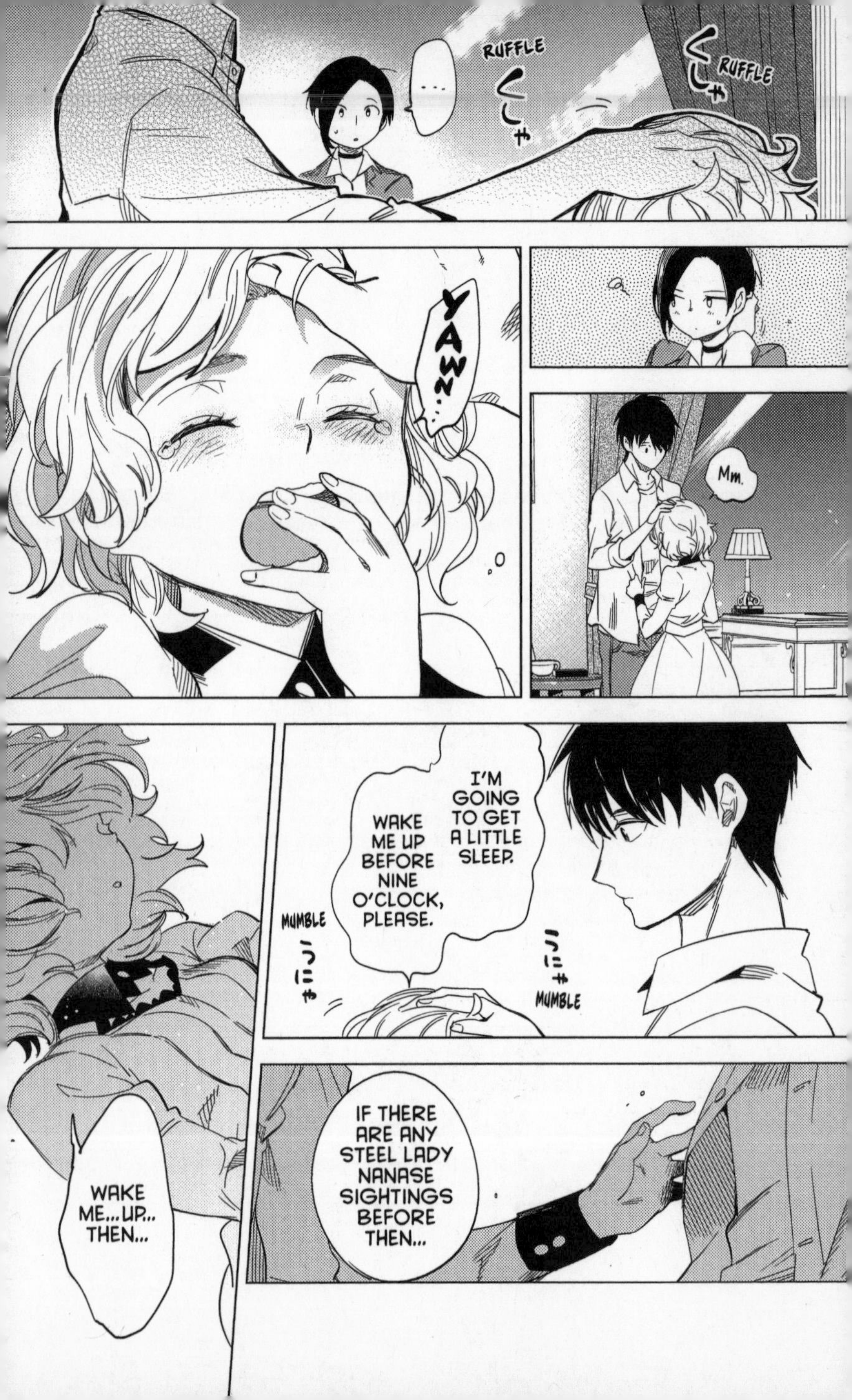

くしゃ RUFFLE
くしゃ RUFFLE
...
Mm.
YAWN...
I'M GOING TO GET A LITTLE SLEEP.
WAKE ME UP BEFORE NINE O'CLOCK, PLEASE.
うにゃ MUMBLE
うにゃ MUMBLE
IF THERE ARE ANY STEEL LADY NANASE SIGHTINGS BEFORE THEN...
WAKE ME...UP... THEN...

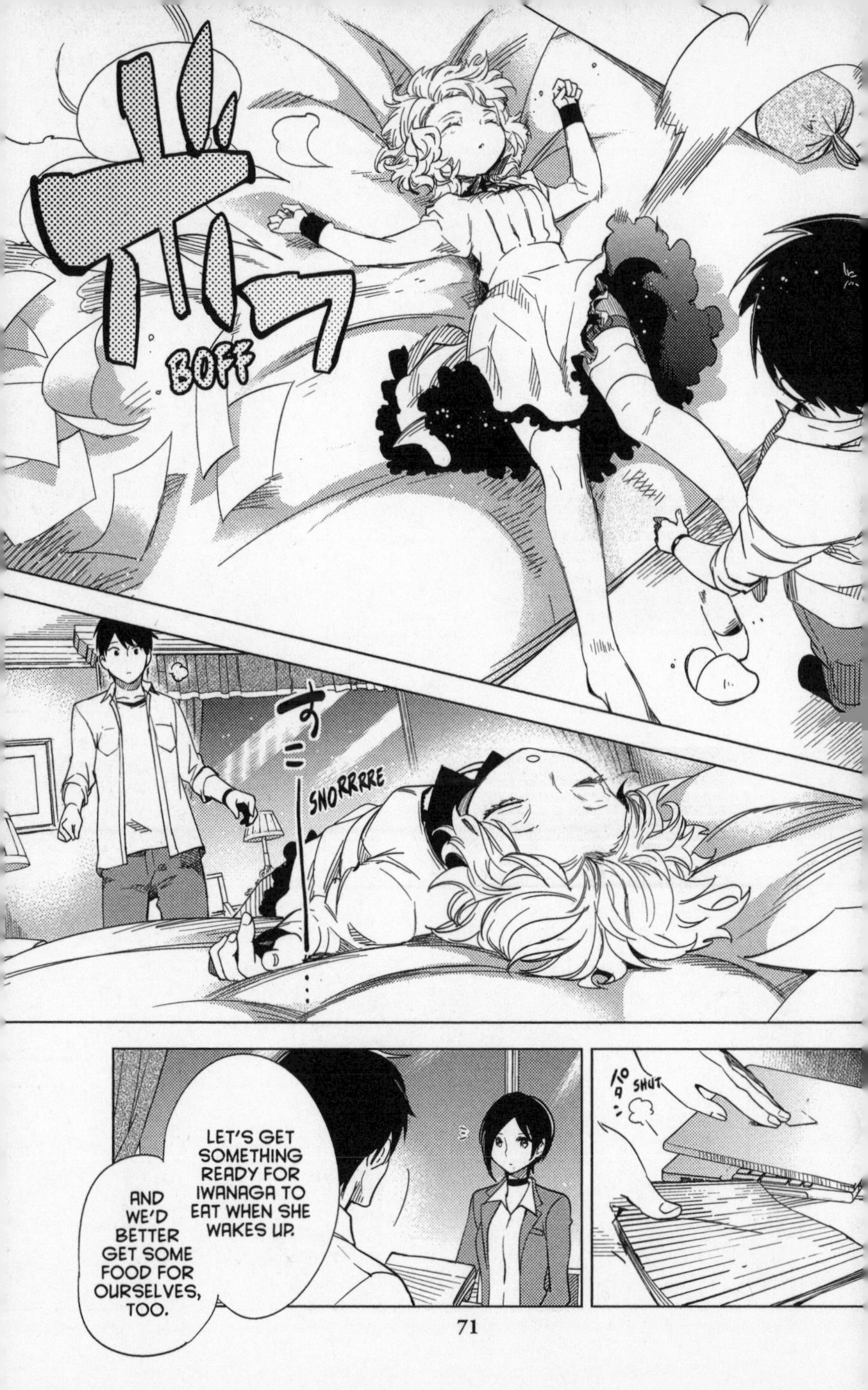
BOFF
SNORRRRE
...
SHUT
LET'S GET SOMETHING READY FOR IWANAGA TO EAT WHEN SHE WAKES UP.
AND WE'D BETTER GET SOME FOOD FOR OURSELVES, TOO.

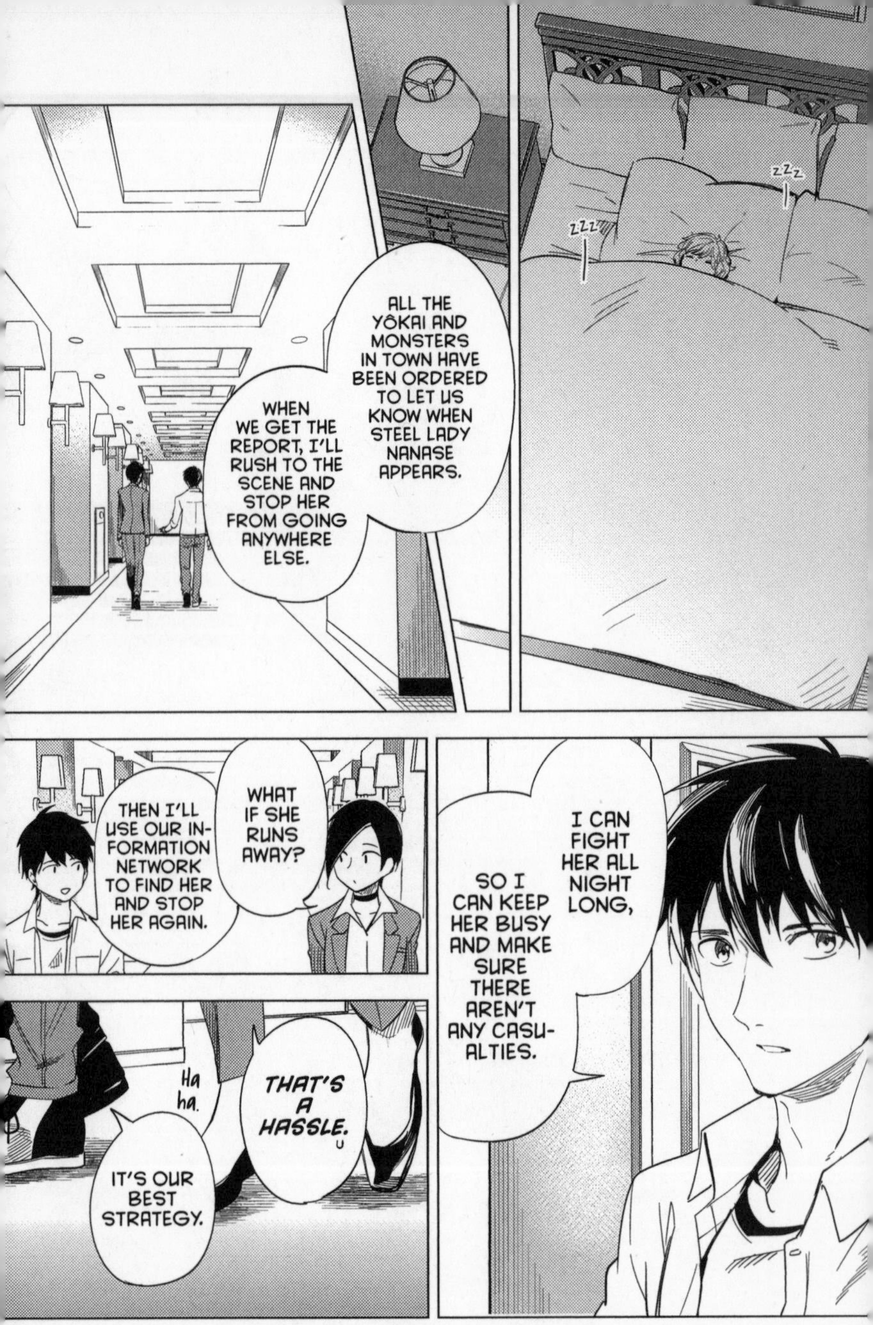
ZZZ
ZZZ
ALL THE YÔKAI AND MONSTERS IN TOWN HAVE BEEN ORDERED TO LET US KNOW WHEN STEEL LADY NANASE APPEARS.
WHEN WE GET THE REPORT, I'LL RUSH TO THE SCENE AND STOP HER FROM GOING ANYWHERE ELSE.
I CAN FIGHT HER ALL NIGHT LONG,
SO I CAN KEEP HER BUSY AND MAKE SURE THERE AREN'T ANY CASU-ALTIES.
WHAT IF SHE RUNS AWAY?
THEN I'LL USE OUR IN-FORMATION NETWORK TO FIND HER AND STOP HER AGAIN.
THAT'S A HASSLE.
Ha ha.
IT'S OUR BEST STRATEGY.

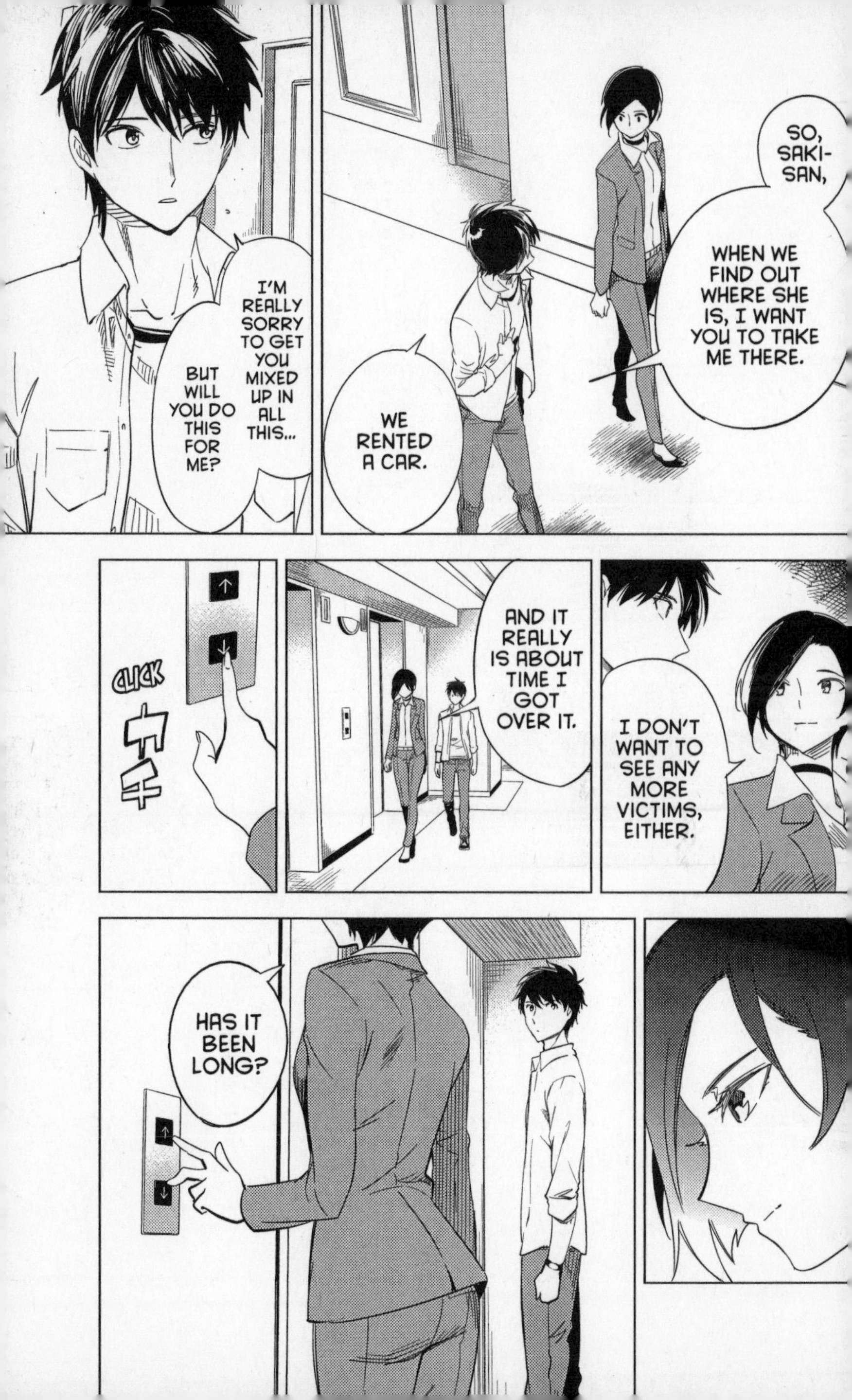
SO, SAKI-SAN,
WHEN WE FIND OUT WHERE SHE IS, I WANT YOU TO TAKE ME THERE.
WE RENTED A CAR.
I'M REALLY SORRY TO GET YOU MIXED UP IN ALL THIS...
BUT WILL YOU DO THIS FOR ME?
I DON'T WANT TO SEE ANY MORE VICTIMS, EITHER.
AND IT REALLY IS ABOUT TIME I GOT OVER IT.
CLICK
カチ
HAS IT BEEN LONG?

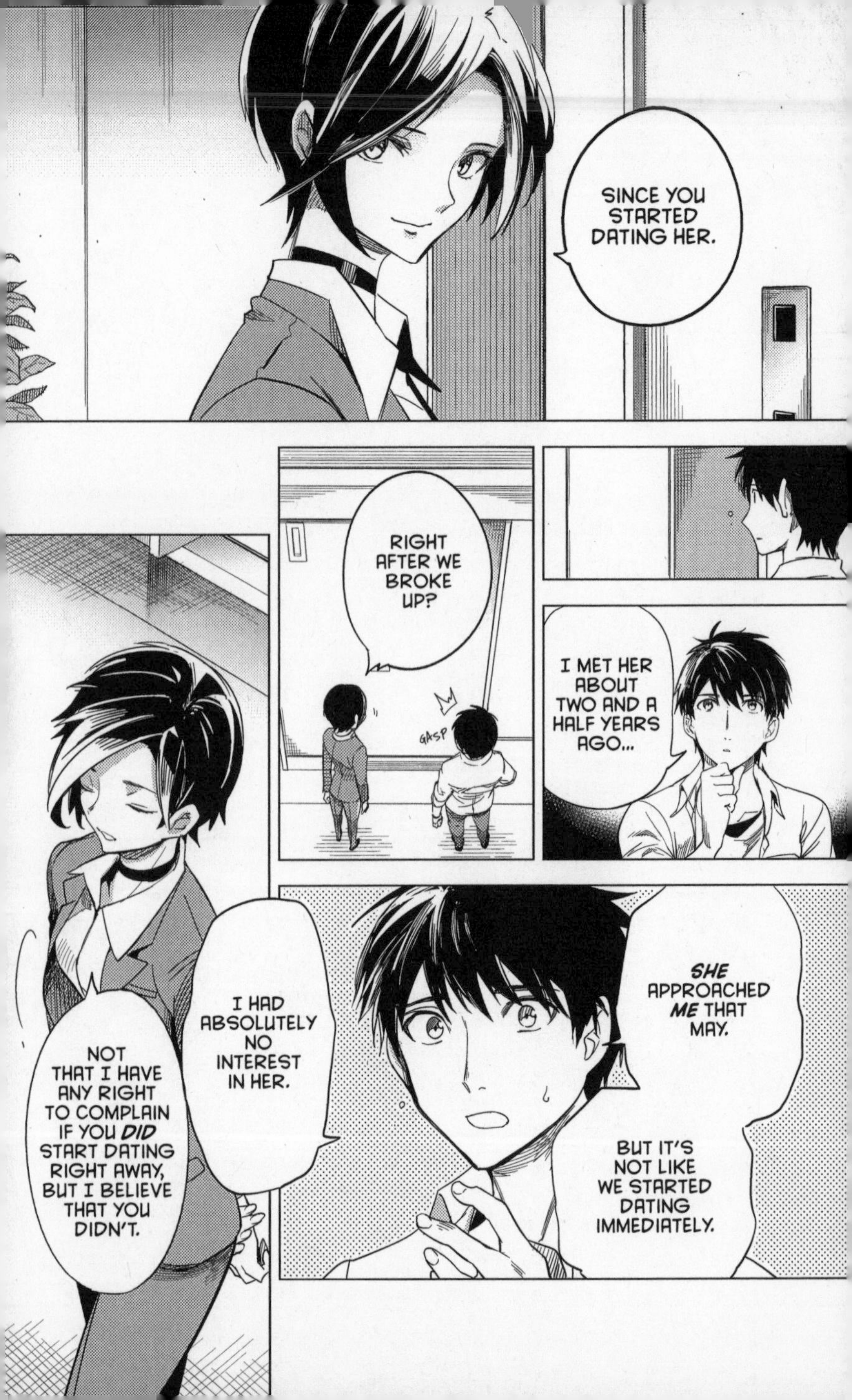
SINCE YOU STARTED DATING HER.
I MET HER ABOUT TWO AND A HALF YEARS AGO...
RIGHT AFTER WE BROKE UP?
GASP
*SHE* APPROACHED *ME* THAT MAY.
BUT IT'S NOT LIKE WE STARTED DATING IMMEDIATELY.
I HAD ABSOLUTELY NO INTEREST IN HER.
NOT THAT I HAVE ANY RIGHT TO COMPLAIN IF YOU *DID* START DATING RIGHT AWAY, BUT I BELIEVE THAT YOU DIDN'T.

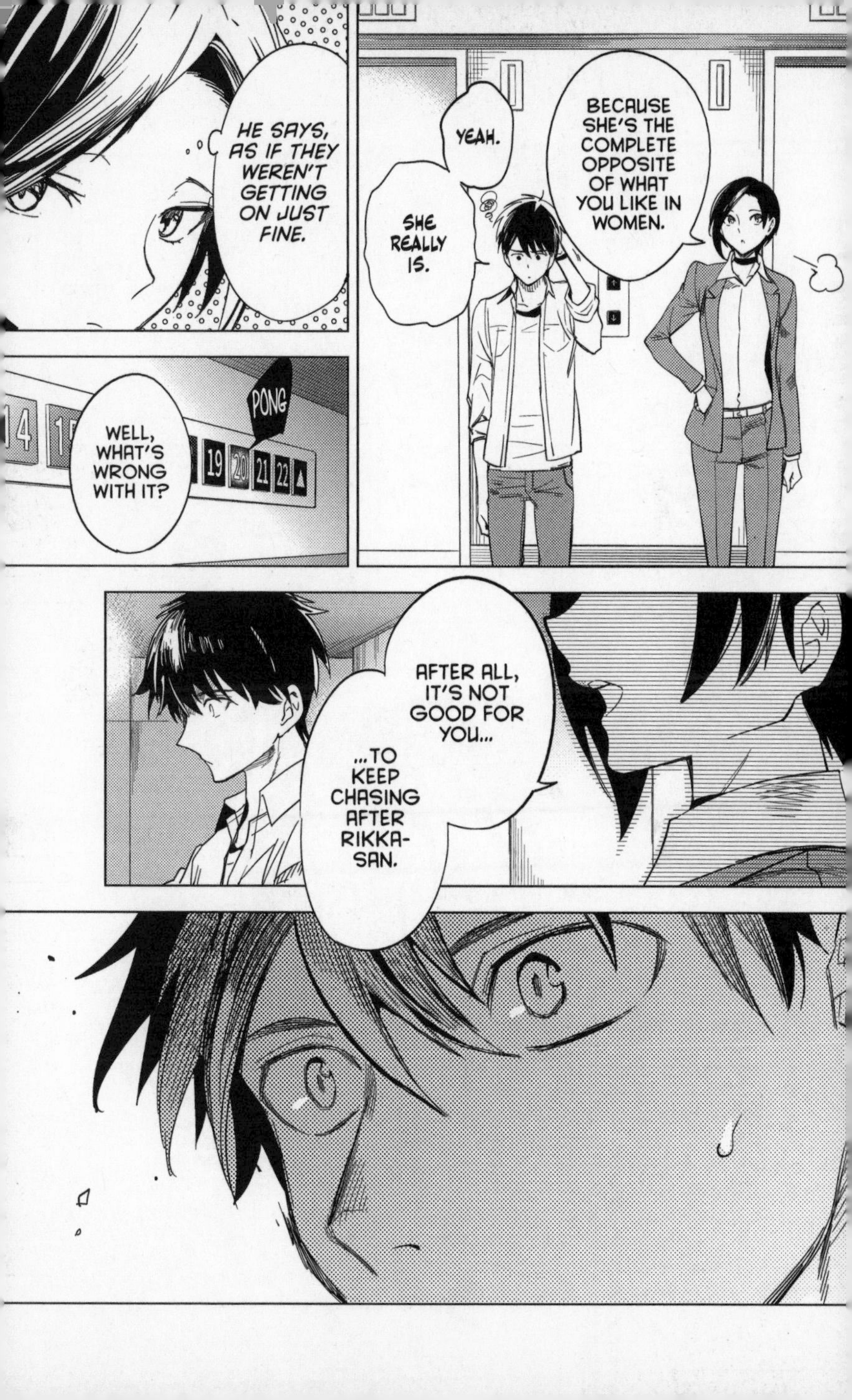
BECAUSE SHE'S THE COMPLETE OPPOSITE OF WHAT YOU LIKE IN WOMEN.
YEAH.
SHE REALLY IS.
HE SAYS, AS IF THEY WEREN'T GETTING ON JUST FINE.
PONG
WELL, WHAT'S WRONG WITH IT?
AFTER ALL, IT'S NOT GOOD FOR YOU...
...TO KEEP CHASING AFTER RIKKA-SAN.

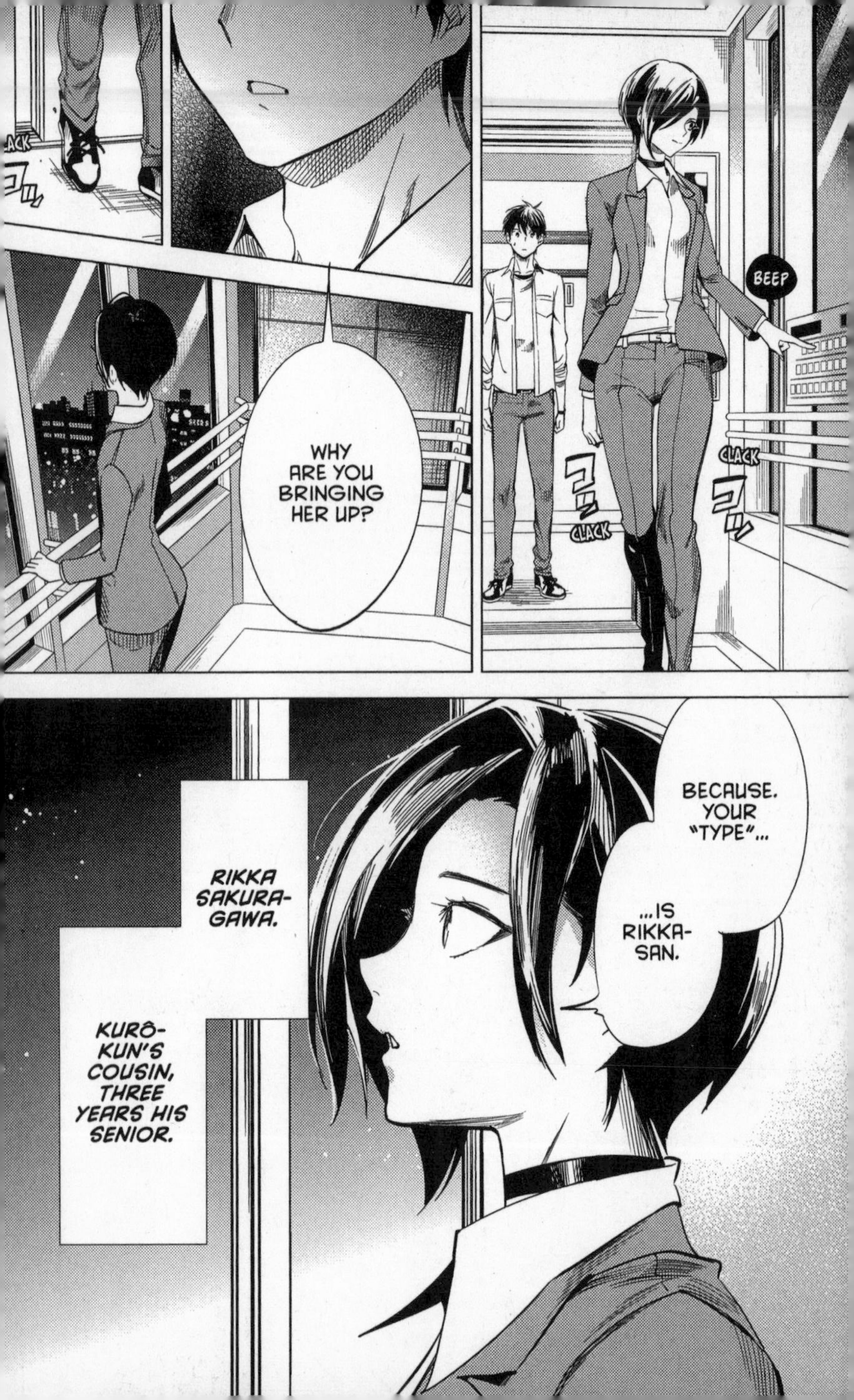
BEEP
CLACK
CLACK
WHY ARE YOU BRINGING HER UP?
BECAUSE. YOUR "TYPE"...
...IS RIKKA-SAN.
RIKKA SAKURA-GAWA.
KURÔ-KUN'S COUSIN, THREE YEARS HIS SENIOR.

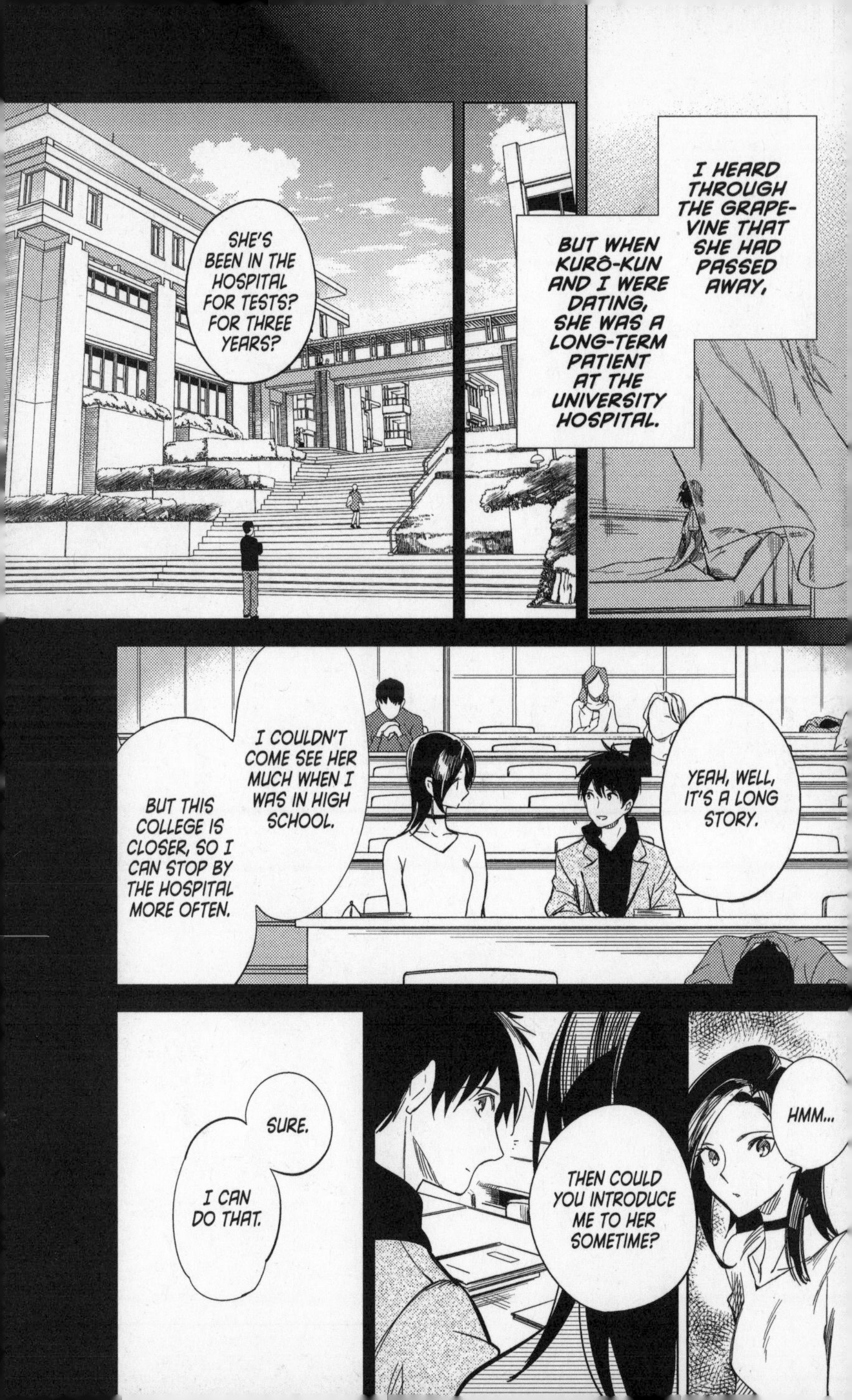
I HEARD THROUGH THE GRAPEVINE THAT SHE HAD PASSED AWAY,
BUT WHEN KURÔ-KUN AND I WERE DATING, SHE WAS A LONG-TERM PATIENT AT THE UNIVERSITY HOSPITAL.
SHE'S BEEN IN THE HOSPITAL FOR TESTS? FOR THREE YEARS?
YEAH, WELL, IT'S A LONG STORY.
I COULDN'T COME SEE HER MUCH WHEN I WAS IN HIGH SCHOOL.
BUT THIS COLLEGE IS CLOSER, SO I CAN STOP BY THE HOSPITAL MORE OFTEN.
HMM...
THEN COULD YOU INTRODUCE ME TO HER SOMETIME?
SURE.
I CAN DO THAT.

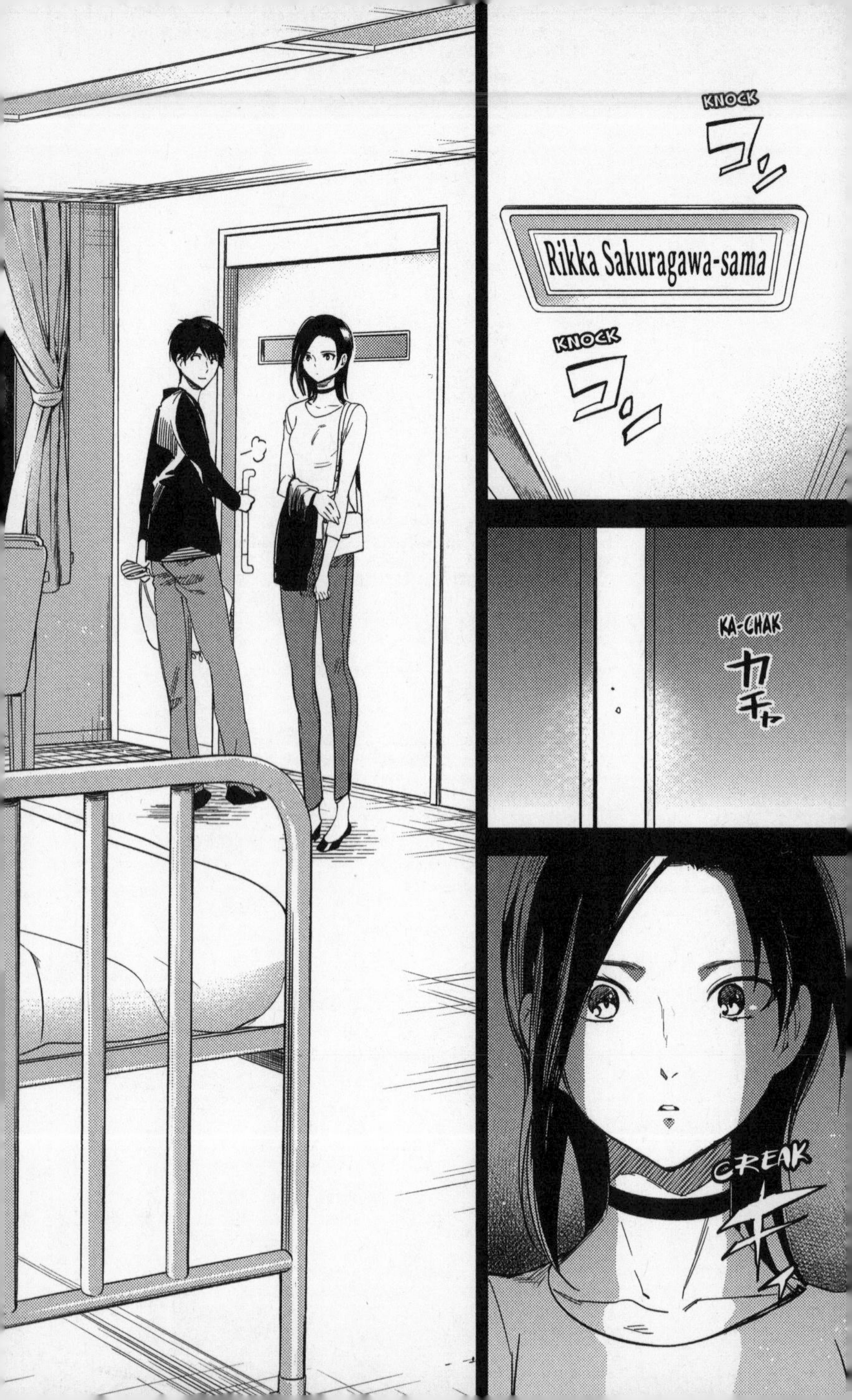
KNOCK
コン
Rikka Sakuragawa-sama
KNOCK
コン
KA-CHAK
カチャ
CREAK

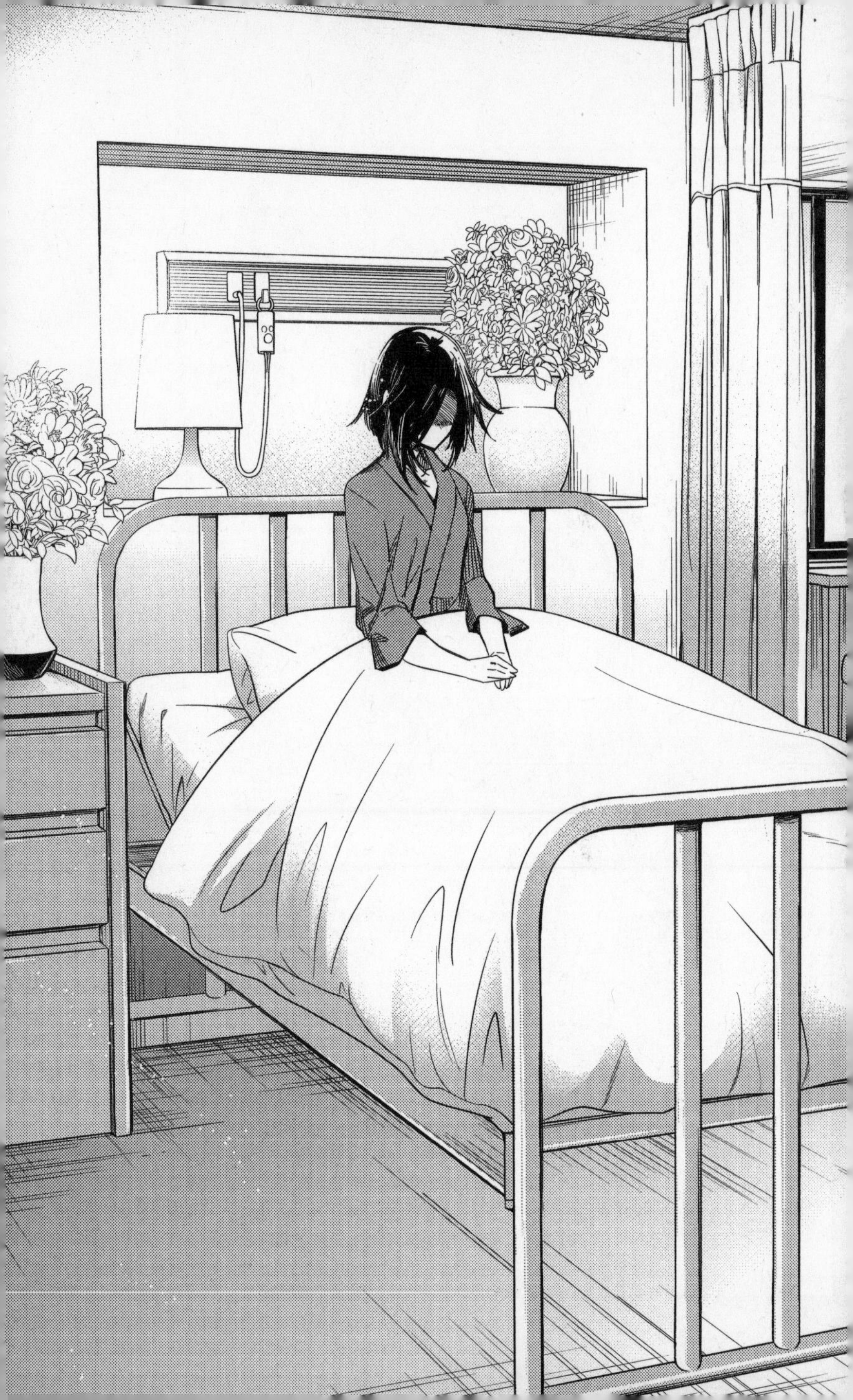

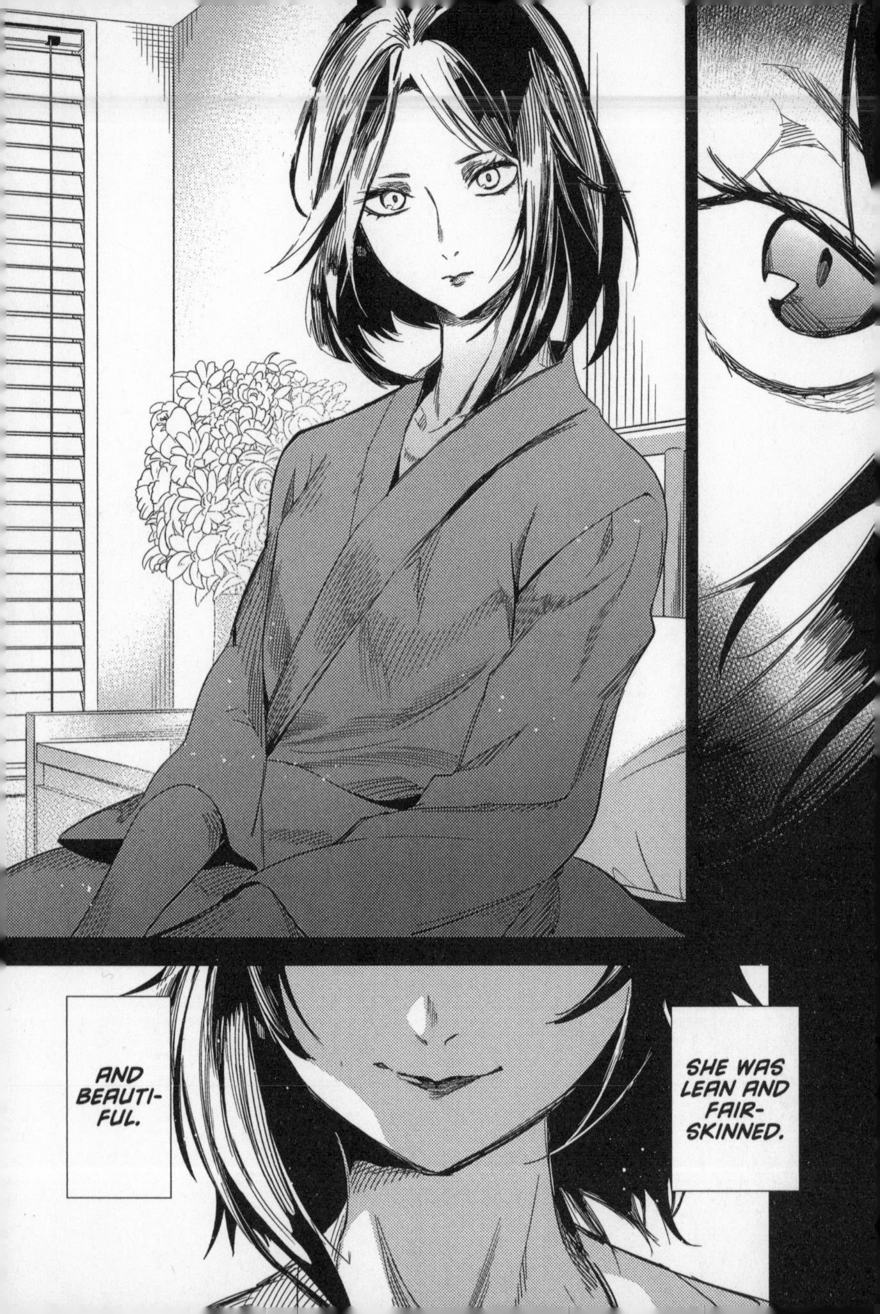
SHE WAS LEAN AND FAIR-SKINNED.
AND BEAUTI-FUL.

IN/SPECTRE

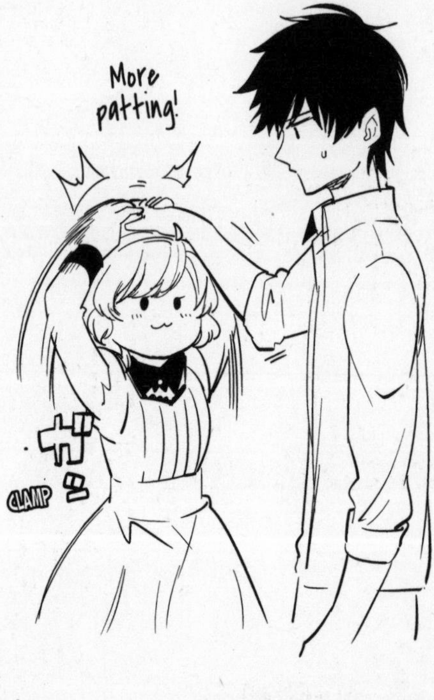
More patting!
ガ
CLAMP

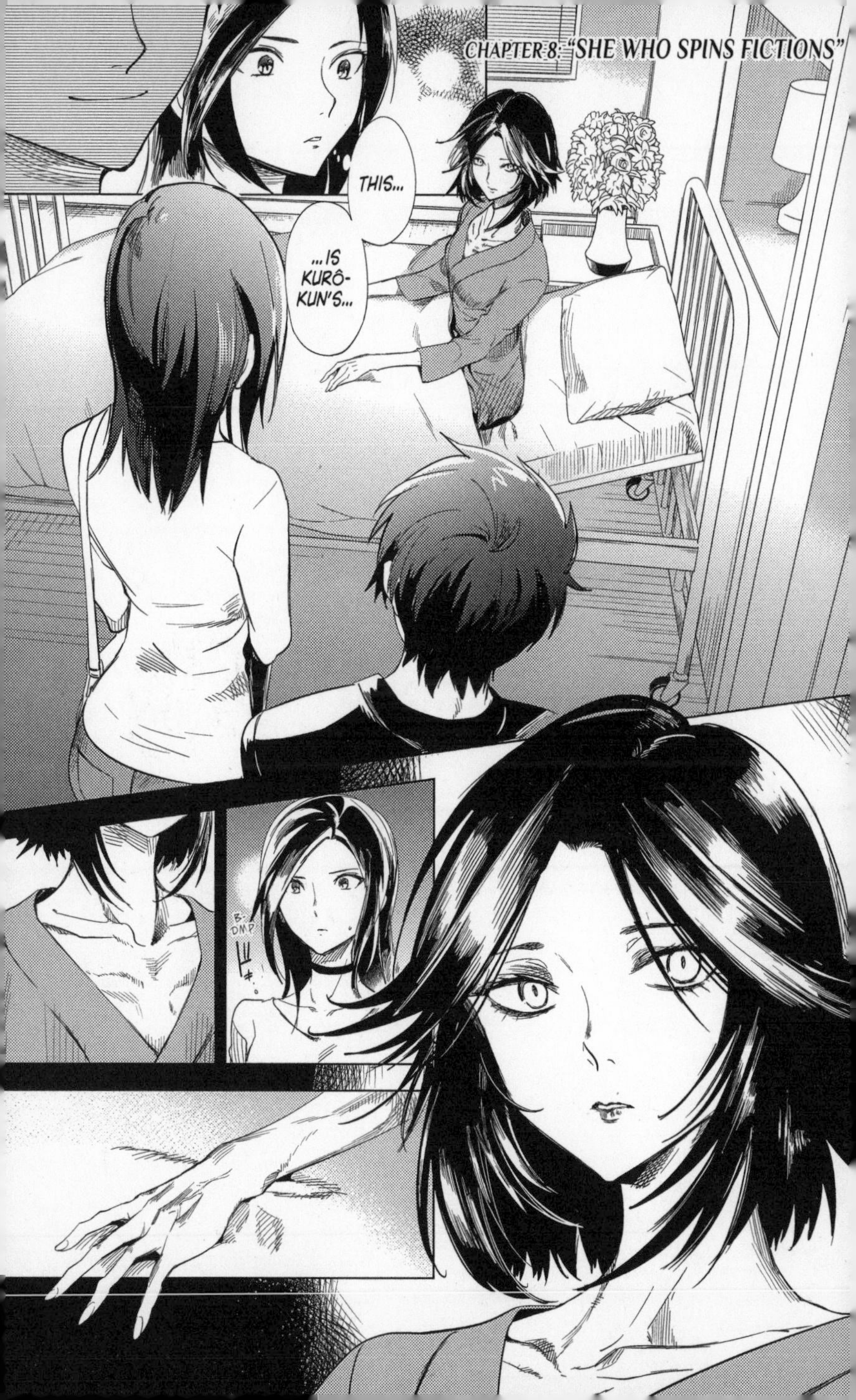
CHAPTER 8: "SHE WHO SPINS FICTIONS"
THIS...
...IS KURÔ-KUN'S...
B-DMP

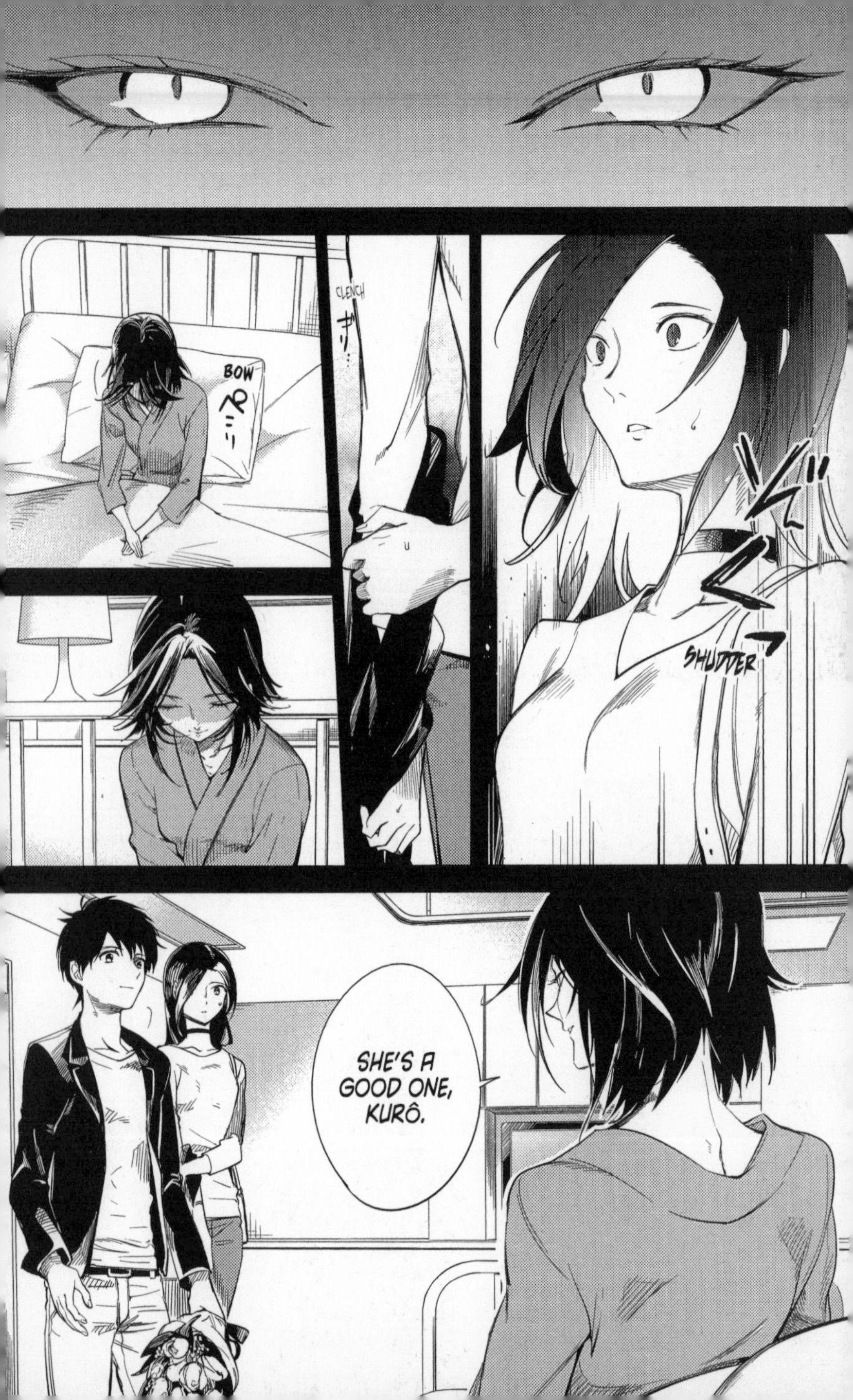
SHUDDER
CLENCH
BOW
SHE'S A GOOD ONE, KURÔ.

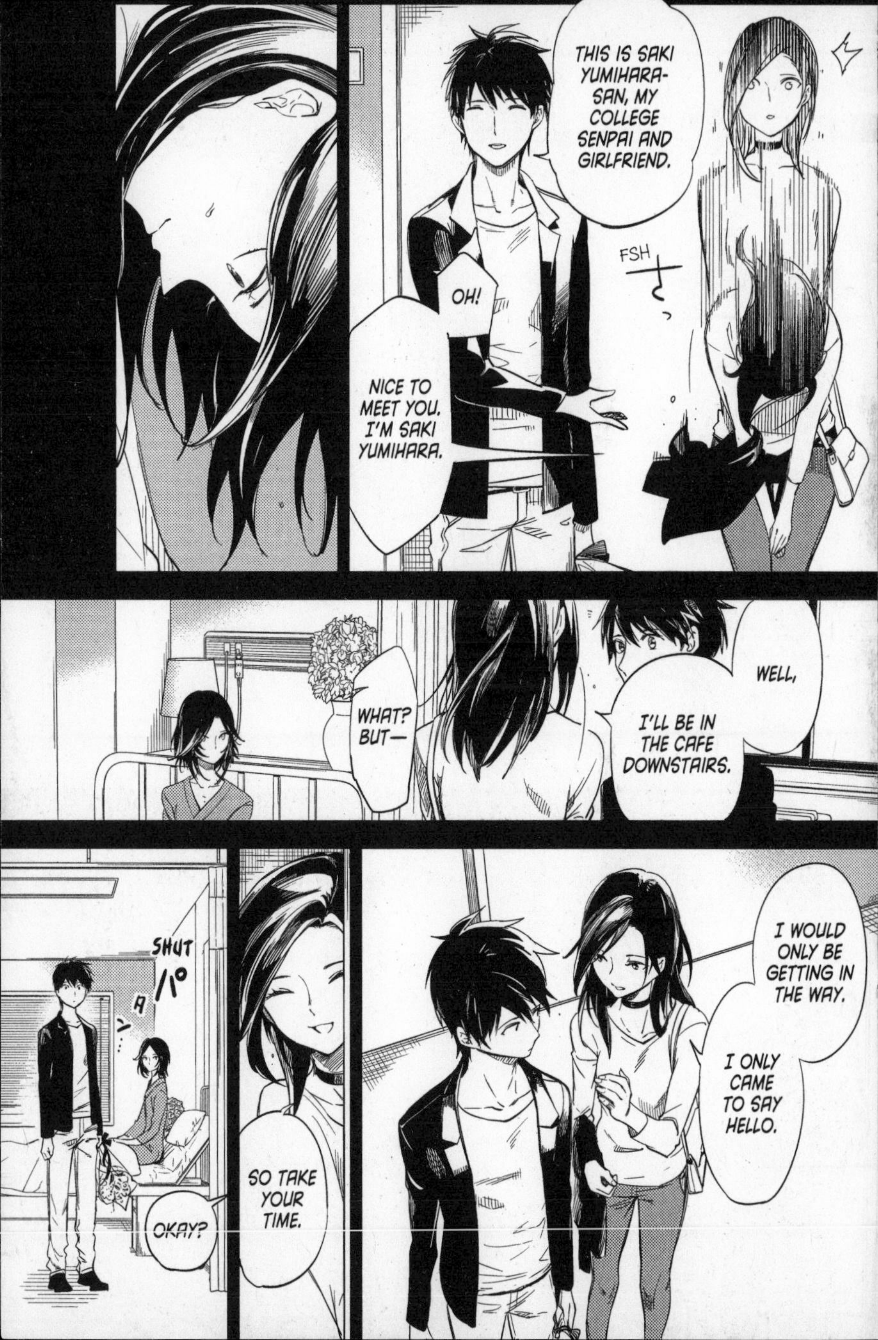
THIS IS SAKI YUMIHARA-SAN, MY COLLEGE SENPAI AND GIRLFRIEND.
FSH
OH!
NICE TO MEET YOU. I'M SAKI YUMIHARA.
WELL,
I'LL BE IN THE CAFE DOWNSTAIRS.
WHAT? BUT—
I WOULD ONLY BE GETTING IN THE WAY.
I ONLY CAME TO SAY HELLO.
SO TAKE YOUR TIME.
OKAY?
SHUT

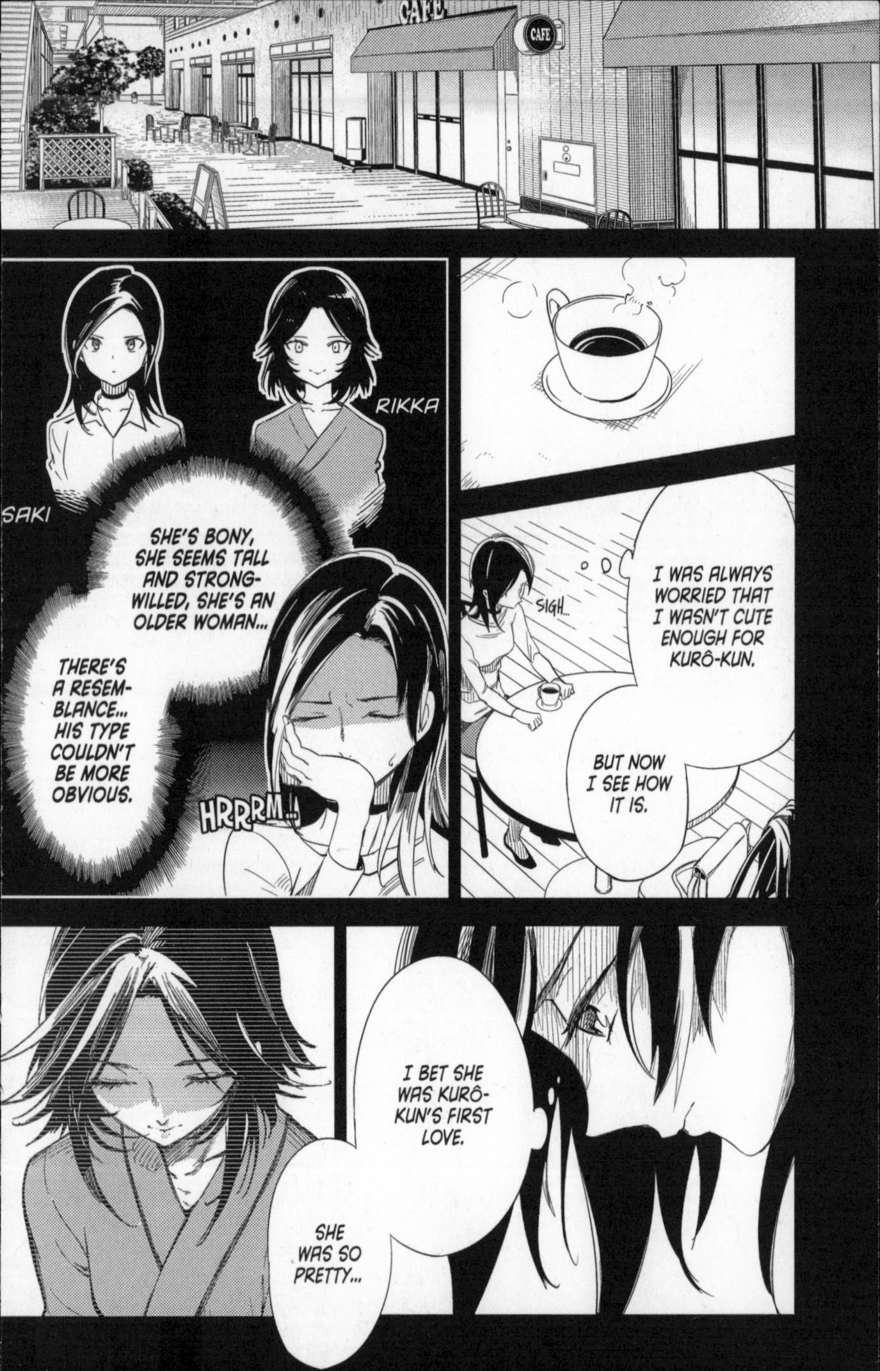
CAFE
CAFE
I WAS ALWAYS WORRIED THAT I WASN'T CUTE ENOUGH FOR KURÔ-KUN.
SIGH...
BUT NOW I SEE HOW IT IS.
RIKKA
SAKI
SHE'S BONY, SHE SEEMS TALL AND STRONG-WILLED, SHE'S AN OLDER WOMAN...
THERE'S A RESEMBLANCE... HIS TYPE COULDN'T BE MORE OBVIOUS.
HRRRM...
I BET SHE WAS KURÔ-KUN'S FIRST LOVE.
SHE WAS SO PRETTY...

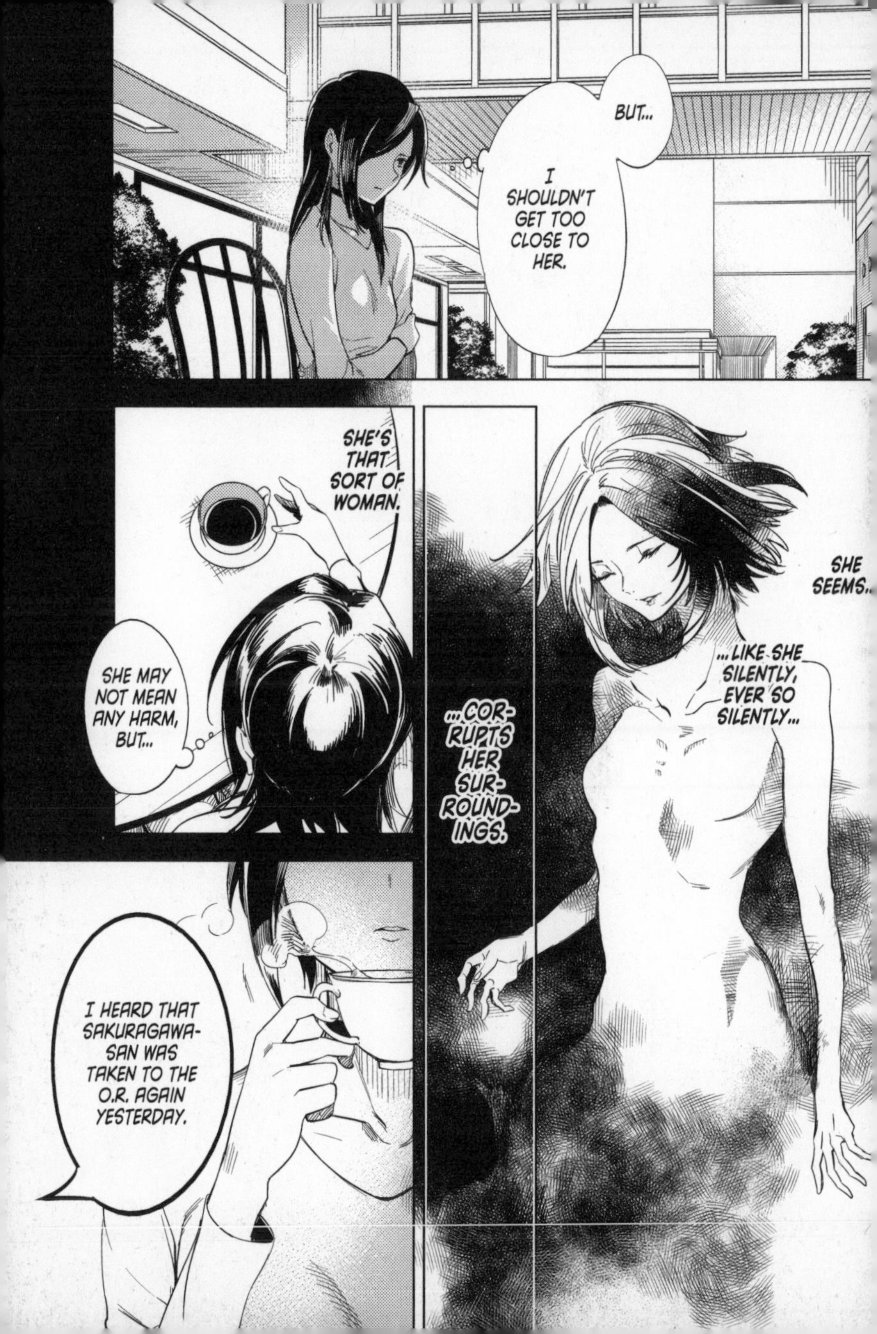
BUT...
I SHOULDN'T GET TOO CLOSE TO HER.
SHE SEEMS...
...LIKE SHE SILENTLY, EVER SO SILENTLY...
...CORRUPTS HER SURROUNDINGS.
SHE'S THAT SORT OF WOMAN.
SHE MAY NOT MEAN ANY HARM, BUT...
I HEARD THAT SAKURAGAWA-SAN WAS TAKEN TO THE O.R. AGAIN YESTERDAY.

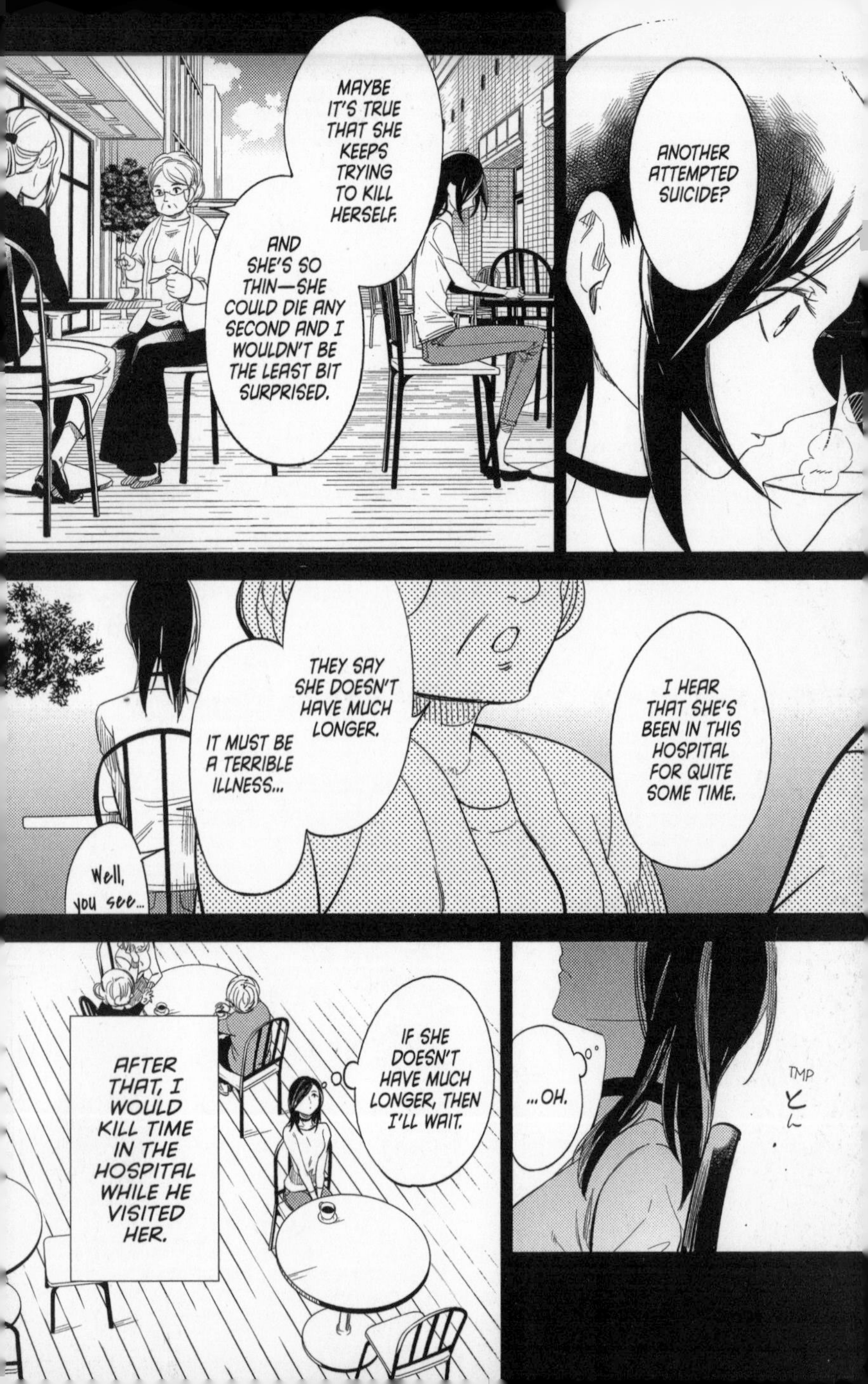
ANOTHER ATTEMPTED SUICIDE?
MAYBE IT'S TRUE THAT SHE KEEPS TRYING TO KILL HERSELF.
AND SHE'S SO THIN—SHE COULD DIE ANY SECOND AND I WOULDN'T BE THE LEAST BIT SURPRISED.
I HEAR THAT SHE'S BEEN IN THIS HOSPITAL FOR QUITE SOME TIME.
THEY SAY SHE DOESN'T HAVE MUCH LONGER.
IT MUST BE A TERRIBLE ILLNESS...
Well, you see...
...OH.
TMP
とん
IF SHE DOESN'T HAVE MUCH LONGER, THEN I'LL WAIT.
AFTER THAT, I WOULD KILL TIME IN THE HOSPITAL WHILE HE VISITED HER.

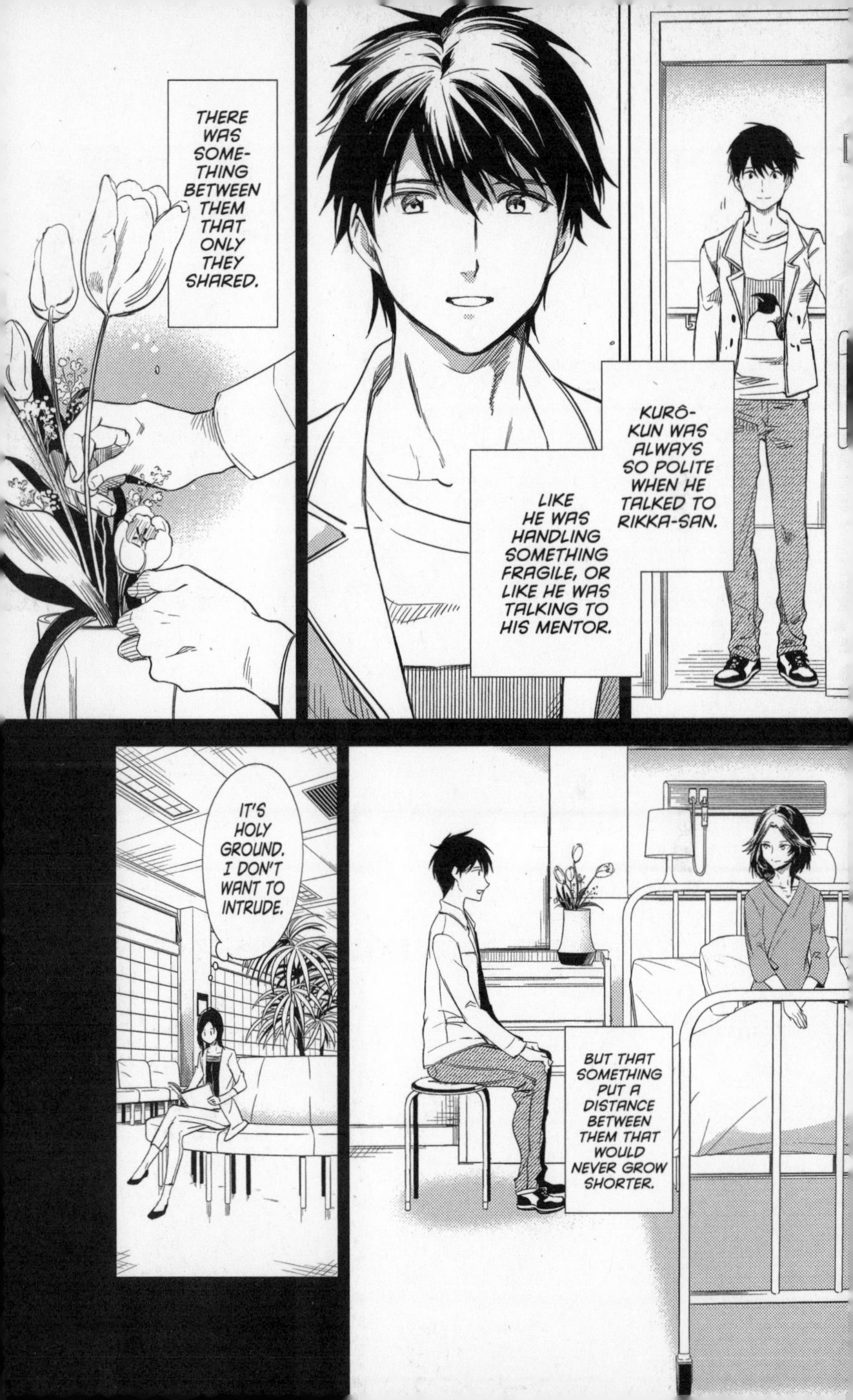
KURÔ-KUN WAS ALWAYS SO POLITE WHEN HE TALKED TO RIKKA-SAN.
LIKE HE WAS HANDLING SOMETHING FRAGILE, OR LIKE HE WAS TALKING TO HIS MENTOR.
THERE WAS SOME-THING BETWEEN THEM THAT ONLY THEY SHARED.
BUT THAT SOMETHING PUT A DISTANCE BETWEEN THEM THAT WOULD NEVER GROW SHORTER.
IT'S HOLY GROUND. I DON'T WANT TO INTRUDE.

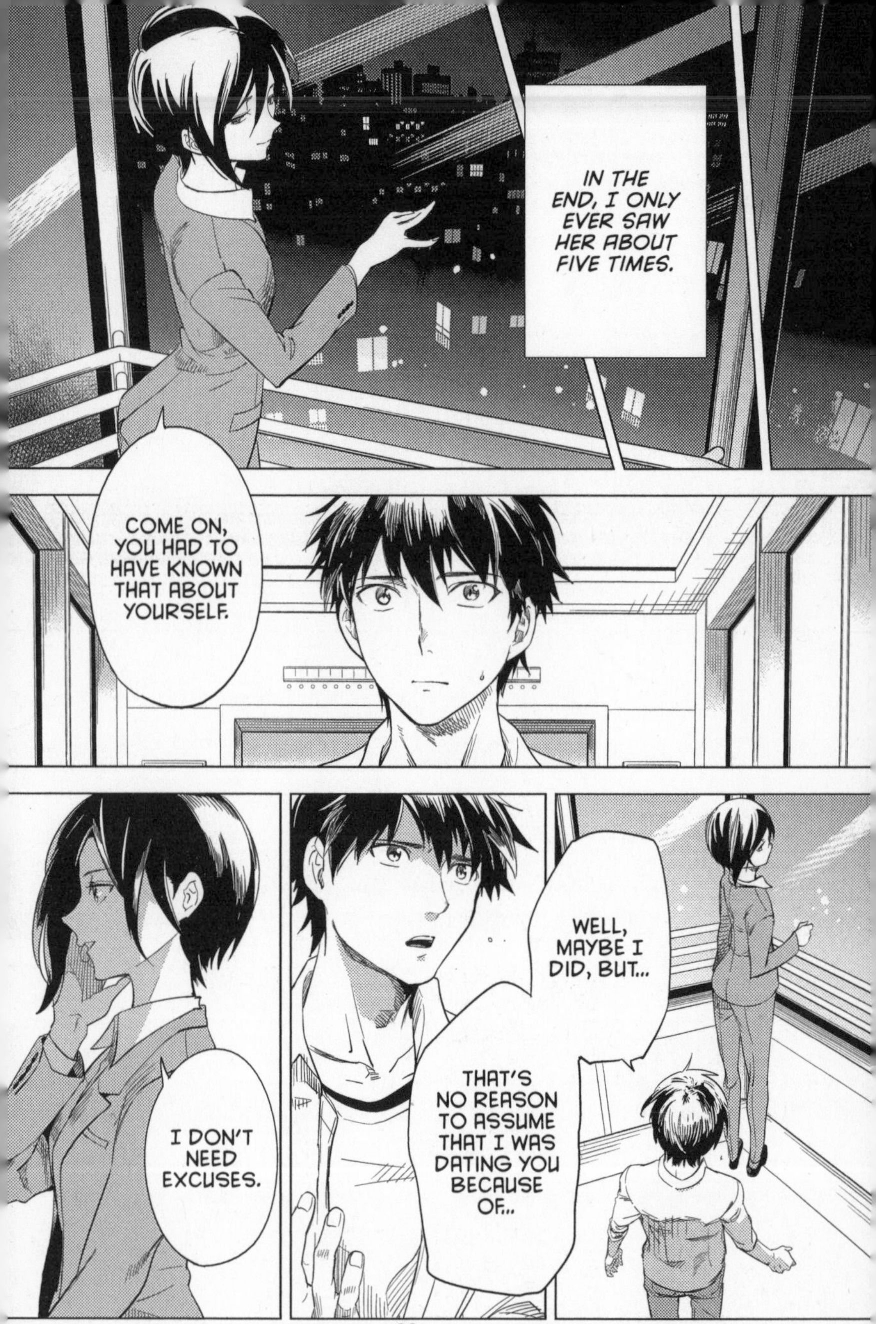
IN THE END, I ONLY EVER SAW HER ABOUT FIVE TIMES.
COME ON, YOU HAD TO HAVE KNOWN THAT ABOUT YOURSELF.
WELL, MAYBE I DID, BUT...
THAT'S NO REASON TO ASSUME THAT I WAS DATING YOU BECAUSE OF...
I DON'T NEED EXCUSES.

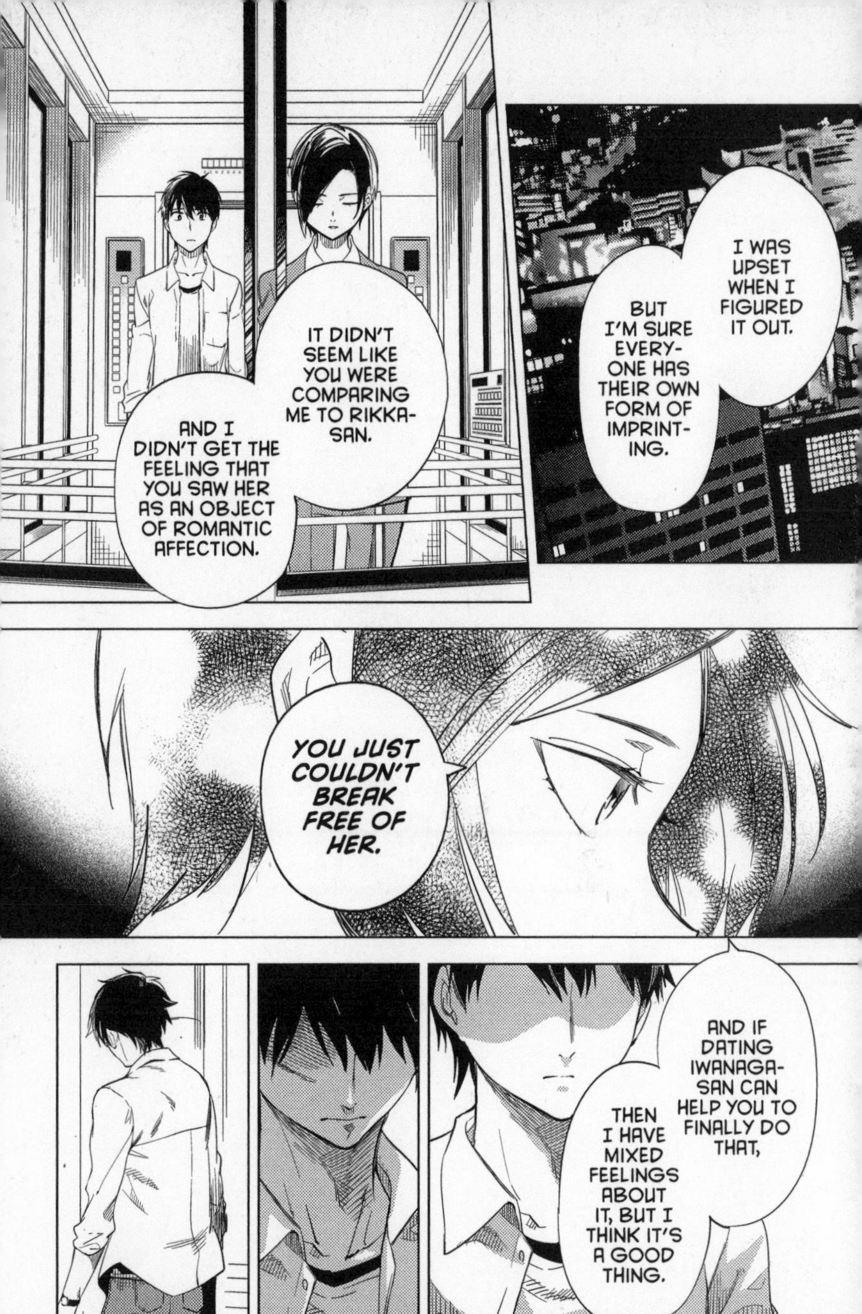
I WAS UPSET WHEN I FIGURED IT OUT.
BUT I'M SURE EVERY-ONE HAS THEIR OWN FORM OF IMPRINT-ING.
IT DIDN'T SEEM LIKE YOU WERE COMPARING ME TO RIKKA-SAN.
AND I DIDN'T GET THE FEELING THAT YOU SAW HER AS AN OBJECT OF ROMANTIC AFFECTION.
*YOU JUST COULDN'T BREAK FREE OF HER.*
AND IF DATING IWANAGA-SAN CAN HELP YOU TO FINALLY DO THAT,
THEN I HAVE MIXED FEELINGS ABOUT IT, BUT I THINK IT'S A GOOD THING.

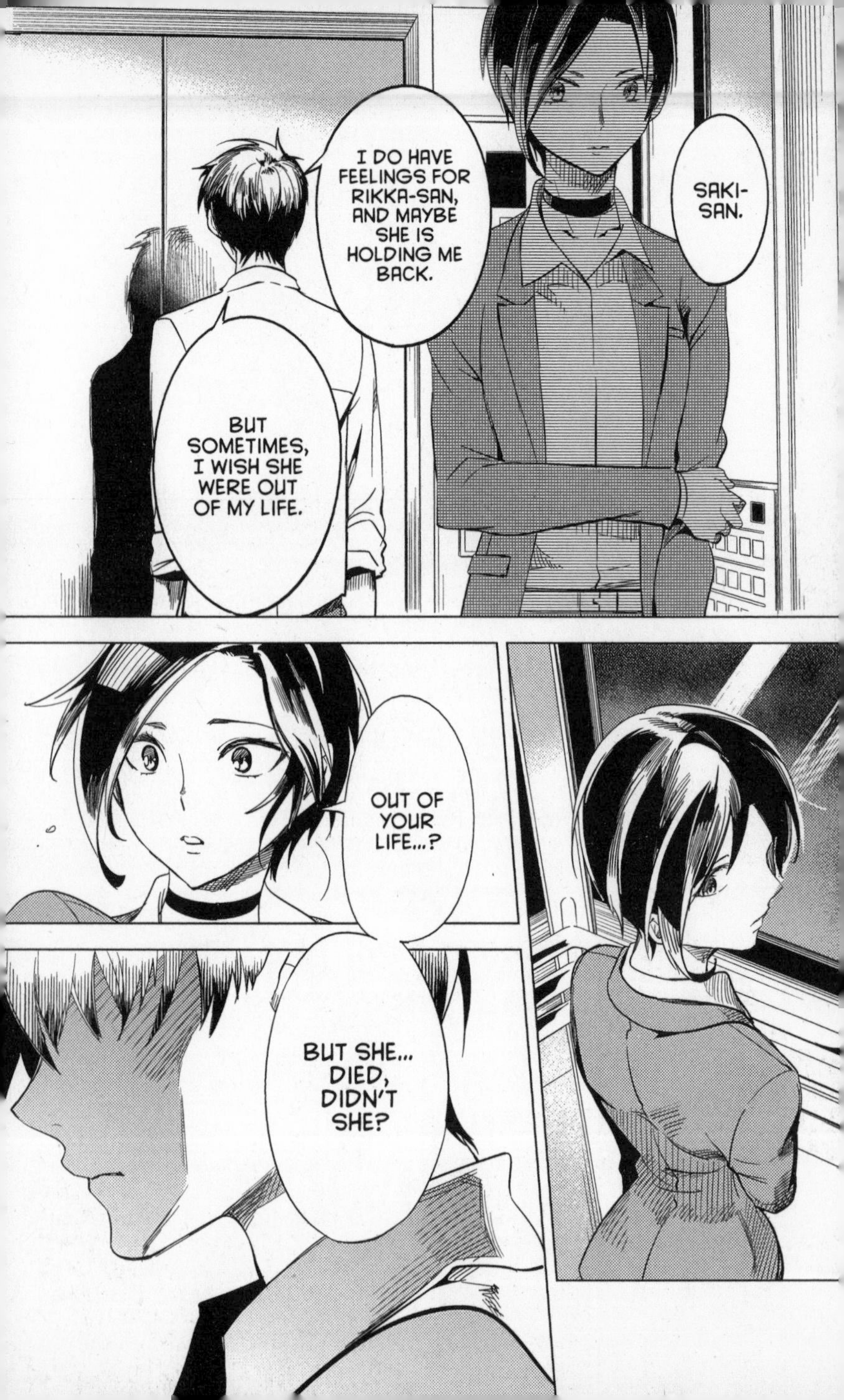
SAKI-SAN.
I DO HAVE FEELINGS FOR RIKKA-SAN, AND MAYBE SHE IS HOLDING ME BACK.
BUT SOMETIMES, I WISH SHE WERE OUT OF MY LIFE.
OUT OF YOUR LIFE...?
BUT SHE... DIED, DIDN'T SHE?

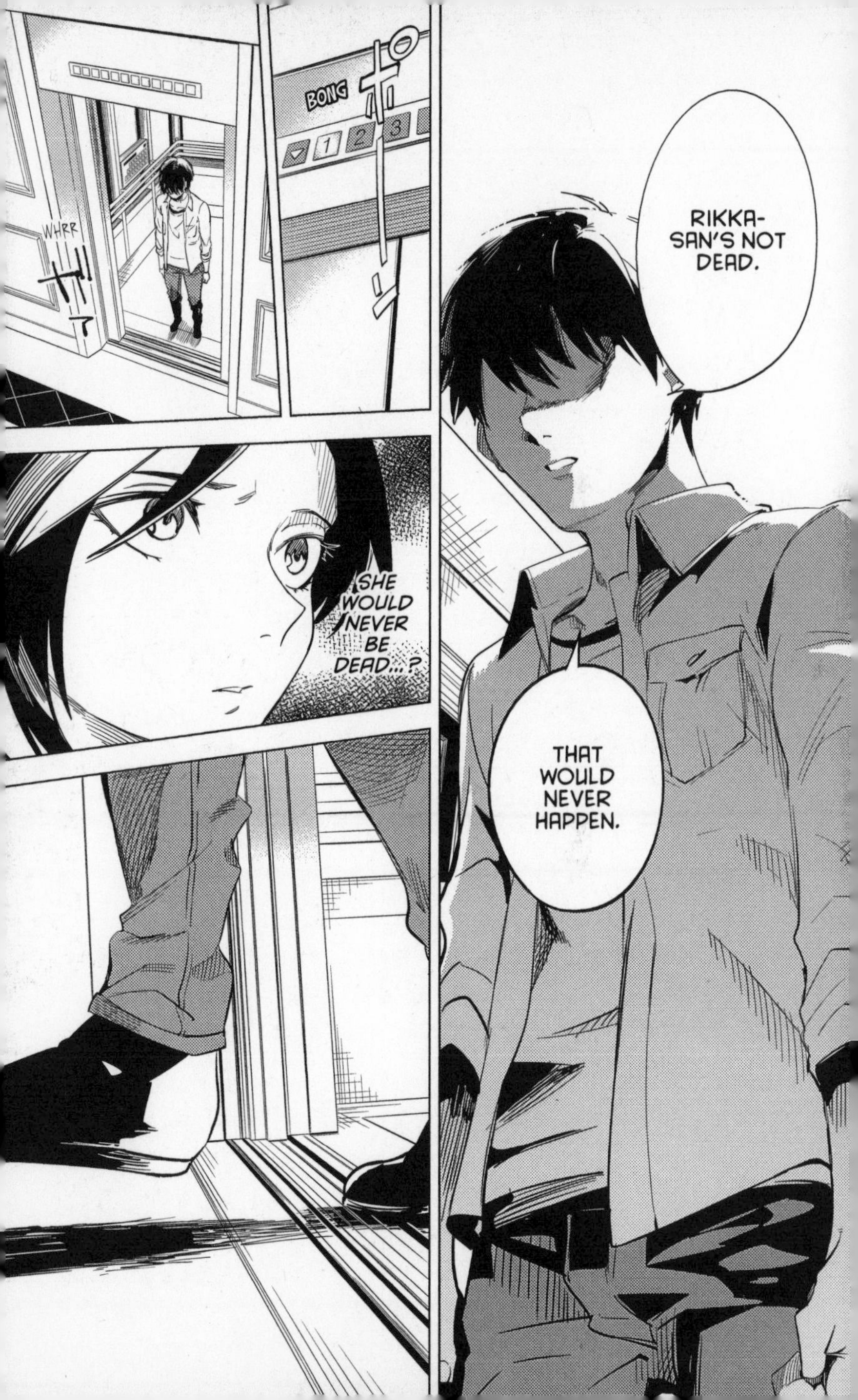
RIKKA-SAN'S NOT DEAD.
THAT WOULD NEVER HAPPEN.
BONG
WHRR
SHE WOULD NEVER BE DEAD...?

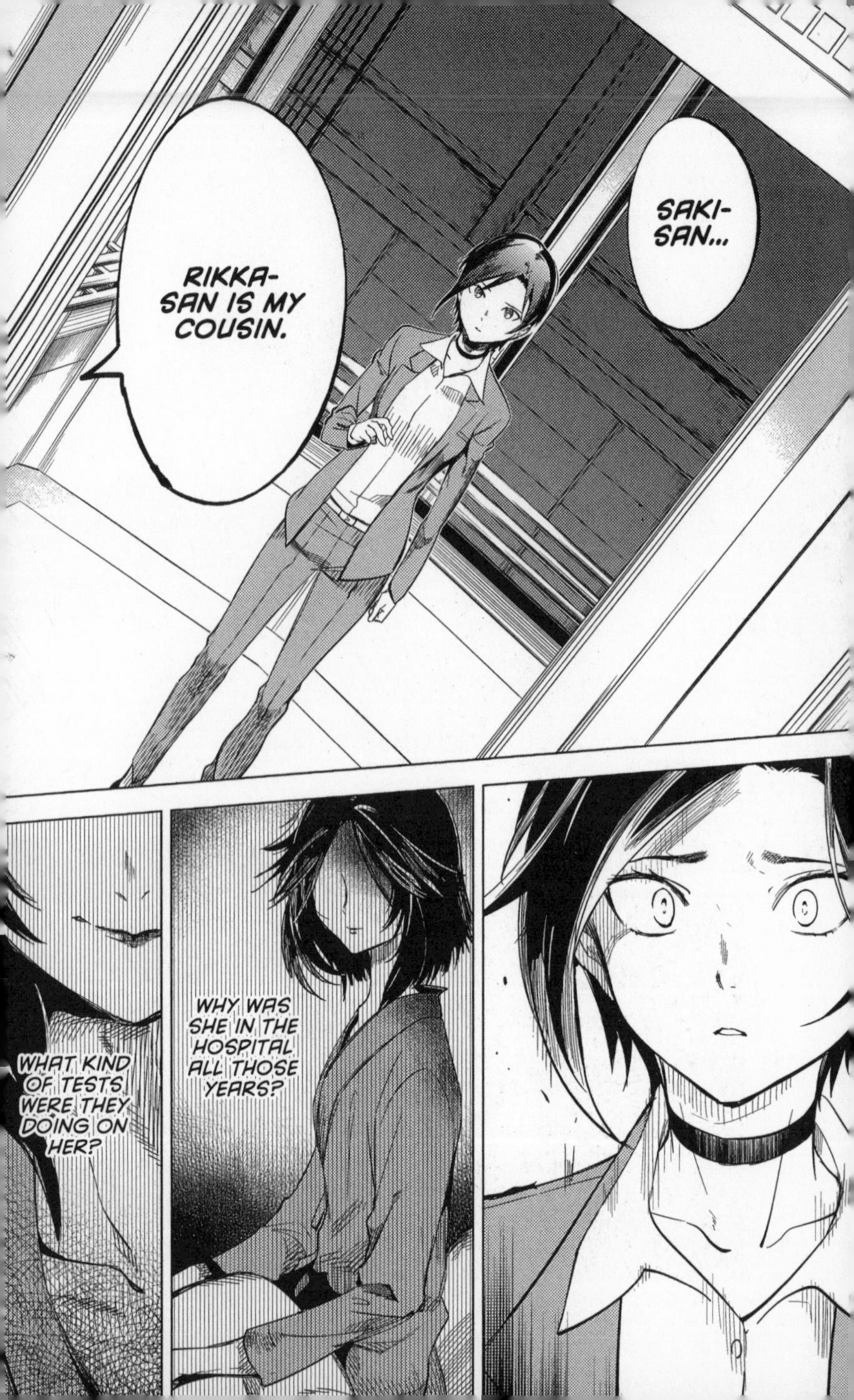
SAKI-SAN...
RIKKA-SAN IS MY COUSIN.
WHY WAS SHE IN THE HOSPITAL ALL THOSE YEARS?
WHAT KIND OF TESTS WERE THEY DOING ON HER?

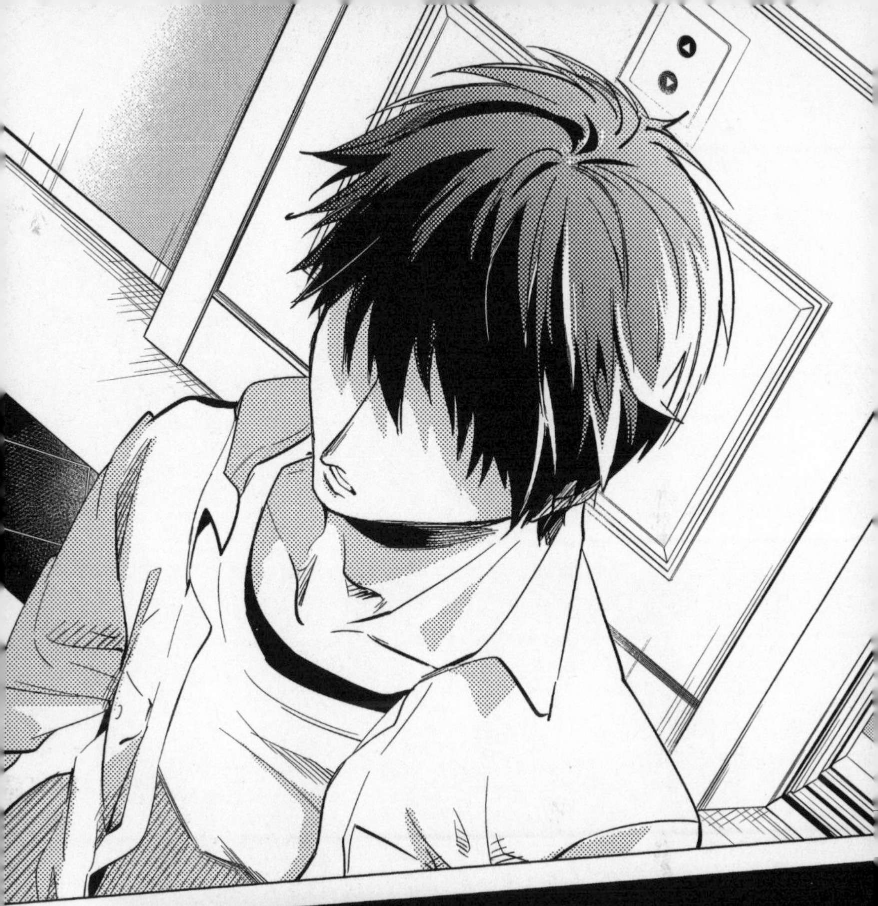

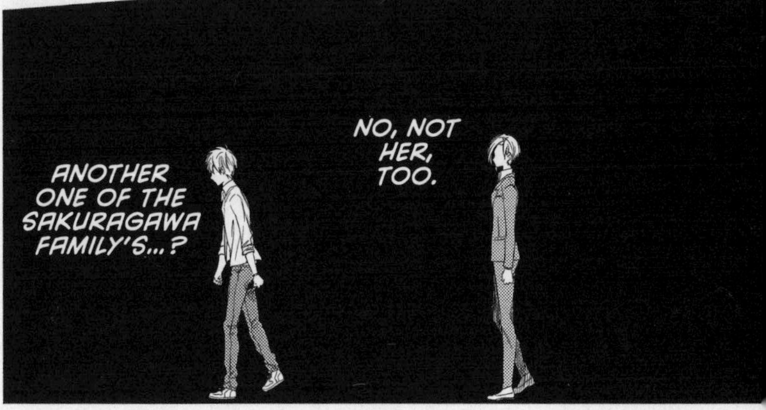
NO, NOT HER, TOO.
ANOTHER ONE OF THE SAKURAGAWA FAMILY'S...?

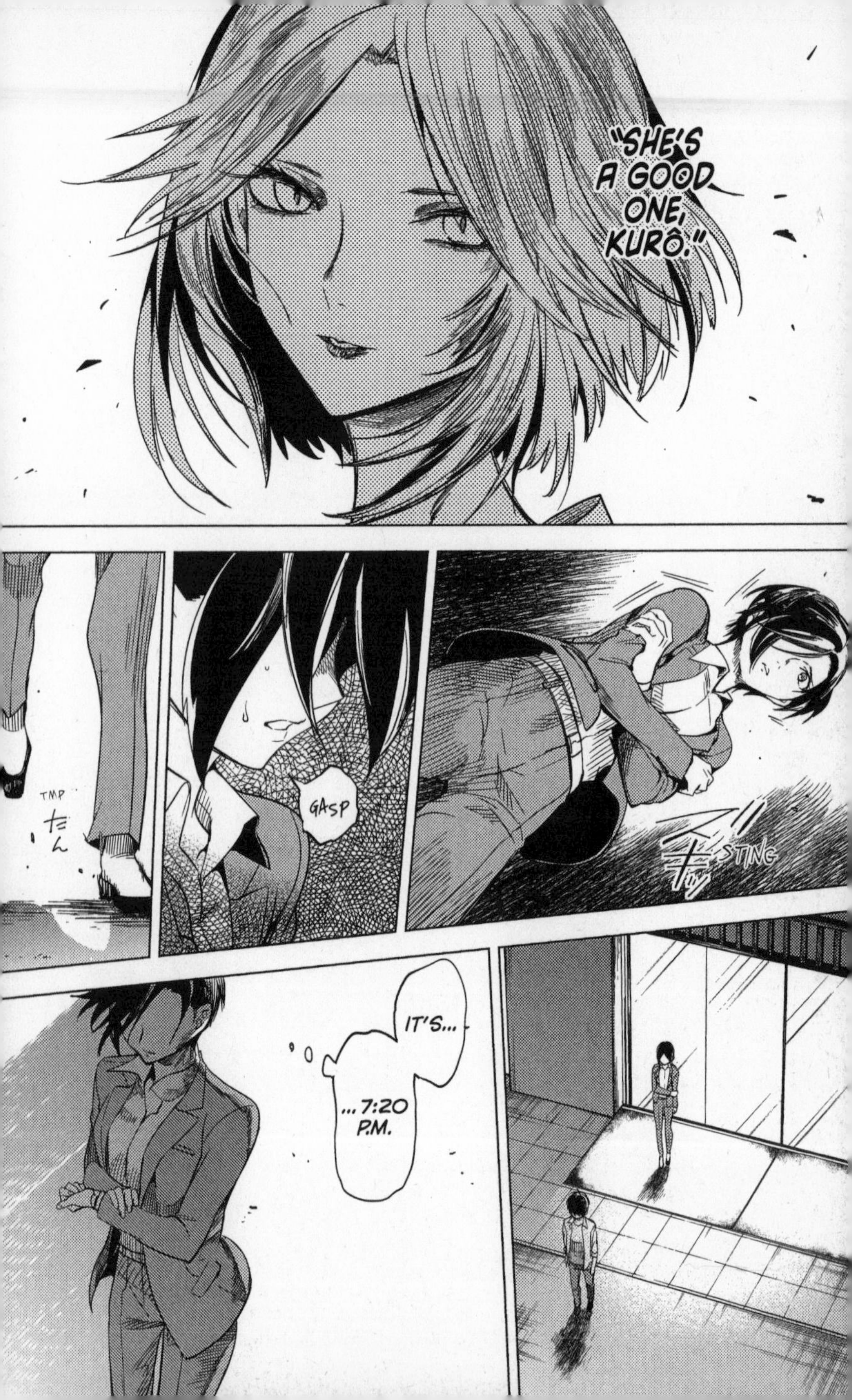
"SHE'S A GOOD ONE, KURÔ."
STING
GASP
TMP
たん
IT'S...
...7:20 P.M.

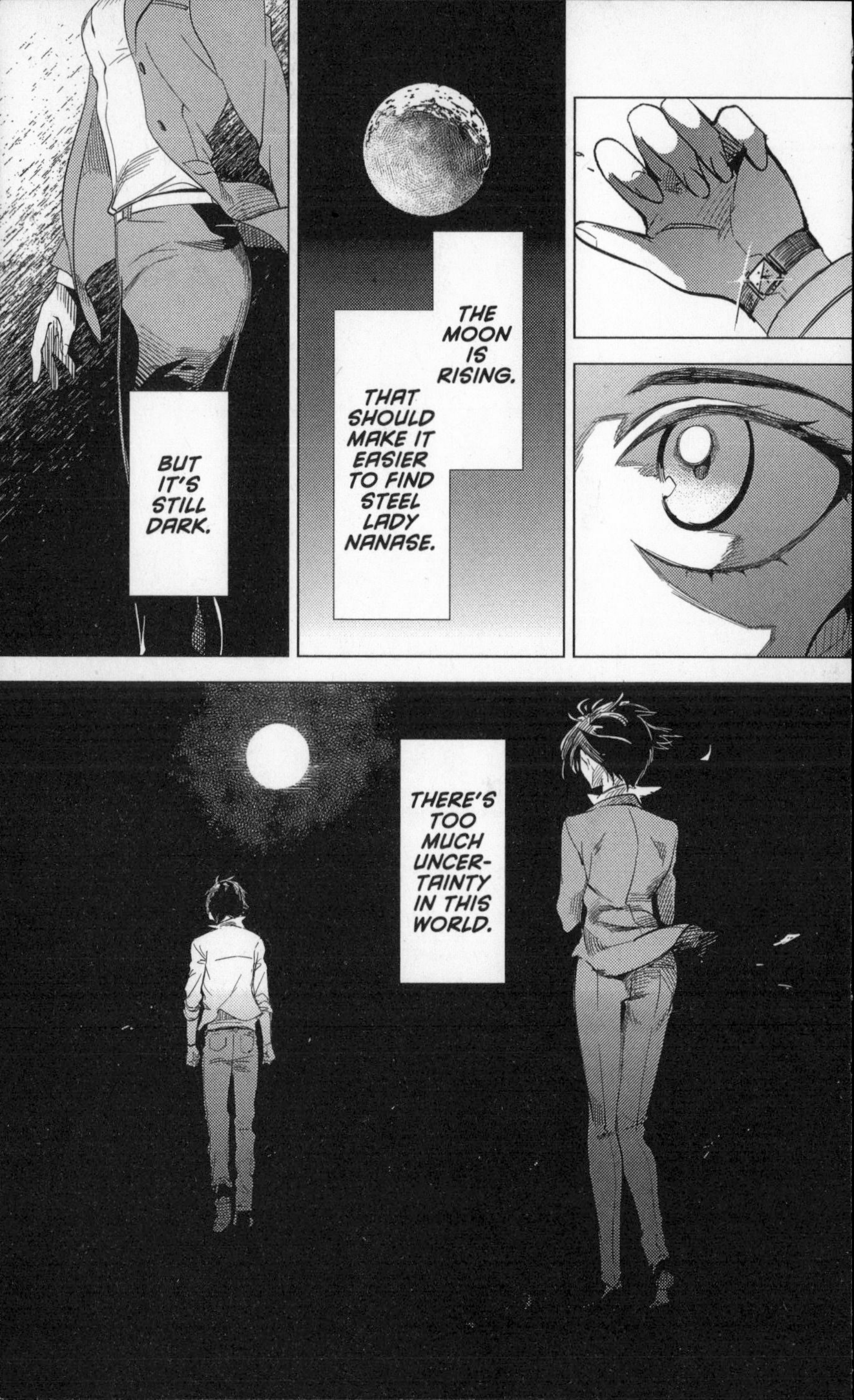
THE MOON IS RISING.
THAT SHOULD MAKE IT EASIER TO FIND STEEL LADY NANASE.
BUT IT'S STILL DARK.
THERE'S TOO MUCH UNCER-TAINTY IN THIS WORLD.

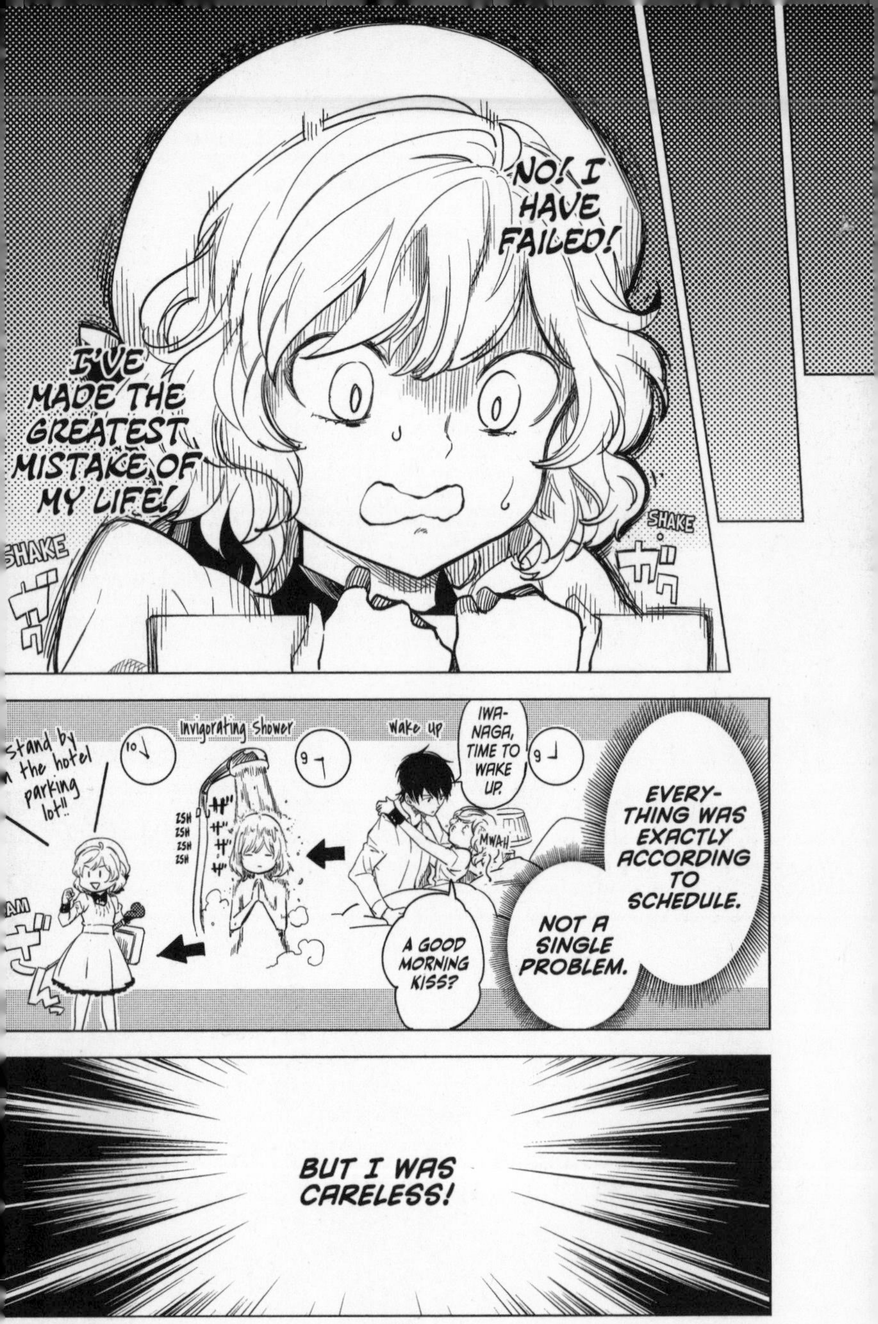
NO! I HAVE FAILED!
I'VE MADE THE GREATEST MISTAKE OF MY LIFE!
SHAKE
SHAKE
EVERY-THING WAS EXACTLY ACCORDING TO SCHEDULE.
NOT A SINGLE PROBLEM.
Wake up
IWA-NAGA, TIME TO WAKE UP.
MWAH
A GOOD MORNING KISS?
Invigorating Shower
ZSH
ZSH
ZSH
ZSH
stand by
n the hotel
parking lot!!
BUT I WAS CARELESS!

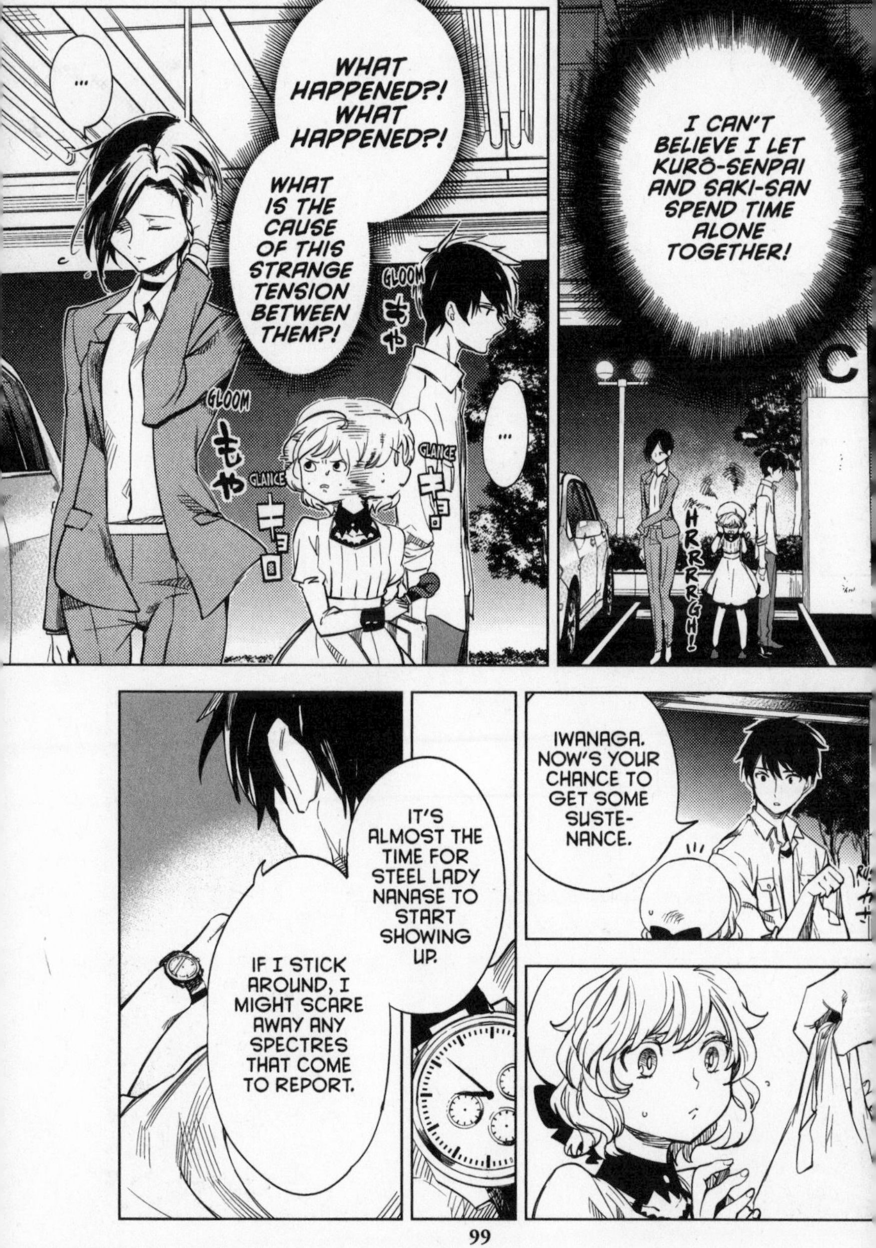

I CAN'T BELIEVE I LET KURÔ-SENPAI AND SAKI-SAN SPEND TIME ALONE TOGETHER!
HRRRRGH!
...
WHAT HAPPENED?! WHAT HAPPENED?!
WHAT IS THE CAUSE OF THIS STRANGE TENSION BETWEEN THEM?!
GLOOM
GLOOM
...
GLANCE
GLANCE
IWANAGA. NOW'S YOUR CHANCE TO GET SOME SUSTE- NANCE.
IT'S ALMOST THE TIME FOR STEEL LADY NANASE TO START SHOWING UP.
IF I STICK AROUND, I MIGHT SCARE AWAY ANY SPECTRES THAT COME TO REPORT.

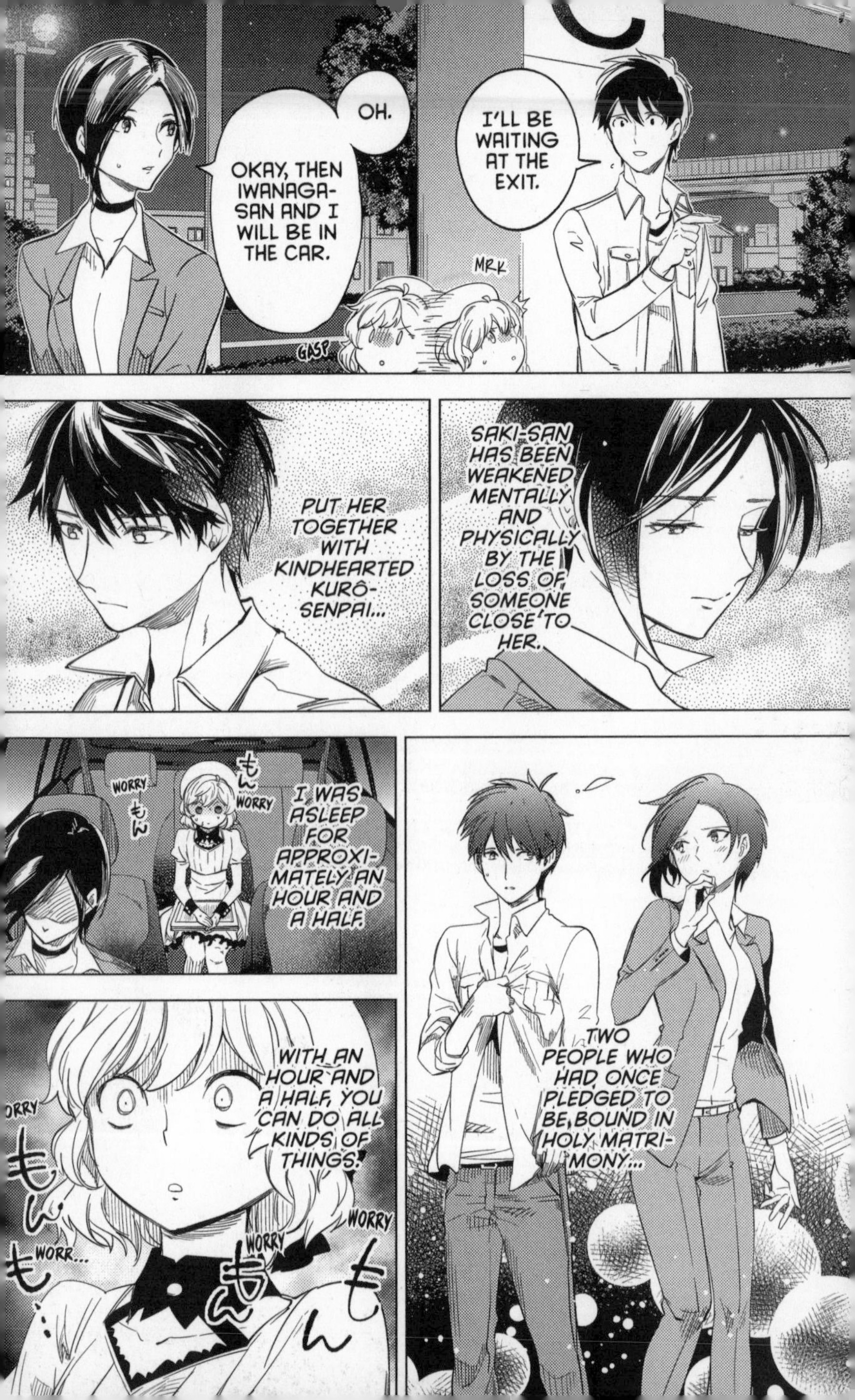

I'LL BE WAITING AT THE EXIT.
OH.
OKAY, THEN IWANAGA-SAN AND I WILL BE IN THE CAR.
MRK
GASP
SAKI-SAN HAS BEEN WEAKENED MENTALLY AND PHYSICALLY BY THE LOSS OF SOMEONE CLOSE TO HER.
PUT HER TOGETHER WITH KINDHEARTED KURÔ-SENPAI...
TWO PEOPLE WHO HAD ONCE PLEDGED TO BE BOUND IN HOLY MATRI-MONY...
I WAS ASLEEP FOR APPROXI-MATELY AN HOUR AND A HALF.
もん
WORRY
WORRY
もん
WITH AN HOUR AND A HALF, YOU CAN DO ALL KINDS OF THINGS!
WORRY
もん
WORRY
もん
WORRY
もん
WORR...
も...

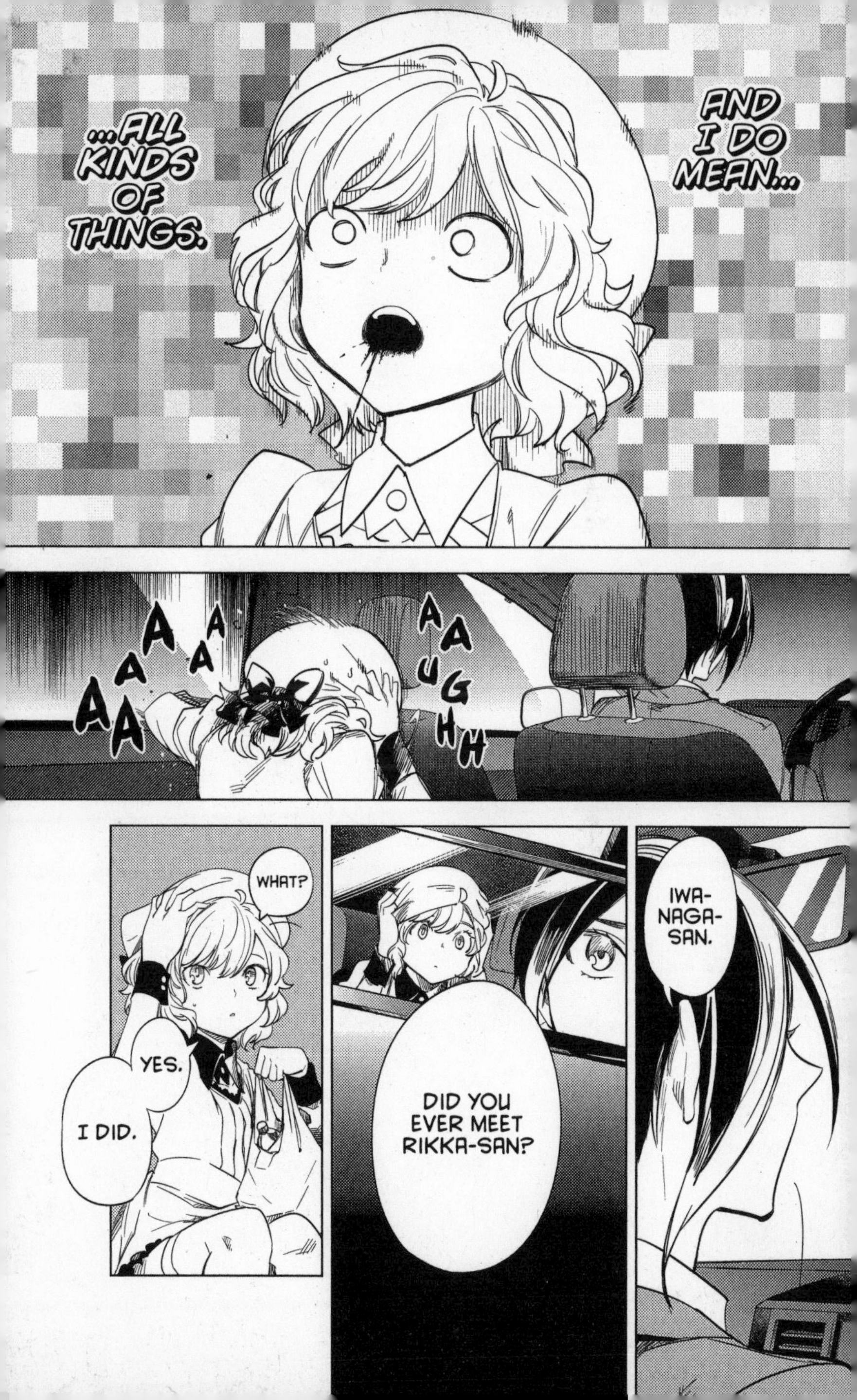
AND I DO MEAN...
...ALL KINDS OF THINGS.
AAUGHH
AAAAAAA
IWA-NAGA-SAN.
DID YOU EVER MEET RIKKA-SAN?
WHAT?
YES.
I DID.

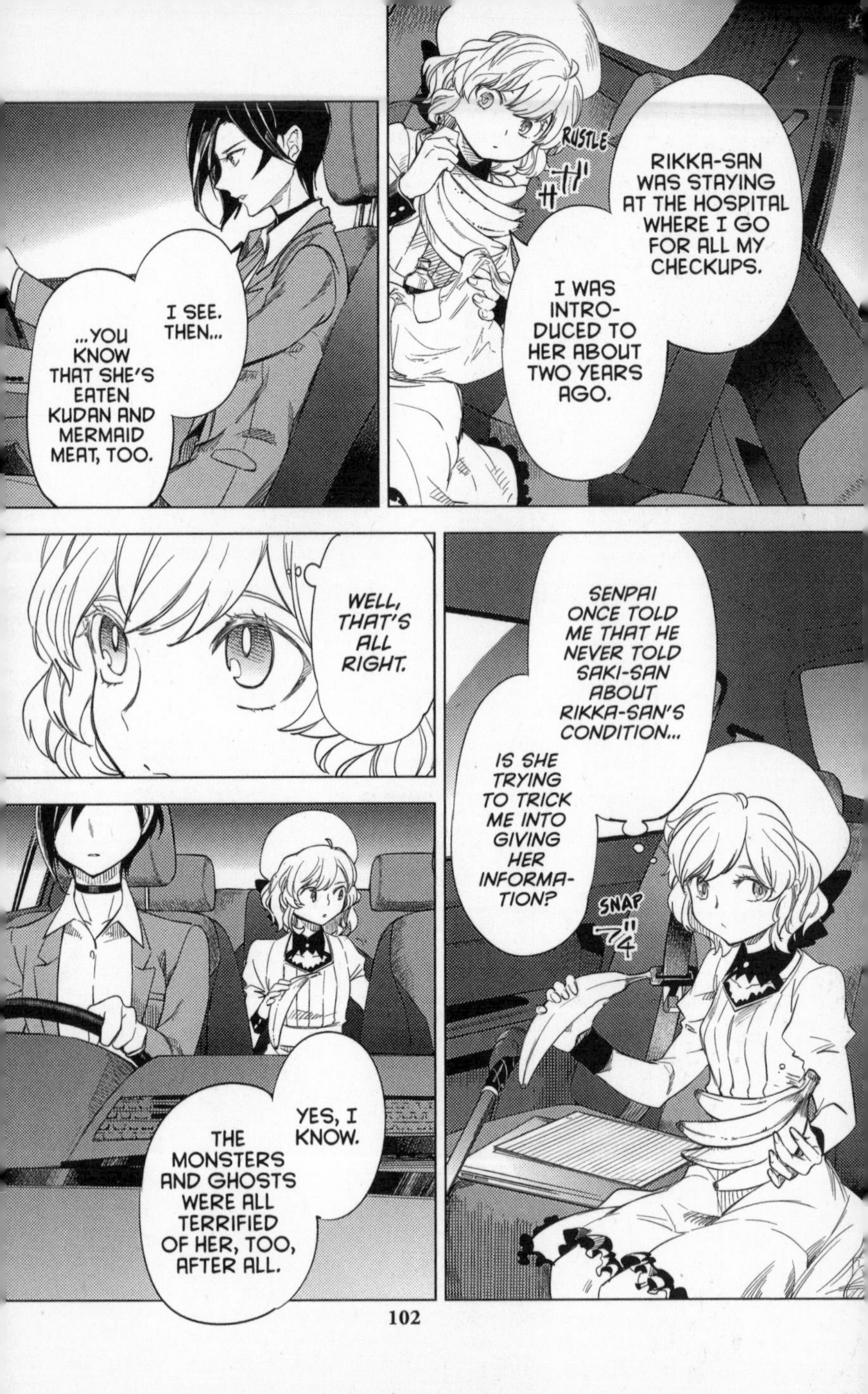
RUSTLE
RIKKA-SAN WAS STAYING AT THE HOSPITAL WHERE I GO FOR ALL MY CHECKUPS.
I WAS INTRO-DUCED TO HER ABOUT TWO YEARS AGO.
I SEE. THEN...
...YOU KNOW THAT SHE'S EATEN KUDAN AND MERMAID MEAT, TOO.
SENPAI ONCE TOLD ME THAT HE NEVER TOLD SAKI-SAN ABOUT RIKKA-SAN'S CONDITION...
IS SHE TRYING TO TRICK ME INTO GIVING HER INFORMA-TION?
SNAP
WELL, THAT'S ALL RIGHT.
YES, I KNOW.
THE MONSTERS AND GHOSTS WERE ALL TERRIFIED OF HER, TOO, AFTER ALL.

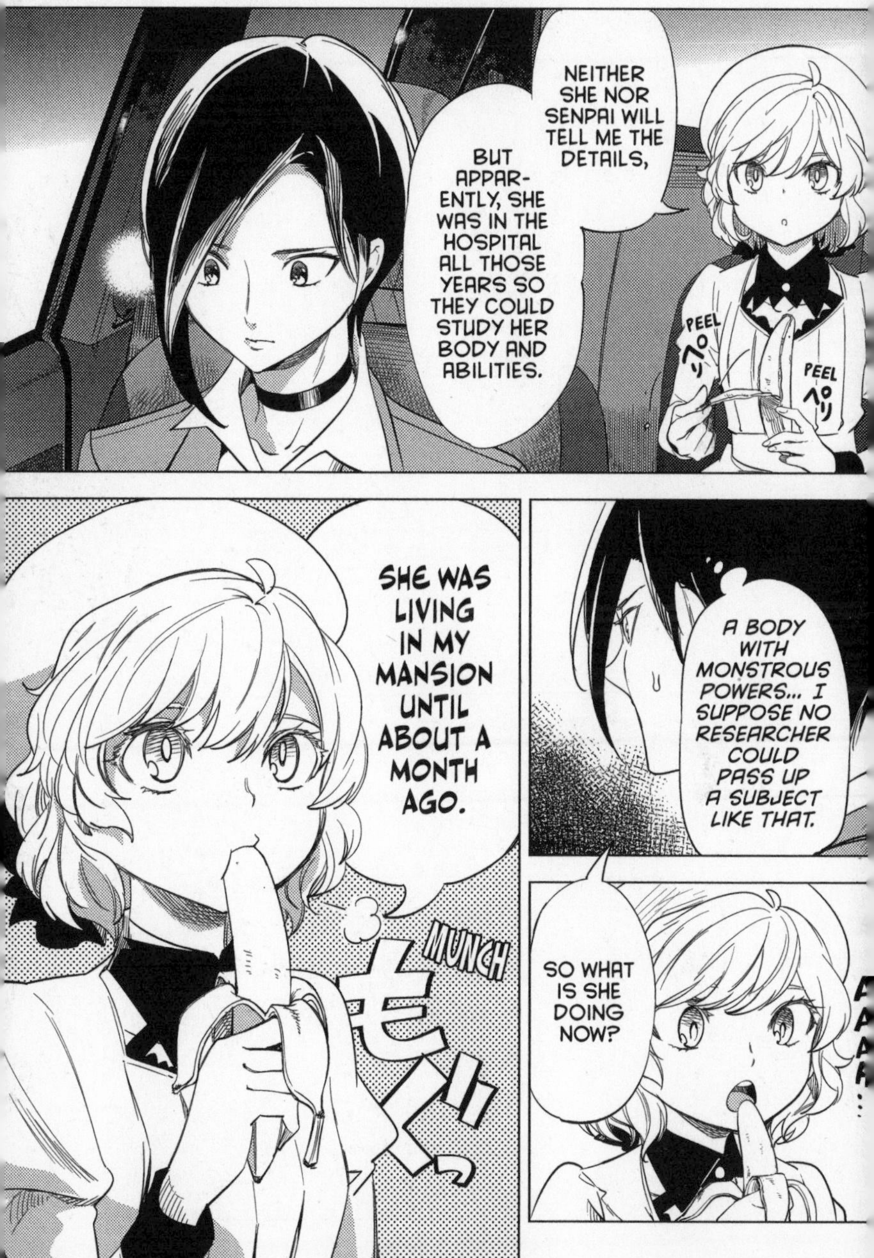
NEITHER SHE NOR SENPAI WILL TELL ME THE DETAILS,
BUT APPARENTLY, SHE WAS IN THE HOSPITAL ALL THOSE YEARS SO THEY COULD STUDY HER BODY AND ABILITIES.
PEEL
PEEL
A BODY WITH MONSTROUS POWERS... I SUPPOSE NO RESEARCHER COULD PASS UP A SUBJECT LIKE THAT.
SO WHAT IS SHE DOING NOW?
SHE WAS LIVING IN MY MANSION UNTIL ABOUT A MONTH AGO.
MUNCH

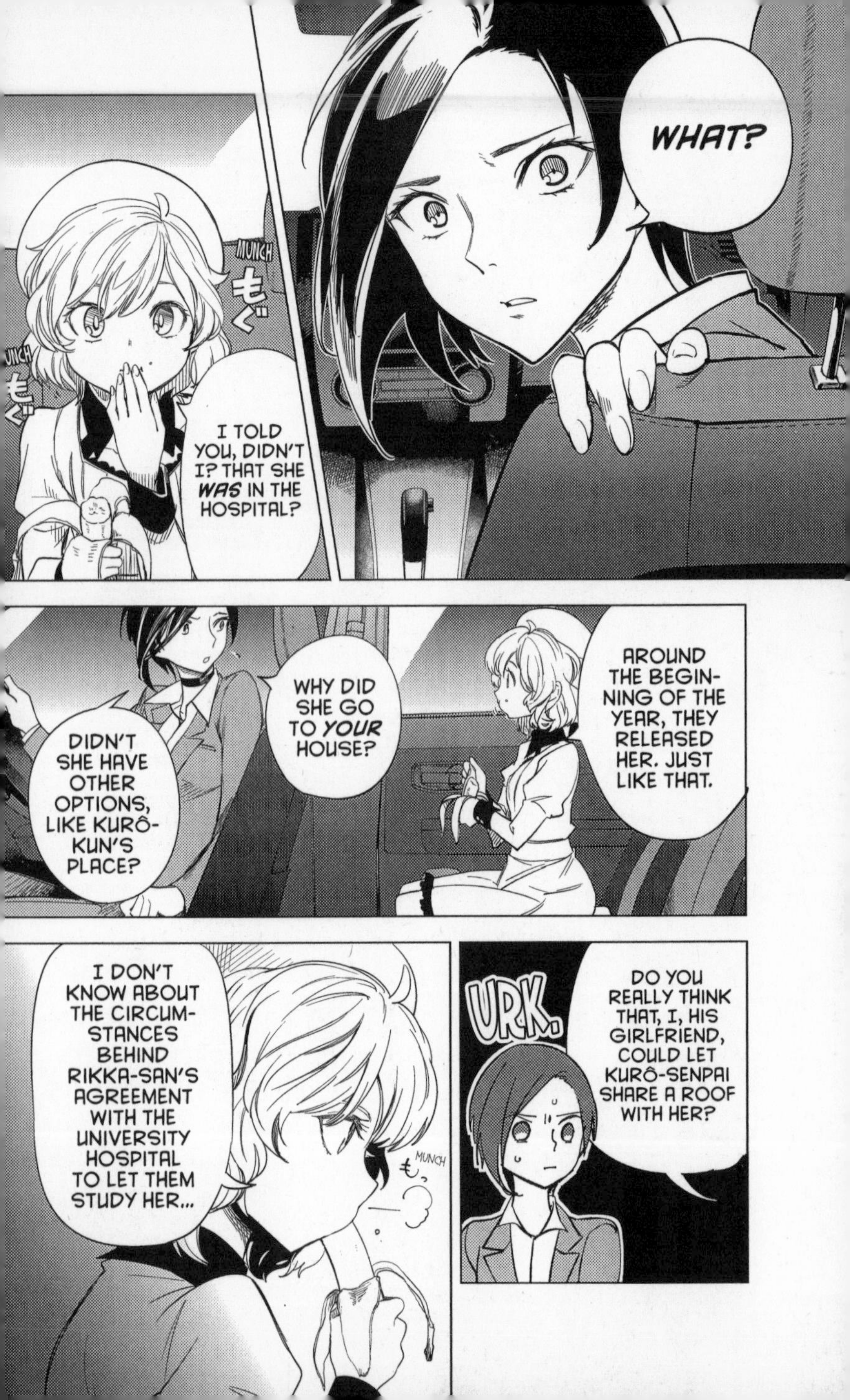
WHAT?
MUNCH
もぐ
もぐ
I TOLD YOU, DIDN'T I? THAT SHE *WAS* IN THE HOSPITAL?
AROUND THE BEGIN-NING OF THE YEAR, THEY RELEASED HER. JUST LIKE THAT.
WHY DID SHE GO TO *YOUR* HOUSE?
DIDN'T SHE HAVE OTHER OPTIONS, LIKE KURÔ-KUN'S PLACE?
URK.
DO YOU REALLY THINK THAT, I, HIS GIRLFRIEND, COULD LET KURÔ-SENPAI SHARE A ROOF WITH HER?
I DON'T KNOW ABOUT THE CIRCUM-STANCES BEHIND RIKKA-SAN'S AGREEMENT WITH THE UNIVERSITY HOSPITAL TO LET THEM STUDY HER...
MUNCH
もっ

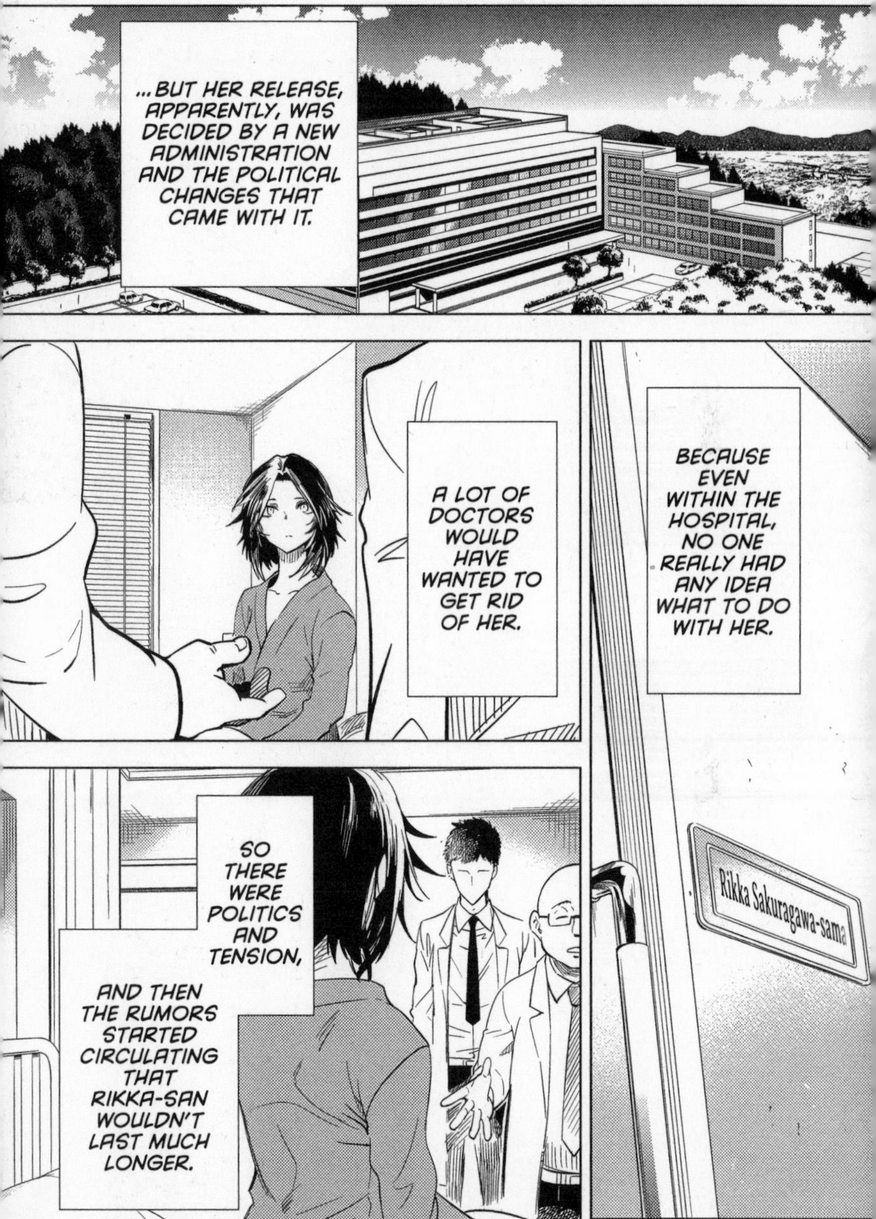
...BUT HER RELEASE, APPARENTLY, WAS DECIDED BY A NEW ADMINISTRATION AND THE POLITICAL CHANGES THAT CAME WITH IT.
BECAUSE EVEN WITHIN THE HOSPITAL, NO ONE REALLY HAD ANY IDEA WHAT TO DO WITH HER.
Rikka Sakuragawa-sama
A LOT OF DOCTORS WOULD HAVE WANTED TO GET RID OF HER.
SO THERE WERE POLITICS AND TENSION,
AND THEN THE RUMORS STARTED CIRCULATING THAT RIKKA-SAN WOULDN'T LAST MUCH LONGER.

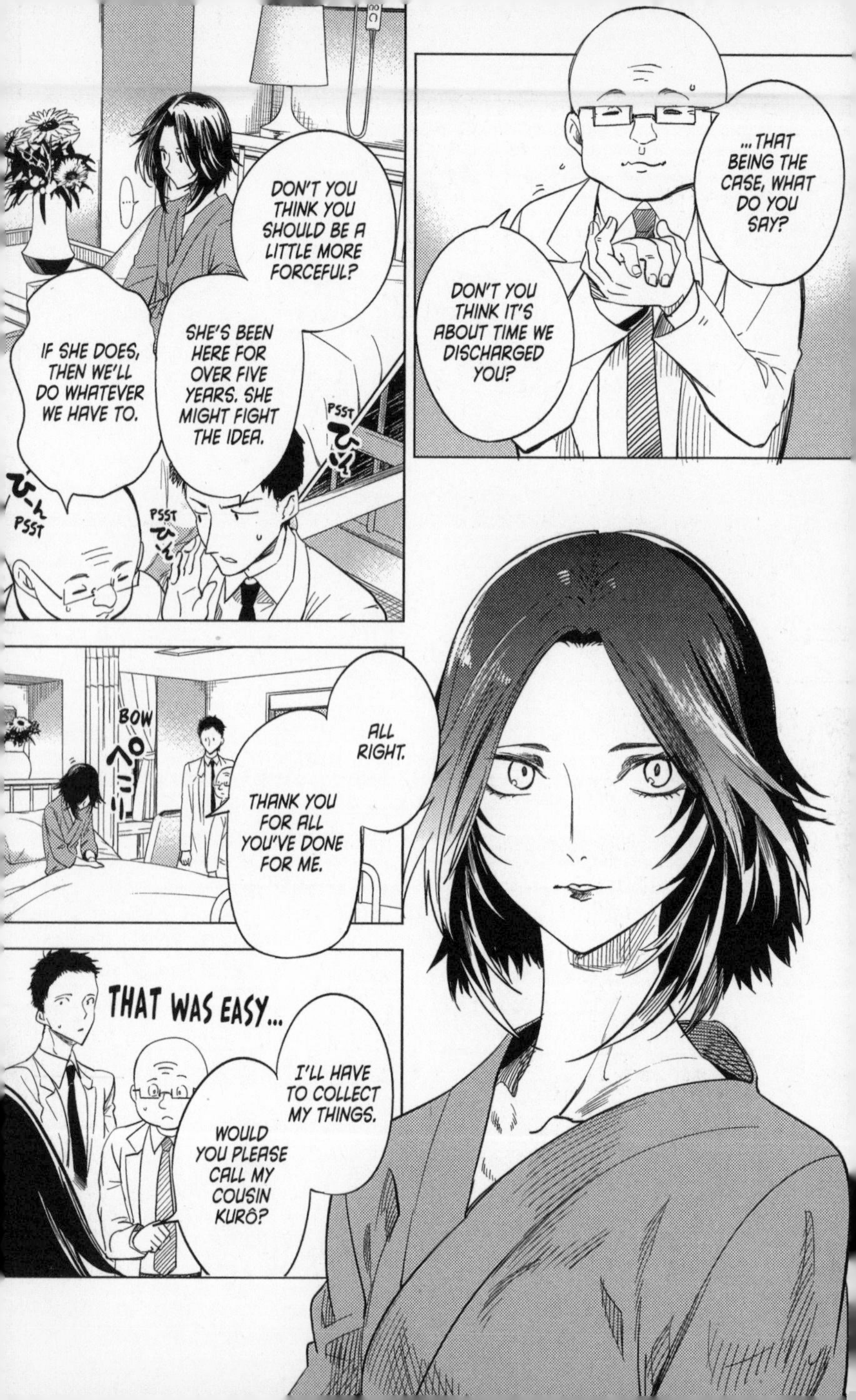
...THAT BEING THE CASE, WHAT DO YOU SAY?
DON'T YOU THINK IT'S ABOUT TIME WE DISCHARGED YOU?
DON'T YOU THINK YOU SHOULD BE A LITTLE MORE FORCEFUL?
...
SHE'S BEEN HERE FOR OVER FIVE YEARS. SHE MIGHT FIGHT THE IDEA.
PSST
IF SHE DOES, THEN WE'LL DO WHATEVER WE HAVE TO.
PSST
PSST
ALL RIGHT.
THANK YOU FOR ALL YOU'VE DONE FOR ME.
BOW
THAT WAS EASY...
I'LL HAVE TO COLLECT MY THINGS.
WOULD YOU PLEASE CALL MY COUSIN KURÔ?

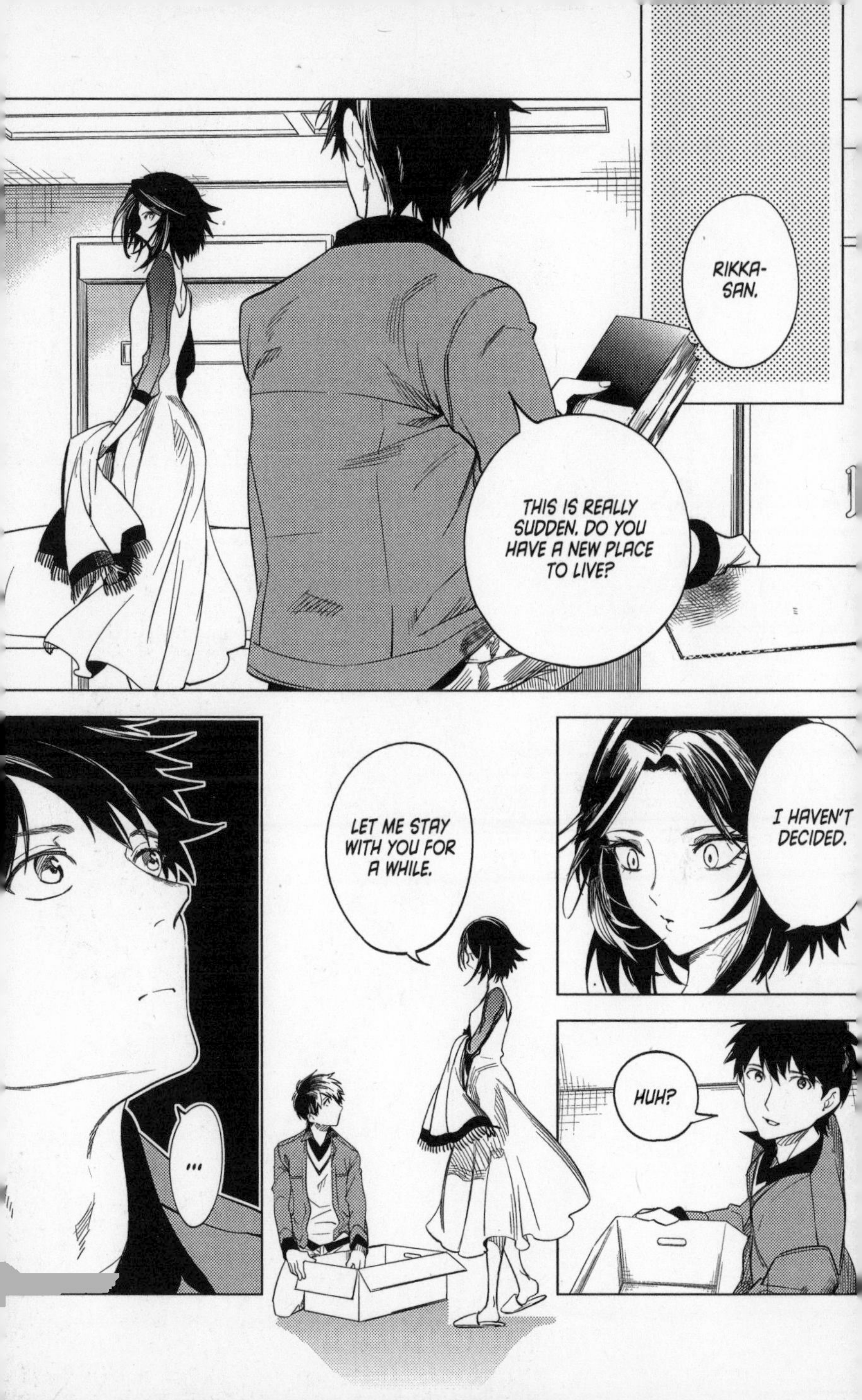
RIKKA-SAN.
THIS IS REALLY SUDDEN. DO YOU HAVE A NEW PLACE TO LIVE?
I HAVEN'T DECIDED.
HUH?
LET ME STAY WITH YOU FOR A WHILE.
...

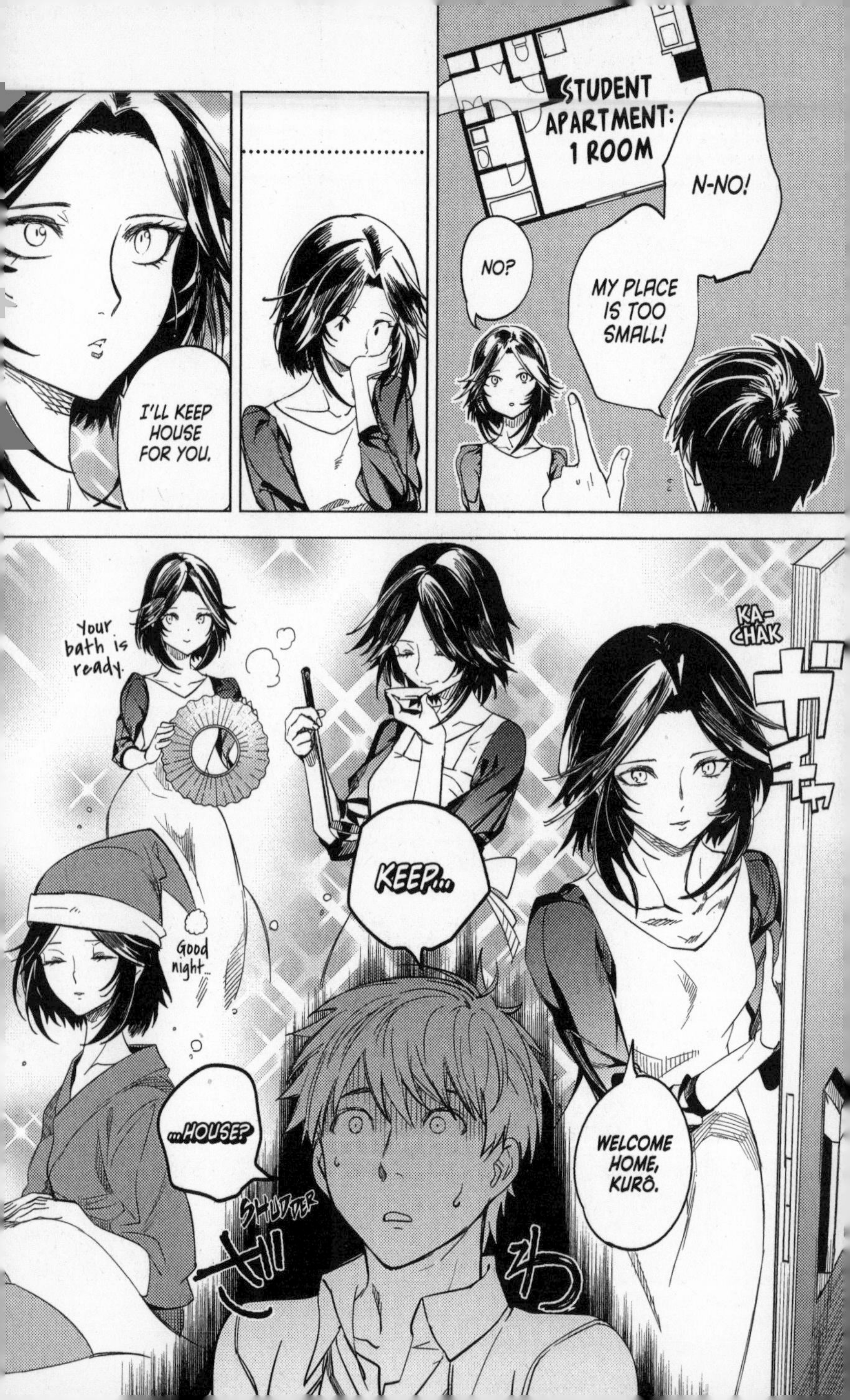
STUDENT APARTMENT: 1 ROOM
N-NO!
NO?
MY PLACE IS TOO SMALL!
........
I'LL KEEP HOUSE FOR YOU.
KA-CHAK
WELCOME HOME, KURŌ.
KEEP...
Your bath is ready.
Good night...
...HOUSE?
SHUDDER

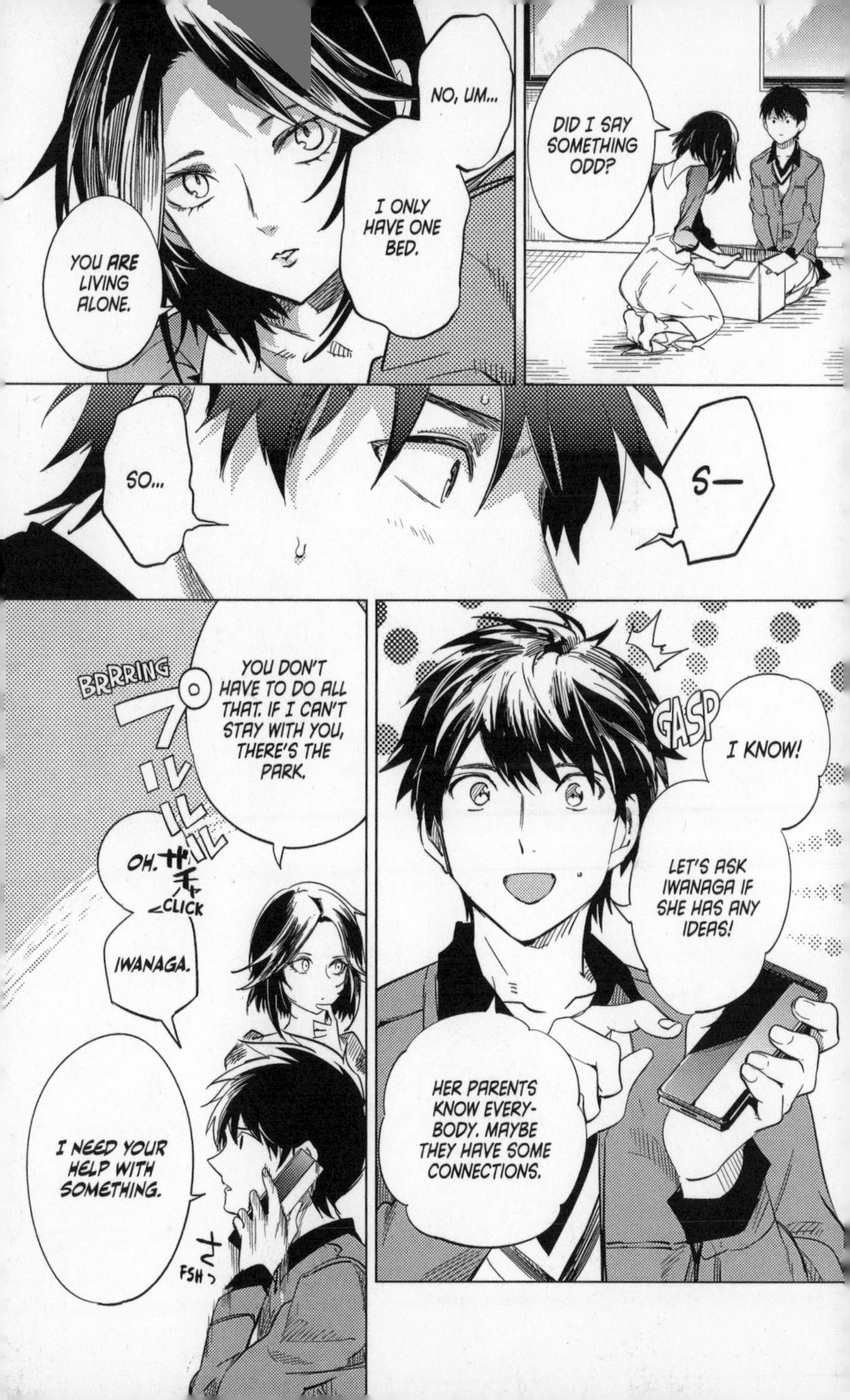
DID I SAY SOMETHING ODD?
NO, UM...
I ONLY HAVE ONE BED.
YOU ARE LIVING ALONE.
S—
SO...
GASP
I KNOW!
LET'S ASK IWANAGA IF SHE HAS ANY IDEAS!
HER PARENTS KNOW EVERY-BODY. MAYBE THEY HAVE SOME CONNECTIONS.
YOU DON'T HAVE TO DO ALL THAT. IF I CAN'T STAY WITH YOU, THERE'S THE PARK.
BRRRING
OH.
CLICK
IWANAGA.
I NEED YOUR HELP WITH SOMETHING.
FSH

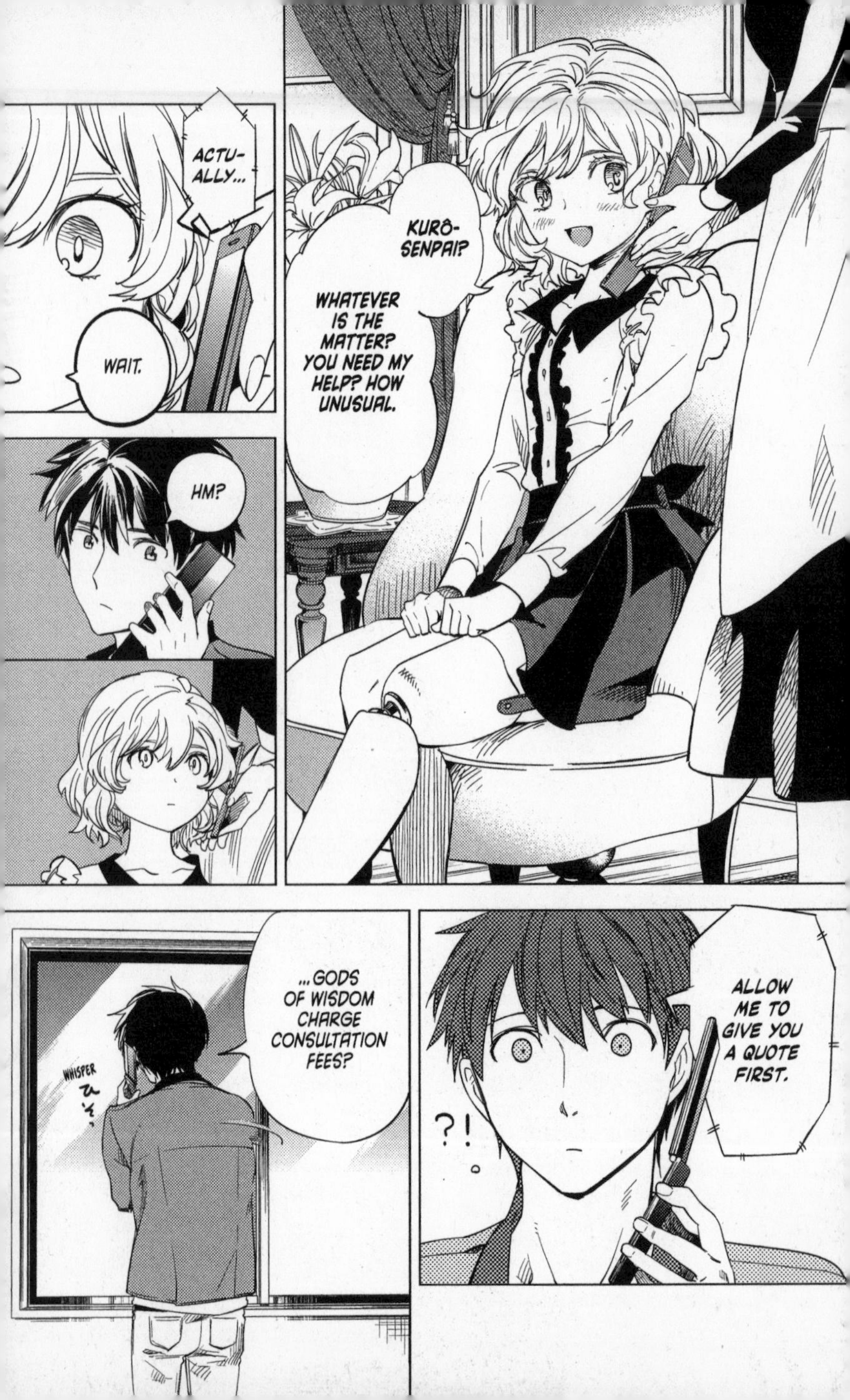
KURÔ-SENPAI?
WHATEVER IS THE MATTER? YOU NEED MY HELP? HOW UNUSUAL.
ACTU-ALLY...
WAIT.
HM?
ALLOW ME TO GIVE YOU A QUOTE FIRST.
?!
...GODS OF WISDOM CHARGE CONSULTATION FEES?
WHISPER
ひそ

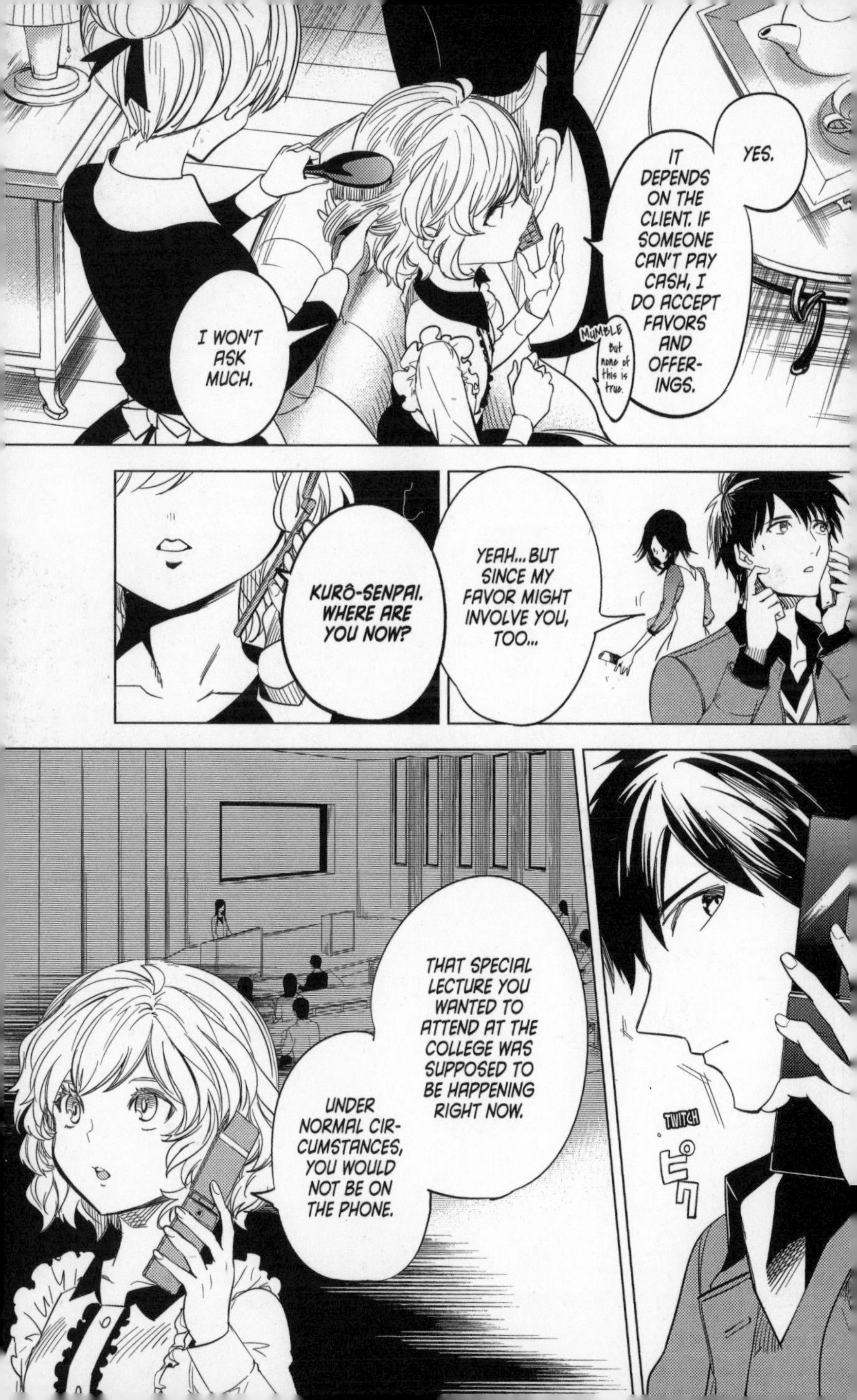
YES.
IT DEPENDS ON THE CLIENT. IF SOMEONE CAN'T PAY CASH, I DO ACCEPT FAVORS AND OFFER-INGS.
MUMBLE
But none of this is true.
I WON'T ASK MUCH.
YEAH...BUT SINCE MY FAVOR MIGHT INVOLVE YOU, TOO...
KURÔ-SENPAI. WHERE ARE YOU NOW?
TWITCH
ピク
THAT SPECIAL LECTURE YOU WANTED TO ATTEND AT THE COLLEGE WAS SUPPOSED TO BE HAPPENING RIGHT NOW.
UNDER NORMAL CIR-CUMSTANCES, YOU WOULD NOT BE ON THE PHONE.

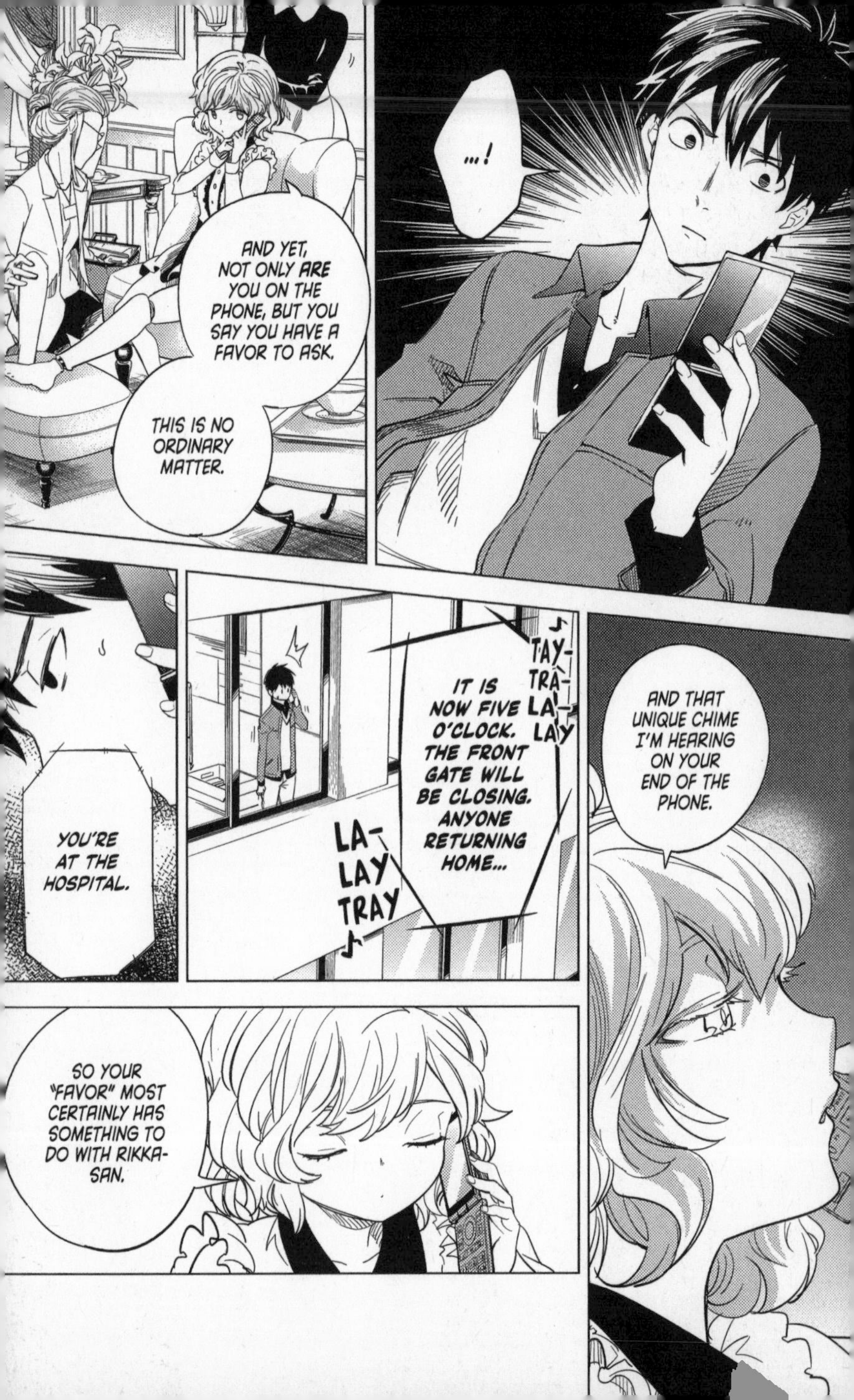
...!
AND YET, NOT ONLY ARE YOU ON THE PHONE, BUT YOU SAY YOU HAVE A FAVOR TO ASK.
THIS IS NO ORDINARY MATTER.
AND THAT UNIQUE CHIME I'M HEARING ON YOUR END OF THE PHONE.
TAY-TRÀ-LA-LAY
IT IS NOW FIVE O'CLOCK. THE FRONT GATE WILL BE CLOSING. ANYONE RETURNING HOME...
LA-LAY TRAY
YOU'RE AT THE HOSPITAL.
SO YOUR "FAVOR" MOST CERTAINLY HAS SOMETHING TO DO WITH RIKKA-SAN.

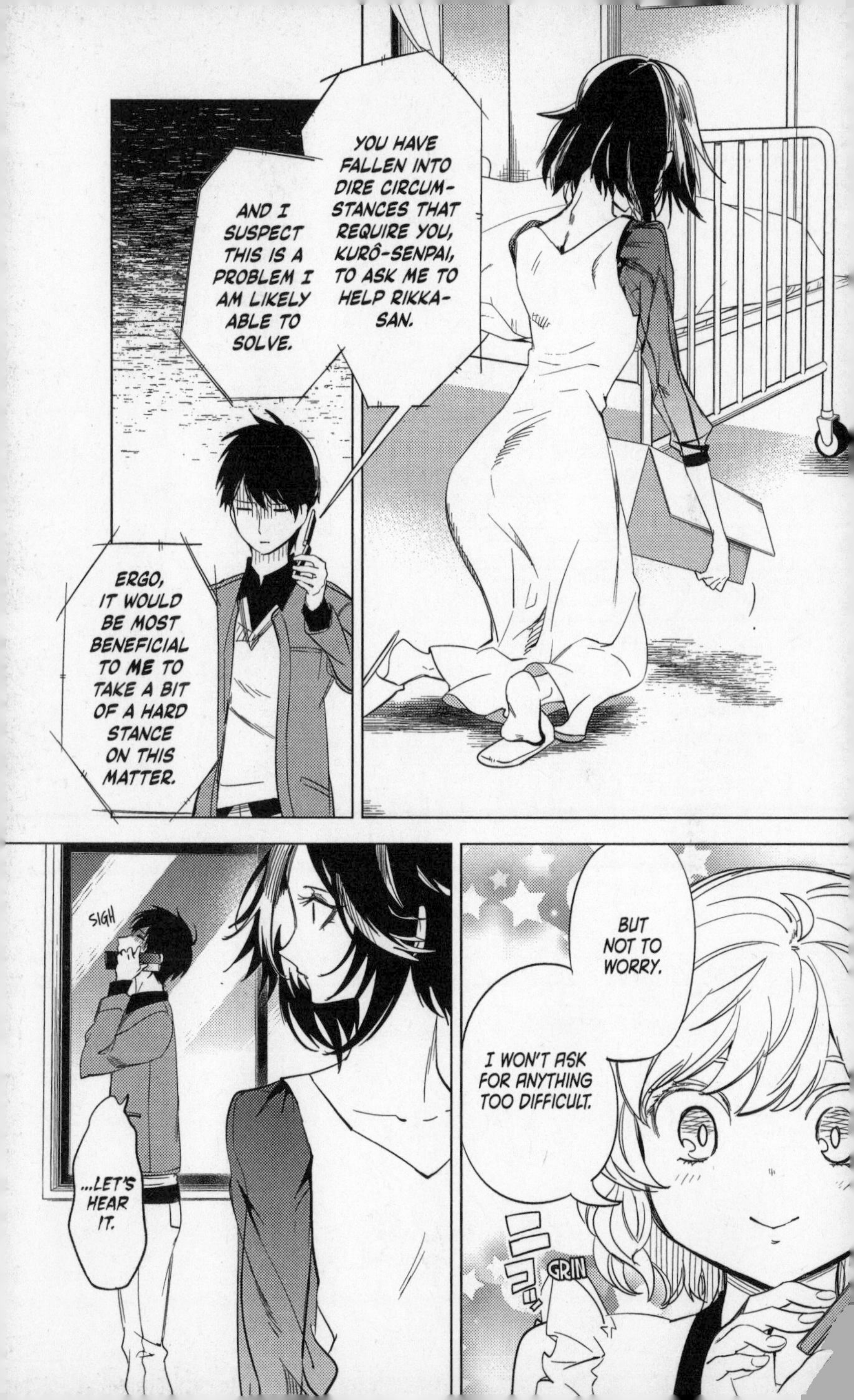
YOU HAVE FALLEN INTO DIRE CIRCUM-STANCES THAT REQUIRE YOU, KURÔ-SENPAI, TO ASK ME TO HELP RIKKA-SAN.
AND I SUSPECT THIS IS A PROBLEM I AM LIKELY ABLE TO SOLVE.
ERGO, IT WOULD BE MOST BENEFICIAL TO ME TO TAKE A BIT OF A HARD STANCE ON THIS MATTER.
BUT NOT TO WORRY.
I WON'T ASK FOR ANYTHING TOO DIFFICULT.
GRIN
SIGH
...LET'S HEAR IT.

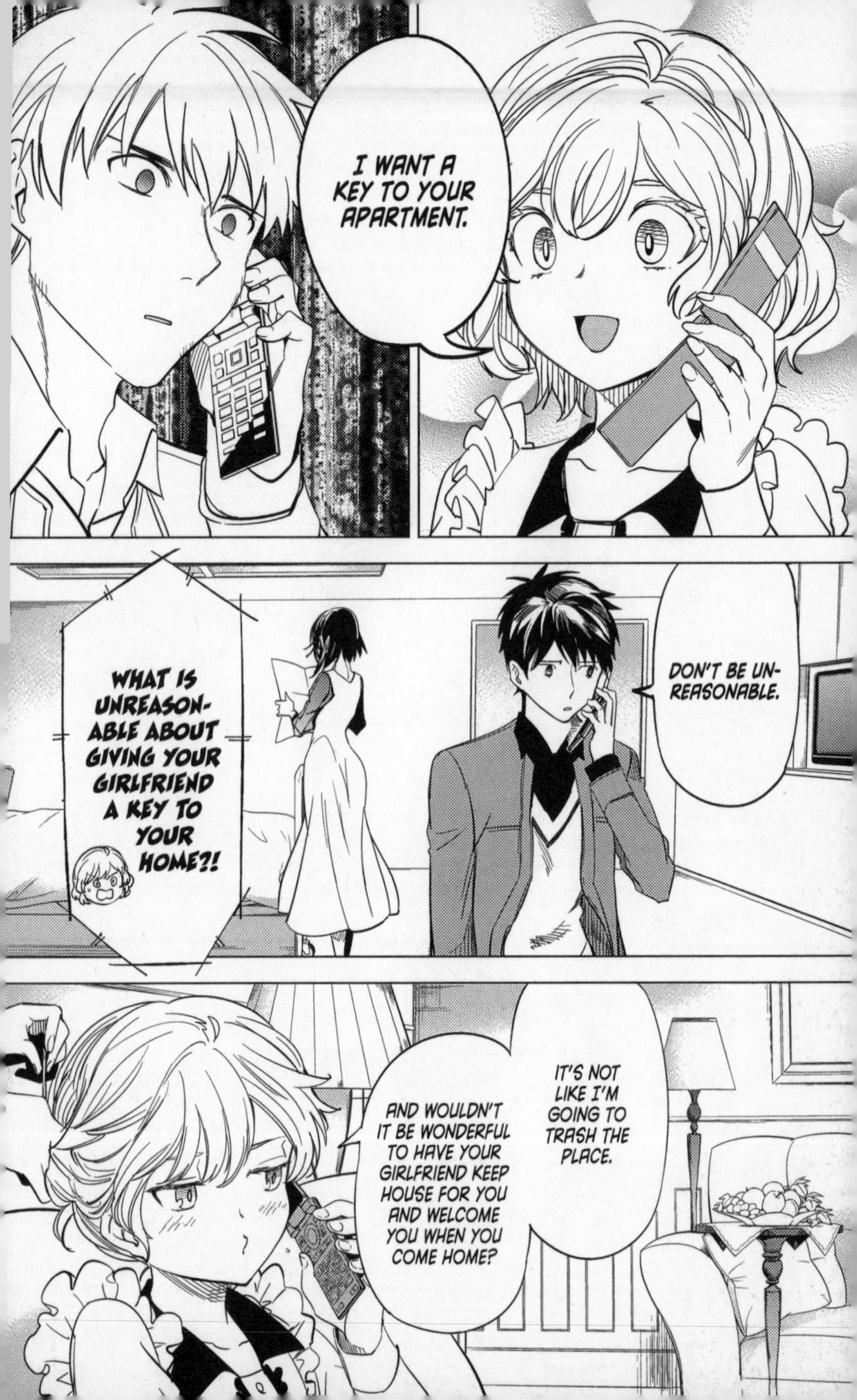
I WANT A KEY TO YOUR APARTMENT.
DON'T BE UN-REASONABLE.
WHAT IS UNREASON-ABLE ABOUT GIVING YOUR GIRLFRIEND A KEY TO YOUR HOME?!
IT'S NOT LIKE I'M GOING TO TRASH THE PLACE.
AND WOULDN'T IT BE WONDERFUL TO HAVE YOUR GIRLFRIEND KEEP HOUSE FOR YOU AND WELCOME YOU WHEN YOU COME HOME?

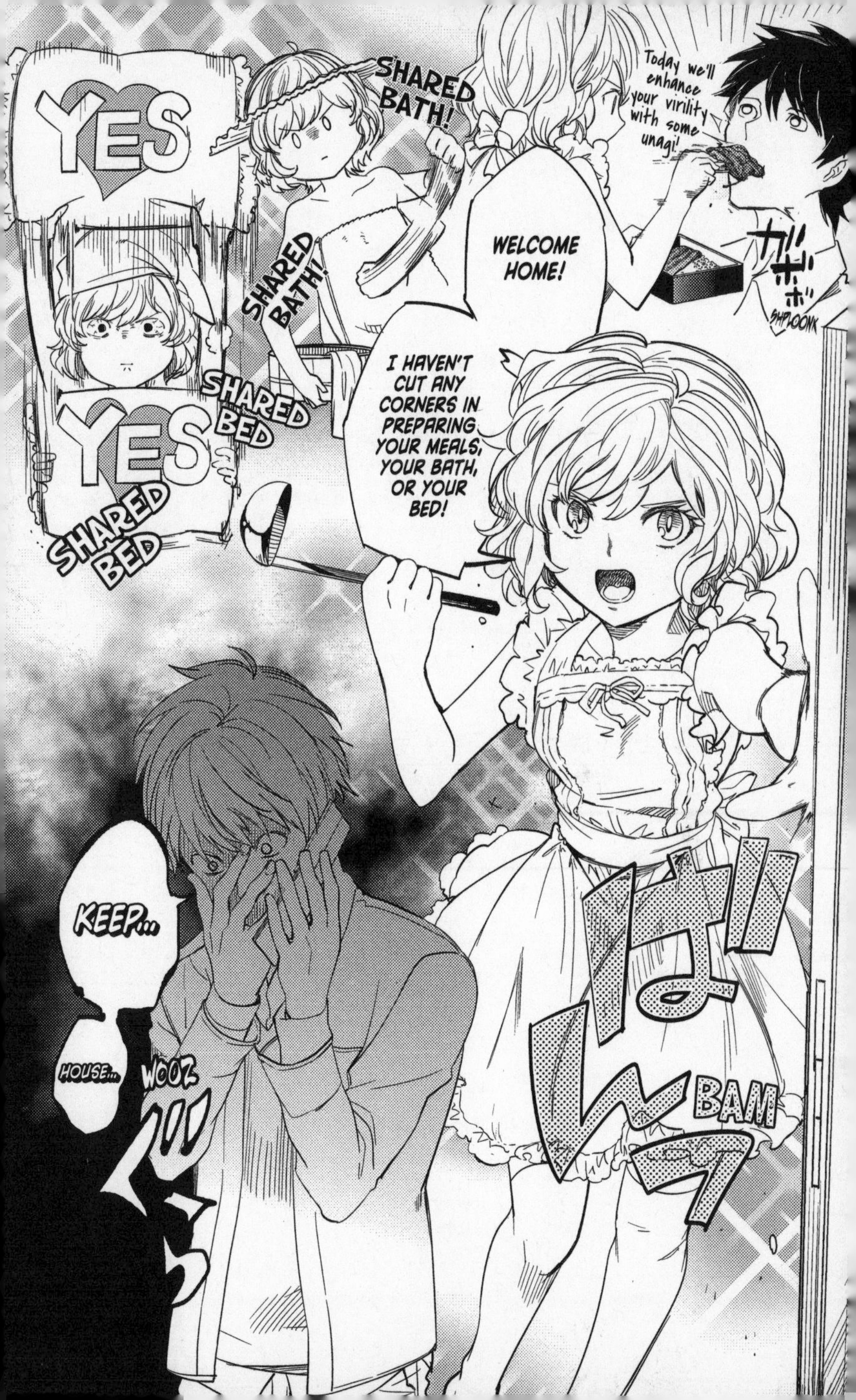
Today we'll enhance your virility with some unagi!
SHPLOONK
WELCOME HOME!
SHARED BATH!
SHARED BATH!
YES
YES
SHARED BED
SHARED BED
I HAVEN'T CUT ANY CORNERS IN PREPARING YOUR MEALS, YOUR BATH, OR YOUR BED!
BAM
KEEP...
HOUSE...
WOOZ

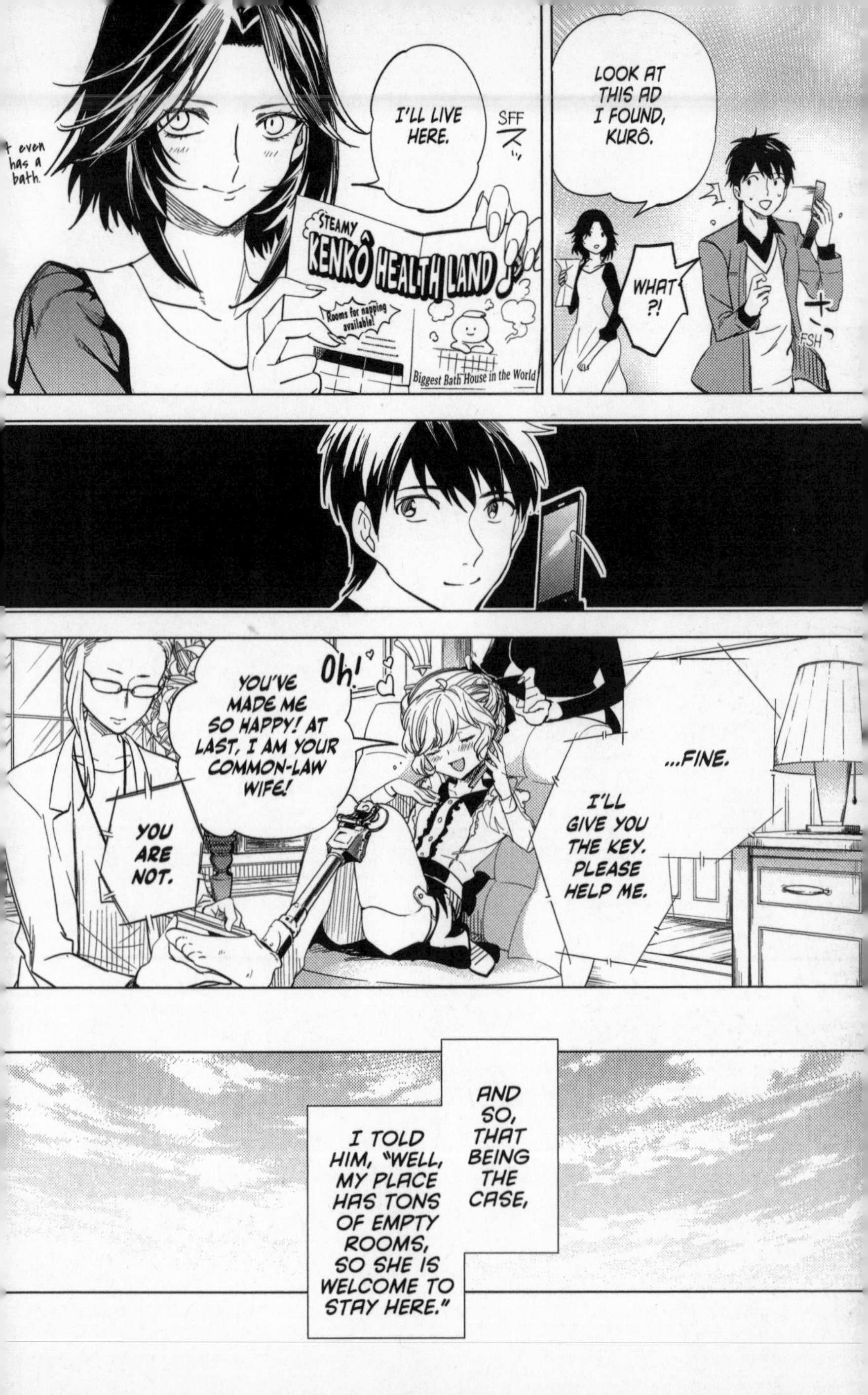
LOOK AT THIS AD I FOUND, KURÔ.
WHAT ?!
FSH
SFF
I'LL LIVE HERE.
t even has a bath.
STEAMY
KENKÔ HEALTH LAND
Rooms for napping available!
Biggest Bath House in the World
...FINE.
I'LL GIVE YOU THE KEY. PLEASE HELP ME.
Oh!
YOU'VE MADE ME SO HAPPY! AT LAST, I AM YOUR COMMON-LAW WIFE!
YOU ARE NOT.
AND SO, THAT BEING THE CASE,
I TOLD HIM, "WELL, MY PLACE HAS TONS OF EMPTY ROOMS, SO SHE IS WELCOME TO STAY HERE."

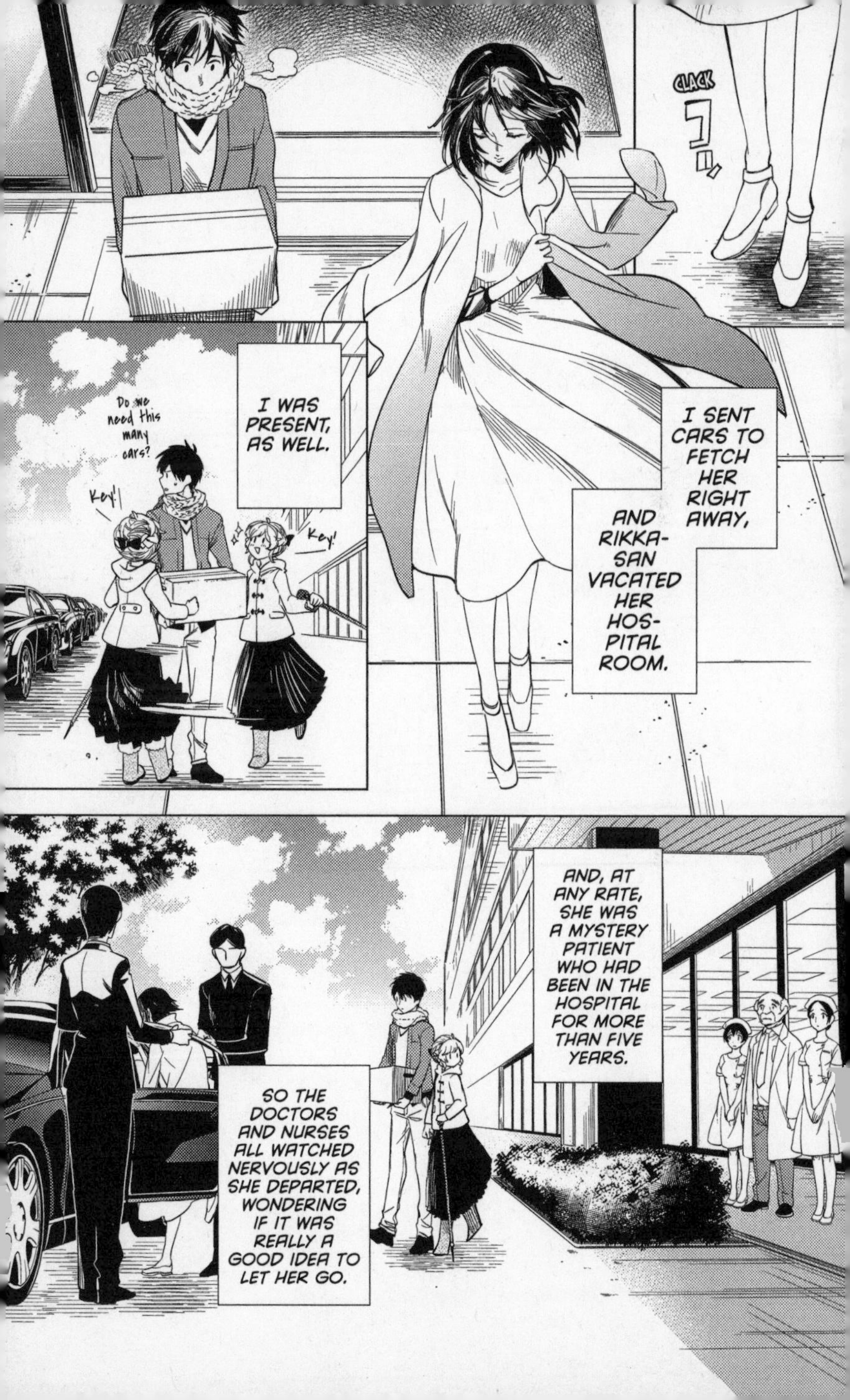
CLACK
I SENT CARS TO FETCH HER RIGHT AWAY,
AND RIKKA-SAN VACATED HER HOSPITAL ROOM.
I WAS PRESENT, AS WELL.
Do we need this many cars?
Key!
Key!
AND, AT ANY RATE, SHE WAS A MYSTERY PATIENT WHO HAD BEEN IN THE HOSPITAL FOR MORE THAN FIVE YEARS.
SO THE DOCTORS AND NURSES ALL WATCHED NERVOUSLY AS SHE DEPARTED, WONDERING IF IT WAS REALLY A GOOD IDEA TO LET HER GO.

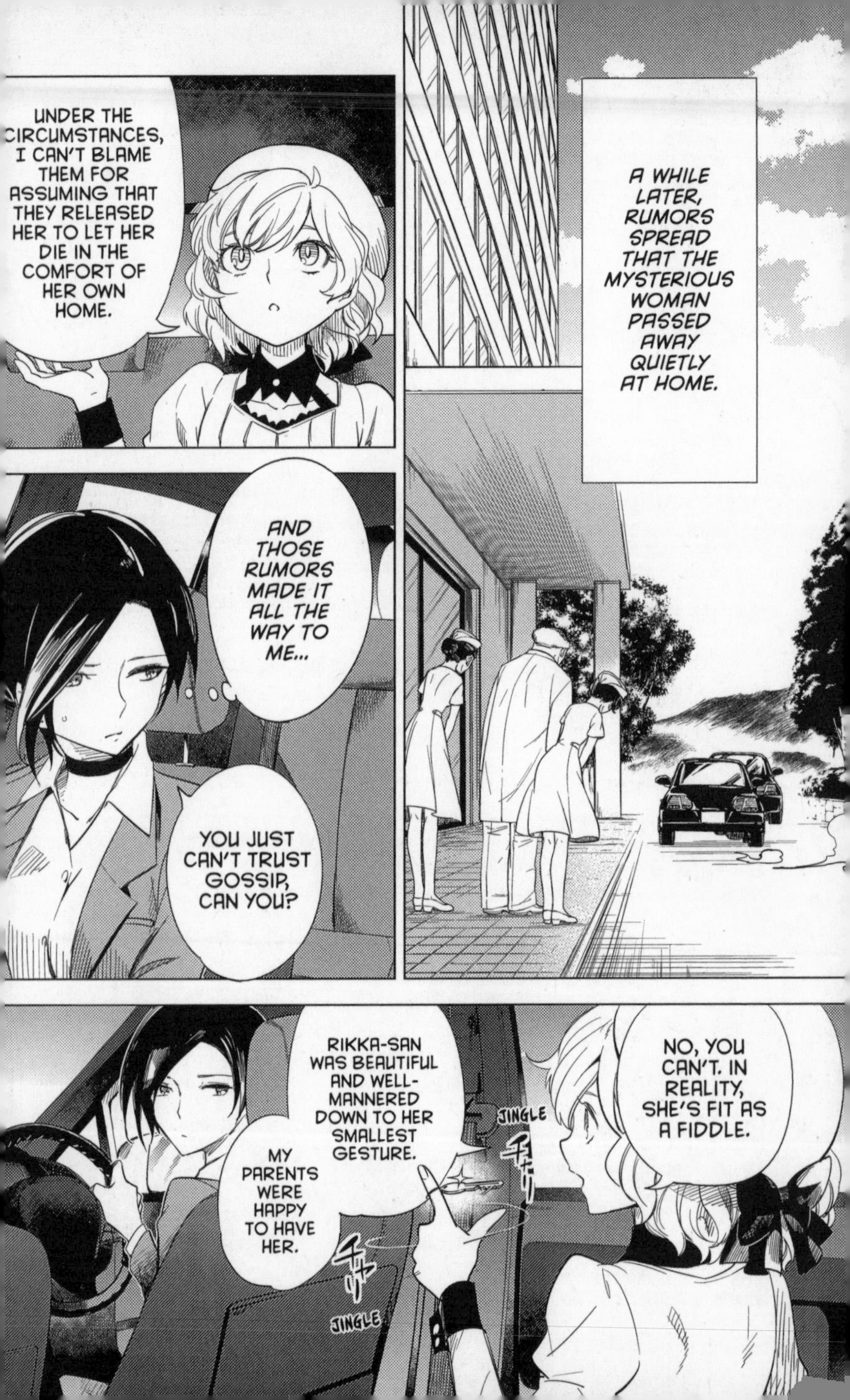
A WHILE LATER, RUMORS SPREAD THAT THE MYSTERIOUS WOMAN PASSED AWAY QUIETLY AT HOME.
UNDER THE CIRCUMSTANCES, I CAN'T BLAME THEM FOR ASSUMING THAT THEY RELEASED HER TO LET HER DIE IN THE COMFORT OF HER OWN HOME.
AND THOSE RUMORS MADE IT ALL THE WAY TO ME...
YOU JUST CAN'T TRUST GOSSIP, CAN YOU?
NO, YOU CAN'T. IN REALITY, SHE'S FIT AS A FIDDLE.
JINGLE
RIKKA-SAN WAS BEAUTIFUL AND WELL-MANNERED DOWN TO HER SMALLEST GESTURE.
MY PARENTS WERE HAPPY TO HAVE HER.
JINGLE

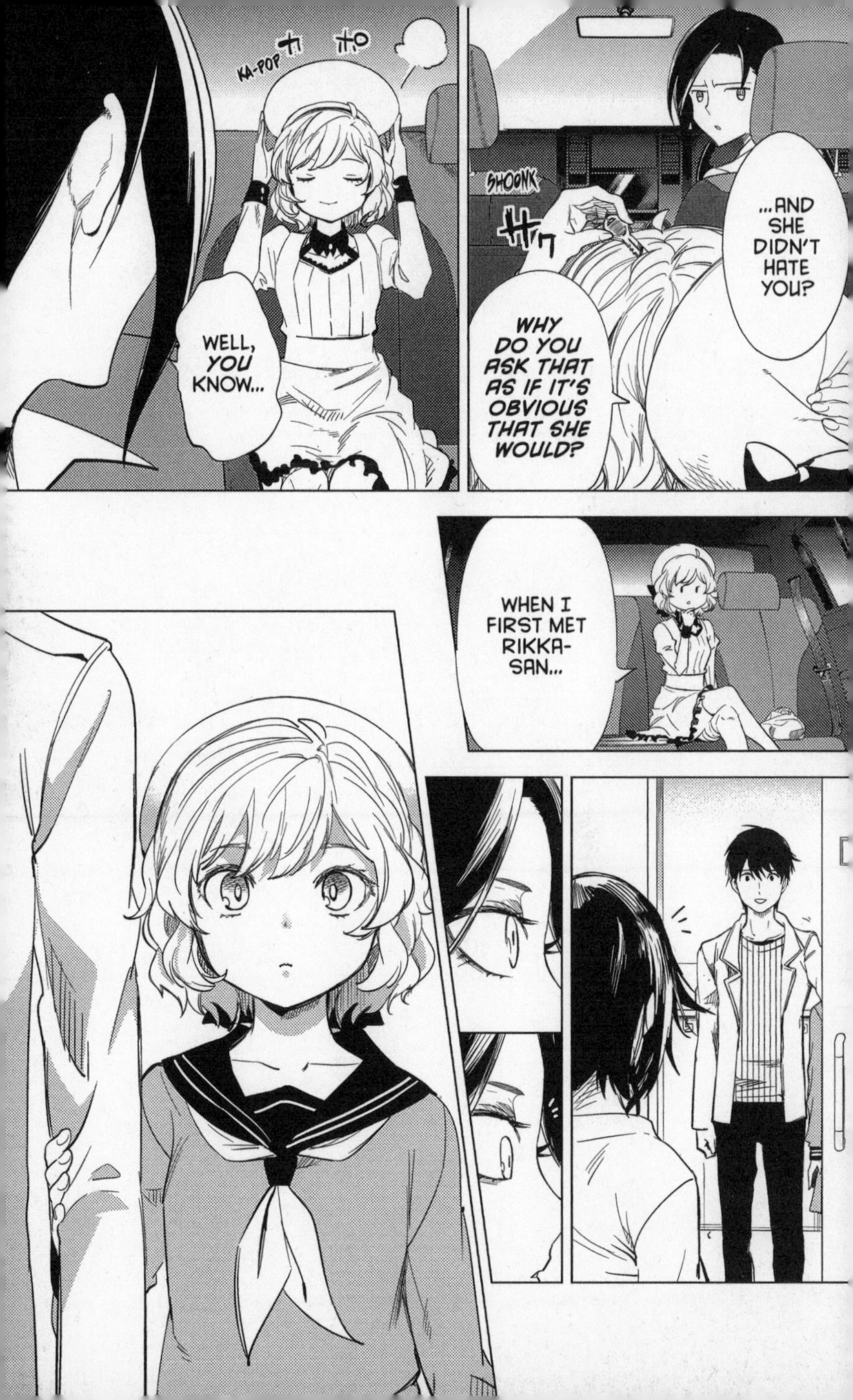
...AND SHE DIDN'T HATE YOU?
SHOONK
サク
WHY DO YOU ASK THAT AS IF IT'S OBVIOUS THAT SHE WOULD?
KA-POP
カ ポ
WELL, YOU KNOW...
WHEN I FIRST MET RIKKA-SAN...

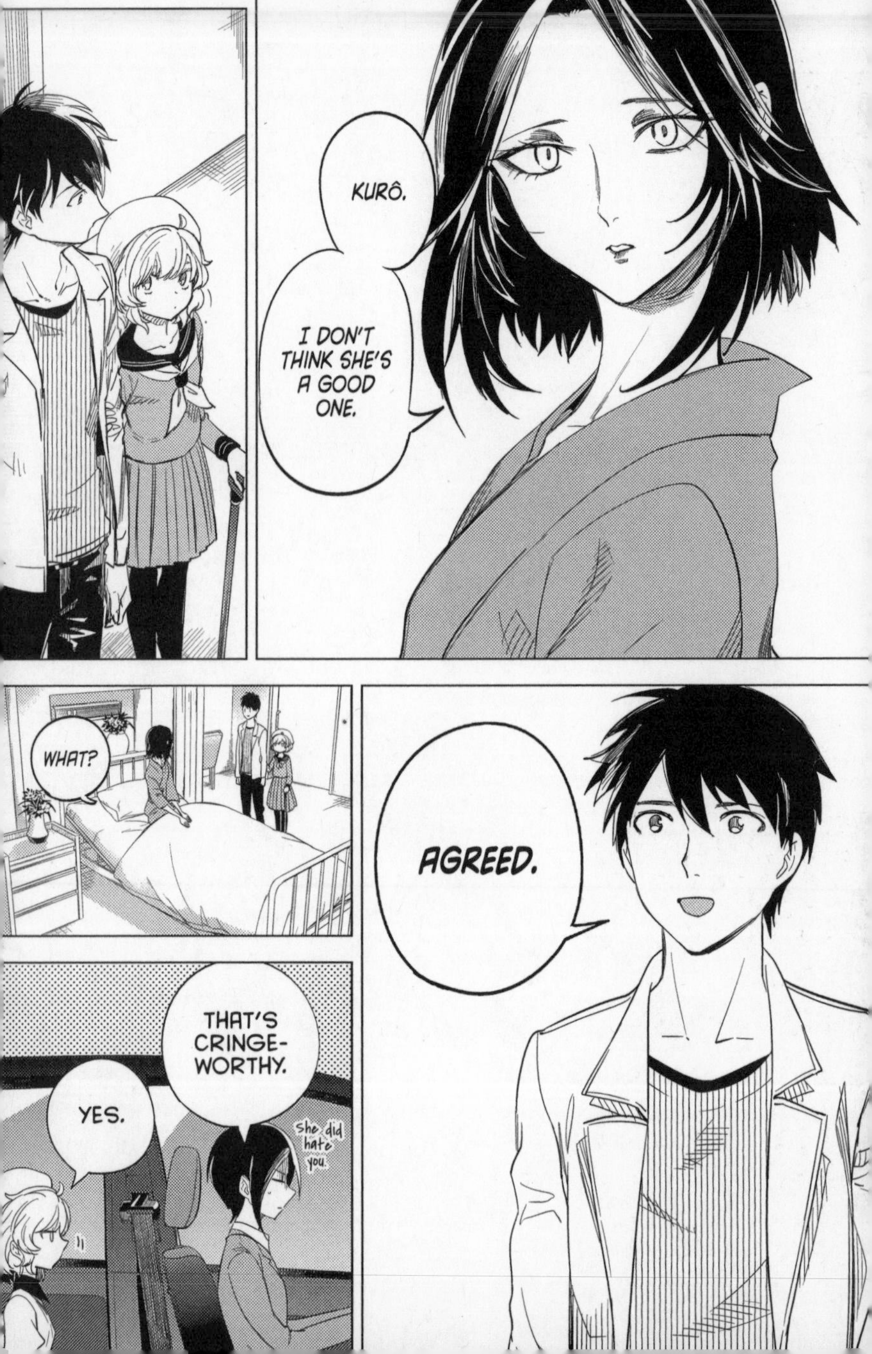
KURÔ.
I DON'T THINK SHE'S A GOOD ONE.
AGREED.
WHAT?
THAT'S CRINGE-WORTHY.
YES.
She did hate you.

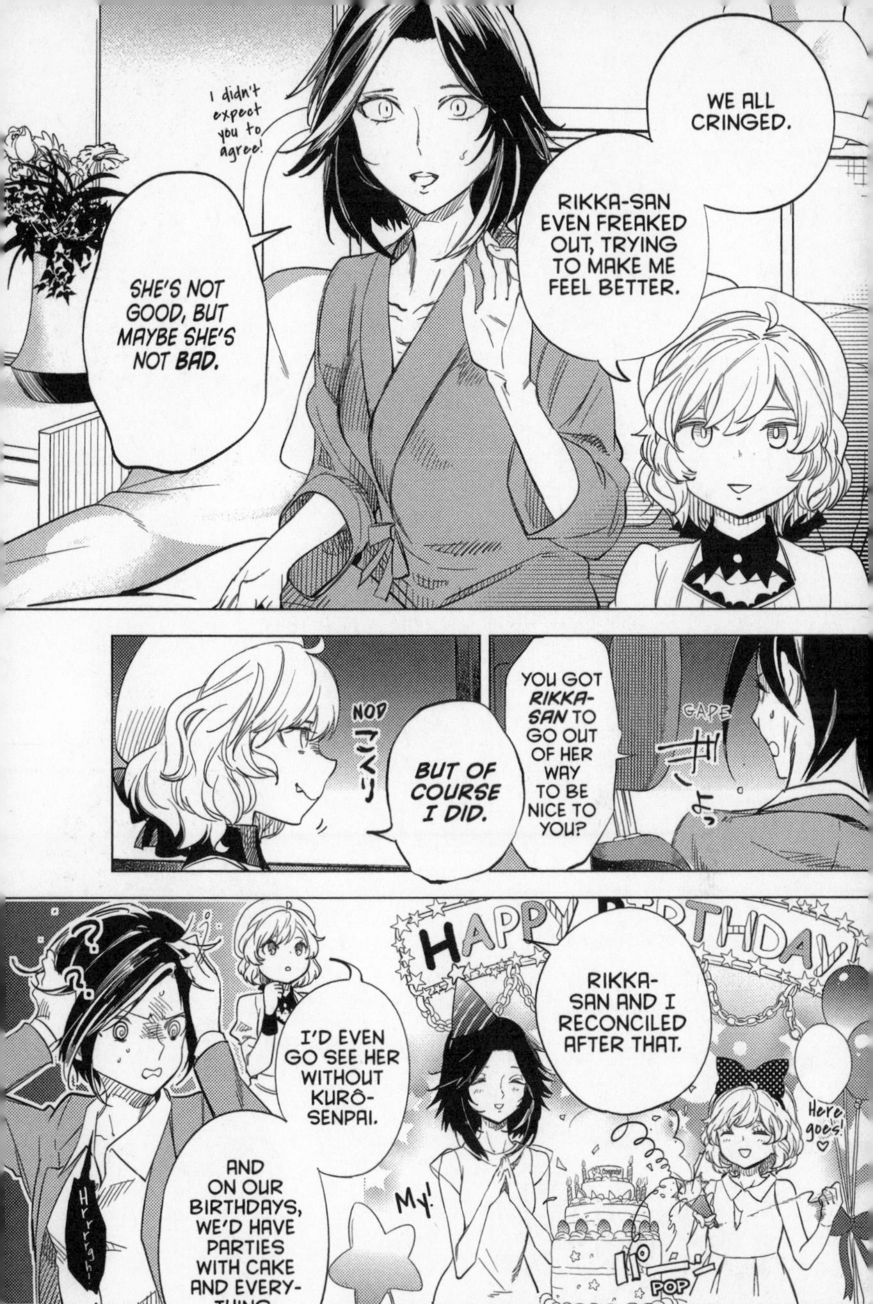
WE ALL CRINGED.
RIKKA-SAN EVEN FREAKED OUT, TRYING TO MAKE ME FEEL BETTER.
I didn't expect you to agree!
SHE'S NOT GOOD, BUT MAYBE SHE'S NOT BAD.
GAPE
YOU GOT RIKKA-SAN TO GO OUT OF HER WAY TO BE NICE TO YOU?
BUT OF COURSE I DID.
NOD
RIKKA-SAN AND I RECONCILED AFTER THAT.
HAPPY BIRTHDAY
Here goes!
POP
My!
I'D EVEN GO SEE HER WITHOUT KURÔ-SENPAI.
AND ON OUR BIRTHDAYS, WE'D HAVE PARTIES WITH CAKE AND EVERY-THING.
Hrrrgh!

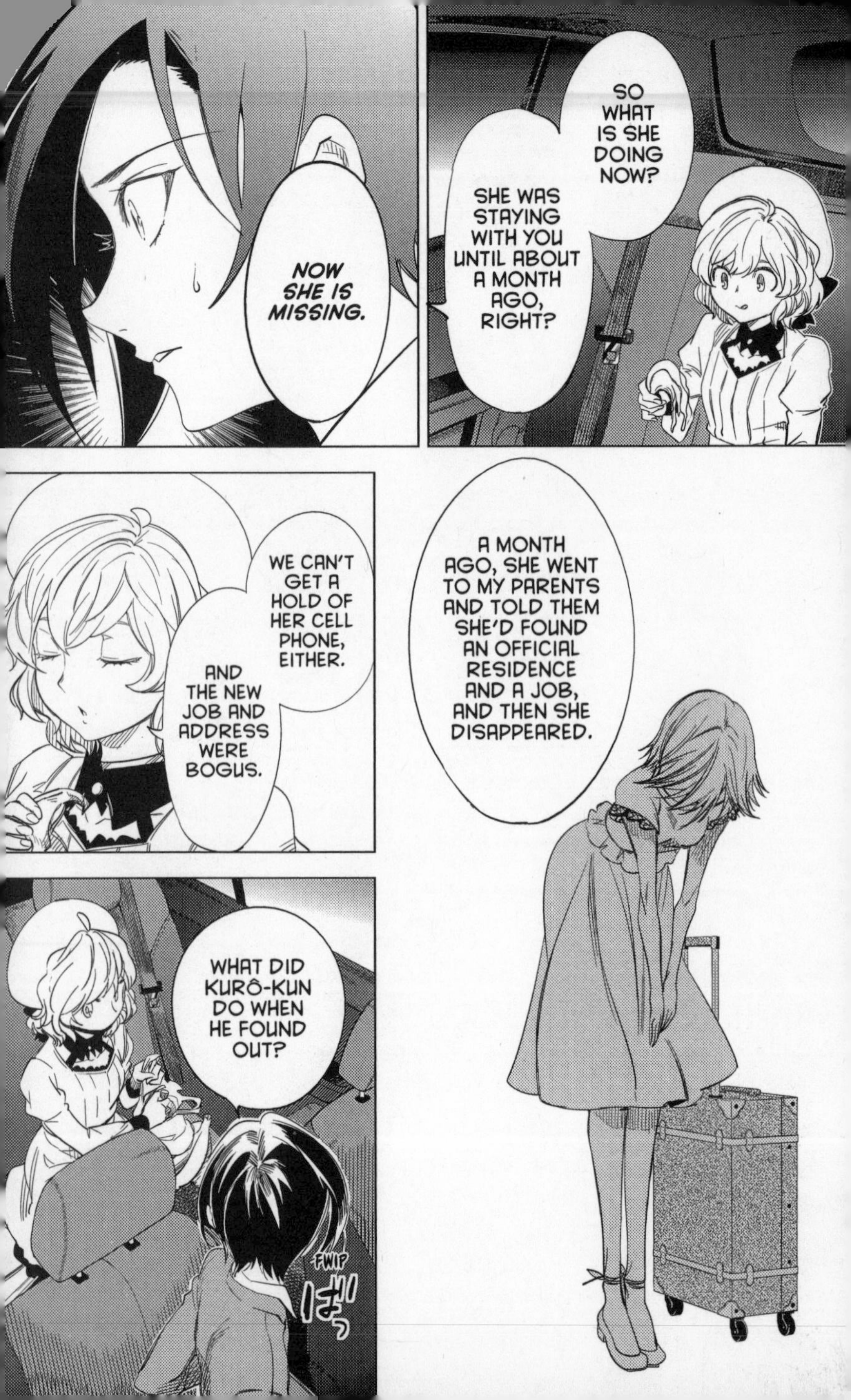
SO WHAT IS SHE DOING NOW?
SHE WAS STAYING WITH YOU UNTIL ABOUT A MONTH AGO, RIGHT?
NOW SHE IS MISSING.
A MONTH AGO, SHE WENT TO MY PARENTS AND TOLD THEM SHE'D FOUND AN OFFICIAL RESIDENCE AND A JOB, AND THEN SHE DISAPPEARED.
WE CAN'T GET A HOLD OF HER CELL PHONE, EITHER.
AND THE NEW JOB AND ADDRESS WERE BOGUS.
WHAT DID KURÔ-KUN DO WHEN HE FOUND OUT?
FWIP
ぱっ

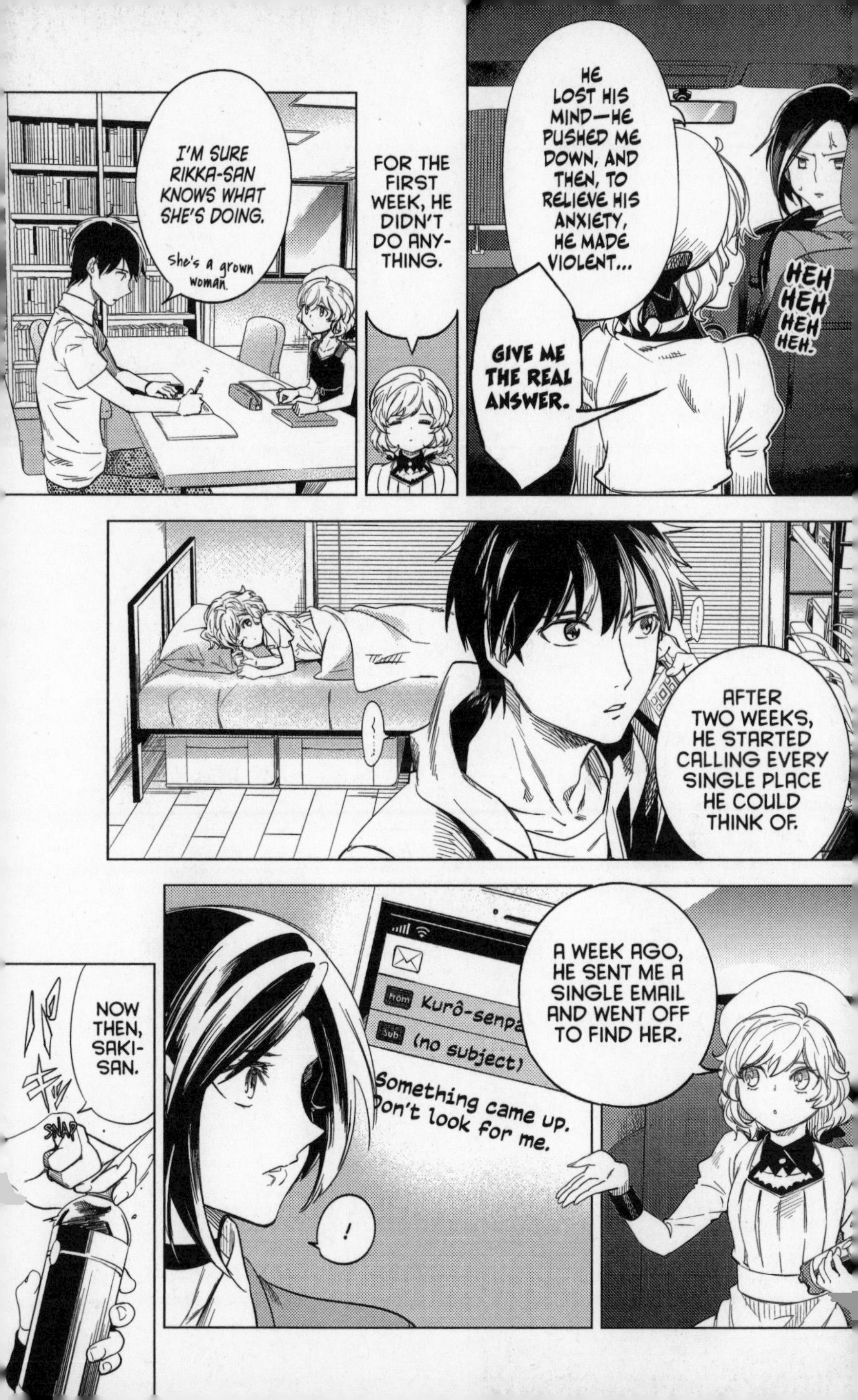
HE LOST HIS MIND—HE PUSHED ME DOWN, AND THEN, TO RELIEVE HIS ANXIETY, HE MADE VIOLENT...
GIVE ME THE REAL ANSWER.
HEH HEH HEH HEH.
FOR THE FIRST WEEK, HE DIDN'T DO ANY-THING.
I'M SURE RIKKA-SAN KNOWS WHAT SHE'S DOING.
She's a grown woman.
AFTER TWO WEEKS, HE STARTED CALLING EVERY SINGLE PLACE HE COULD THINK OF.
A WEEK AGO, HE SENT ME A SINGLE EMAIL AND WENT OFF TO FIND HER.
From Kurô-senpa
Sub (no subject)
Something came up. Don't look for me.
!
NOW THEN, SAKI-SAN.
SNAP

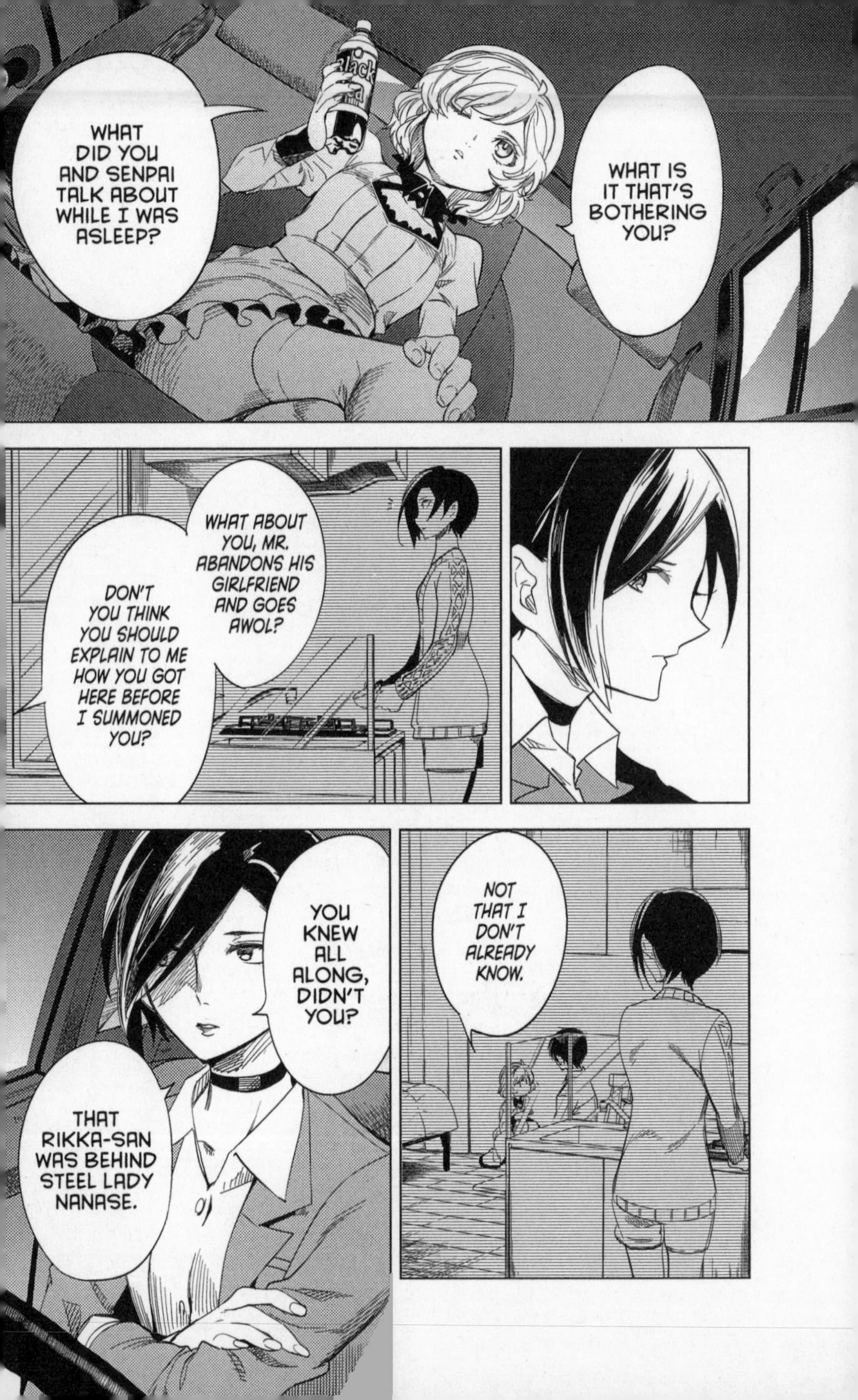
WHAT IS IT THAT'S BOTHERING YOU?
WHAT DID YOU AND SENPAI TALK ABOUT WHILE I WAS ASLEEP?
WHAT ABOUT YOU, MR. ABANDONS HIS GIRLFRIEND AND GOES AWOL?
DON'T YOU THINK YOU SHOULD EXPLAIN TO ME HOW YOU GOT HERE BEFORE I SUMMONED YOU?
NOT THAT I DON'T ALREADY KNOW.
YOU KNEW ALL ALONG, DIDN'T YOU?
THAT RIKKA-SAN WAS BEHIND STEEL LADY NANASE.

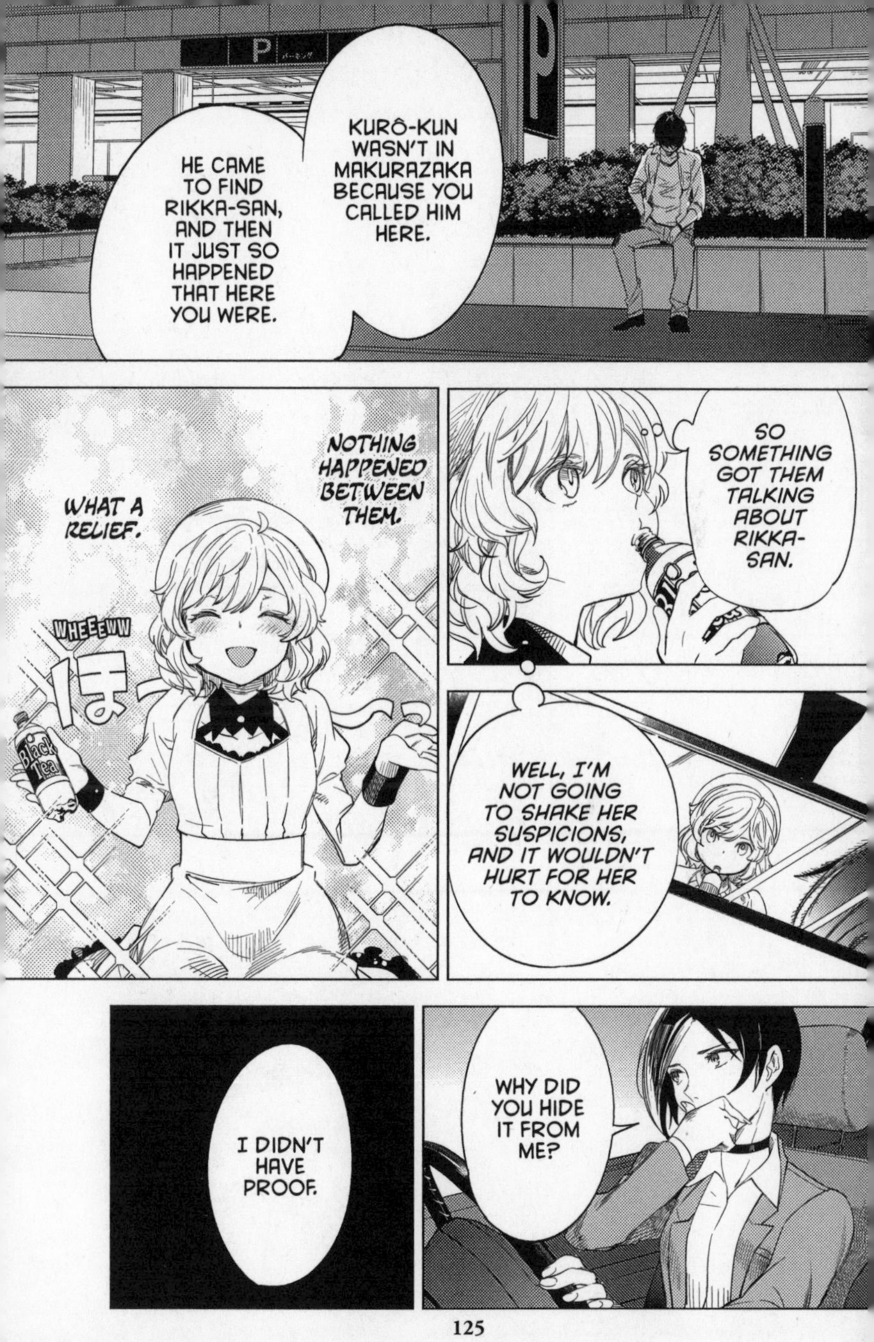
KURÔ-KUN WASN'T IN MAKURAZAKA BECAUSE YOU CALLED HIM HERE.
HE CAME TO FIND RIKKA-SAN, AND THEN IT JUST SO HAPPENED THAT HERE YOU WERE.
SO SOMETHING GOT THEM TALKING ABOUT RIKKA-SAN.
WELL, I'M NOT GOING TO SHAKE HER SUSPICIONS, AND IT WOULDN'T HURT FOR HER TO KNOW.
NOTHING HAPPENED BETWEEN THEM.
WHAT A RELIEF.
WHEEEWW
ほーっ
Black Tea
WHY DID YOU HIDE IT FROM ME?
I DIDN'T HAVE PROOF.

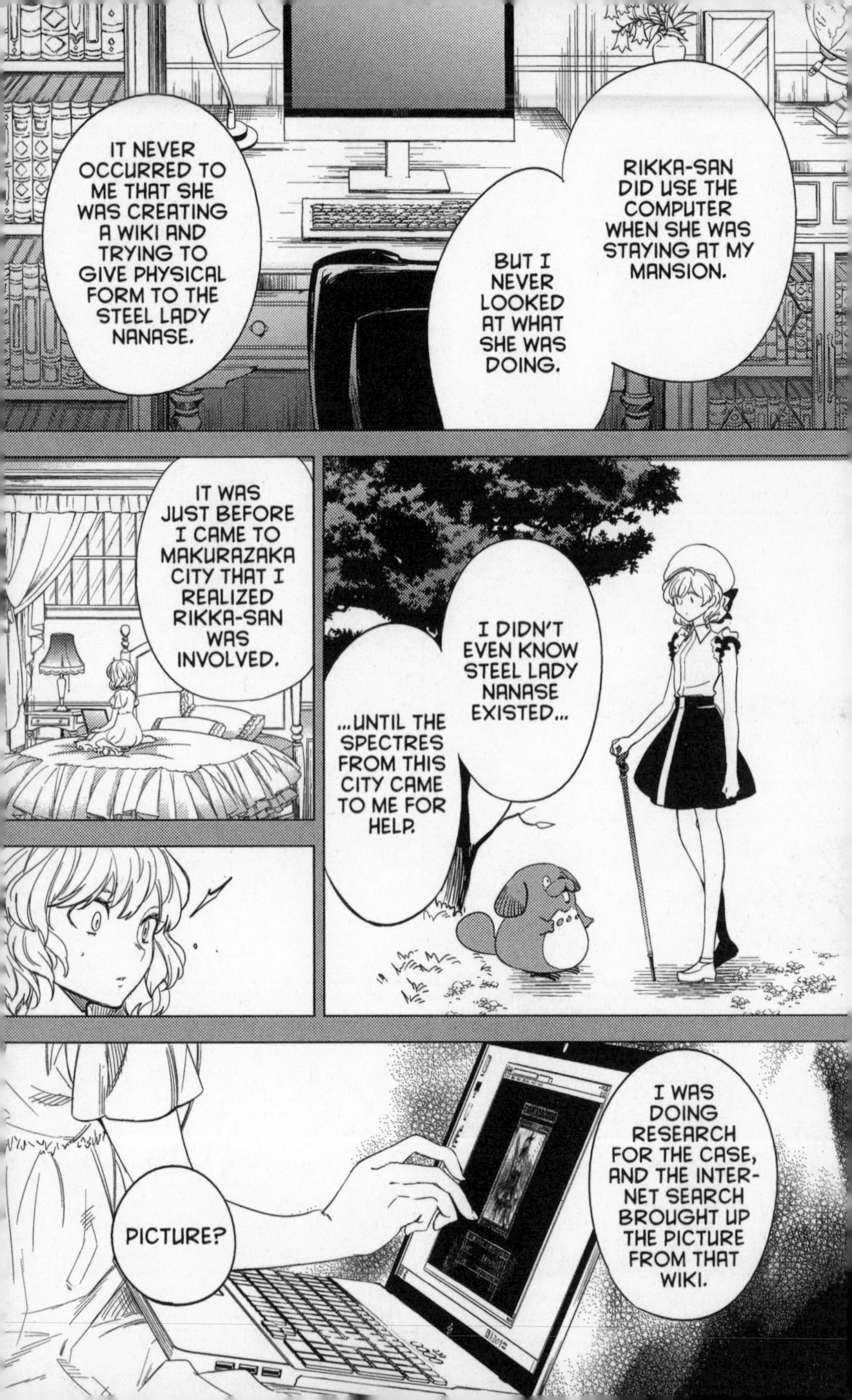
RIKKA-SAN DID USE THE COMPUTER WHEN SHE WAS STAYING AT MY MANSION.
BUT I NEVER LOOKED AT WHAT SHE WAS DOING.
IT NEVER OCCURRED TO ME THAT SHE WAS CREATING A WIKI AND TRYING TO GIVE PHYSICAL FORM TO THE STEEL LADY NANASE.
I DIDN'T EVEN KNOW STEEL LADY NANASE EXISTED...
...UNTIL THE SPECTRES FROM THIS CITY CAME TO ME FOR HELP.
IT WAS JUST BEFORE I CAME TO MAKURAZAKA CITY THAT I REALIZED RIKKA-SAN WAS INVOLVED.
I WAS DOING RESEARCH FOR THE CASE, AND THE INTER-NET SEARCH BROUGHT UP THE PICTURE FROM THAT WIKI.
PICTURE?

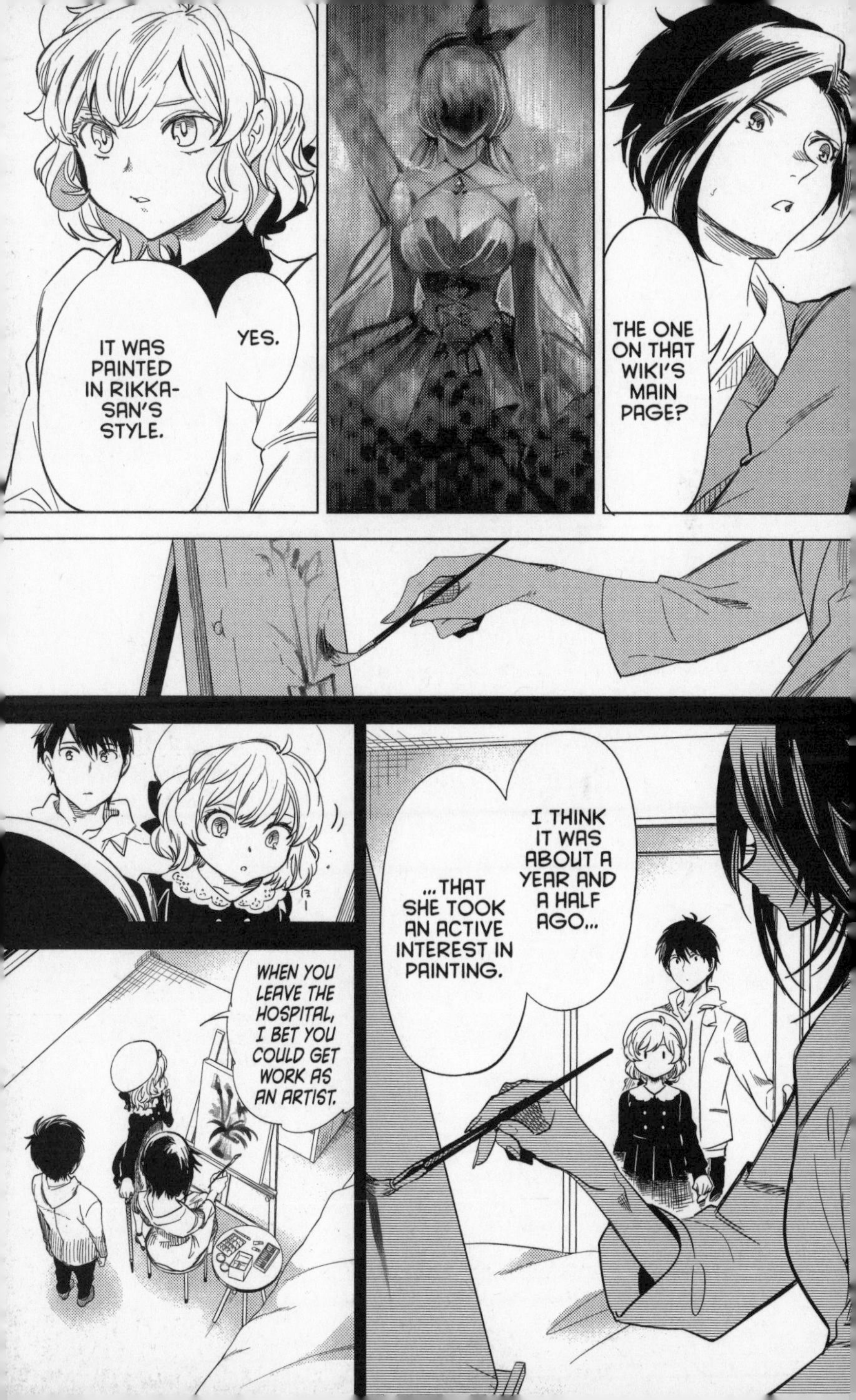
THE ONE ON THAT WIKI'S MAIN PAGE?
YES.
IT WAS PAINTED IN RIKKA-SAN'S STYLE.
I THINK IT WAS ABOUT A YEAR AND A HALF AGO...
...THAT SHE TOOK AN ACTIVE INTEREST IN PAINTING.
WHEN YOU LEAVE THE HOSPITAL, I BET YOU COULD GET WORK AS AN ARTIST.

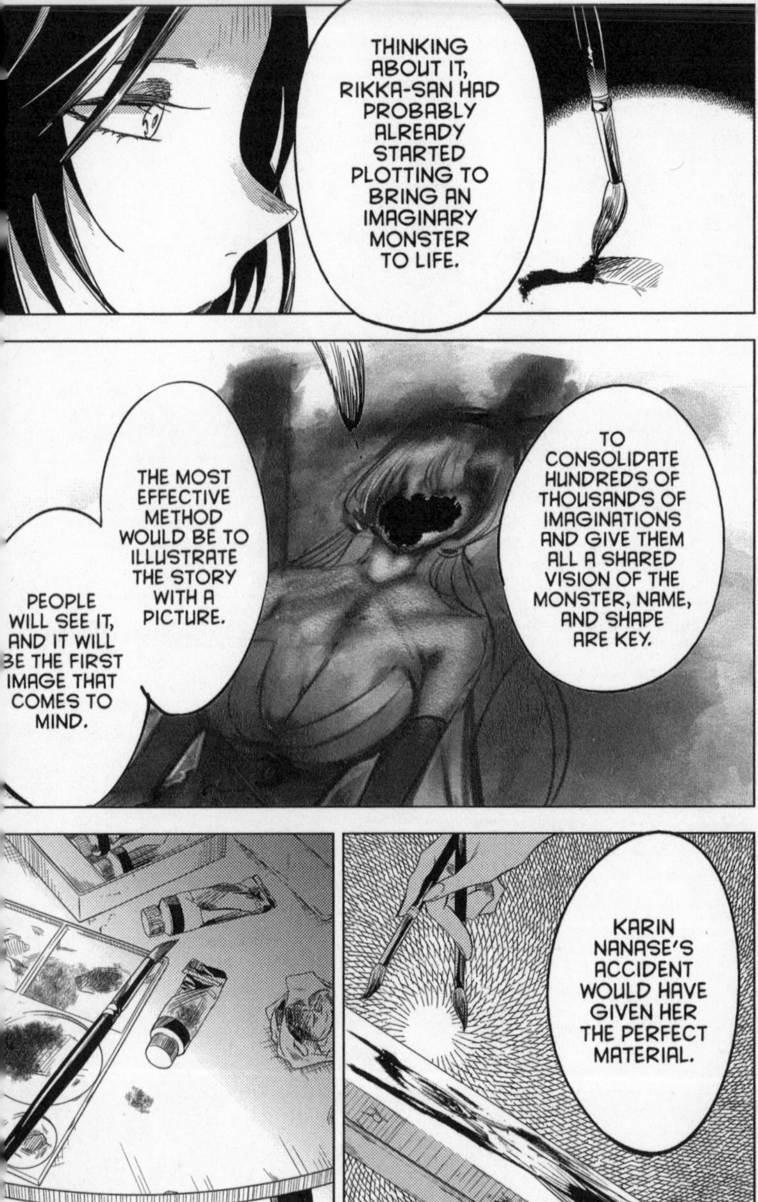
THINKING ABOUT IT, RIKKA-SAN HAD PROBABLY ALREADY STARTED PLOTTING TO BRING AN IMAGINARY MONSTER TO LIFE.
TO CONSOLIDATE HUNDREDS OF THOUSANDS OF IMAGINATIONS AND GIVE THEM ALL A SHARED VISION OF THE MONSTER, NAME, AND SHAPE ARE KEY.
THE MOST EFFECTIVE METHOD WOULD BE TO ILLUSTRATE THE STORY WITH A PICTURE.
PEOPLE WILL SEE IT, AND IT WILL BE THE FIRST IMAGE THAT COMES TO MIND.
KARIN NANASE'S ACCIDENT WOULD HAVE GIVEN HER THE PERFECT MATERIAL.

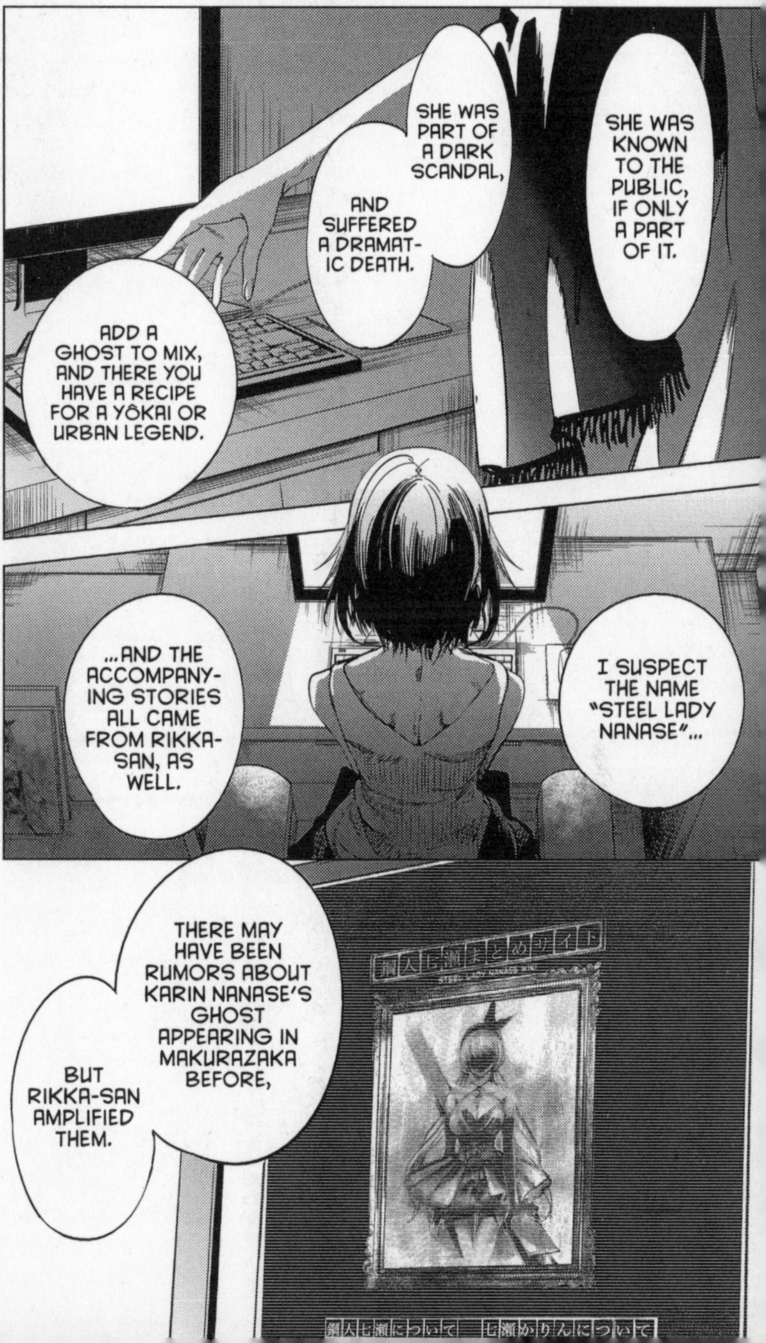
SHE WAS KNOWN TO THE PUBLIC, IF ONLY A PART OF IT.
SHE WAS PART OF A DARK SCANDAL,
AND SUFFERED A DRAMAT-IC DEATH.
ADD A GHOST TO MIX, AND THERE YOU HAVE A RECIPE FOR A YÔKAI OR URBAN LEGEND.
I SUSPECT THE NAME "STEEL LADY NANASE"...
...AND THE ACCOMPANY-ING STORIES ALL CAME FROM RIKKA-SAN, AS WELL.
THERE MAY HAVE BEEN RUMORS ABOUT KARIN NANASE'S GHOST APPEARING IN MAKURAZAKA BEFORE,
BUT RIKKA-SAN AMPLIFIED THEM.
鋼人七瀬まとめサイト
STEEL LADY NANASE WIKI
鋼人七瀬について
七瀬かりんについて

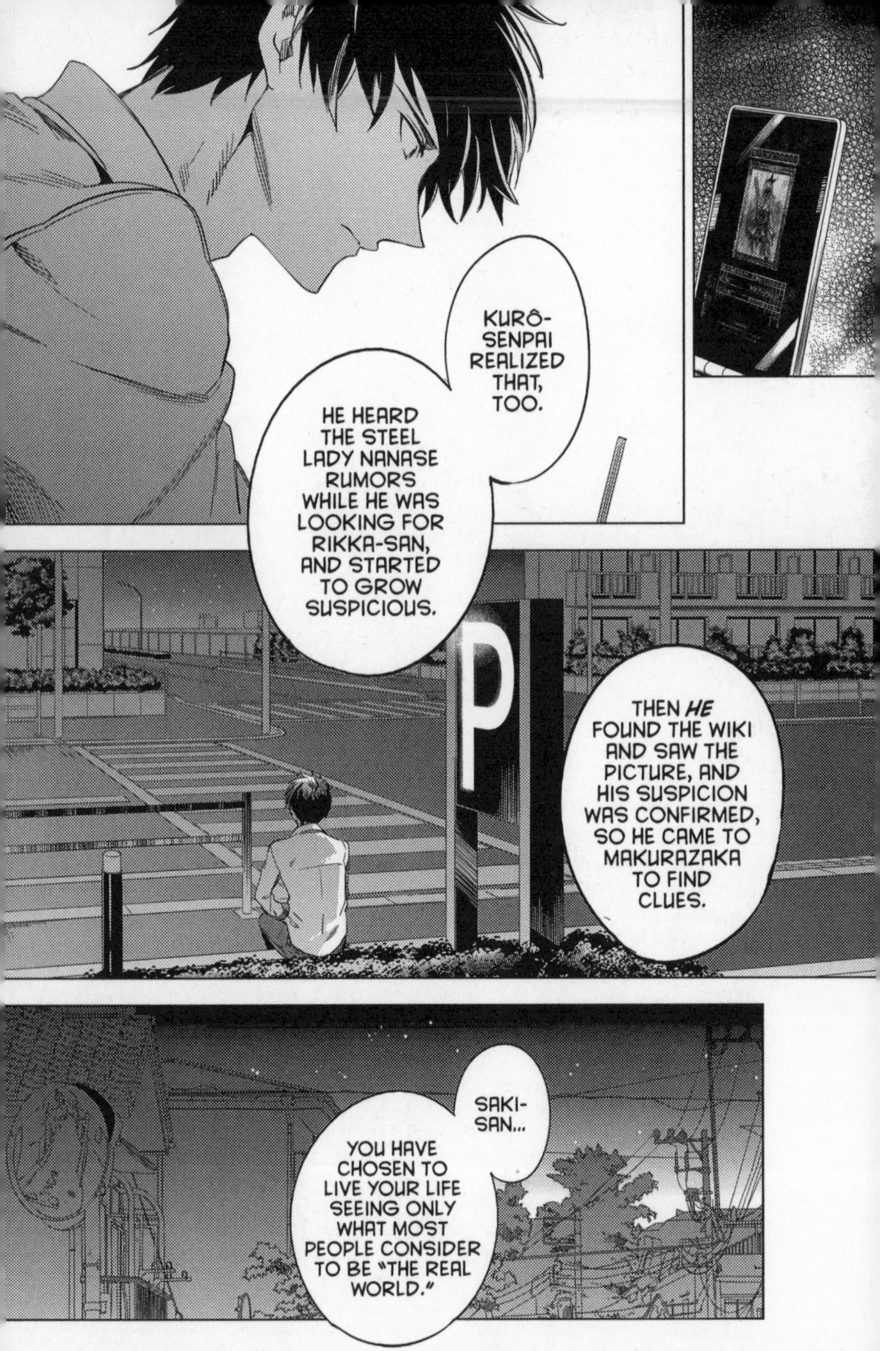
KURÔ-SENPAI REALIZED THAT, TOO.
HE HEARD THE STEEL LADY NANASE RUMORS WHILE HE WAS LOOKING FOR RIKKA-SAN, AND STARTED TO GROW SUSPICIOUS.
THEN *HE* FOUND THE WIKI AND SAW THE PICTURE, AND HIS SUSPICION WAS CONFIRMED, SO HE CAME TO MAKURAZAKA TO FIND CLUES.
SAKI-SAN...
YOU HAVE CHOSEN TO LIVE YOUR LIFE SEEING ONLY WHAT MOST PEOPLE CONSIDER TO BE "THE REAL WORLD."

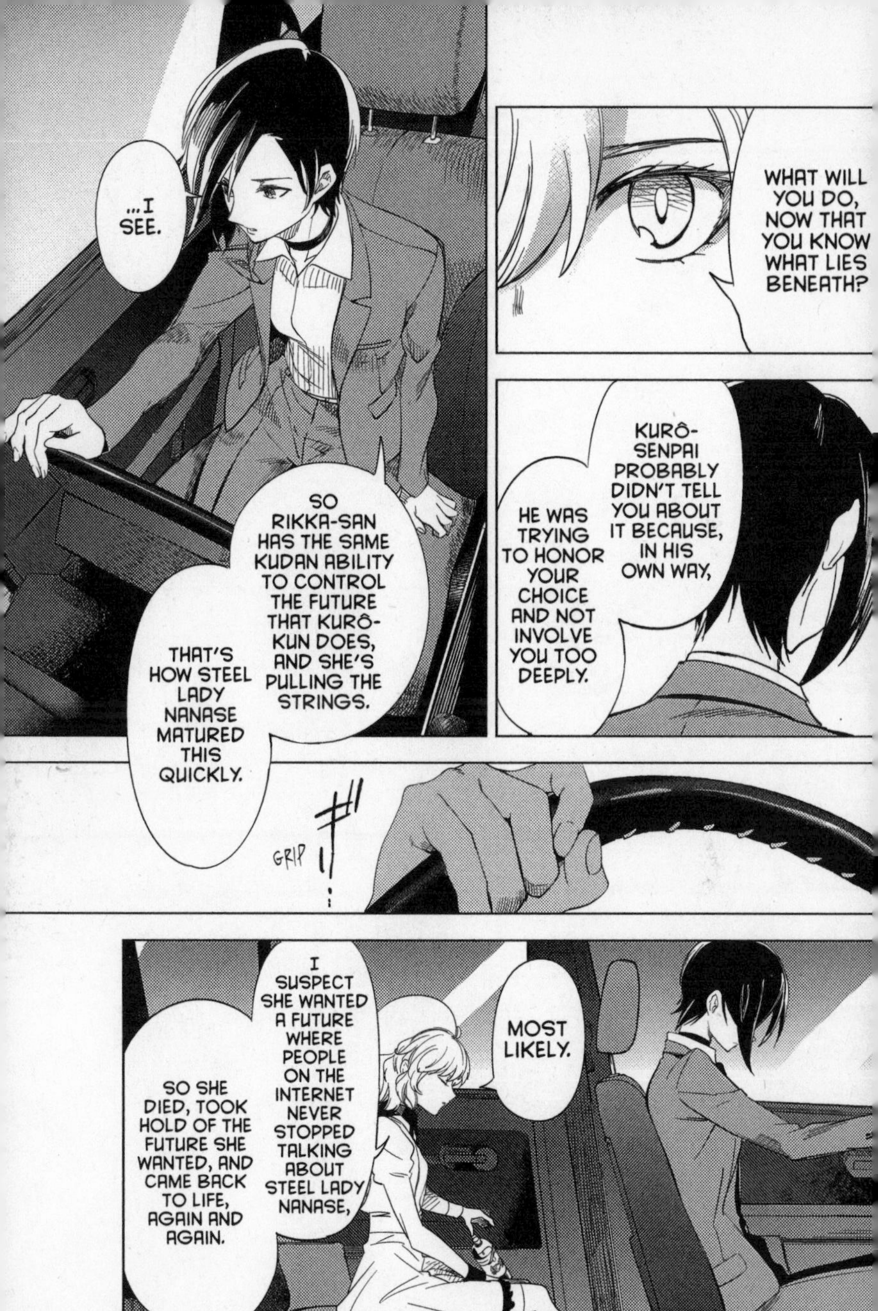
WHAT WILL YOU DO, NOW THAT YOU KNOW WHAT LIES BENEATH?
KURÔ-SENPAI PROBABLY DIDN'T TELL YOU ABOUT IT BECAUSE, IN HIS OWN WAY,
HE WAS TRYING TO HONOR YOUR CHOICE AND NOT INVOLVE YOU TOO DEEPLY.
...I SEE.
SO RIKKA-SAN HAS THE SAME KUDAN ABILITY TO CONTROL THE FUTURE THAT KURÔ-KUN DOES, AND SHE'S PULLING THE STRINGS.
THAT'S HOW STEEL LADY NANASE MATURED THIS QUICKLY.
GRIP
MOST LIKELY.
I SUSPECT SHE WANTED A FUTURE WHERE PEOPLE ON THE INTERNET NEVER STOPPED TALKING ABOUT STEEL LADY NANASE,
SO SHE DIED, TOOK HOLD OF THE FUTURE SHE WANTED, AND CAME BACK TO LIFE, AGAIN AND AGAIN.

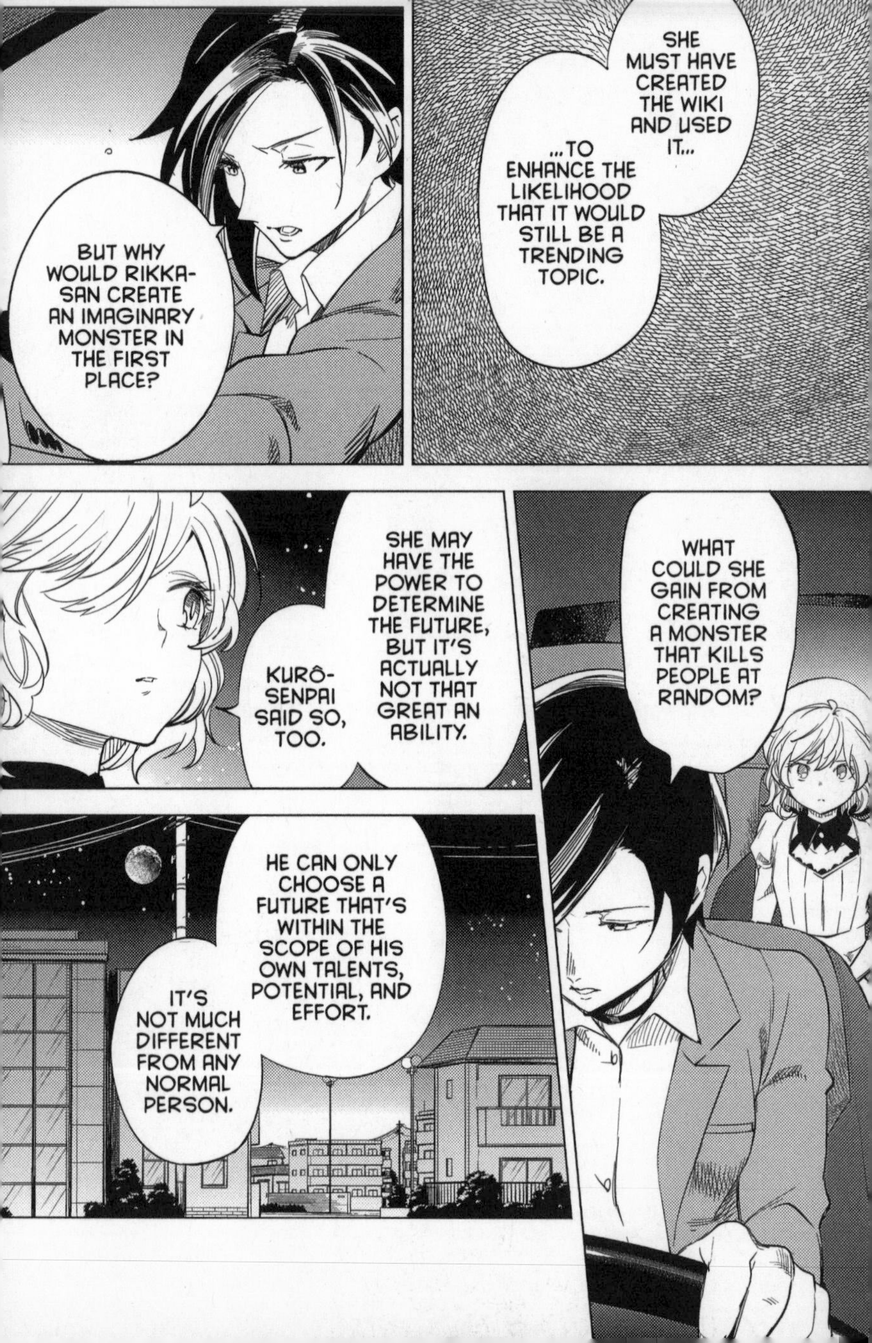
SHE MUST HAVE CREATED THE WIKI AND USED IT...
...TO ENHANCE THE LIKELIHOOD THAT IT WOULD STILL BE A TRENDING TOPIC.
BUT WHY WOULD RIKKA-SAN CREATE AN IMAGINARY MONSTER IN THE FIRST PLACE?
WHAT COULD SHE GAIN FROM CREATING A MONSTER THAT KILLS PEOPLE AT RANDOM?
SHE MAY HAVE THE POWER TO DETERMINE THE FUTURE, BUT IT'S ACTUALLY NOT THAT GREAT AN ABILITY.
KURÔ-SENPAI SAID SO, TOO.
HE CAN ONLY CHOOSE A FUTURE THAT'S WITHIN THE SCOPE OF HIS OWN TALENTS, POTENTIAL, AND EFFORT.
IT'S NOT MUCH DIFFERENT FROM ANY NORMAL PERSON.

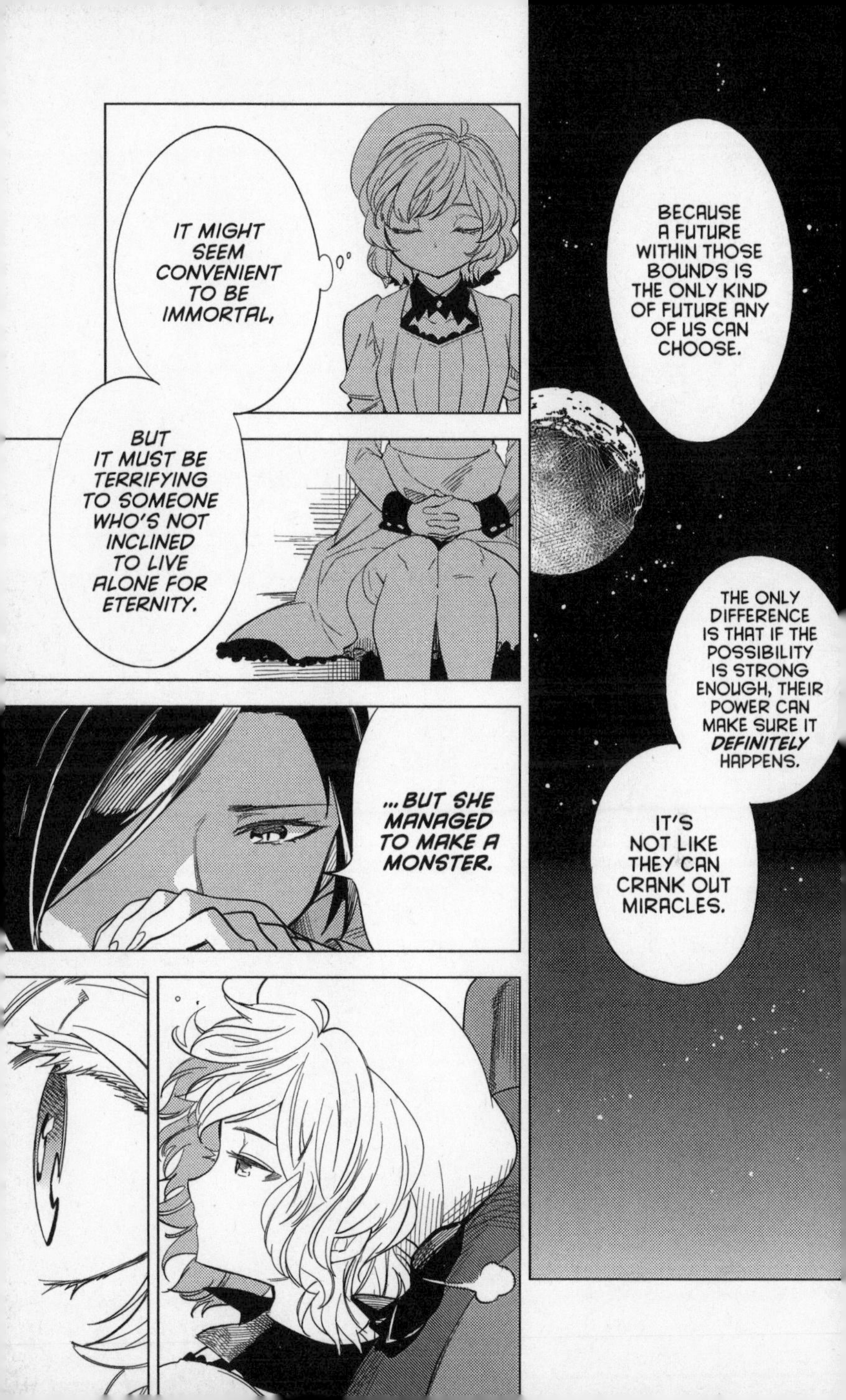
BECAUSE A FUTURE WITHIN THOSE BOUNDS IS THE ONLY KIND OF FUTURE ANY OF US CAN CHOOSE.
THE ONLY DIFFERENCE IS THAT IF THE POSSIBILITY IS STRONG ENOUGH, THEIR POWER CAN MAKE SURE IT *DEFINITELY* HAPPENS.
IT'S NOT LIKE THEY CAN CRANK OUT MIRACLES.
IT MIGHT SEEM CONVENIENT TO BE IMMORTAL,
BUT IT MUST BE TERRIFYING TO SOMEONE WHO'S NOT INCLINED TO LIVE ALONE FOR ETERNITY.
...BUT SHE MANAGED TO MAKE A MONSTER.

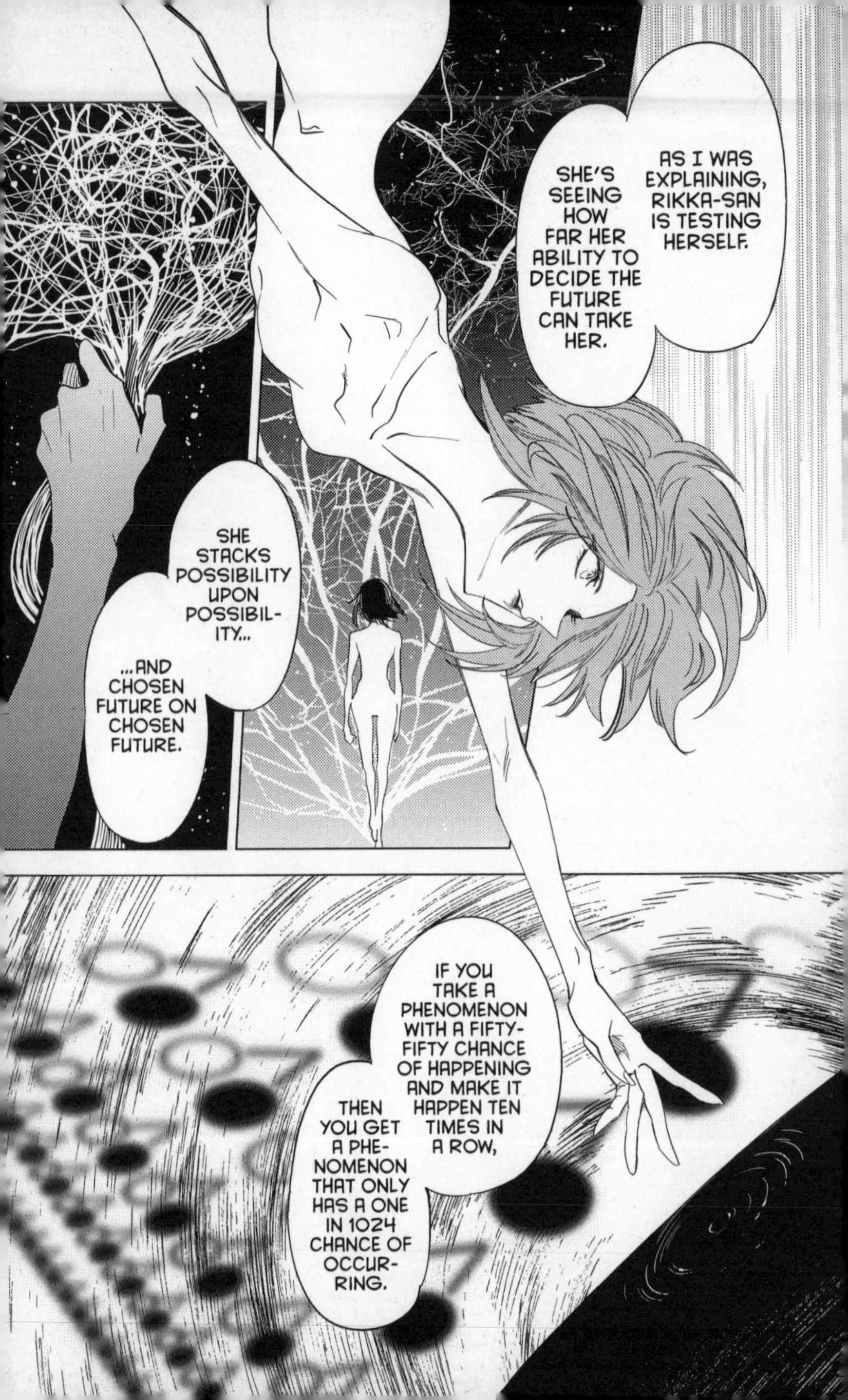
AS I WAS EXPLAINING, RIKKA-SAN IS TESTING HERSELF.
SHE'S SEEING HOW FAR HER ABILITY TO DECIDE THE FUTURE CAN TAKE HER.
SHE STACKS POSSIBILITY UPON POSSIBIL-ITY...
...AND CHOSEN FUTURE ON CHOSEN FUTURE.
IF YOU TAKE A PHENOMENON WITH A FIFTY-FIFTY CHANCE OF HAPPENING AND MAKE IT HAPPEN TEN TIMES IN A ROW,
THEN YOU GET A PHE-NOMENON THAT ONLY HAS A ONE IN 1024 CHANCE OF OCCUR-RING.

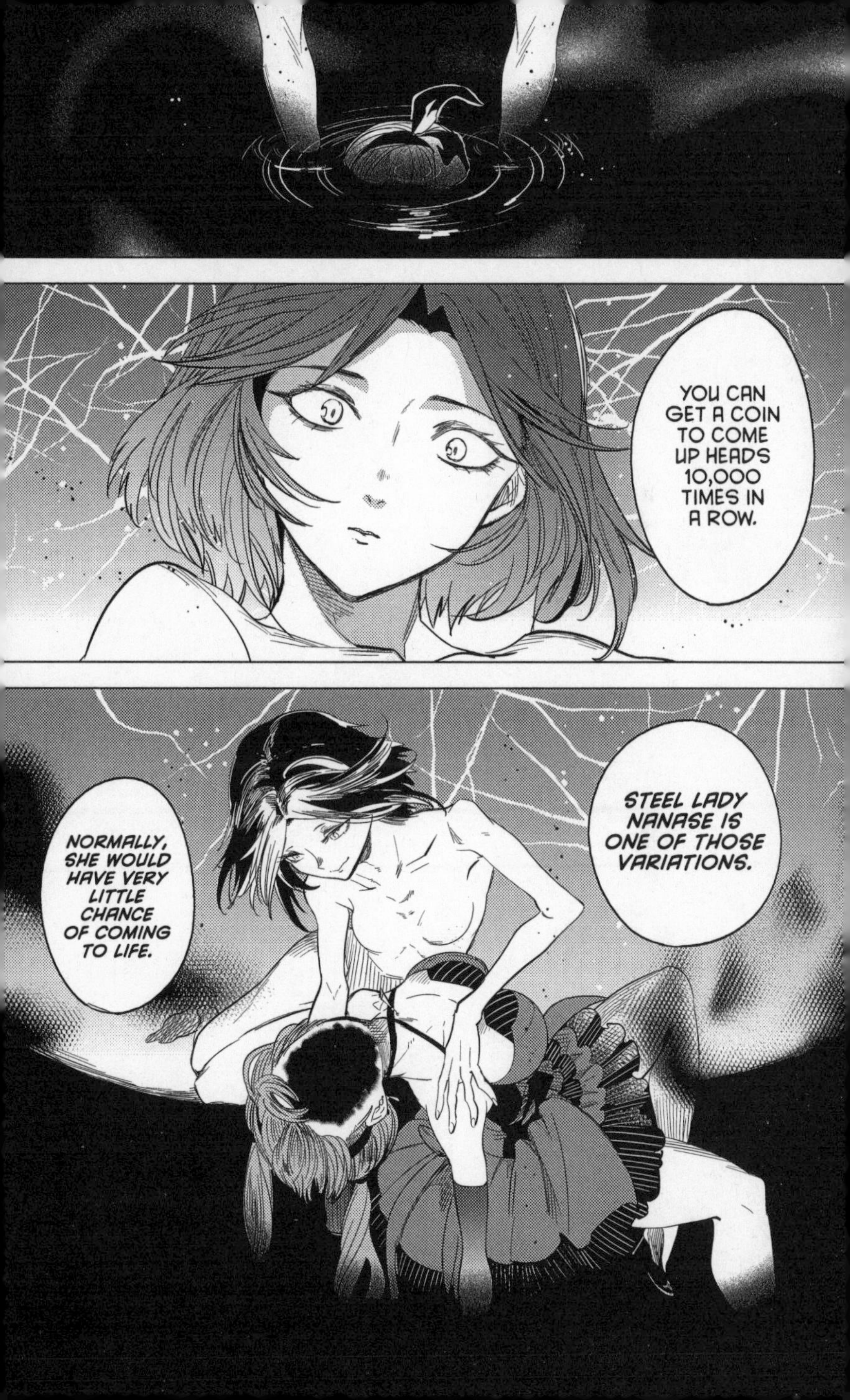
YOU CAN GET A COIN TO COME UP HEADS 10,000 TIMES IN A ROW.
STEEL LADY NANASE IS ONE OF THOSE VARIATIONS.
NORMALLY, SHE WOULD HAVE VERY LITTLE CHANCE OF COMING TO LIFE.

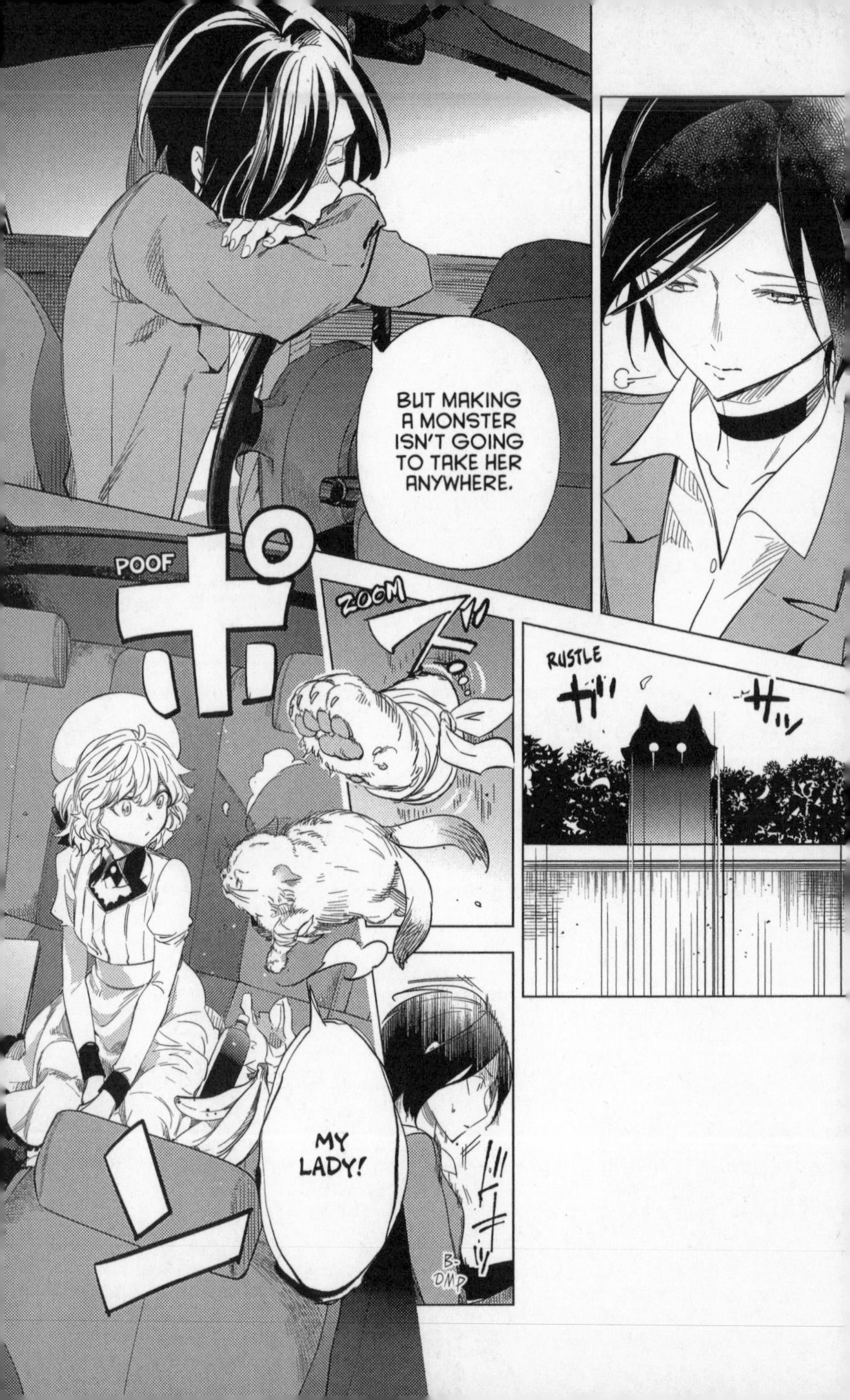
BUT MAKING A MONSTER ISN'T GOING TO TAKE HER ANYWHERE.
RUSTLE
ZOOM
POOF
MY LADY!
B-DMP

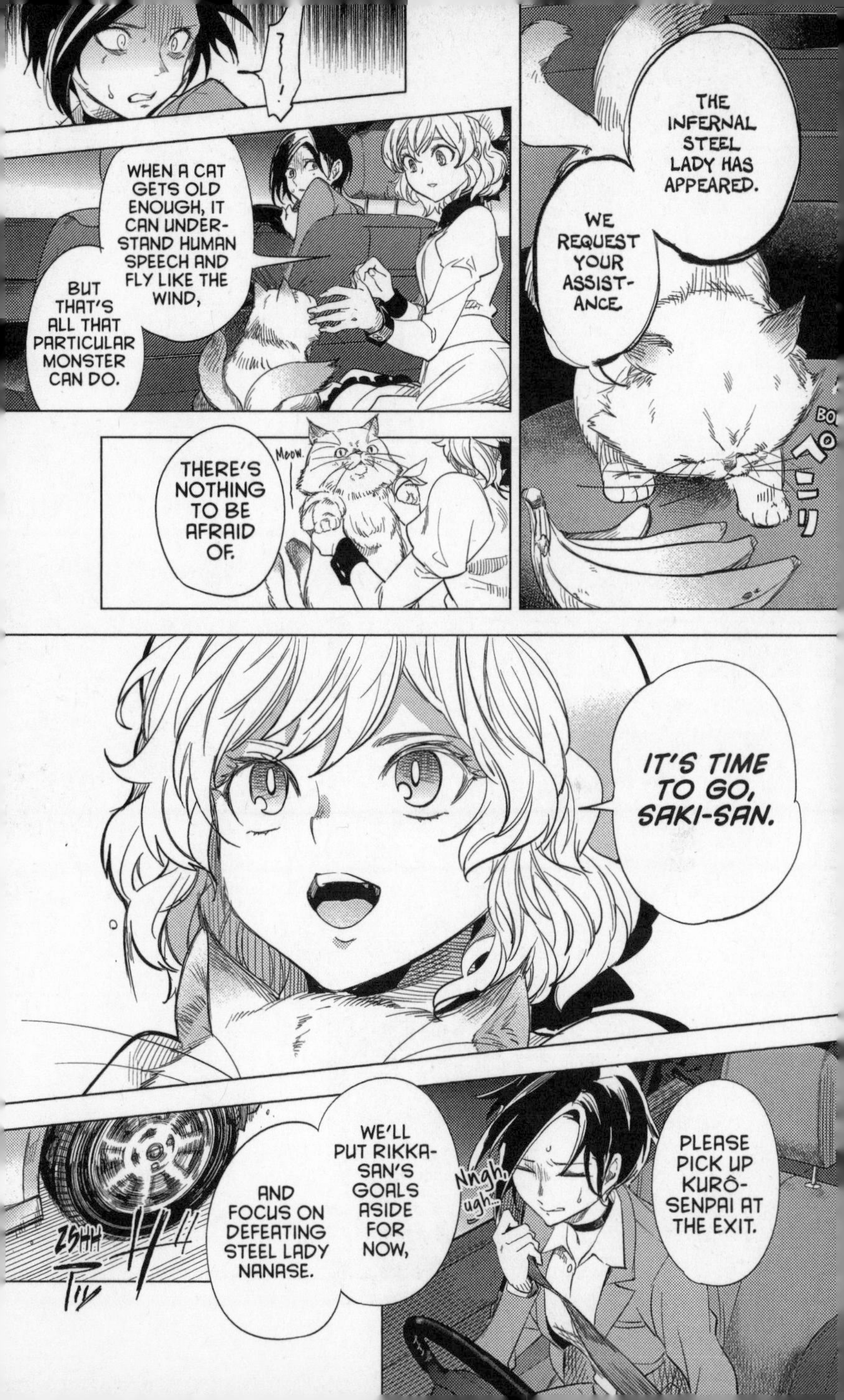
THE INFERNAL STEEL LADY HAS APPEARED.
WE REQUEST YOUR ASSISTANCE.
BO
WHEN A CAT GETS OLD ENOUGH, IT CAN UNDERSTAND HUMAN SPEECH AND FLY LIKE THE WIND,
BUT THAT'S ALL THAT PARTICULAR MONSTER CAN DO.
Meow.
THERE'S NOTHING TO BE AFRAID OF.
IT'S TIME TO GO, SAKI-SAN.
PLEASE PICK UP KURÔ-SENPAI AT THE EXIT.
Nngh, ugh...
WE'LL PUT RIKKA-SAN'S GOALS ASIDE FOR NOW,
AND FOCUS ON DEFEATING STEEL LADY NANASE.
ZSHH

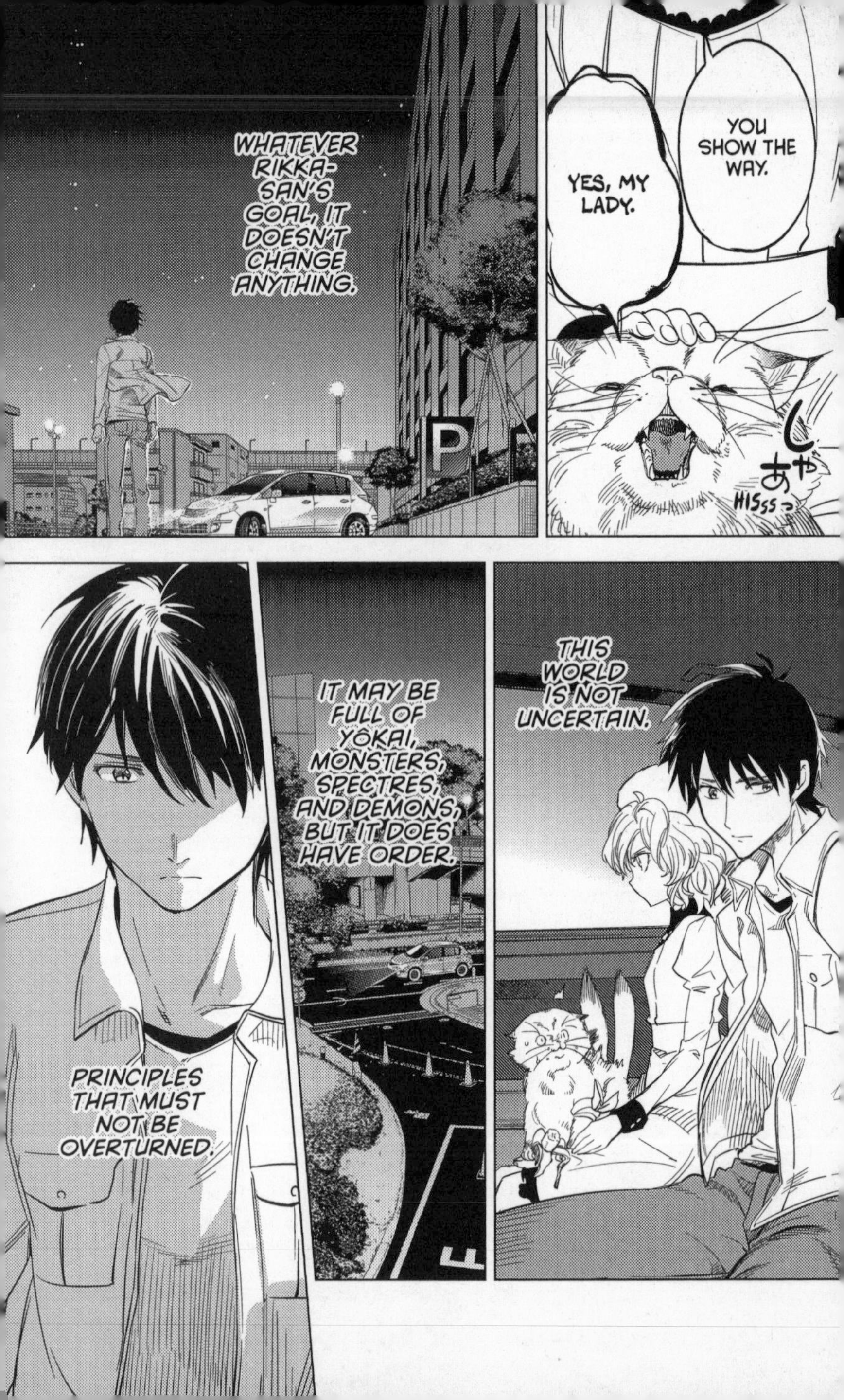
YOU SHOW THE WAY.
YES, MY LADY.
しゃあっ
HISSS
WHATEVER RIKKA-SAN'S GOAL, IT DOESN'T CHANGE ANYTHING.
THIS WORLD IS NOT UNCERTAIN.
IT MAY BE FULL OF YÔKAI, MONSTERS, SPECTRES, AND DEMONS, BUT IT DOES HAVE ORDER.
PRINCIPLES THAT MUST NOT BE OVERTURNED.

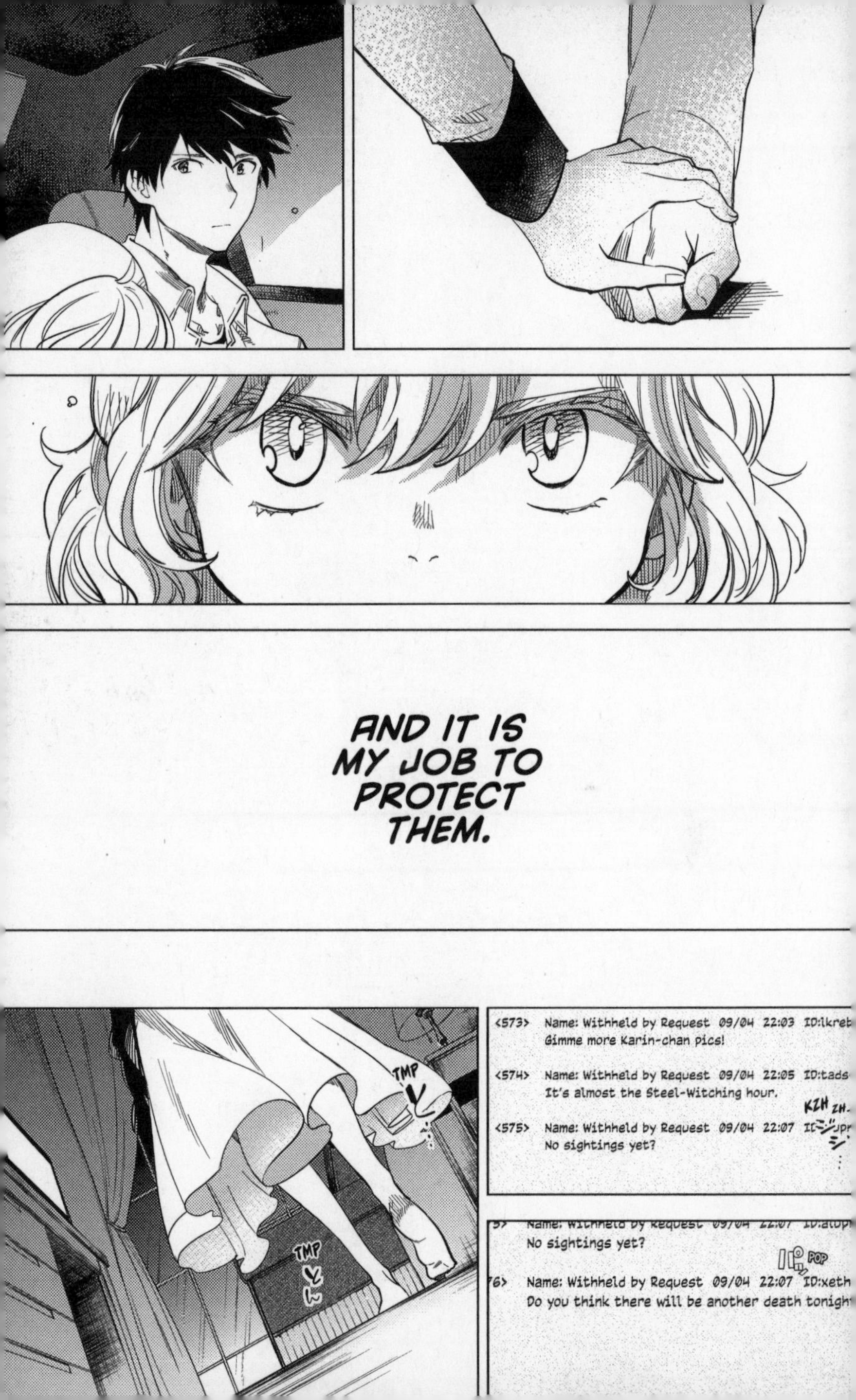

AND IT IS MY JOB TO PROTECT THEM.
<573> Name: Withheld by Request 09/04 22:03 ID:lkreb
Gimme more Karin-chan pics!
<574> Name: Withheld by Request 09/04 22:05 ID:tads
It's almost the Steel-Witching hour.
<575> Name: Withheld by Request 09/04 22:07
No sightings yet?
KZH ZH
No sightings yet?
POP
Name: Withheld by Request 09/04 22:07 ID:xeth
Do you think there will be another death tonigh
TMP
TMP

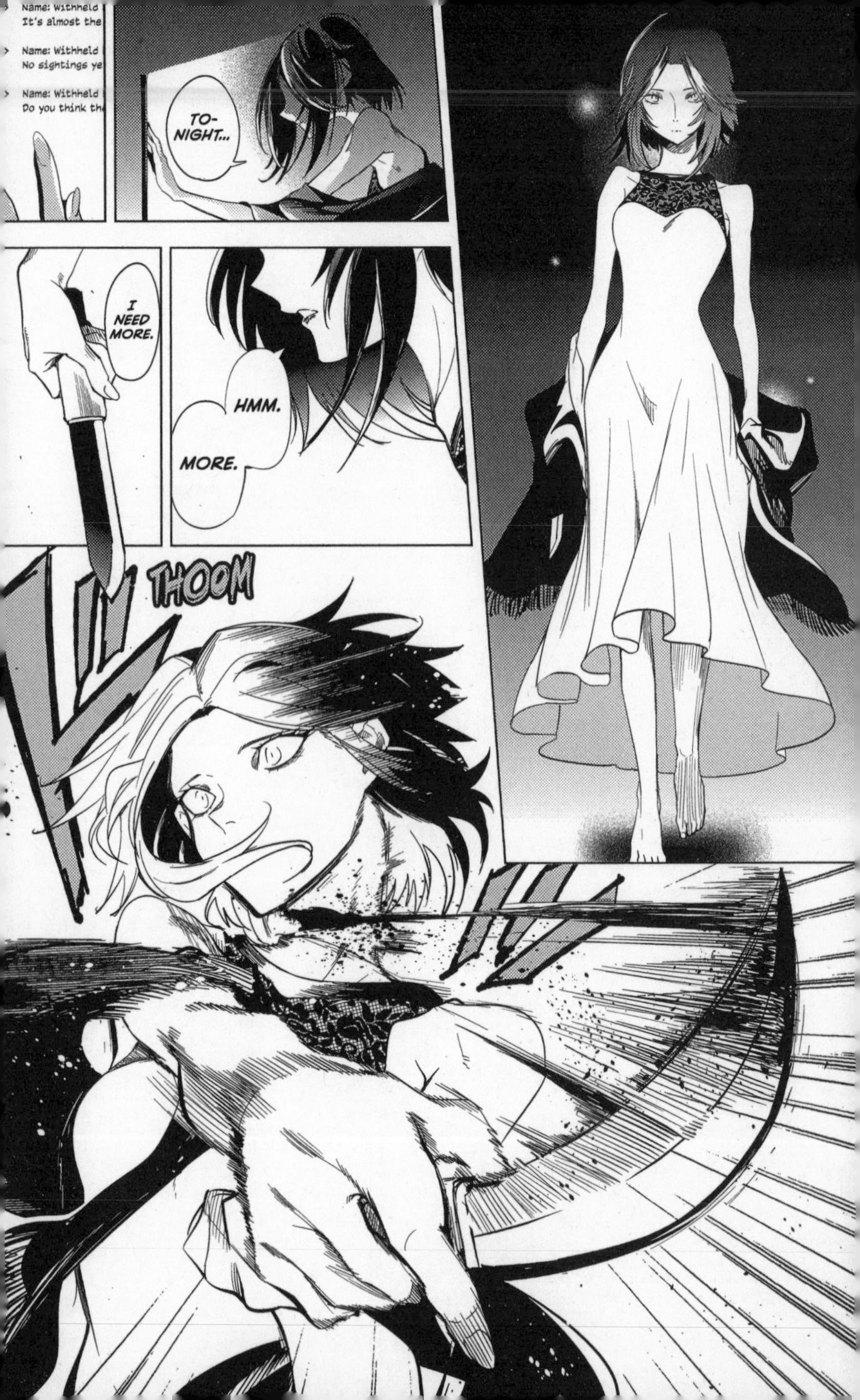
TO-NIGHT...
Name: Withheld
It's almost the
Name: Withheld
No sightings ye
Name: Withheld
Do you think th
HMM.
MORE.
I NEED MORE.
THOOM

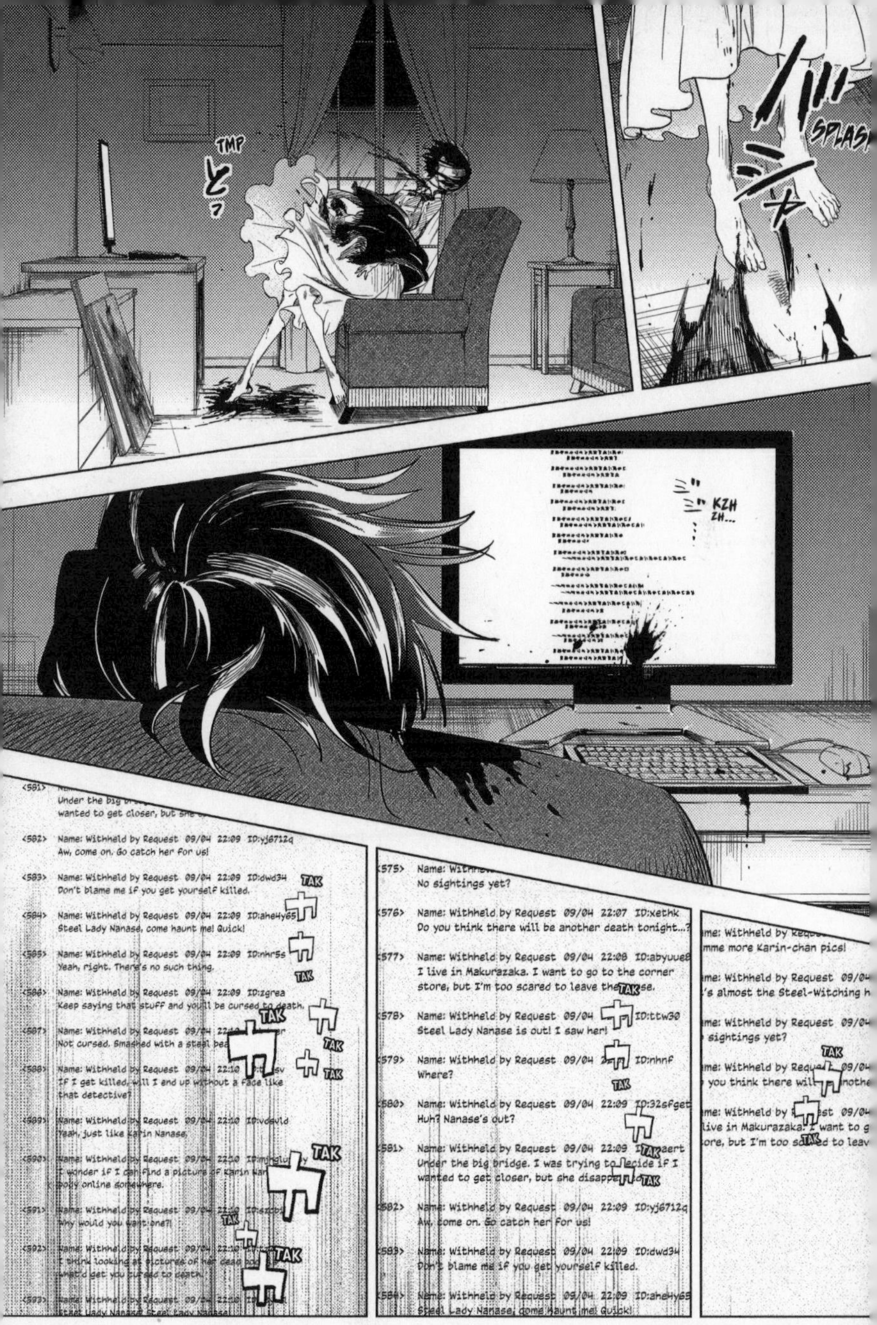
SPLASH
TMP
KZH
ZH...
me: Withheld by Request 09/04
's almost the Steel-Witching h
me: Withheld by Request 09/04
sightings yet?
TAK
you think there wil
live in Makurazaka. want to g
ore, but I'm too s ed to leav
TAK
<575> Name:
No sightings yet?
<576> Name: Withheld by Request 09/04 22:07 ID:xethk
Do you think there will be another death tonight...?
<577> Name: Withheld by Request 09/04 22:08 ID:abyuue8
I live in Makurazaka. I want to go to the corner
store, but I'm too scared to leave the se.
TAK
<578> Name: Withheld by Request 09/04 ID:ttw30
Steel Lady Nanase is out! I saw her!
<579> Name: Withheld by Request 09/04 ID:nhnf
Where?
TAK
<580> Name: Withheld by Request 09/04 22:09 ID:32sfget
Huh? Nanase's out?
<581> Name: Withheld by Request 09/04 22:09
TAK
Under the big bridge. I was trying to ecide if I
TAK
<582> Name: Withheld by Request 09/04 22:09 ID:yj6712q
Aw, come on. Go catch her for us!
<583> Name: Withheld by Request 09/04 22:09 ID:dwd34
Don't blame me if you get yourself killed.
<584> Name: Withheld by Request 09/04 22:09 ID:ahe4y65
Steel Lady Nanase, come haunt me! Quick!
<581>
Under the big
wanted to get closer, but
<582> Name: Withheld by Request 09/04 22:09 ID:yj6712q
Aw, come on. Go catch her for us!
<583> Name: Withheld by Request 09/04 22:09 ID:dwd34
Don't blame me if you get yourself killed.
TAK
<584> Name: Withheld by Request 09/04 22:09 ID:ahe4y65
Steel Lady Nanase, come haunt me! Quick!
<585> Name: Withheld by Request 09/04 22:09 ID:nhr5s
Yeah, right. There's no such thing.
TAK
<586> Name: Withheld by Request 09/04 22:09 ID:zgrea
Keep saying that stuff and you'll be cursed to death.
TAK
<587> Name: Withheld by Request 09/04
Not cursed. Smashed with a steel
TAK
<588> Name: Withheld by Request 09/04 22:10
If I get killed, will I end up without a face like
that detective?
TAK
<589> Name: Withheld by Request 09/04 22:10 ID:vdsvld
Yeah, just like Karin Nanase.
TAK
<590> Name: Withheld by Request 09/04 22:10
I wonder if I can find a picture of Karin
body online somewhere.
<591> Name: Withheld by Request 09/04 22:10
Why would you want one?!
TAK
<592> Name: Withheld by Request 09/04 22:10
I think looking at pictures of her dead
that'd get you cursed to death.
TAK
<593> Name: Withheld by Request 09/04 22:10
Steel Lady Nanase! Steel Lady Nanase!

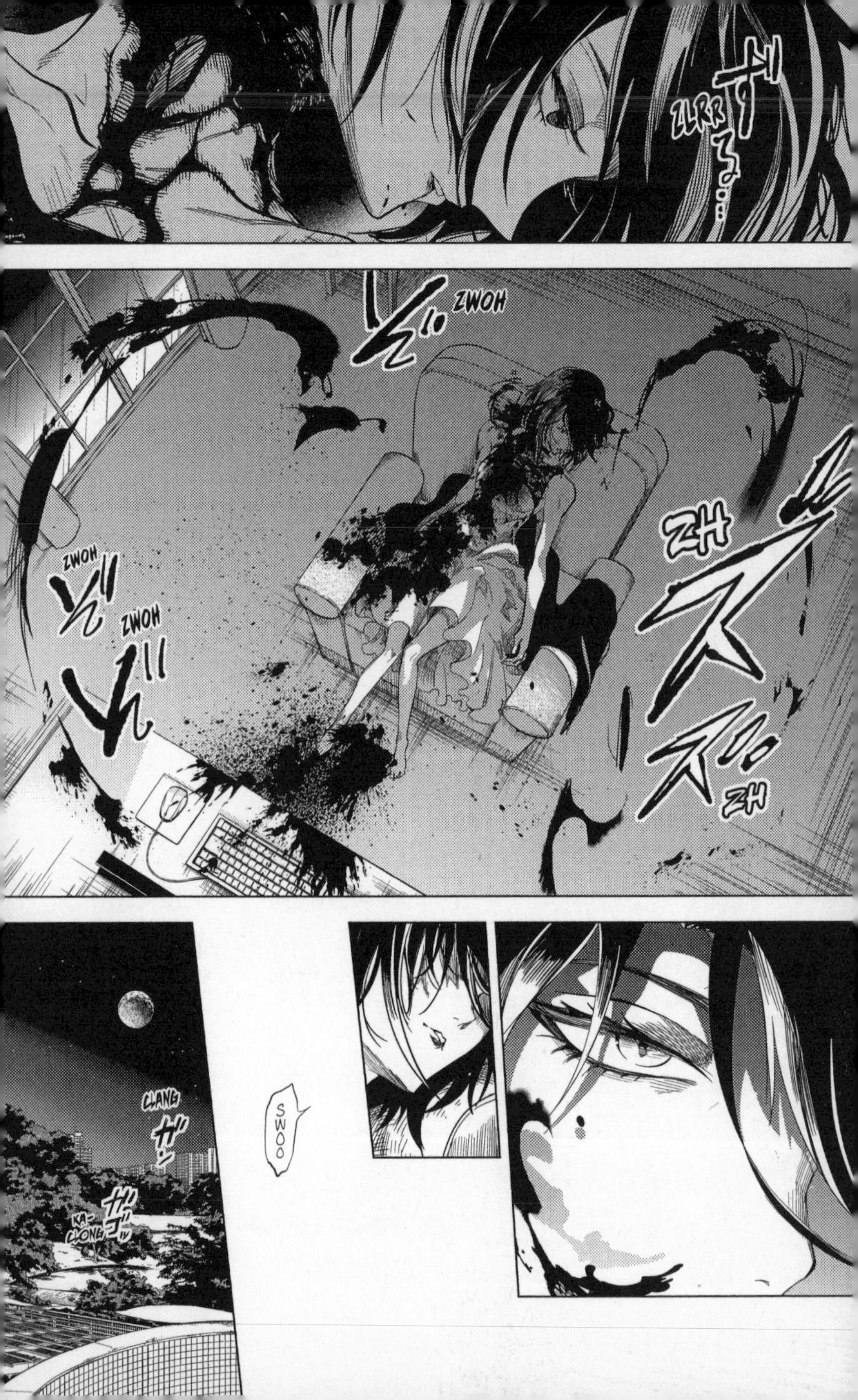
ZLRR
ZH
ZH
ZWOH
ZWOH
ZWOH
SWOO
CLANG
KA-CLONG

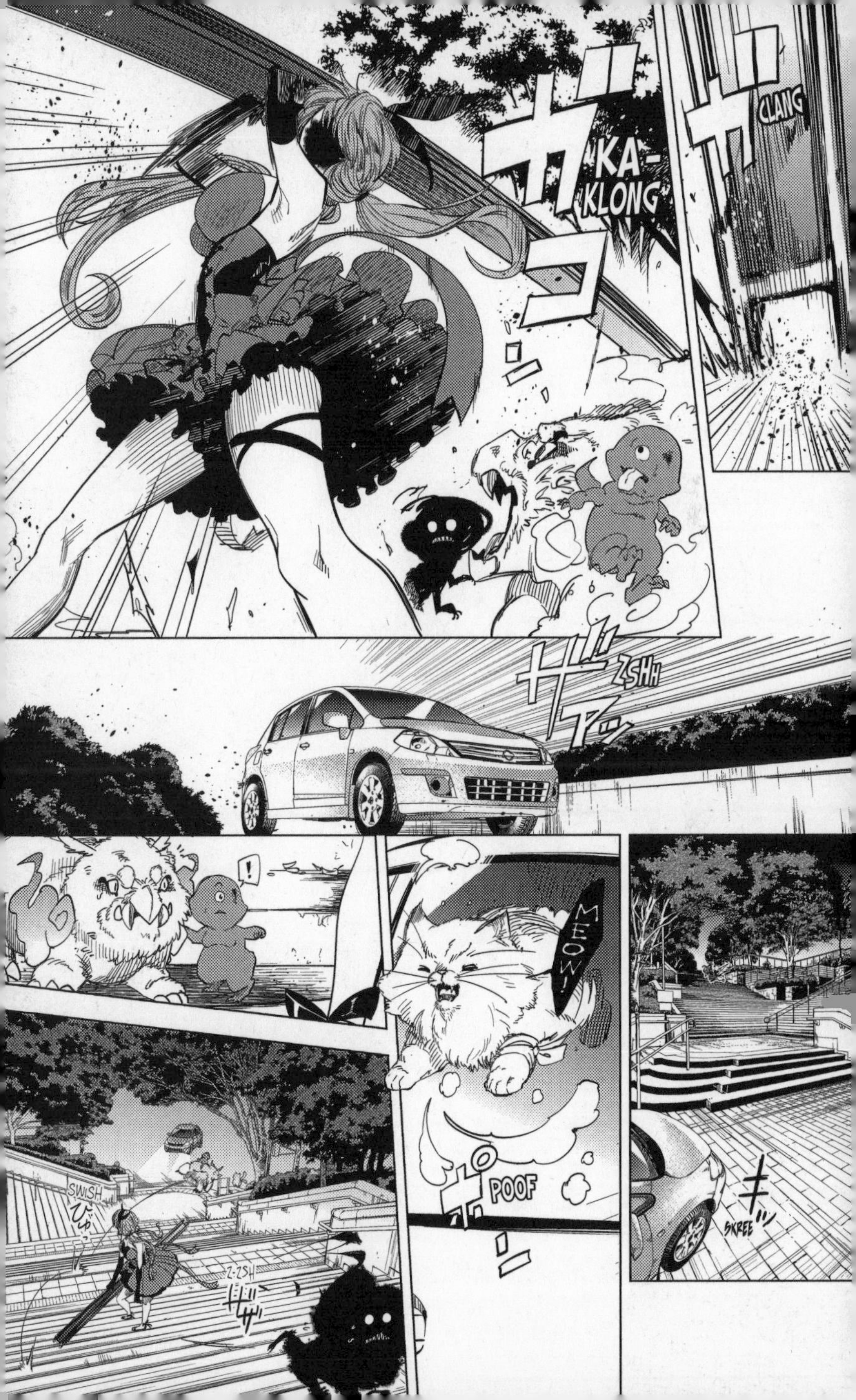
CLANG
KA-KLONG
ZSHH
SKREE
MEOW!
POOF
!
SWISH
Z-ZSH

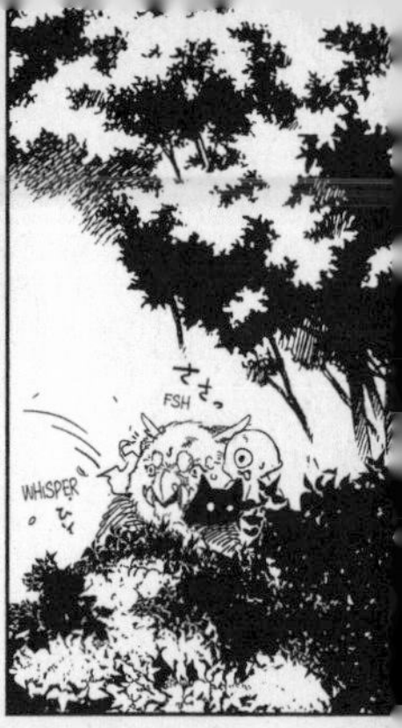
ささっ
FSH
WHISPER
ひそ
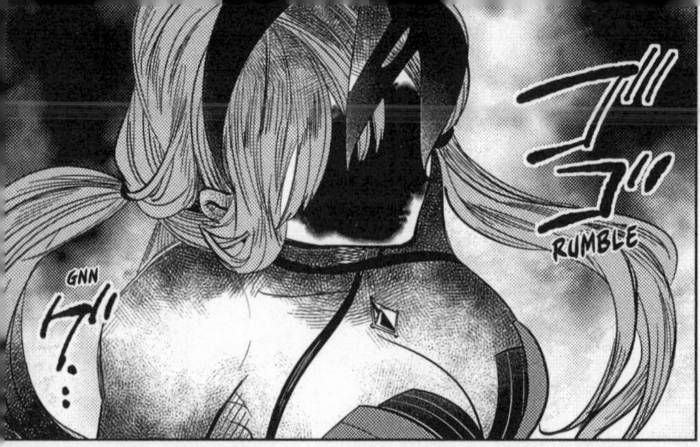
ゴゴ
RUMBLE
GNN
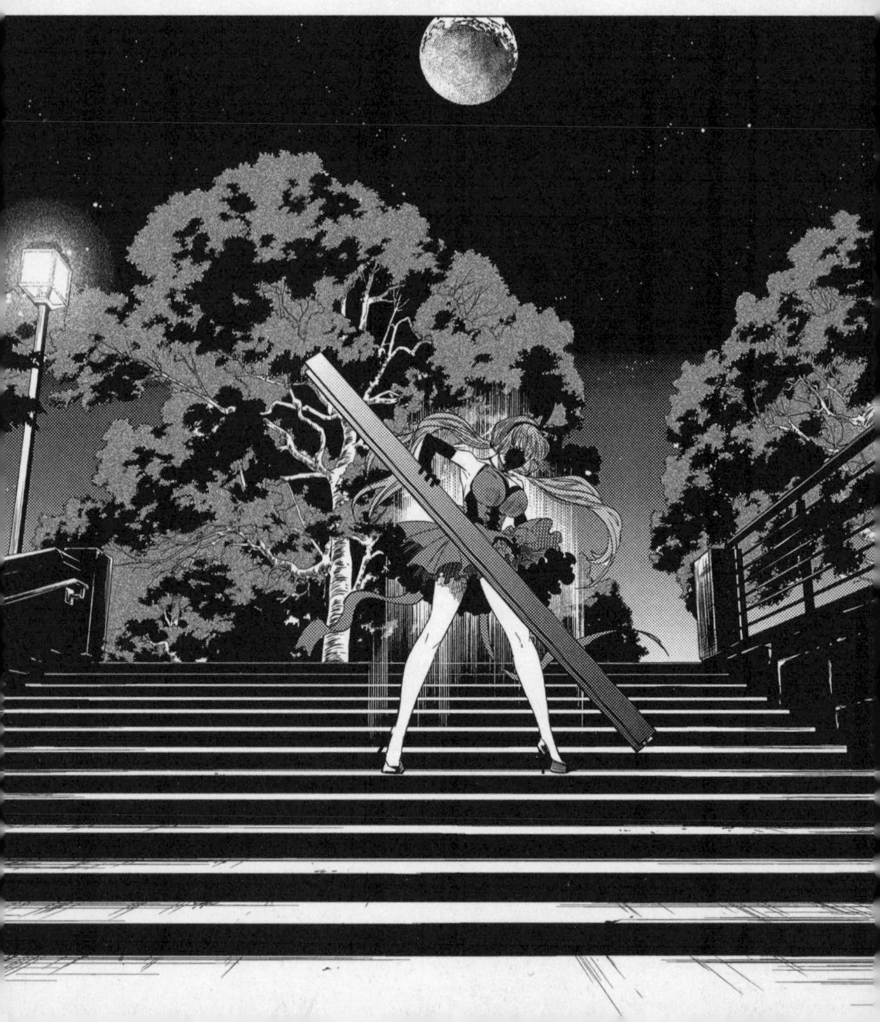

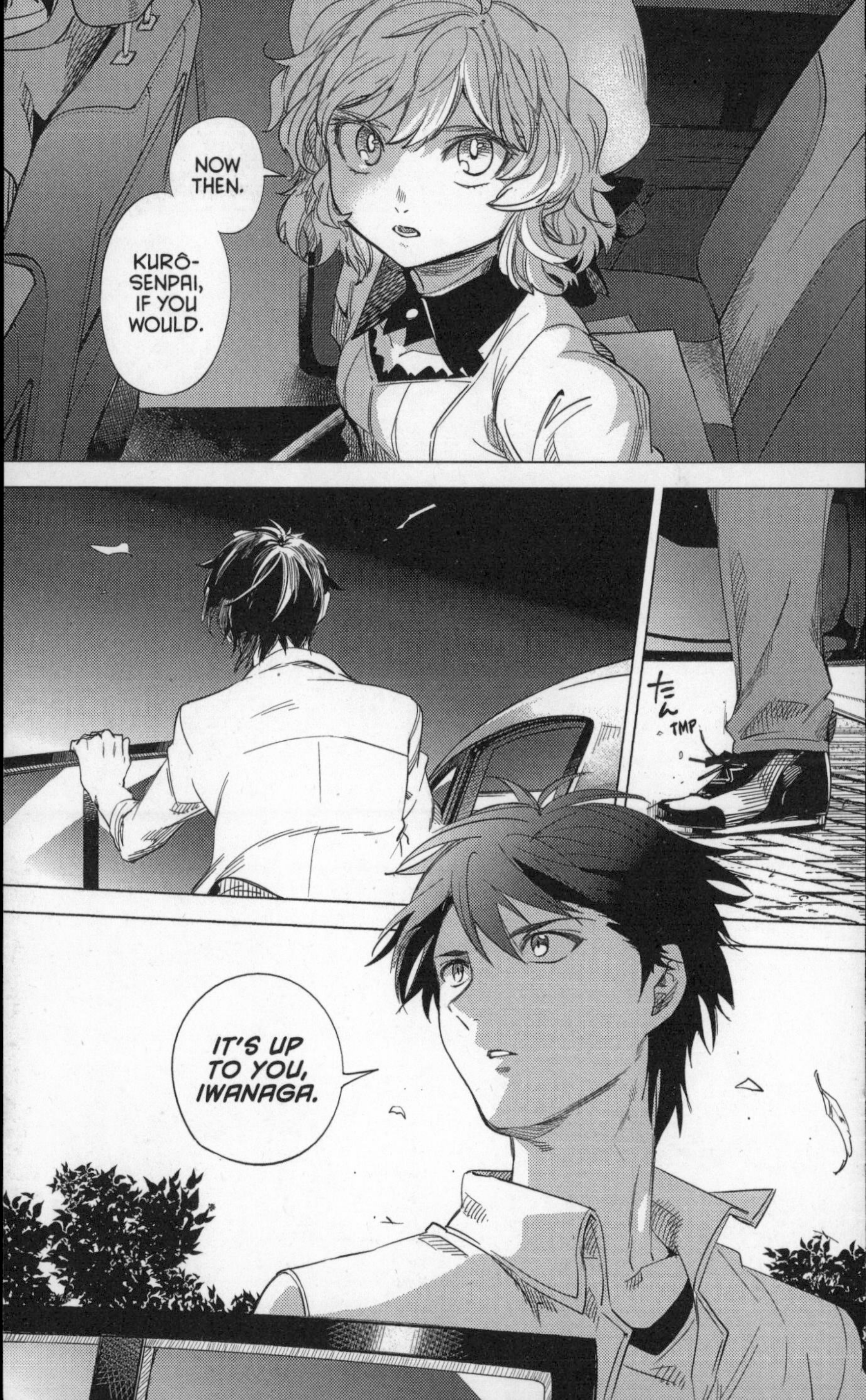
NOW THEN.
KURÔ-SENPAI, IF YOU WOULD.
たん
TMP
IT'S UP TO YOU, IWANAGA.

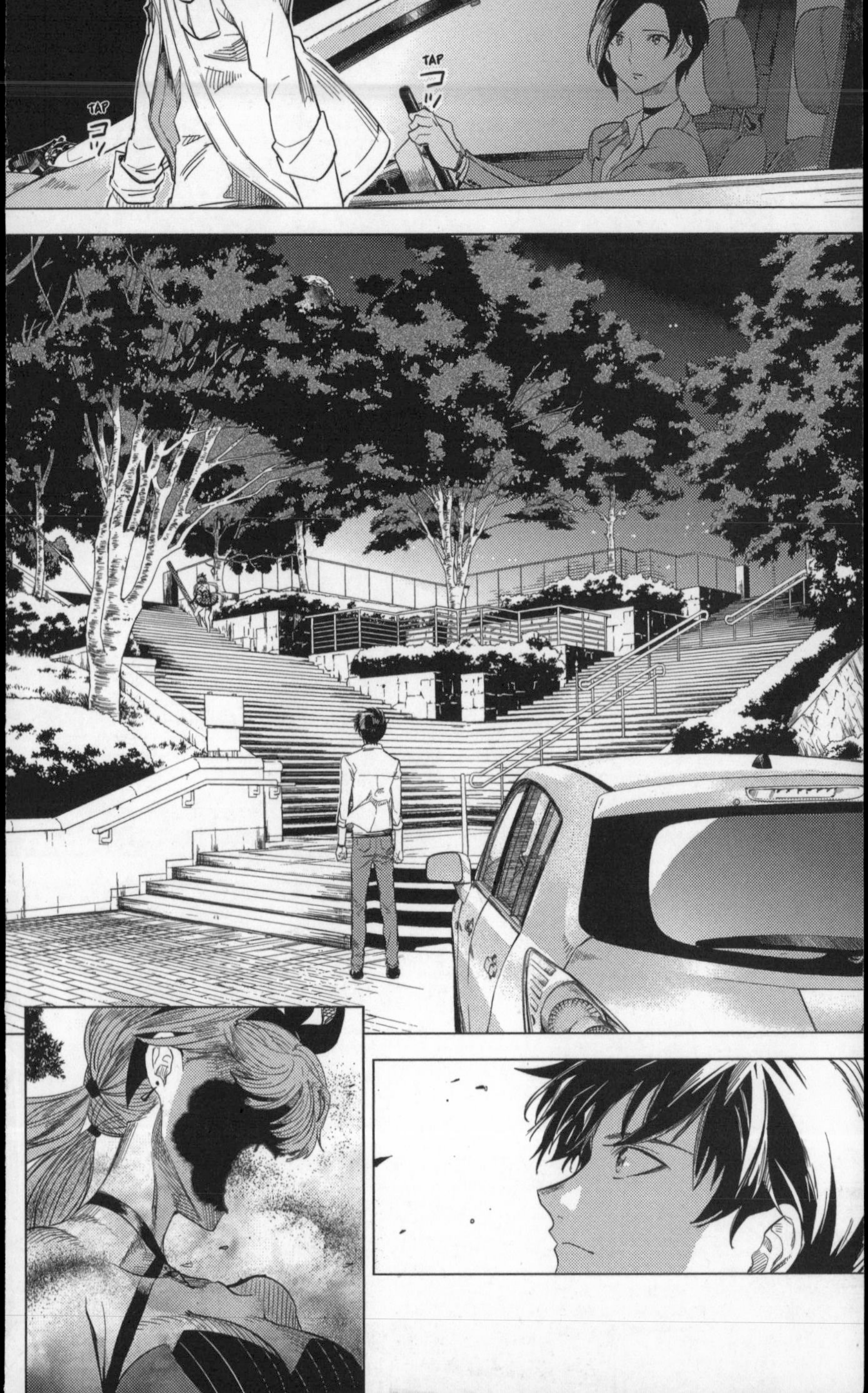
TAP
コツ
TAP
コツ

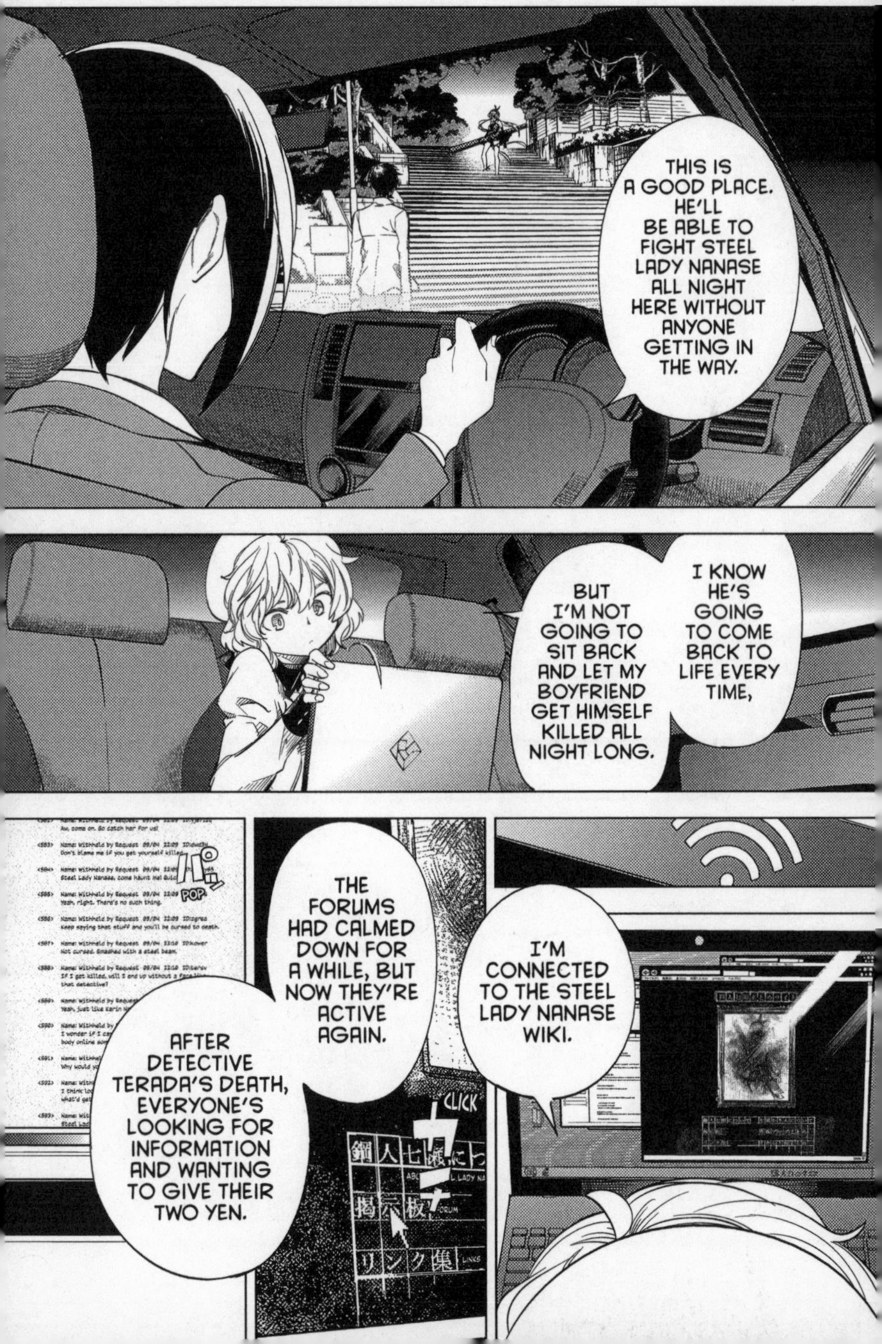
THIS IS A GOOD PLACE. HE'LL BE ABLE TO FIGHT STEEL LADY NANASE ALL NIGHT HERE WITHOUT ANYONE GETTING IN THE WAY.
I KNOW HE'S GOING TO COME BACK TO LIFE EVERY TIME,
BUT I'M NOT GOING TO SIT BACK AND LET MY BOYFRIEND GET HIMSELF KILLED ALL NIGHT LONG.
I'M CONNECTED TO THE STEEL LADY NANASE WIKI.
CLICK
THE FORUMS HAD CALMED DOWN FOR A WHILE, BUT NOW THEY'RE ACTIVE AGAIN.
AFTER DETECTIVE TERADA'S DEATH, EVERYONE'S LOOKING FOR INFORMATION AND WANTING TO GIVE THEIR TWO YEN.
POP

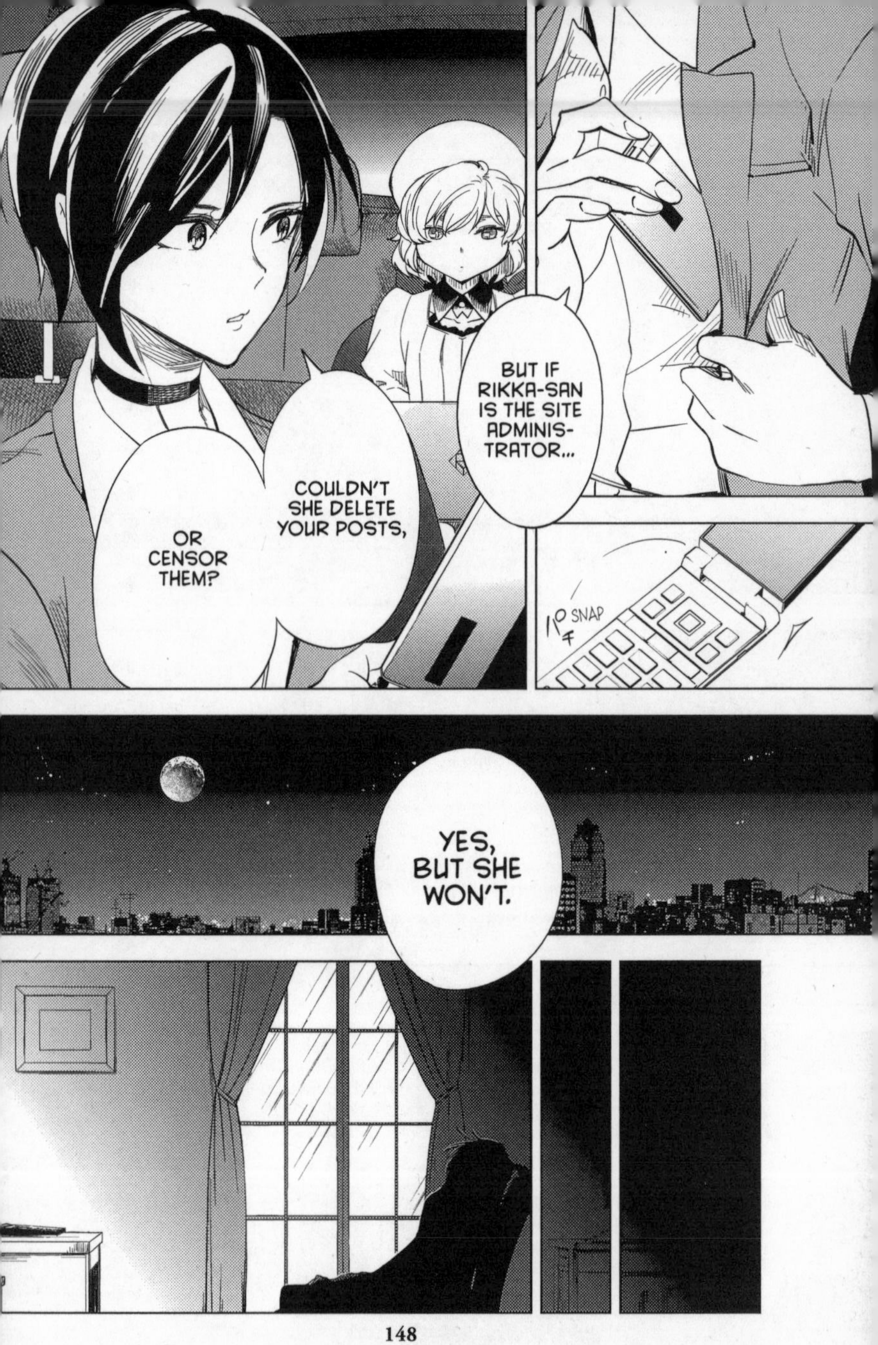
BUT IF RIKKA-SAN IS THE SITE ADMINISTRATOR...
パチ SNAP
COULDN'T SHE DELETE YOUR POSTS,
OR CENSOR THEM?
YES, BUT SHE WON'T.

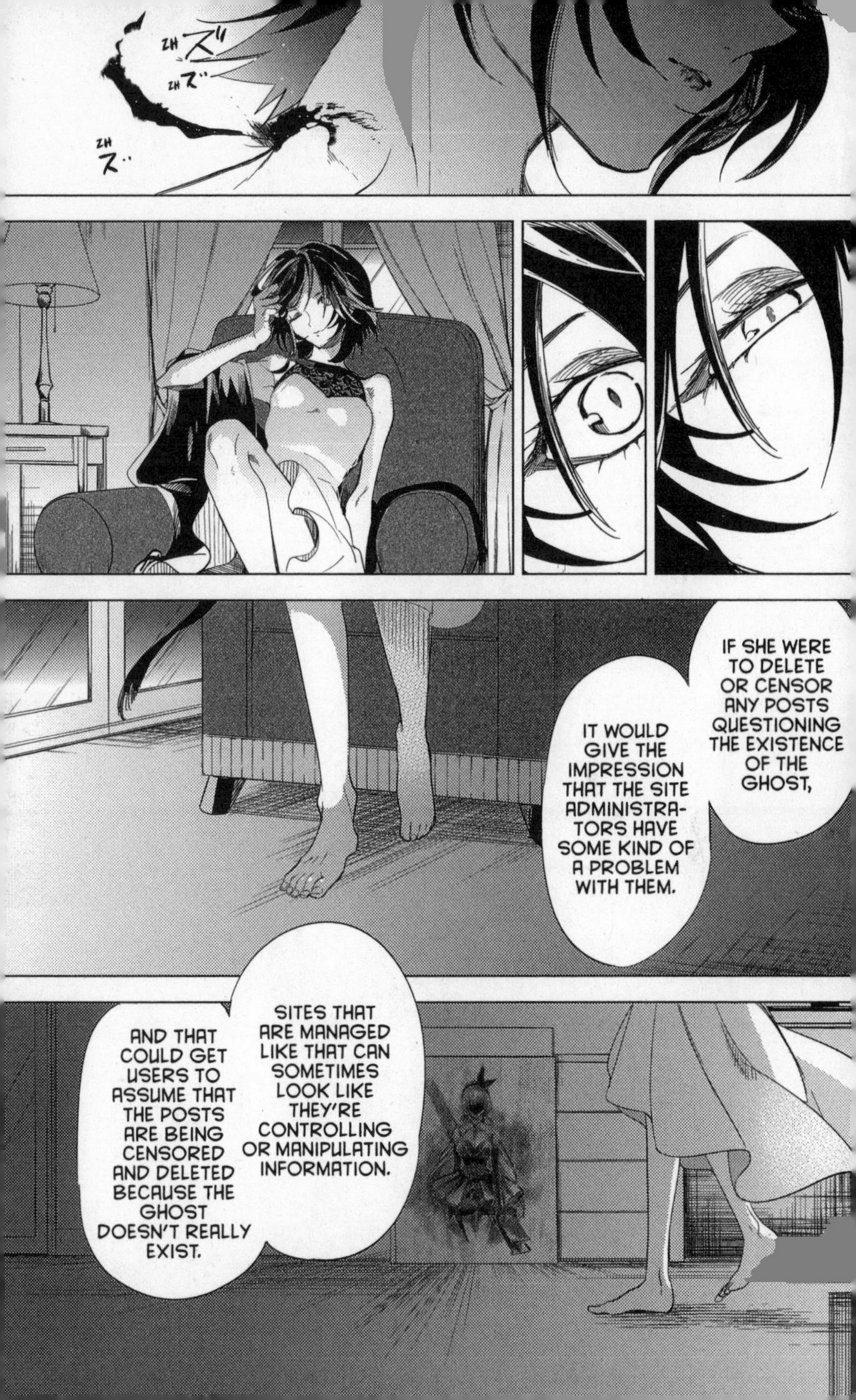
ZH ズ
ZH ズ
ZH ズ..
IF SHE WERE TO DELETE OR CENSOR ANY POSTS QUESTIONING THE EXISTENCE OF THE GHOST,
IT WOULD GIVE THE IMPRESSION THAT THE SITE ADMINISTRA-TORS HAVE SOME KIND OF A PROBLEM WITH THEM.
SITES THAT ARE MANAGED LIKE THAT CAN SOMETIMES LOOK LIKE THEY'RE CONTROLLING OR MANIPULATING INFORMATION.
AND THAT COULD GET USERS TO ASSUME THAT THE POSTS ARE BEING CENSORED AND DELETED BECAUSE THE GHOST DOESN'T REALLY EXIST.

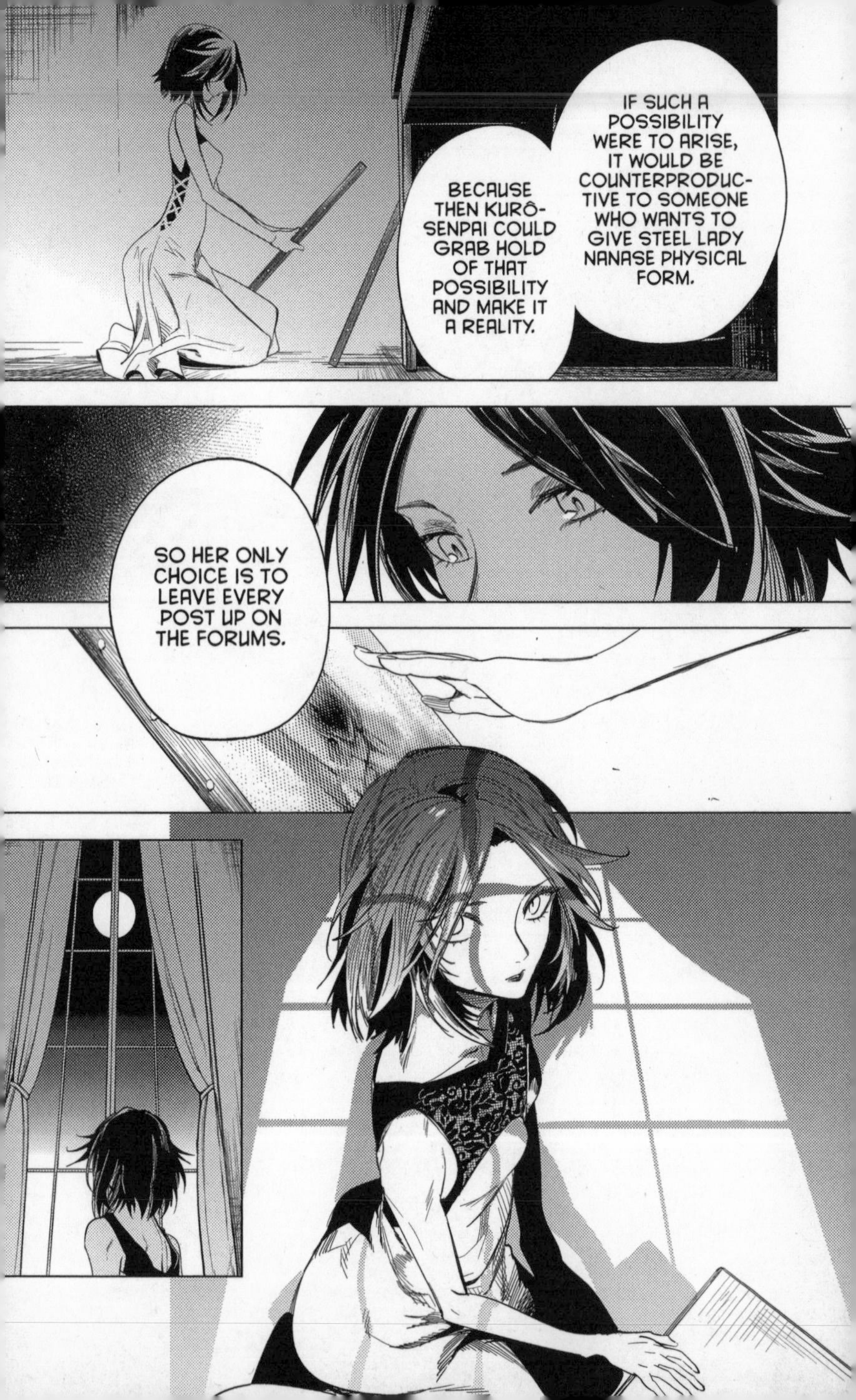
IF SUCH A POSSIBILITY WERE TO ARISE, IT WOULD BE COUNTERPRODUC-TIVE TO SOMEONE WHO WANTS TO GIVE STEEL LADY NANASE PHYSICAL FORM.
BECAUSE THEN KURÔ-SENPAI COULD GRAB HOLD OF THAT POSSIBILITY AND MAKE IT A REALITY.
SO HER ONLY CHOICE IS TO LEAVE EVERY POST UP ON THE FORUMS.

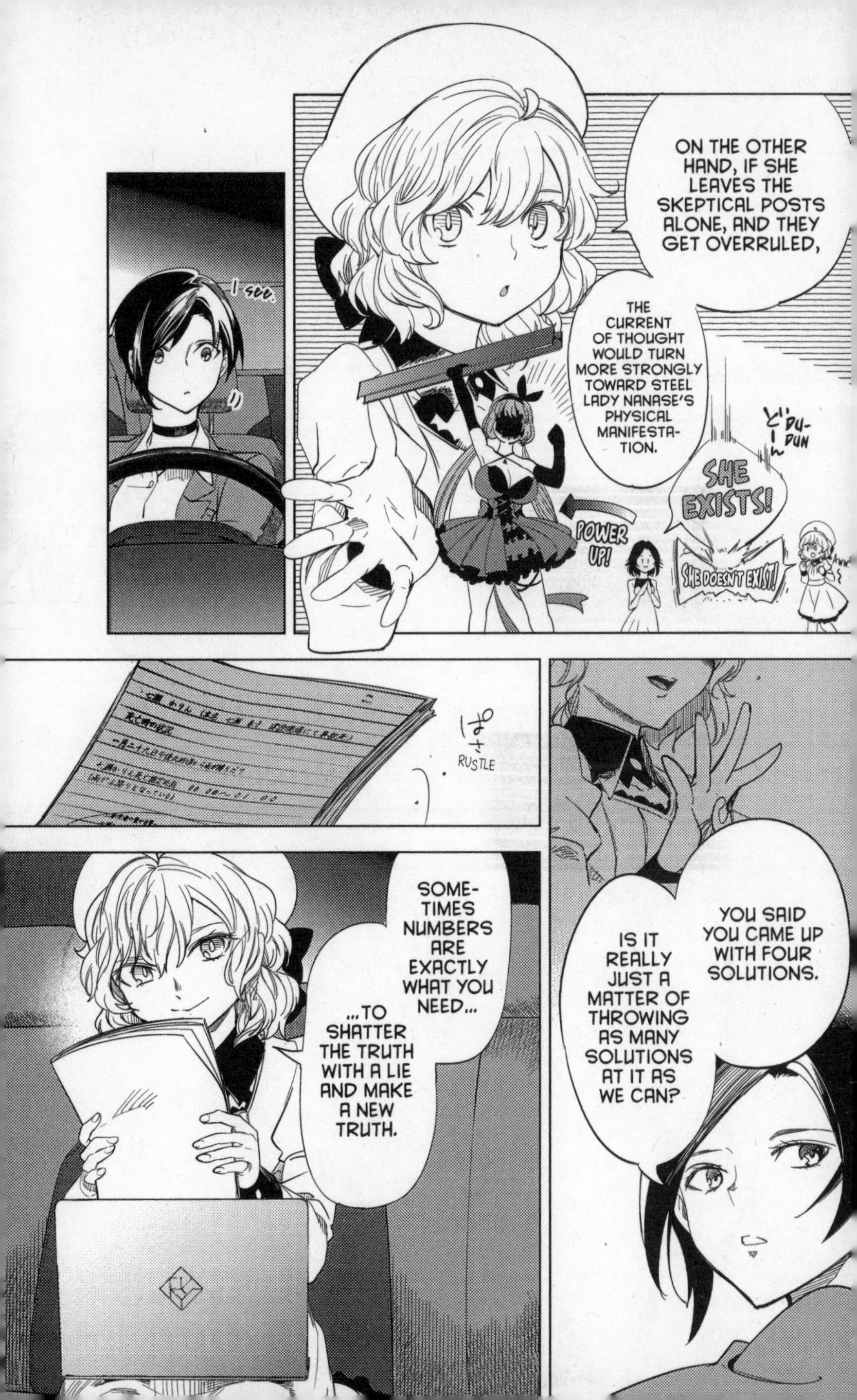
ON THE OTHER HAND, IF SHE LEAVES THE SKEPTICAL POSTS ALONE, AND THEY GET OVERRULED,
THE CURRENT OF THOUGHT WOULD TURN MORE STRONGLY TOWARD STEEL LADY NANASE'S PHYSICAL MANIFESTA-TION.
どーん DU-DUN
SHE EXISTS!
POWER UP!
SHE DOESN'T EXIST!
I see.
YOU SAID YOU CAME UP WITH FOUR SOLUTIONS.
IS IT REALLY JUST A MATTER OF THROWING AS MANY SOLUTIONS AT IT AS WE CAN?
ぱさ RUSTLE
SOME-TIMES NUMBERS ARE EXACTLY WHAT YOU NEED...
...TO SHATTER THE TRUTH WITH A LIE AND MAKE A NEW TRUTH.

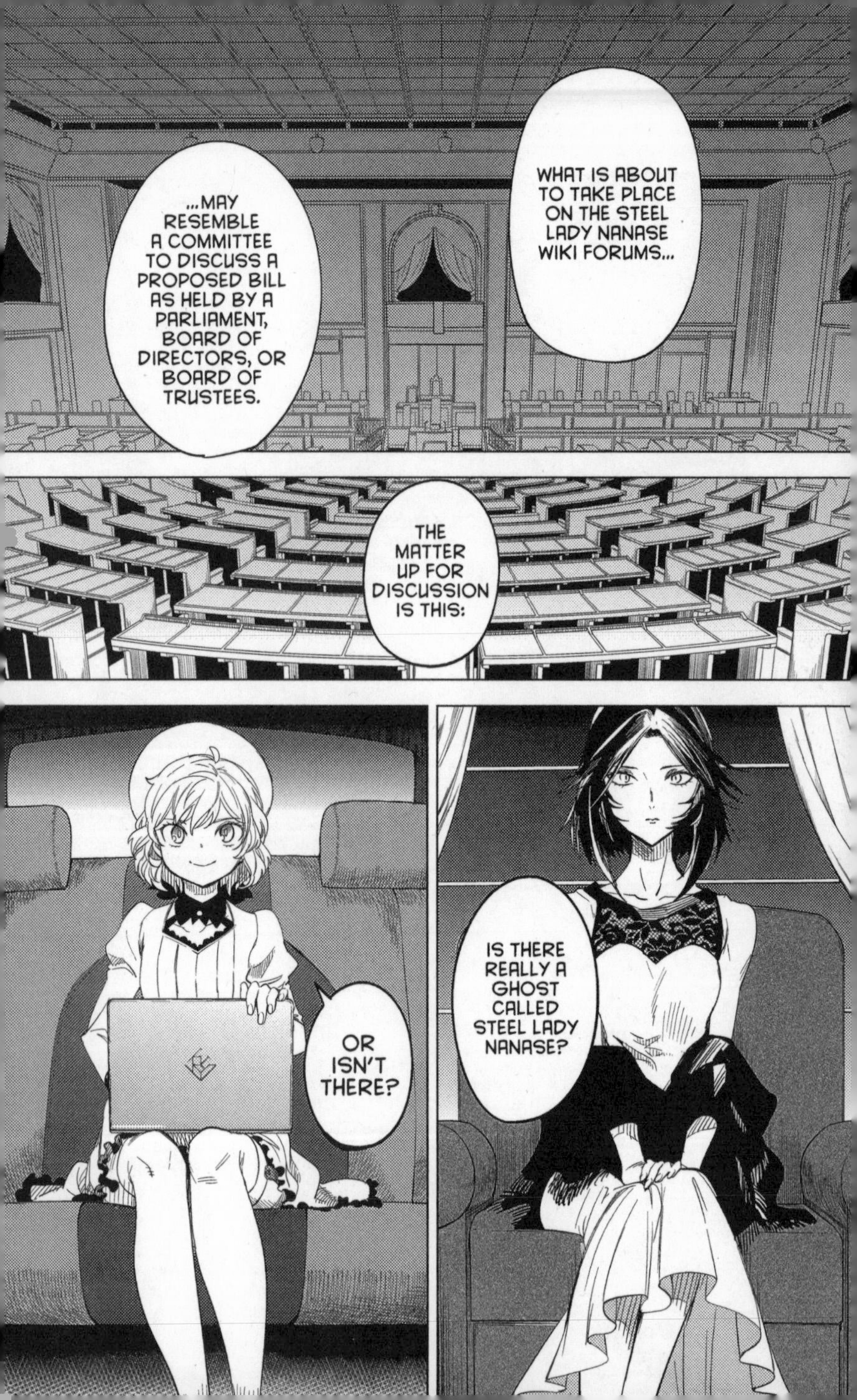
WHAT IS ABOUT TO TAKE PLACE ON THE STEEL LADY NANASE WIKI FORUMS...
...MAY RESEMBLE A COMMITTEE TO DISCUSS A PROPOSED BILL AS HELD BY A PARLIAMENT, BOARD OF DIRECTORS, OR BOARD OF TRUSTEES.
THE MATTER UP FOR DISCUSSION IS THIS:
IS THERE REALLY A GHOST CALLED STEEL LADY NANASE?
OR ISN'T THERE?

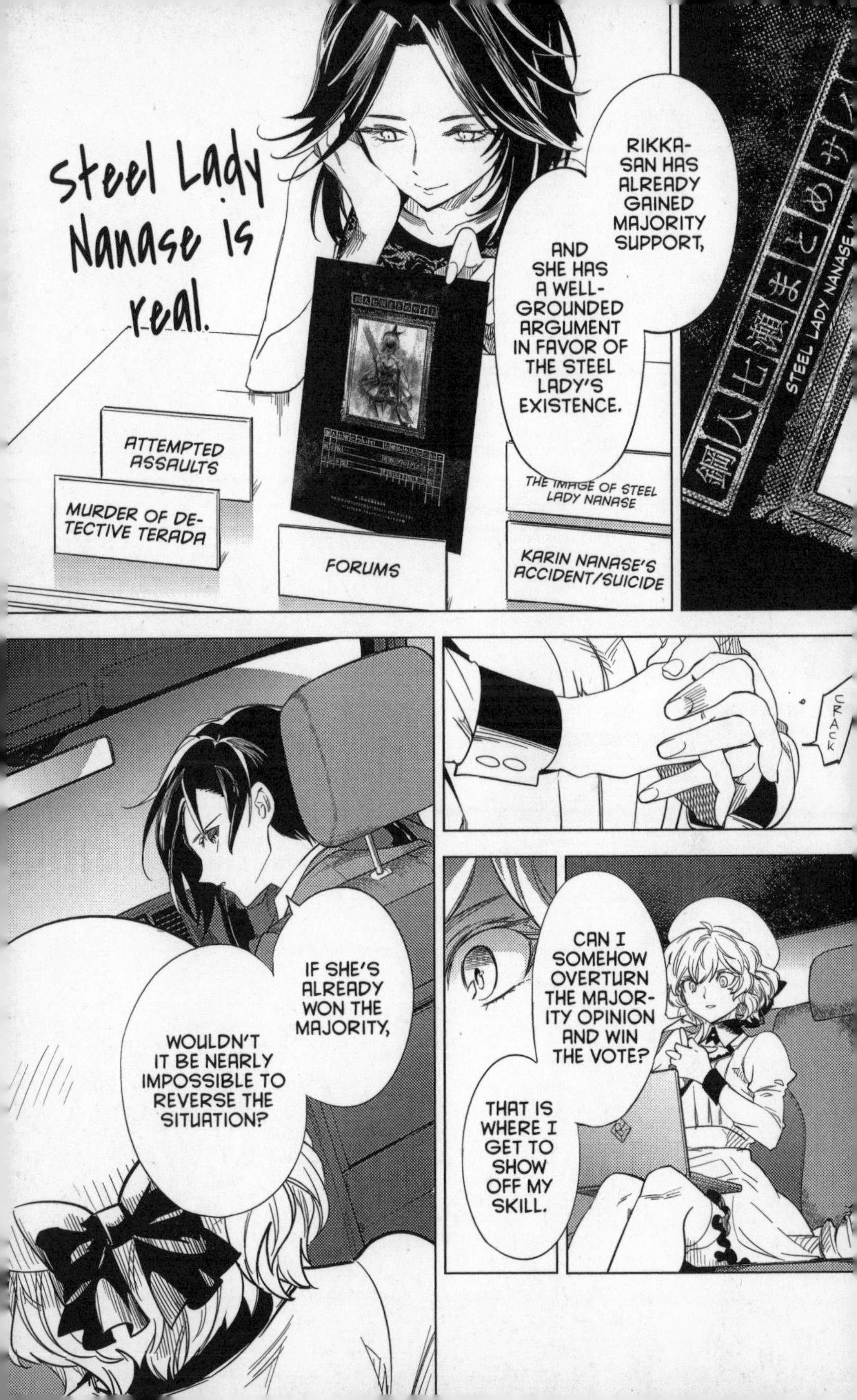
鋼人七瀬まとめサ
STEEL LADY NANASE
RIKKA-SAN HAS ALREADY GAINED MAJORITY SUPPORT,
AND SHE HAS A WELL-GROUNDED ARGUMENT IN FAVOR OF THE STEEL LADY'S EXISTENCE.
THE IMAGE OF STEEL LADY NANASE
KARIN NANASE'S ACCIDENT/SUICIDE
FORUMS
ATTEMPTED ASSAULTS
MURDER OF DETECTIVE TERADA
Steel Lady Nanase is real.
CRACK
CAN I SOMEHOW OVERTURN THE MAJORITY OPINION AND WIN THE VOTE?
THAT IS WHERE I GET TO SHOW OFF MY SKILL.
IF SHE'S ALREADY WON THE MAJORITY,
WOULDN'T IT BE NEARLY IMPOSSIBLE TO REVERSE THE SITUATION?

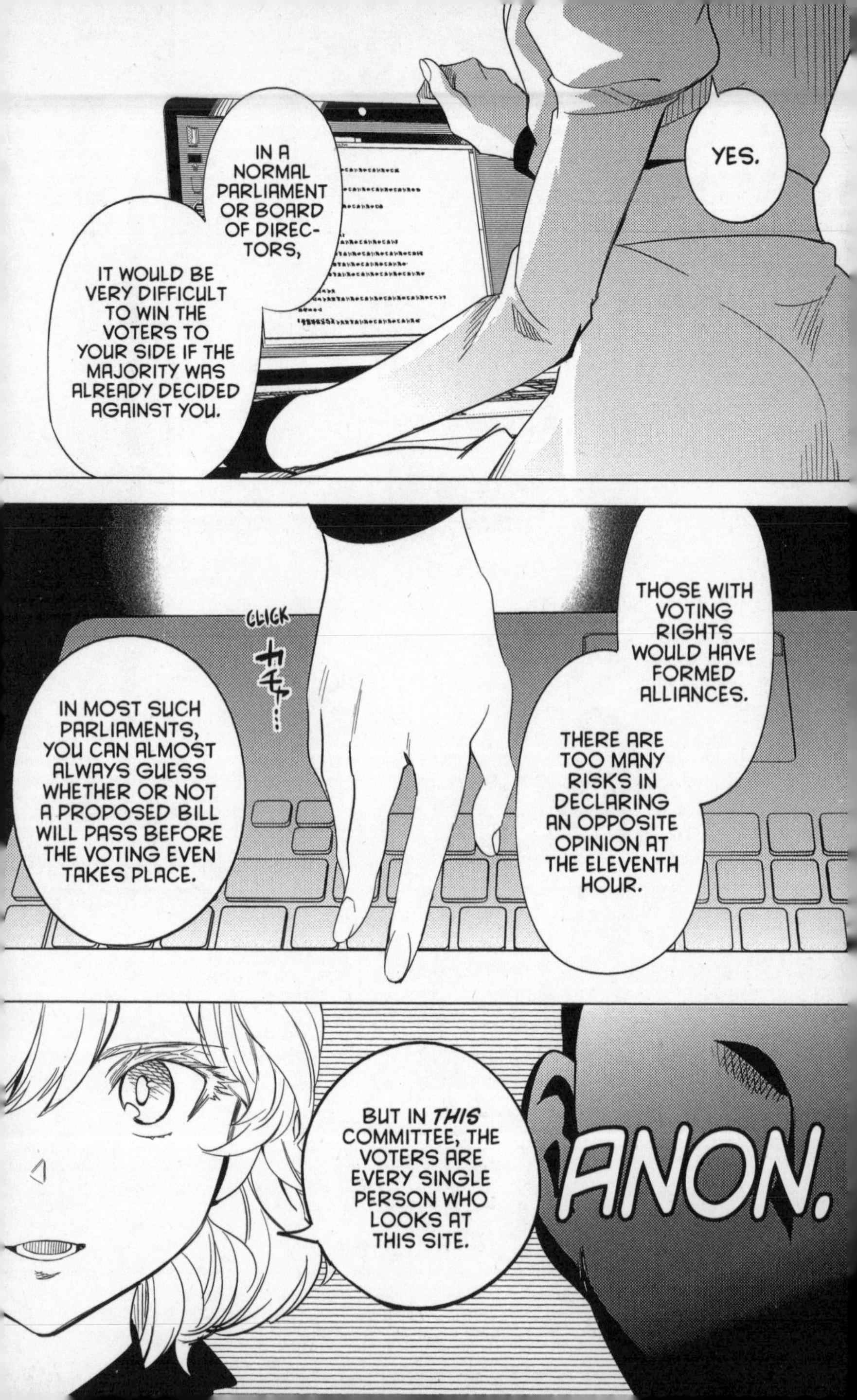
YES.
IN A NORMAL PARLIAMENT OR BOARD OF DIREC-TORS,
IT WOULD BE VERY DIFFICULT TO WIN THE VOTERS TO YOUR SIDE IF THE MAJORITY WAS ALREADY DECIDED AGAINST YOU.
THOSE WITH VOTING RIGHTS WOULD HAVE FORMED ALLIANCES.
THERE ARE TOO MANY RISKS IN DECLARING AN OPPOSITE OPINION AT THE ELEVENTH HOUR.
CLICK
カチャ…
IN MOST SUCH PARLIAMENTS, YOU CAN ALMOST ALWAYS GUESS WHETHER OR NOT A PROPOSED BILL WILL PASS BEFORE THE VOTING EVEN TAKES PLACE.
ANON.
BUT IN *THIS* COMMITTEE, THE VOTERS ARE EVERY SINGLE PERSON WHO LOOKS AT THIS SITE.

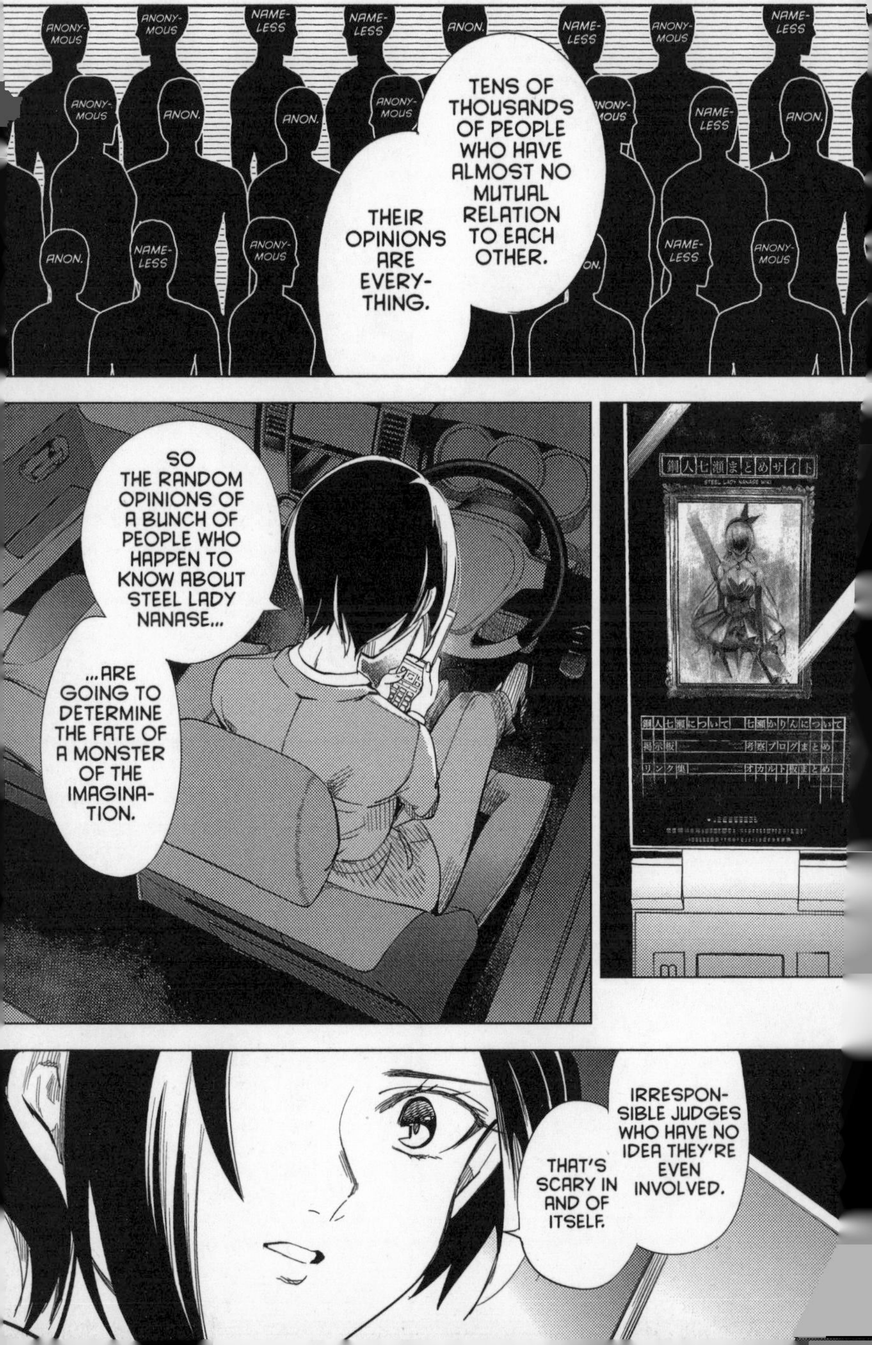
NAME-LESS
ANONY-MOUS
NAME-LESS
ANON.
NAME-LESS
NAME-LESS
ANONY-MOUS
ANON.
NAME-LESS
ANONY-MOUS
ANON.
ANON.
ANONY-MOUS
TENS OF THOUSANDS OF PEOPLE WHO HAVE ALMOST NO MUTUAL RELATION TO EACH OTHER.
THEIR OPINIONS ARE EVERY-THING.
ANONY-MOUS
NAME-LESS
ANONY-MOUS
NAME-LESS
ANON.
鋼人七瀬まとめサイト
STEEL LADY NANASE WIKI
鋼人七瀬について
七瀬かりんについて
掲示板
考察ブログまとめ
リンク集
オカルト板まとめ
SO THE RANDOM OPINIONS OF A BUNCH OF PEOPLE WHO HAPPEN TO KNOW ABOUT STEEL LADY NANASE...
...ARE GOING TO DETERMINE THE FATE OF A MONSTER OF THE IMAGINA-TION.
IRRESPON-SIBLE JUDGES WHO HAVE NO IDEA THEY'RE EVEN INVOLVED.
THAT'S SCARY IN AND OF ITSELF.

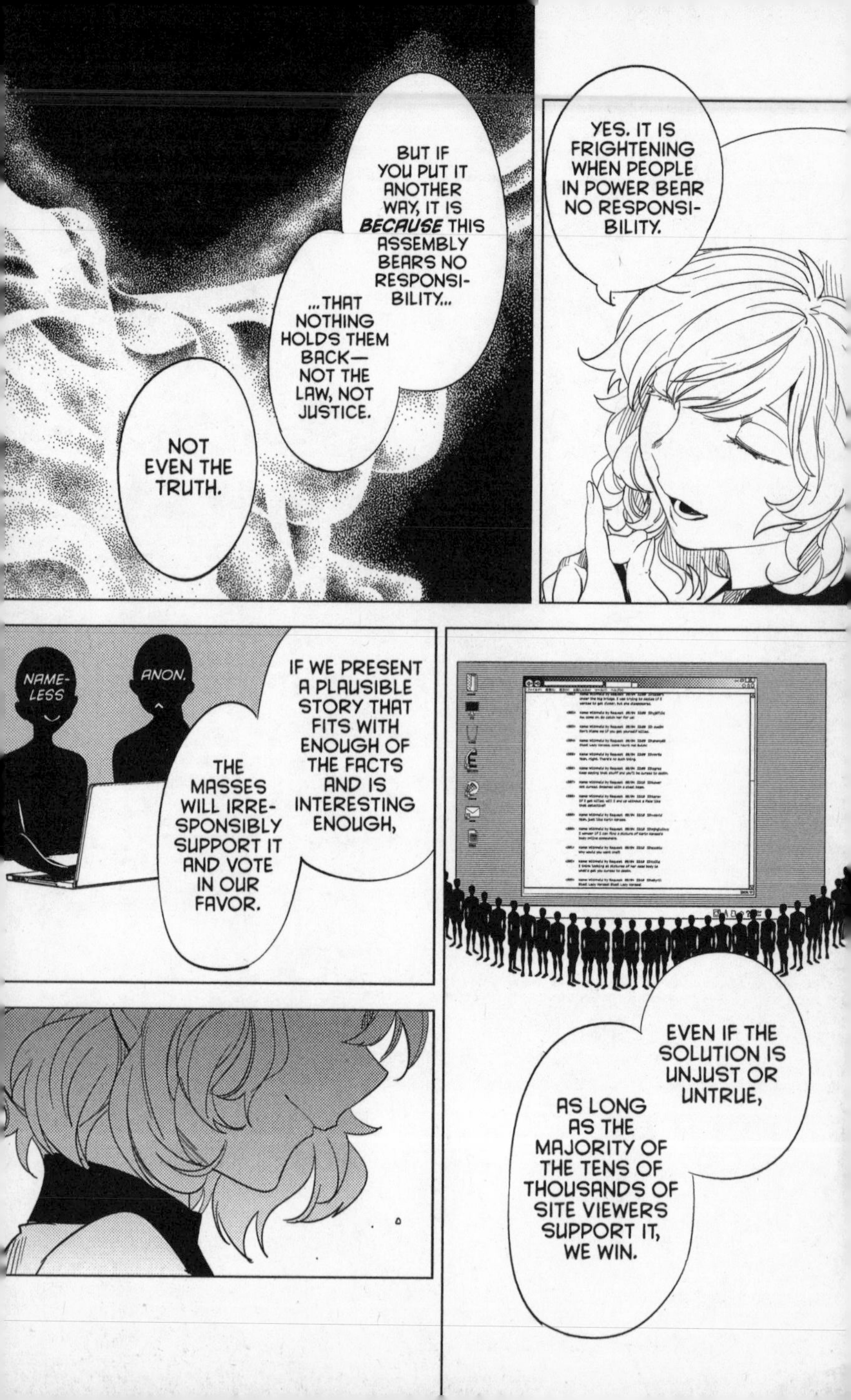
YES. IT IS FRIGHTENING WHEN PEOPLE IN POWER BEAR NO RESPONSI-BILITY.
BUT IF YOU PUT IT ANOTHER WAY, IT IS *BECAUSE* THIS ASSEMBLY BEARS NO RESPONSI-BILITY...
...THAT NOTHING HOLDS THEM BACK—NOT THE LAW, NOT JUSTICE.
NOT EVEN THE TRUTH.
EVEN IF THE SOLUTION IS UNJUST OR UNTRUE,
AS LONG AS THE MAJORITY OF THE TENS OF THOUSANDS OF SITE VIEWERS SUPPORT IT, WE WIN.
ANON.
NAME-LESS
IF WE PRESENT A PLAUSIBLE STORY THAT FITS WITH ENOUGH OF THE FACTS AND IS INTERESTING ENOUGH,
THE MASSES WILL IRRE-SPONSIBLY SUPPORT IT AND VOTE IN OUR FAVOR.

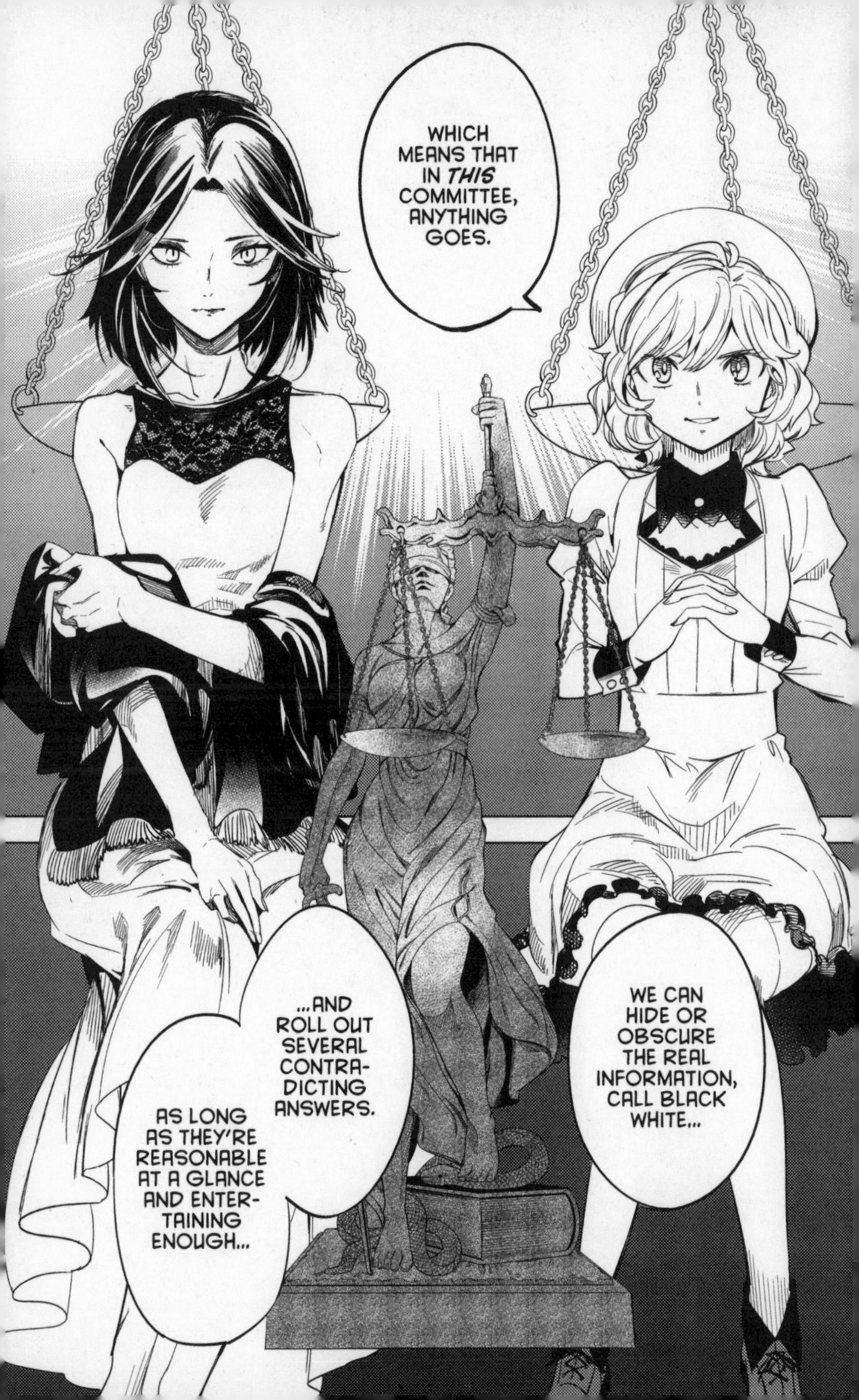
WHICH MEANS THAT IN *THIS* COMMITTEE, ANYTHING GOES.
WE CAN HIDE OR OBSCURE THE REAL INFORMATION, CALL BLACK WHITE...
...AND ROLL OUT SEVERAL CONTRA-DICTING ANSWERS.
AS LONG AS THEY'RE REASONABLE AT A GLANCE AND ENTER-TAINING ENOUGH...

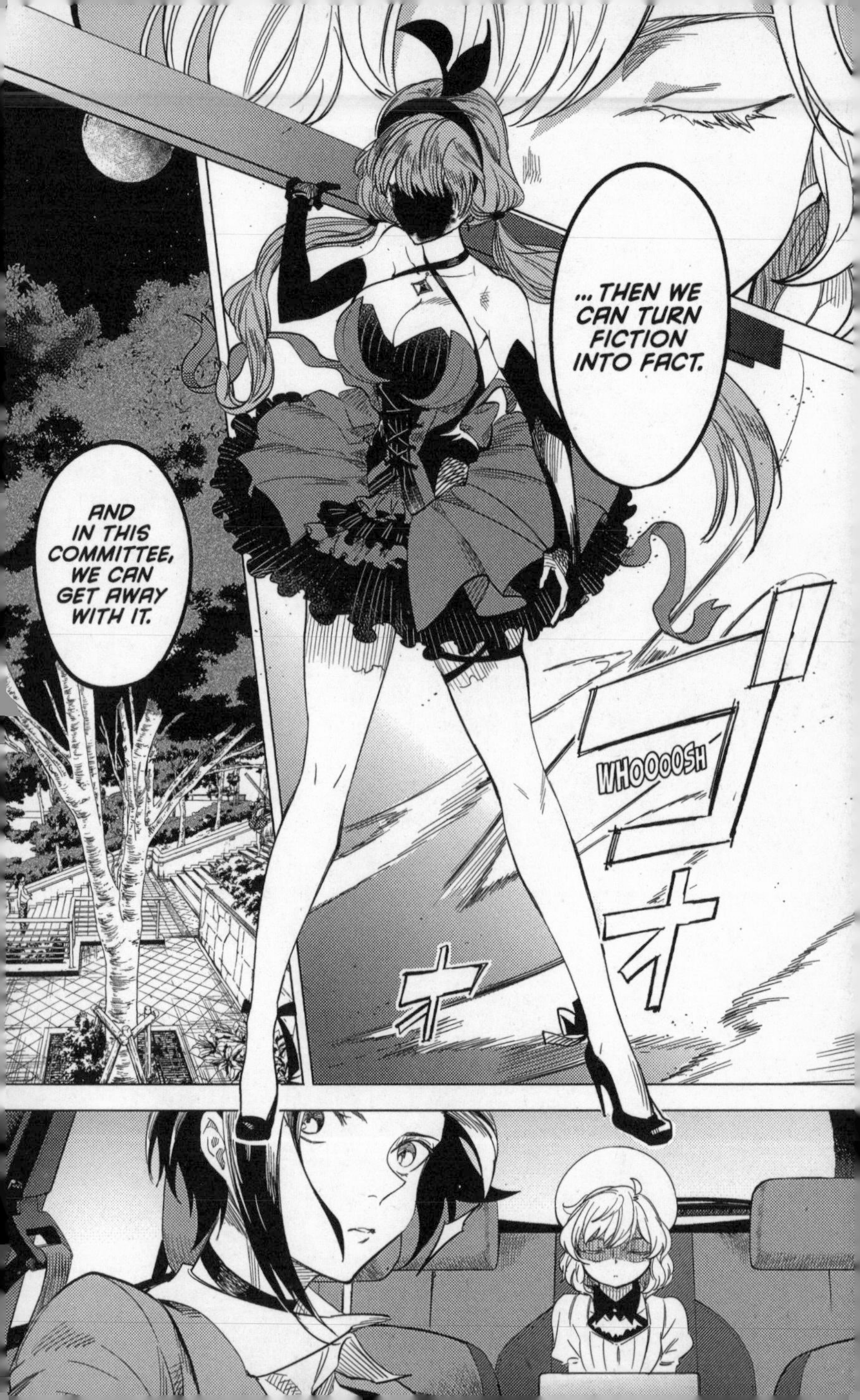
...THEN WE CAN TURN FICTION INTO FACT.
AND IN THIS COMMITTEE, WE CAN GET AWAY WITH IT.
WHOOOOOSH

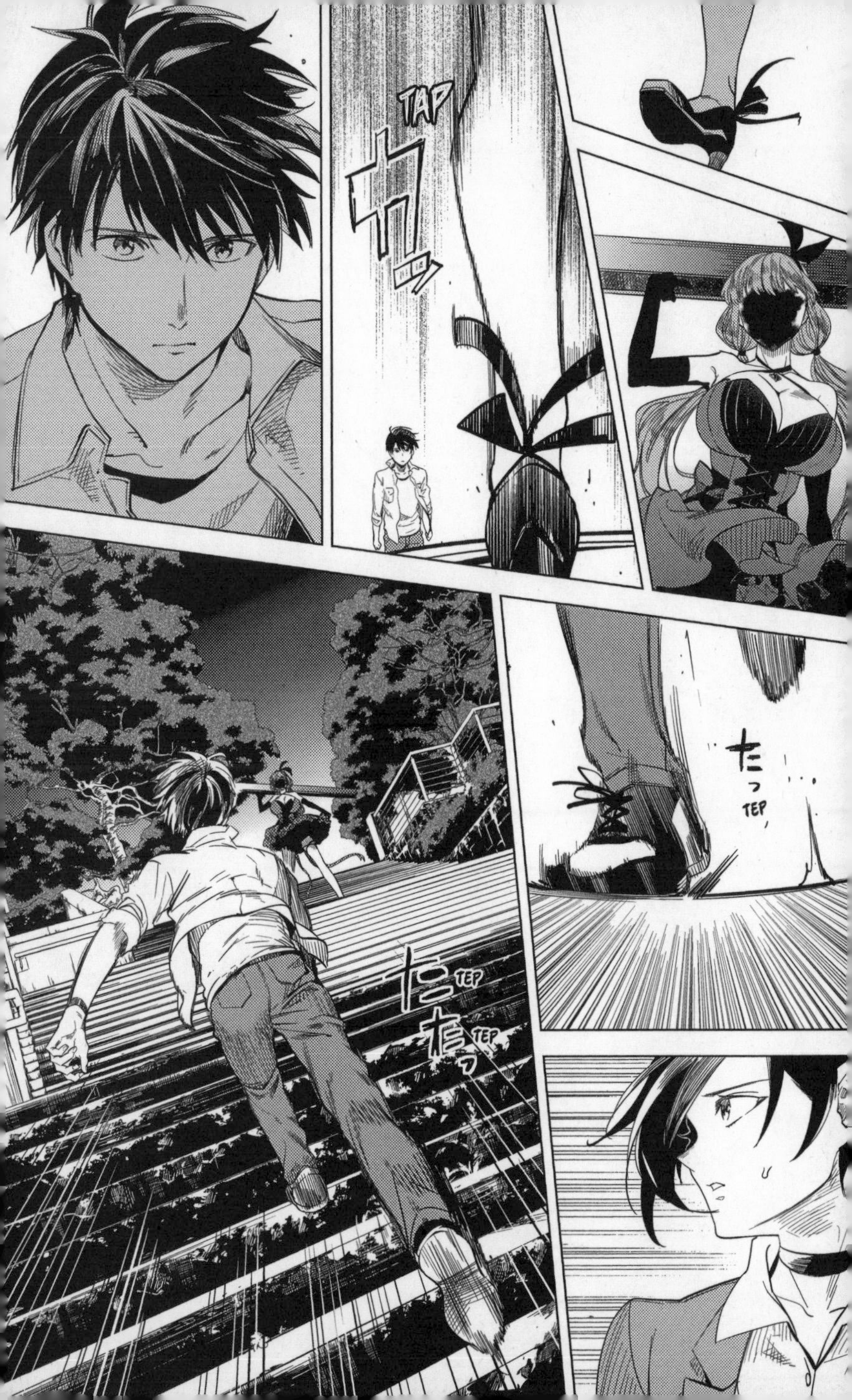
TAP
タッ
たっ
TEP
たっ
TEP
たっ
TEP

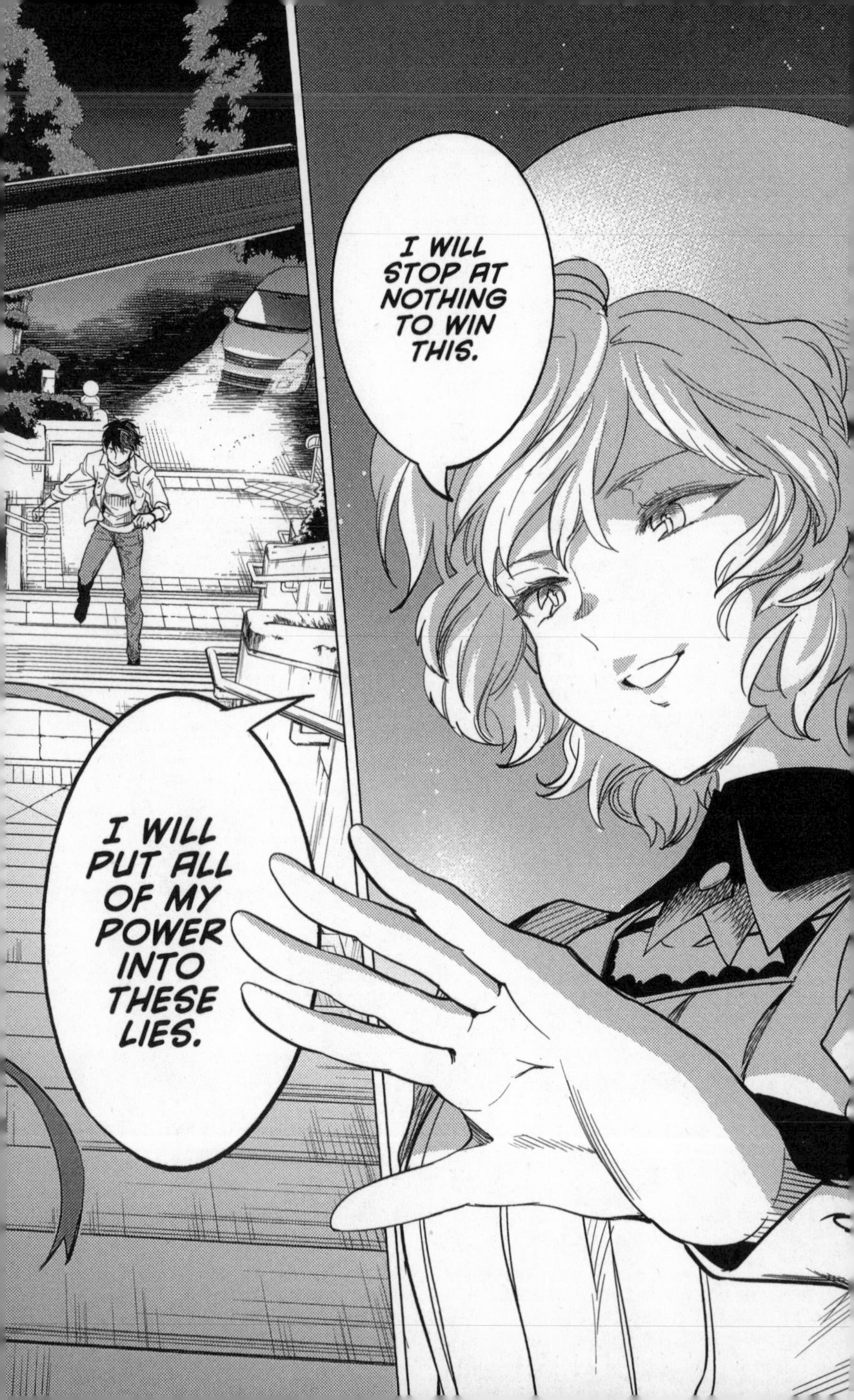
I WILL STOP AT NOTHING TO WIN THIS.
I WILL PUT ALL OF MY POWER INTO THESE LIES.

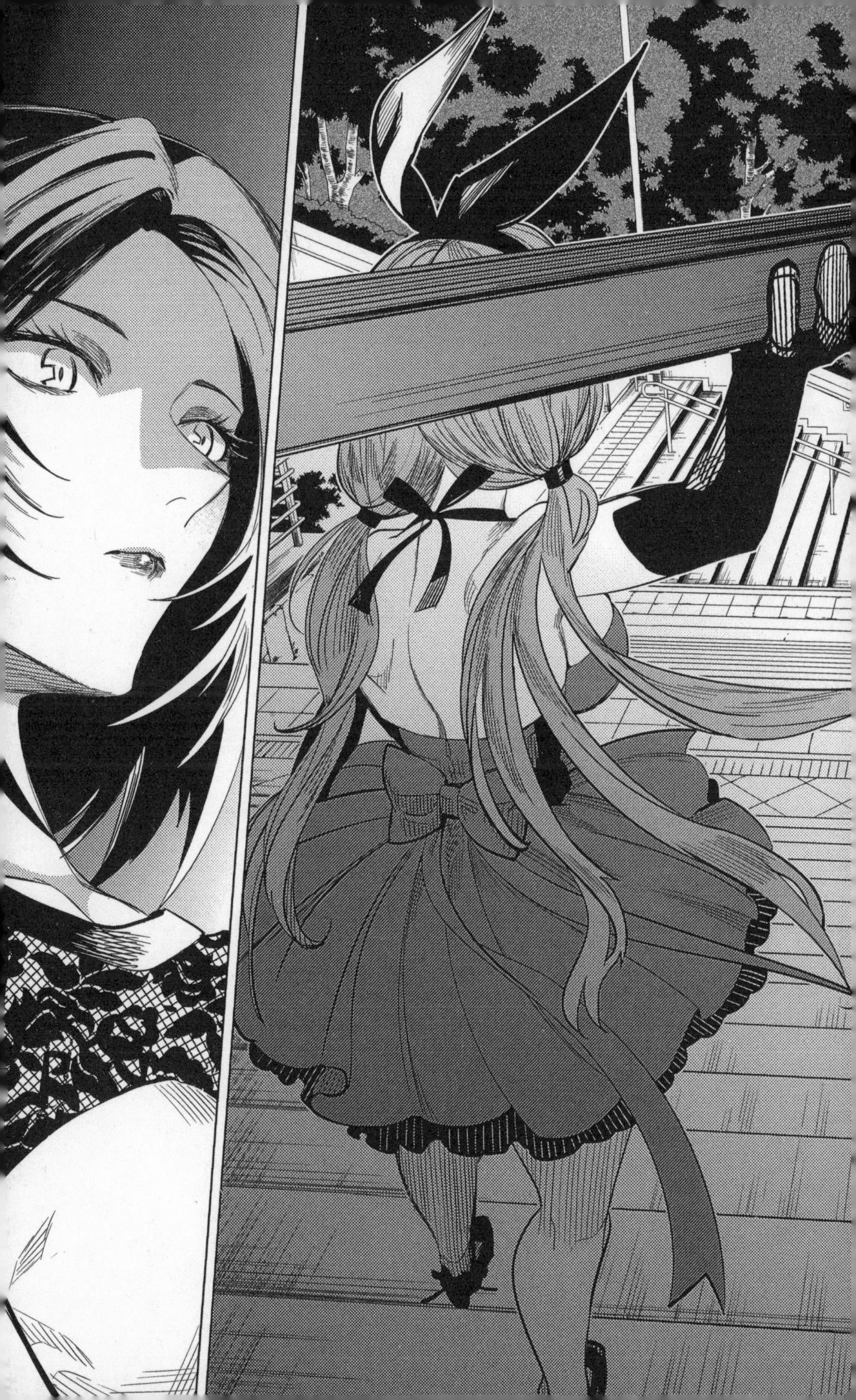

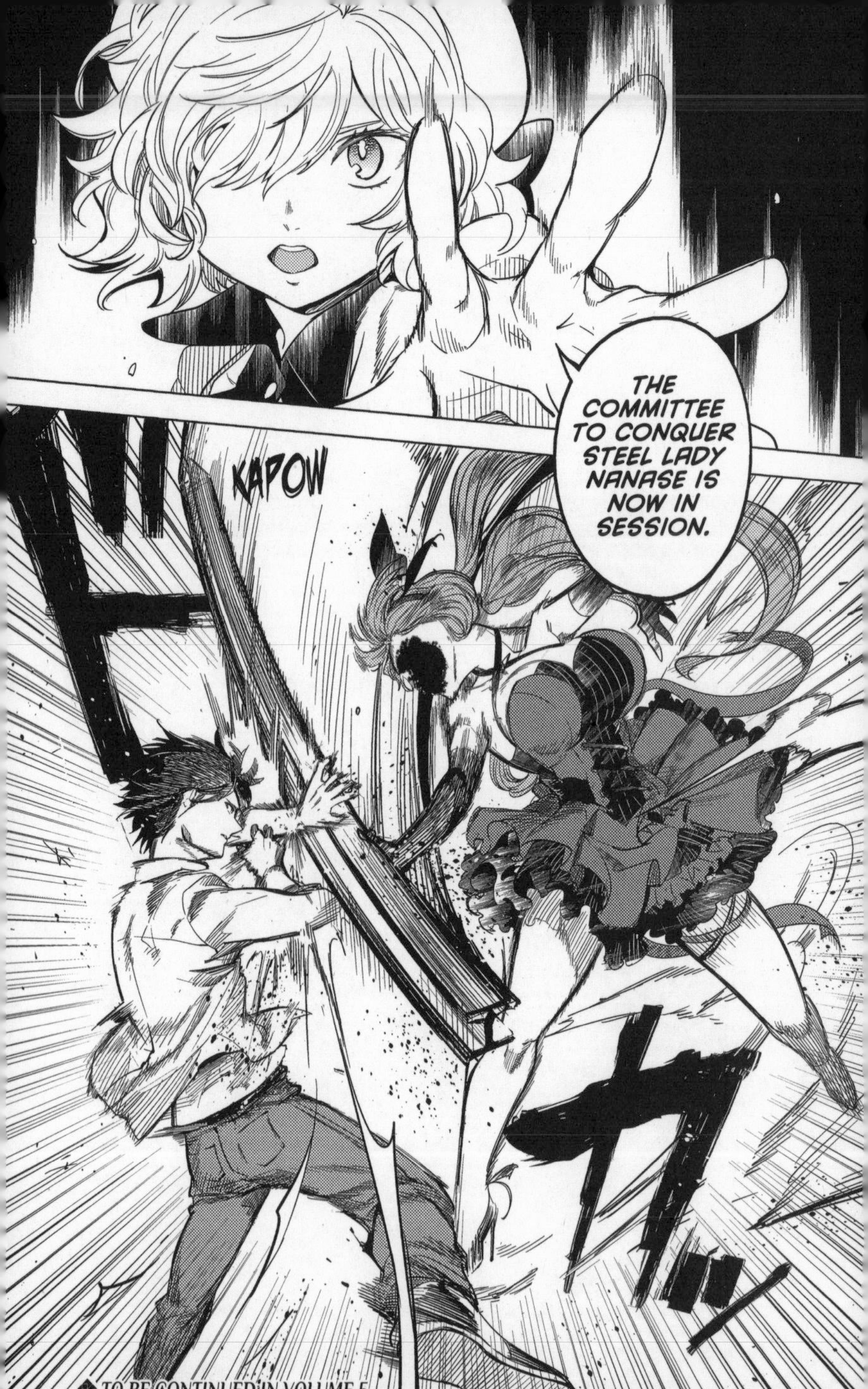
THE COMMITTEE TO CONQUER STEEL LADY NANASE IS NOW IN SESSION.
KAPOW

◆TO BE CONTINUED IN VOLUME 5

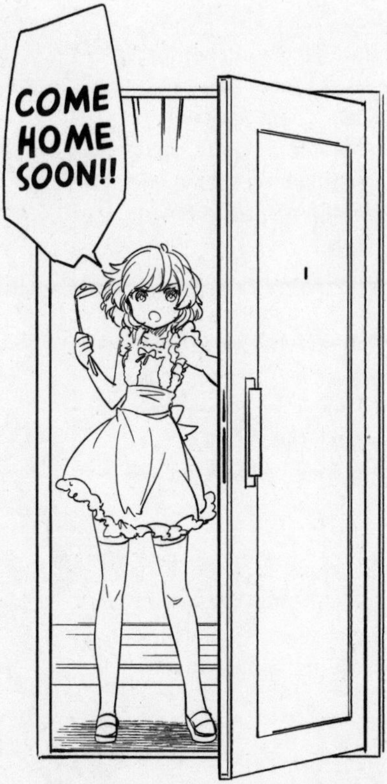
COME HOME SOON!!

# Things an Author Considers

I'm the author, Kyo Shirodaira. We're already at volume four. That was fast.

I'm always saying this, but although I am the original author, I'm not doing anything in particular for the manga. If I had to say I did something, it'd be that what I do is read the new chapter when it's published and tell the editor what I thought of it. I suspect there would be no damage to the manga if I did not offer these opinions, but if I don't show people that, "Yes, I am the author, I do read the manga of my work," people might think, "Wow, you're some kinda jerky author who doesn't even care about your own work, ain't ya?" On the other hand, if all I say is, "That was another good chapter," people might laugh at me behind my back, saying, "Thou hast no esprit, my good fellow," so I'm always doing my best to give intelligent feedback. Although you would be quite right to point out that no, that's not where I should be focusing my effort. And what is "esprit," anyway? I think it's the name of some delicious mineral water.

Putting all of that aside, this story takes place in the modern day, and when writing a "modern day" story, what gets tricky is depicting the normal, everyday aspects. When I write, I can use a phrase that's modern, common, and everyday at the time, but in extreme situations, it may have fallen out of use by the time the book is published, and that immediately makes the work seem outdated.

When I write a novel, I try to avoid anachronisms as much as possible. I never specify the year it takes place; I try not to use trendy words, new words that haven't been established in the vernacular, or overly slangy words; and I intentionally

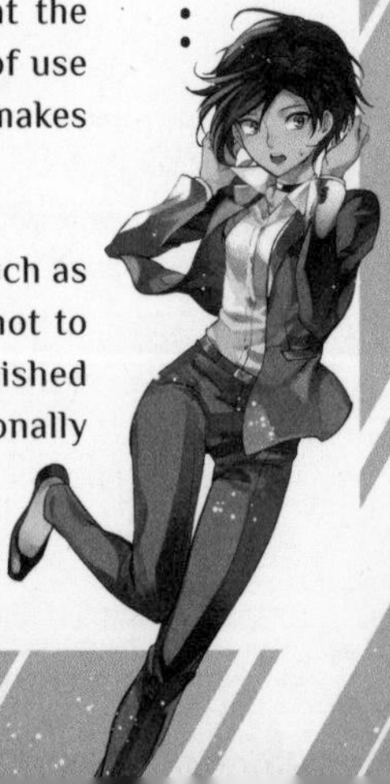

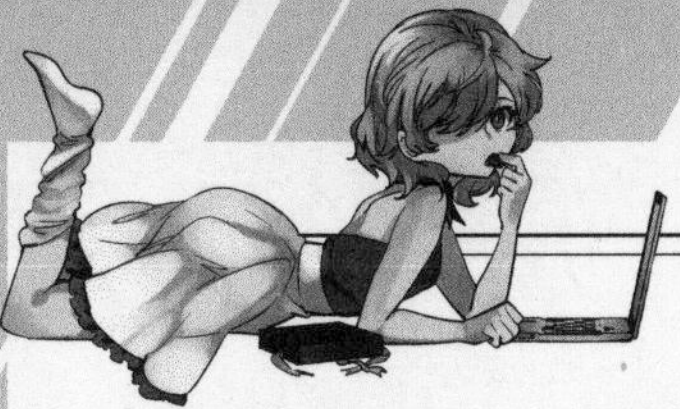



keep the depictions of daily commodities simple. Even so, while I was writing this book, I couldn't have imagined that certain internet and social media services would have become so popular, to the extent that it may seem unnatural that they don't appear in the story. On the other hand, even if I had been able to put them in, it's possible that it wouldn't have been long before they would have outdated the work. Even the shape of cell phones has changed a lot in a short amount of time—when the novel was first printed, there was a phrase, "She popped open her cell phone," that I took out for the new edition. It isn't easy.

And then when it becomes a manga, so many more things need to be presented in a clear picture, so it gets even harder to create the right atmosphere. I thoughtlessly made "modernness" a key part of the story, which must have created several problems for Katase-sensei, who has to draw props and people and backgrounds in a way that doesn't create inconsistency with the setting or the logic that goes with it, and that doesn't make the "modern day" feel old. It must be difficult to maintain this balance. This could be a real test of your esprit.

So what *is* esprit, anyway? Years ago, it would have taken time and effort to look up the word, but now anybody can just do a quick, easy search with their cell phone and get the answer in a split second. Times have changed.

Now then, this is the volume where the person pulling all the strings on the Steel Lady Nanase urban legend is finally identified, and I think it's fairly clear who's behind the crime, how they did it, and why. With so many questions answered, there would only be a few pages left in a normal mystery novel, but for this story, we're only just getting to the good part. The battle of lies to turn a lie-born truth back into a lie is about to begin.

Well, I hope you'll read the next volume.

Kyo Shirodaira

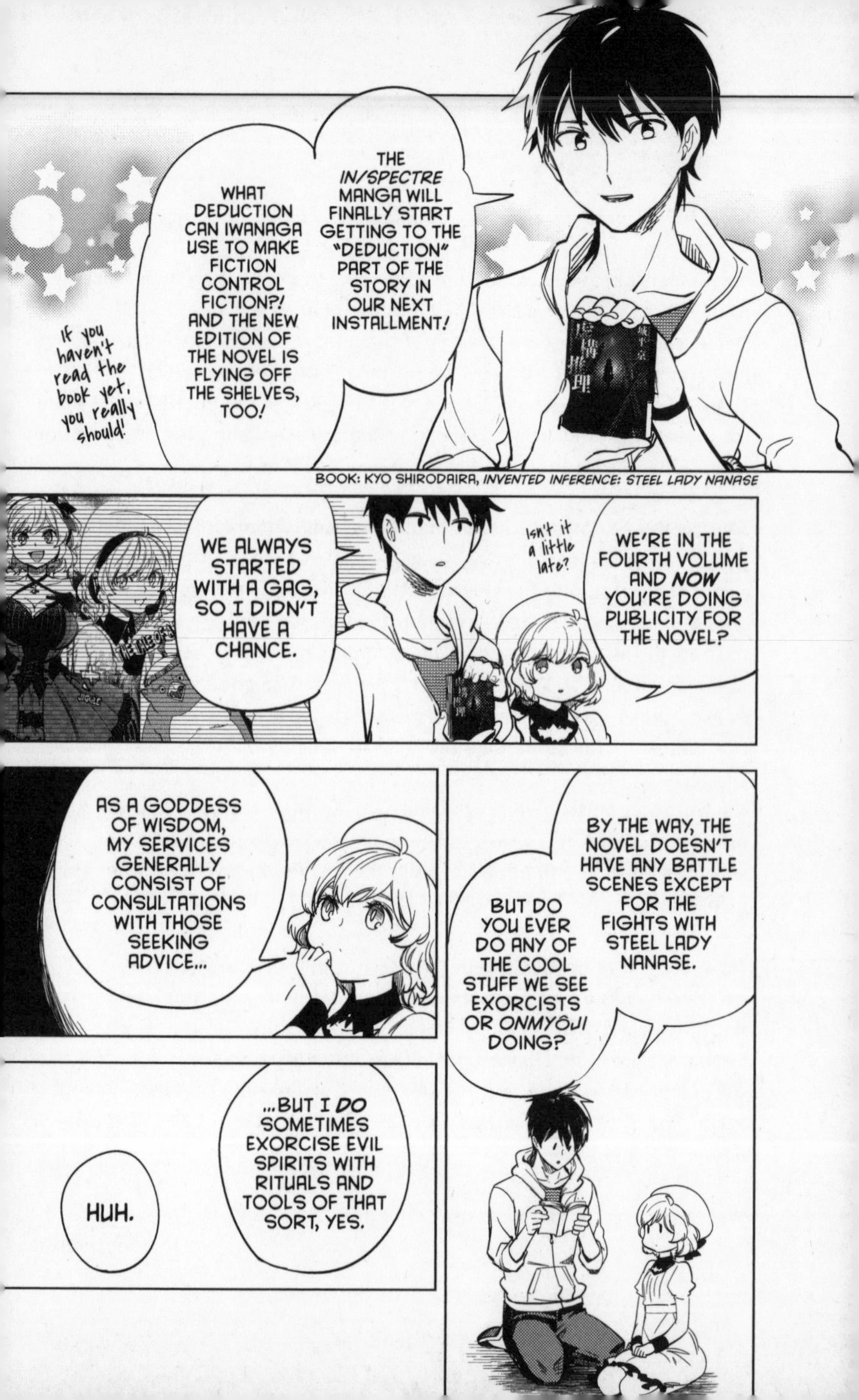
THE *IN/SPECTRE* MANGA WILL FINALLY START GETTING TO THE "DEDUCTION" PART OF THE STORY IN OUR NEXT INSTALLMENT!
WHAT DEDUCTION CAN IWANAGA USE TO MAKE FICTION CONTROL FICTION?! AND THE NEW EDITION OF THE NOVEL IS FLYING OFF THE SHELVES, TOO!
If you haven't read the book yet, you really should!
BOOK: KYO SHIRODAIRA, *INVENTED INFERENCE: STEEL LADY NANASE*
WE'RE IN THE FOURTH VOLUME AND *NOW* YOU'RE DOING PUBLICITY FOR THE NOVEL?
Isn't it a little late?
WE ALWAYS STARTED WITH A GAG, SO I DIDN'T HAVE A CHANCE.
BY THE WAY, THE NOVEL DOESN'T HAVE ANY BATTLE SCENES EXCEPT FOR THE FIGHTS WITH STEEL LADY NANASE.
BUT DO YOU EVER DO ANY OF THE COOL STUFF WE SEE EXORCISTS OR *ONMYŌJI* DOING?
AS A GODDESS OF WISDOM, MY SERVICES GENERALLY CONSIST OF CONSULTATIONS WITH THOSE SEEKING ADVICE...
...BUT I *DO* SOMETIMES EXORCISE EVIL SPIRITS WITH RITUALS AND TOOLS OF THAT SORT, YES.
HUH.

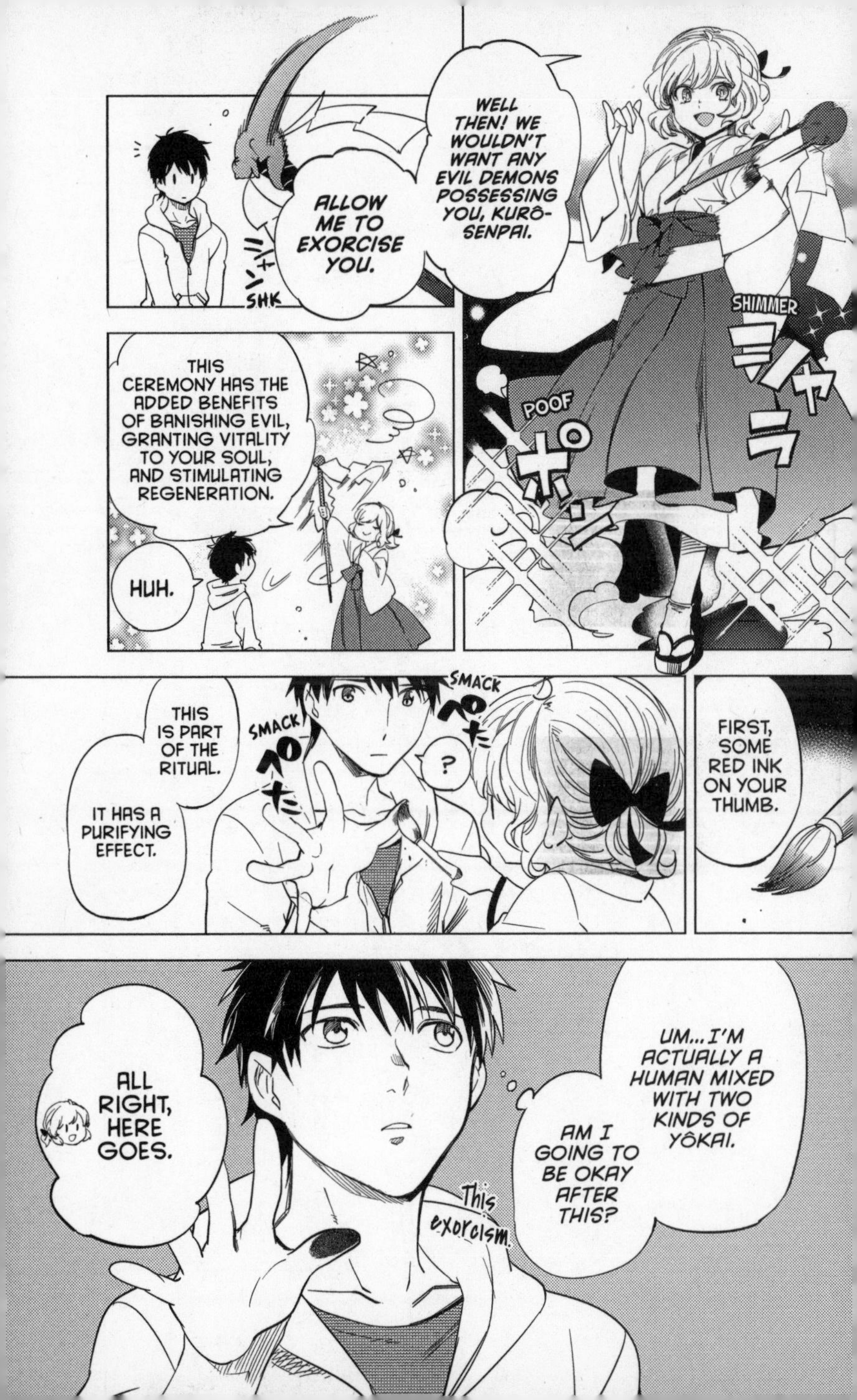
WELL THEN! WE WOULDN'T WANT ANY EVIL DEMONS POSSESSING YOU, KURÔ-SENPAI.
SHIMMER
POOF
ALLOW ME TO EXORCISE YOU.
SHK
THIS CEREMONY HAS THE ADDED BENEFITS OF BANISHING EVIL, GRANTING VITALITY TO YOUR SOUL, AND STIMULATING REGENERATION.
HUH.
FIRST, SOME RED INK ON YOUR THUMB.
SMACK
?
SMACK
THIS IS PART OF THE RITUAL.
IT HAS A PURIFYING EFFECT.
UM...I'M ACTUALLY A HUMAN MIXED WITH TWO KINDS OF YÔKAI.
AM I GOING TO BE OKAY AFTER THIS?
This exorcism.
ALL RIGHT, HERE GOES.

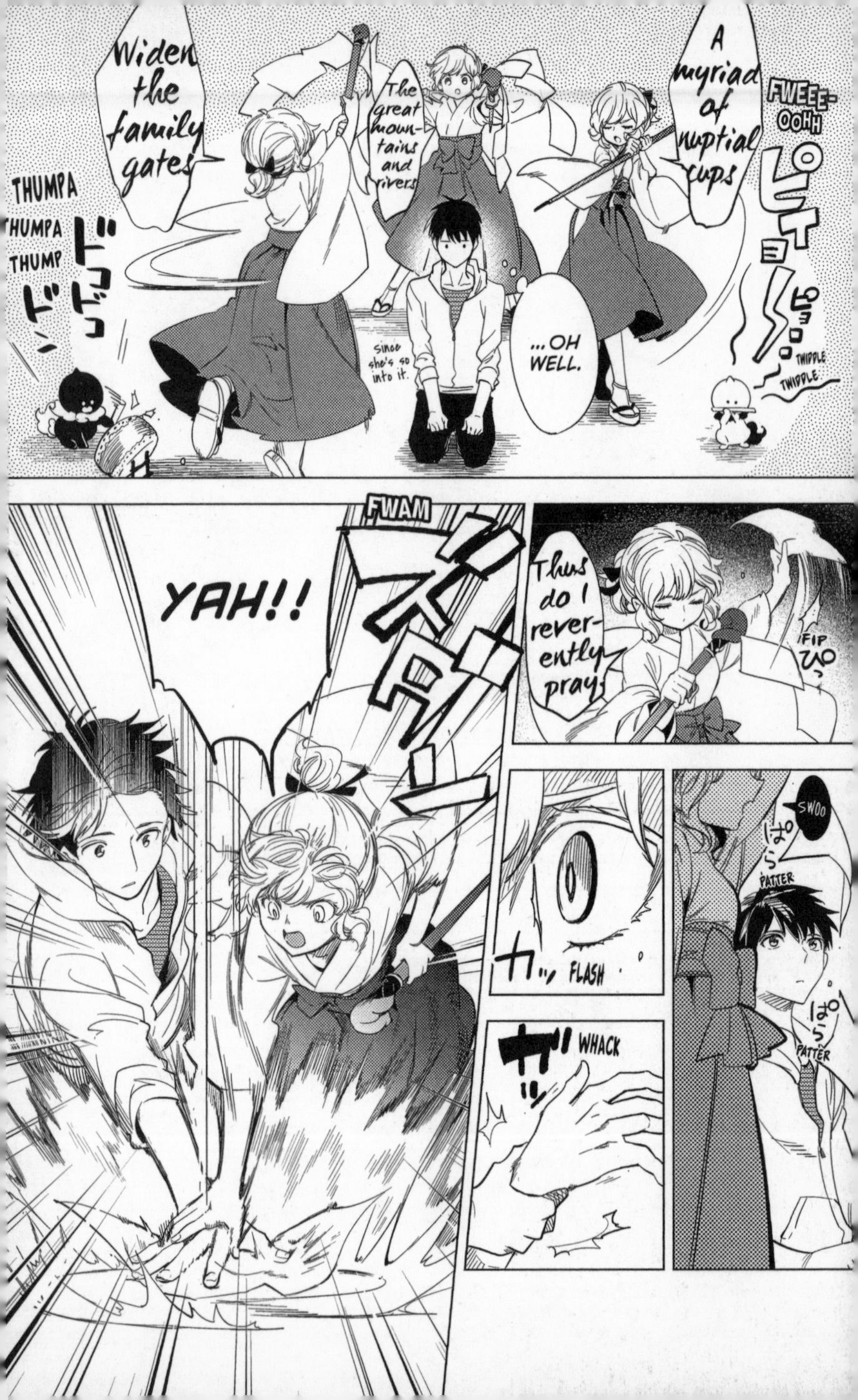
FWEEE-OOHH
A myriad of nuptial cups
The great moun-tains and rivers
Widen the family gates
THUMPA THUMPA THUMP
...OH WELL.
Since she's so into it.
TWIDDLE TWIDDLE
Thus do I rever-ently pray
FIP
SWOO
PATTER
PATTER
FLASH
WHACK
FWAM
YAH!!

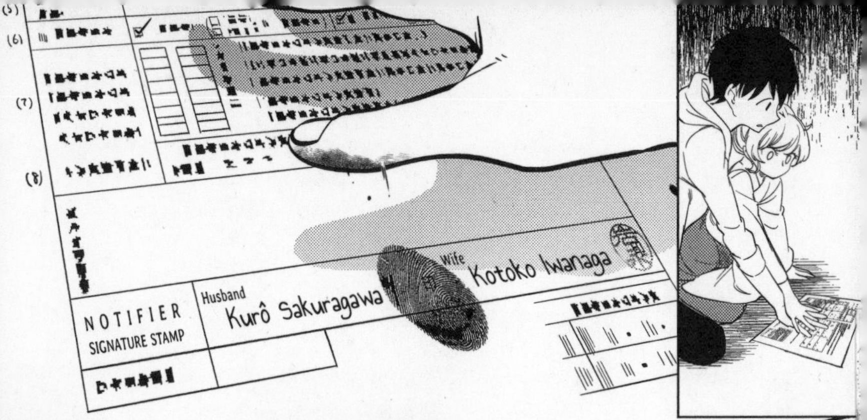
(5)
(6)
(7)
(8)
Wife
Kotoko Iwanaga
Husband
Kurô Sakuragawa
NOTIFIER
SIGNATURE STAMP

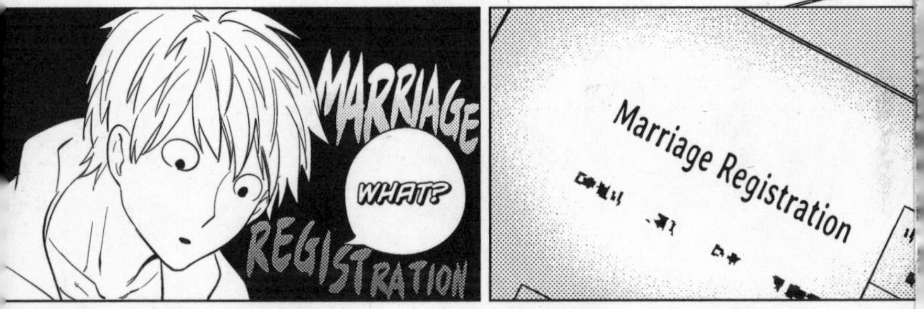
Marriage Registration
MARRIAGE
WHAT?
REGISTRATION

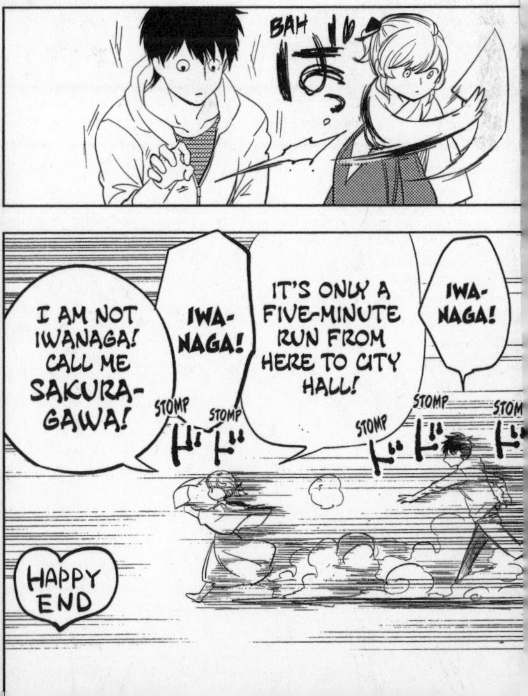
BAH
IWA-
NAGA!
IT'S ONLY A FIVE-MINUTE RUN FROM HERE TO CITY HALL!
IWA-
NAGA!
I AM NOT IWANAGA! CALL ME SAKURA-GAWA!
STOMP
STOMP
STOMP
STOMP
HAPPY END

Thank you for reading! I hope you'll join us for the next volume.
Katago

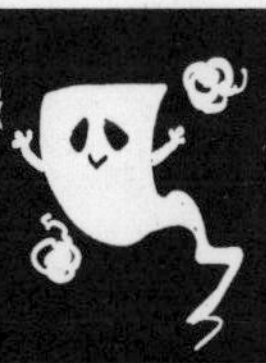

- STAFF -

Otôtamu
Kuro Shima
Tonpu
Yamamoto
Yutsu

-Editors-

O-kawa
T-da

(honorifics excluded)

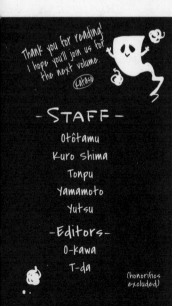

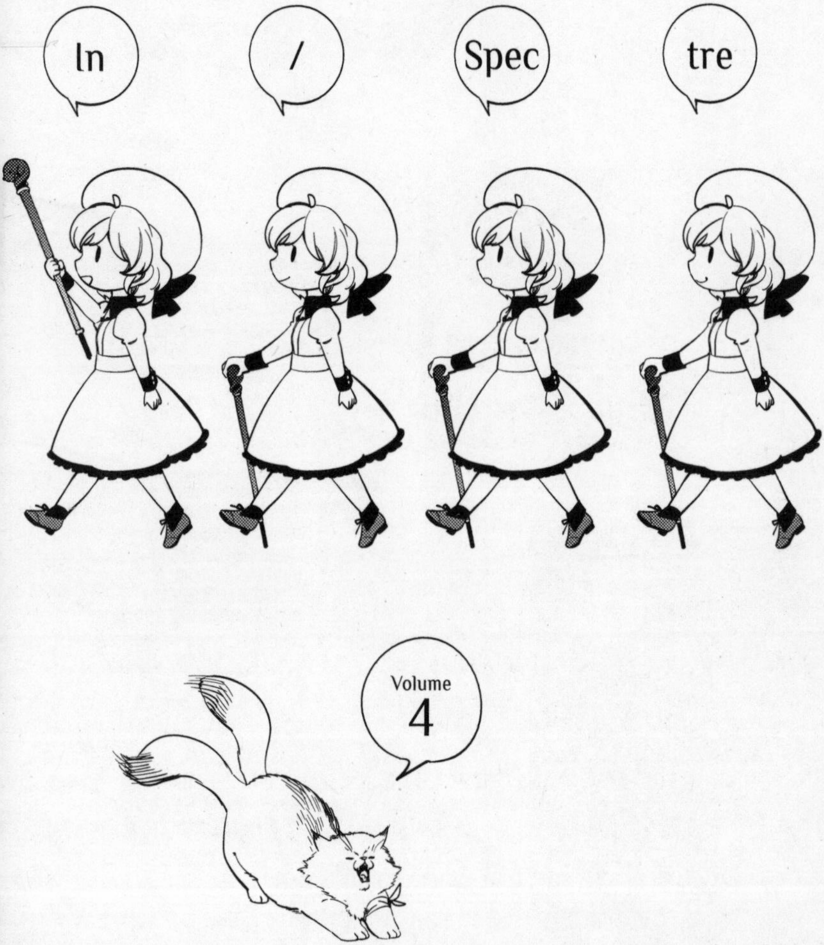
In
/
Spec
tre
Volume
4

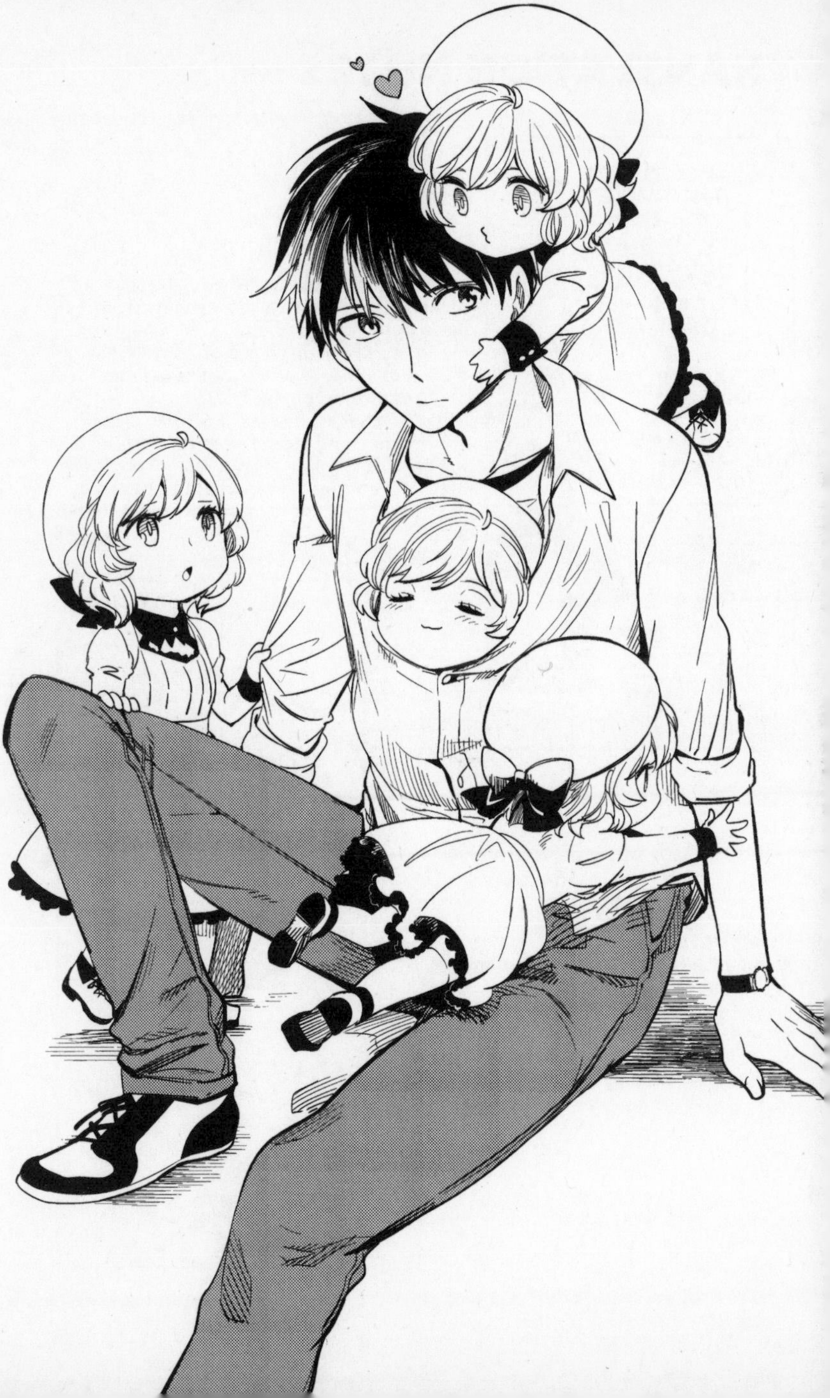

# TRANSLATION NOTES

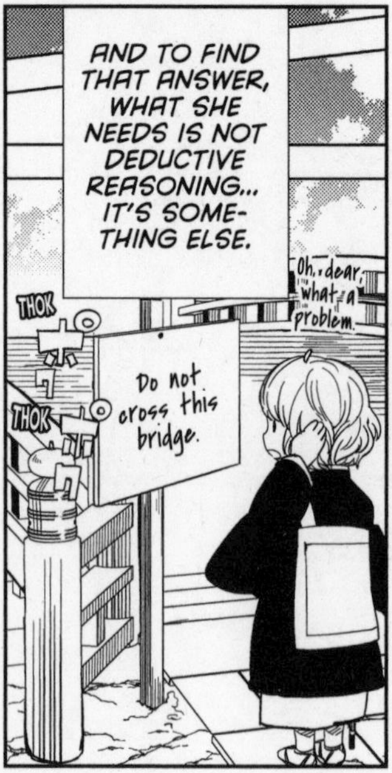
AND TO FIND THAT ANSWER, WHAT SHE NEEDS IS NOT DEDUCTIVE REASONING... IT'S SOME-THING ELSE.
Oh, dear, what a problem.
THOK
THOK
Do not cross this bridge.

**Do not cross this bridge, page 54**

This is a reference to a story about Ikkyû-san, a Buddhist monk known for his quick wit. In this story, he comes across a bridge, in front of which is a sign that says *Kono hashi wataru bekarazu*, or "Do not cross this bridge." Clever as always, Ikkyû-san takes another meaning for the word *hashi* (bridge), and decides the sign means "Do not cross the edges." Therefore, he would not be breaking any rules if he were to cross the bridge in the center.

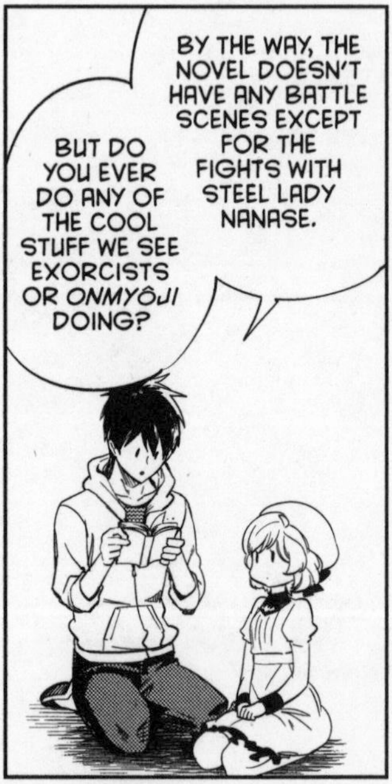
BY THE WAY, THE NOVEL DOESN'T HAVE ANY BATTLE SCENES EXCEPT FOR THE FIGHTS WITH STEEL LADY NANASE.
BUT DO YOU EVER DO ANY OF THE COOL STUFF WE SEE EXORCISTS OR ONMYÔJI DOING?

**Onmyôji, page 166**

An onmyôji is a practitioner of onmyôdô, or the way of Yin and Yang. It is a form of divination that mixes natural science and occultism, using the Five Elements as well as Yin and Yang. An onmyôji specializes in divination and magic, including exorcism.

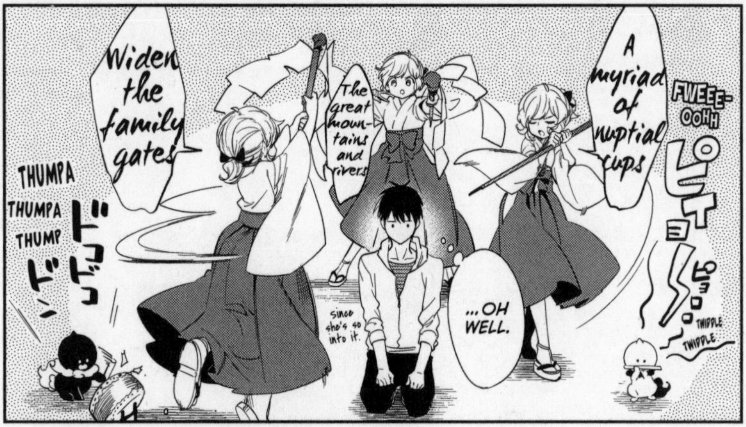
A myriad of nuptial cups
FWEEEE-OOHH
TWIDDLE TWIDDLE
The great moun-tains and rivers
...OH WELL.
Since she's so into it.
Widen the family gates
THUMPA THUMPA THUMP

**A myriad of nuptial cups, page 168**

Here Kotoko is reciting bits and pieces of a Shinto prayer, commonly used for a very specific ceremony. The ceremony usually involves two people and a priest, who prays for the health, happiness, and prosperity of the couple.

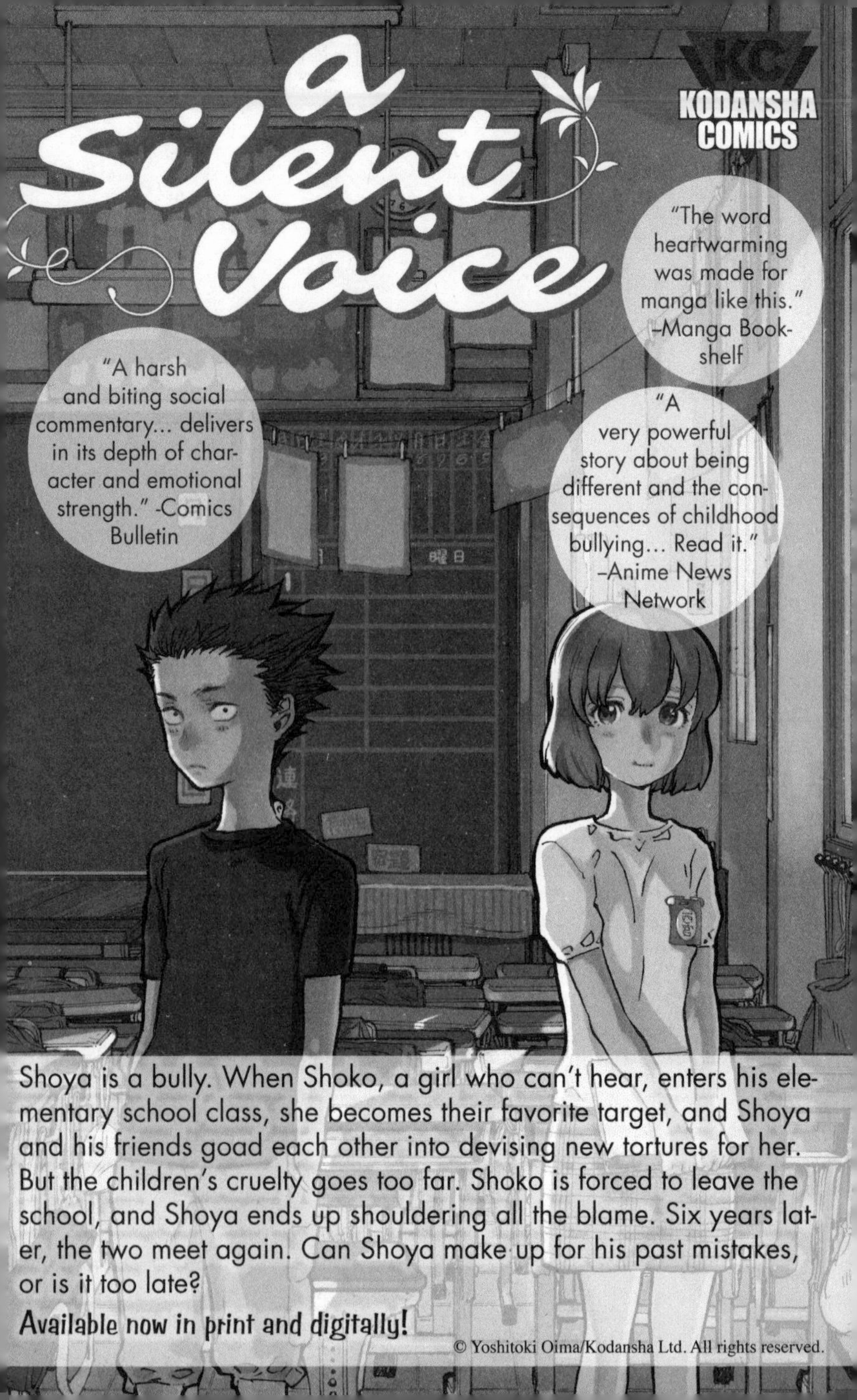
KC
KODANSHA COMICS
a Silent Voice
"The word heartwarming was made for manga like this." –Manga Bookshelf
"A harsh and biting social commentary... delivers in its depth of character and emotional strength." -Comics Bulletin
"A very powerful story about being different and the consequences of childhood bullying... Read it." –Anime News Network
Shoya is a bully. When Shoko, a girl who can't hear, enters his elementary school class, she becomes their favorite target, and Shoya and his friends goad each other into devising new tortures for her. But the children's cruelty goes too far. Shoko is forced to leave the school, and Shoya ends up shouldering all the blame. Six years later, the two meet again. Can Shoya make up for his past mistakes, or is it too late?
Available now in print and digitally!
© Yoshitoki Oima/Kodansha Ltd. All rights reserved.

# INUYASHIKI

**A superhero like none you've ever seen, from the creator of "Gantz"!**

ICHIRO INUYASHIKI IS DOWN ON HIS LUCK. HE LOOKS MUCH OLDER THAN HIS 58 YEARS, HIS CHILDREN DESPISE HIM, AND HIS WIFE THINKS HE'S A USELESS COWARD. SO WHEN HE'S DIAGNOSED WITH STOMACH CANCER AND GIVEN THREE MONTHS TO LIVE, IT SEEMS THE ONLY ONE WHO'LL MISS HIM IS HIS DOG.

THEN A BLINDING LIGHT FILLS THE SKY, AND THE OLD MAN IS KILLED... ONLY TO WAKE UP LATER IN A BODY HE ALMOST RECOGNIZES AS HIS OWN. CAN IT BE THAT ICHIRO INUYASHIKI IS NO LONGER HUMAN?

COMES IN EXTRA-LARGE EDITIONS WITH COLOR PAGES!

KODANSHA COMICS

Inuyashiki © Hiroya Oku/Kodansha Ltd. All rights reserved.

*In/Spectre* volume 4 is a work of fiction. Names, characters, places, and incidents are the products of the author's imagination or are used fictitiously. Any resemblance to actual events, locales, or persons, living or dead, is entirely coincidental.

A Kodansha Comics Trade Paperback Original.

*In/Spectre* volume 4 copyright © 2016 Kyo Shirodaira/Chashiba Katase
English translation copyright © 2017 Kyo Shirodaira/Chashiba Katase

All rights reserved.

Published in the United States by Kodansha Comics,
an imprint of Kodansha USA Publishing, LLC, New York.

Publication rights for this English edition arranged through Kodansha Ltd., Tokyo.

First published in Japan in 2016 by Kodansha Ltd., Tokyo, as *Kyokou Suiri* volume 4.

ISBN 978-1-63236-395-4

Printed in the United States of America.

www.kodanshacomics.com

9 8 7 6 5 4 3 2 1

Translation: Alethea Nibley & Athena Nibley
Lettering: Lys Blakeslee
Editing: Ajani Oloye
Kodansha Comics edition cover design: Phil Balsman